The Rosie Cru

Their Excellent Method
of Making Medicines of Metals
also
Their Lawes and Mysteries

The Rosie Crucian Secrets

Their Excellent Method
of making Medicines of Metals
also
their Lawes and Mysteries

Edited
with a Preface and Introduction
and
Critical and Explanatory Notes
by
E. J. Langford Garstin
Foreword by Ithell Colquhoun

THE AQUARIAN PRESS
Wellingborough, Northamptonshire

First published 1985

© THE AQUARIAN PRESS 1985

All rights reserved. No part of this book may be reproduced or utilized in any form or by any means, electronic or mechanical, including photocopying, recording or by any information storage and retrieval system, without permission in writing from the Publisher.

British Library Cataloguing in Publication Data

Dee, Dr John, *1527-1608*
  The Rosie Crucian secrets: their excellent method
  of making medicines of metals, also their lawes
  and mysteries.
  1. Rosicrucians
  I. Title   II. Garstin, E. J. Langford
  135'.43   BF1623.R7

ISBN 0-85030-441-5

The Aquarian Press is part of the Thorsons Publishing Group

Printed and bound in Great Britain

CONTENTS[1]

	Page
Foreword	7
Preface	11
Introduction	23
PART I The Rosie Crucian Secrets — Their Excellent Method of Making Medicines of Metals	31
The Letter of Dr John Frederick Helvetius	188
PART II Clavis Chymicus — An Explanation of Certain Chymical Hard Words Alphabetically Digested	199
PART III Of the Laws and Mysteries of the Rosie Crucians	217
References	264

FOREWORD

Edward John Langford Garstin, though a somewhat distant cousin, was familiar to me by the name of Eddie from my early childhood. I don't recall in what connection I first heard of him but his name seemed to come up in any talk of family relations. I did not meet him until 1928 when I was studying art at the Slade School and had joined The Quest Society. This group was run on fairly informal lines by G.R.S. Mead, one time secretary to Mme Blavatsky, and author of many works on Gnosticism. Edward was a prominent member of The Quest and I made myself known to him at one of its meetings. I have told something of my association with him in my study of MacGregor Mathers and the Golden Dawn, *The Sword of Wisdom* (Spearman, 1975).

I am not certain of the date of Edward's birth, but if, as I believe, he was 62 at the time of his death on June 26, 1955, this could make it about 1893. I am hazy about his exact connection with my family, but I have traced record of a certain Louisa Charlotte, daughter of General Garstin and wife of Charles (Andrew?) Colebrooke Sutherland who was in the Bengal Civil Service. This lady died at sea in 1838, presumably on the way to or from India, having produced two daughters. One of them married James Colquhoun and became the mother of my grandfather, James Andrew Sutherland Colquhoun, b. 1839. I suppose that Edward's great-great grandfather was the above mentioned General Garstin who must have been active at the end of the eighteenth century, but there was certainly another General Garstin among his immediate forebears — his father or grandfather.

My impression is that there was no link with the writer Crosbie Garstin and his father Norman, who was a founder member of the Newlyn School of Painters and settled in Cornwall towards the end of last century.

In appearance Edward was above middle height and of sandy colouring with pale blue eyes. In features he resembled the photograph of the French Alchemist, Claude d'Ygé de Lablatinièrs (1912-1964), which appeared on the cover of the review *L'Initiation et Science*, No. 63, Paris 1965, marking the occasion of the latter's death.

Edward was dogged by ill-luck all his life, both in business and in affairs of the heart. The fate of his occult work recalls a phrase used by W.B. Yeats in a similar connection, being 'neither paid nor praised'. Edward was an excellent dancer and married young, one of his wife's attractions being that she was able to partner him in ballroom dancing championships, many of which they won. The 1914-18 War broke up this partnership when the Army claimed Edward. On his return from active service with the rank of Captain, he found no sign of his wife, except numerous debts. She had vanished, having sold the contents of their flat and spent all the money in their joint account. In an attempt to re-establish himself Edward embarked on various business ventures but with a notable lack of success. So it came about that when I met him he was sharing a flat with his widowed mother in a less than modish area of Kensington, unemployed except for his esoteric studies. He found out that he was also a good cook and this proved useful in their straightened circumstances. He was a vegetarian at this time, probably following the example of Mathers. Later, he was to be glad to have food of any kind.

I take it that he was already an occult student when he met Mrs Morgan Boyd, who had helped Moina MacGregor Mathers to establish the A∴O∴ Lodge of the Golden Dawn, when the latter moved to London from Paris, soon after Mathers' death in 1918. So Edward must have been initiated into this Lodge by the early 1920s. Moina had died when I met him but he had known her well. I do not think he would have had the opportunity of meeting Mathers himself, and whether he had joined The Quest before his initiation I don't know. Certainly for some years between the two Wars he was investigating the groups and personalities then active on the London occult scene. He hoped to marry Mrs Boyd's daughter Esme, who was also a member of the Lodge, but she married a stockbroker instead.

In about 1930 Mr Mead decided to close down The Quest Society and magazine, relinquishing the lease of the two studios used as premises, Edward tried to carry on a similar group under the name of The Search Society. This lacked not only The Quest's headquarters but most of its prestigious membership, though Dr W. B. Crow and Hugh Schonfield were among its supporters. The latter co-edited with Edward a quarterly review *The Search*,[1] produced by the Search Publishing Company, a venture in which they were joined as I recall, by a third partner, Cazimir de Prozynski. They brought out some few titles, but in a year or two, all three 'searches' — society, review, and company — had collapsed.

After I left the Slade School, I went to live abroad for a while, and when I returned to London was much occupied with my work as a painter. I had gradually lost touch with Edward after the refusal of Mrs Boyd to admit me to their Lodge — as recounted in *The Sword of Wisdom*. [2] (It was hasty of me, as I now see, to take this No for an answer, since it is common practice with some secret associations to refuse a candidate the *first* time around.) Later I heard that with the outbreak of the 1939-45 War, Edward was recalled to the Army, in which he finally reached the rank of acting Colonel, but this was never confirmed and he returned to civilian life as a Major, much to his disappointment in view of his family traditions. Such traditions must have been important to him, since he used his family motto, Animo et Fide, as his magical name.

Edward's mother had died and he married again, this time a redhaired charmer, formerly the wife of the commercial artist Beresford Egan. This second marriage was no more successful than the first. The ex-Mrs Egan had no sympathy with Edward's occult interests, which were a topic of ridicule between her and her boyfriends. After the war, she departed with one of these, a G.I., taking most of Edward's furniture and all his family portraits with her to the U.S.A.

When I next made contact with Edward, in the early 1950s, he was living in a service flat at Scarsdale Villas, W.8. He was unemployed except for a partnership, again with de Prozynski, in a concern called the Anglo-Brazilian Trading Company, which dealt in mechanical spare-parts of some kind. Unfortunately no commercial activity in this line was possible, since all trade with Brazil was barred by the British Government for some years. I presume the partner had some other means of subsistance, but Edward complained of being badly hit by the ban. Though I did not understand how near he was to destitution, I wondered why he did not exchange his flat for a simple room in a less expensive area, and take any kind of job until he could find something more congenial. I suggested that he asked Mrs Boyd's help, as she had some useful contacts in the business world, but he maintained that she could do nothing. (I was later told that she had already come to his rescue financially on occasion — now either she was unwilling to do so again, or he was unwilling to ask her.) Finally , he was obliged to give up the flat and sell his small but well-chosen library of occult books to Geoffrey Watkins.

Next he migrated to one of the remoter suburbs, lodging for a time with a chemist and his wife in return for assistance in running their business. Lastly he exchanged these rather cramped quarters for a room in the flat of A. C. (Tony) Windyard's parents in Battersea. Tony, since deceased, was then a young teacher of mathematics and much interested in esoteric subjects. I do not know how long this arrangement lasted, but it was not long. Afterwards Tony related to me that one evening they had a discussion on some point of Qabalah and on retiring Edward had seemed calm and collected. But next morning his door was locked and a note pinned outside directed Tony to push the key through and pull it under the door to open. He found Edward dead from an overdose of some drug.

Mrs Boyd was shocked at this news and insisted that consequent on the suicide, Tony should destroy Edward's Order Papers, implements and any items directly connected with his G.D. work, all of which he had kept together in a trunk.[3]

I was out of London for some weeks at this time and only heard of Edward's death by letter from Tony after the inquest and funeral at Morden Cemetary were over. I remembered Edward's remarking some time previously, that he had no inhibitions about suicide, but I felt sure that he could have found some happier solution to his problems. He must have been severely depressed and thus unable to foresee anything but a burdensome old age.

His life story reminds one of a warning passage from Eliphas Lévi, which recounts the frequent lot of the occult explorer, and finishes.

> 'Inheritor of so many victims, he does not dare the less, but he understands better the necessity for silence.'

ITHELL COLQUHOUN
(First published in *The Hermetic Journal*, Number 6, Winter 1979).

1. *The Search. A Quarterly Review* survived for fourteen issues between January 1931 and April 1934. Garstin's company was also responsible for publishing his own book on alchemy, *The Secret Fire, an Alchemical Study*, (1932) and for producing an abridged edition of W. Marsham Adams's *The Book of the Master of the Hidden Places* (1933), which Garstin edited and provided with a Foreword, Notes and an Appendix. His earlier book, *Theurgy or the Hermetic Practice. A Treatise on Spiritual Alchemy*, had been published in 1930 by Rider & Co.

2. pp. 19-22. Mrs Boyd is referred to as 'Mrs Evan Weir'

3. Some, at least, were not destroyed. A number of Garstin's G∴D∴ papers came into the hands of Geoffrey Watkins, together with the present text of his edition of *The Rosie Crucian Secrets*.

PREFACE

The Rosie Crucian Secrets exists only in one known copy, which is No. 6485 of the Harleian MSS. It purports to be a copy of a manuscript by Dr John Dee, the celebrated Elizabethan mathematician, physician, astrologer, magician and alchemist, and is credited to him in Cooper's *Athenae Cantabrigiensis*. Apparently the authority for this ascription is the fact that the MS, which consists of 501 beautifully written folios and has no title page, gives throughout, as marginal notes, the numbers of 'the Sheets of Dr Dee'. The work is in three parts, of which the first is purely alchemical and medical; the second is a short alchemical lexicon; and the third deals with the Laws of the Order. A fresh numbering of the sheets 'according to Dr Dee' commences with each part.

As far as I am aware, no doubt as to the authenticity of this manuscript obtained until 1893, when Mr A. E. Waite suggested that it was a forgery on the following grounds.[2] (1) That a critical examination of the first part shows it to be little else but an adaptation of John Heydon's *Elharvareuna, or Rosicrucian Medicines of Metals*, first published in 1665. (2) That at the end of the first part is included a letter said to be from Dr John Frederick Helvetius to Dr John Dee, giving an account of a transmutation by Elias Artista, which historical transmutation took place at the end of 1666, more than half a century after the death of Dee.[3] (3) That the lexicon, which purports to explain certain hard words which occur in the writings of Dr Dee, consists almost entirely of words not found in the extant works of that author. (4) That the third part is an adapted translation of Michael Maier's *Themis Aurea*, which appeared in 1618.[4]

One other objection has been raised,[5] namely that the Rosicrucians only came into existence about the time of Dee's death. This argument is, however, almost entirely negligible beside those brought forward by Mr Waite, which must be considered in some detail.

Before commencing such an examination, it would, perhaps, be as well to make one point clear. The MS does not in any way claim to be an autograph, but merely a copy, and the copyist has indicated the date of the commencement of his labours. March 12th 1713, by inscribing it in the floriated title at the head of the manuscript. For the moment we will ignore the identity of the copyist, though this will also have to be considered as having some bearing on the question of forgery.

As regards Mr Waite's first point, anyone who cares to compare the *Rosie Crucian Secrets* with Heydon's *Elharvareuna* will find that as far as the end of the second paragraph of what is stated to be 'the thirty-eighth sheet, Dr Dee',[6] the one is certainly an adaptation of the other, though without further evidence it is impossible to say who is guilty of the plagiarism. Our MS, however,[7] extends to some ninety-four sheets of Dr Dee, so that *Elharvareuna* can account only for a little over one third of it. The remaining two thirds I have been unable to identify anywhere — except for Helvetius' letter — and Mr Waite has neither indicated a source nor pointed out that one is lacking. His last published pronouncement on the subject merely states that 'the text is alchemical as far as folio 352[8] and draws much from Heydon'.[9] I will return to this point again, but in the meantime I would merely suggest that as evidence of forgery it is inconclusive and inaccurately stated.

Mr Waite's three remaining arguments seem to me to be far more to the point. Indeed so cogent are they that in the absence of any other theory to explain what must at once be admitted to be correct, I should be compelled to agree that he has proved his case. As I have already remarked, he might, indeed, have further pointed out with regard to Maier's *Themis Aurea* that Part III of our MS is almost a verbatim transcript of the first and only English translation of this work, which appeared in 1656. I shall endeavour later to put forward an alternative explanation of these facts.

I must first, however, deal with the suggestion that Rosicrucianism only came into existence about the time of Dee's death.[10] As I shall have to enter rather more fully into the question at a later stage, I will, for the moment, content myself with saying that unfortunately for its value as an argument, this statement has never been proved, despite the large number of books that have been published dealing with the origin and history of the Fraternity, nor is it probable that the problem will be taken much further. Mr Waite has, perhaps, been more painstaking than any other contemporary scholar, but his findings can only be regarded by the impartial reader as inconclusive, as is the case with so much historical research. We are left, therefore, with no precise knowledge as to the date of the foundation of the Order in Germany,[11] and hence no grounds for stating that Dee could not, as tradition relates, have been a member.[12]

At this stage it becomes necessary to take into consideration the identity of the copyist, seeing that he has been accused of forgery on what must be described as a wholesale scale.[13] He is one Peter Smart, who describes himself as M.A. of London, and he would seem to have been occupied in copying various MSS during the years 1699 to 1714, but mostly from 1712 to 1714.

The charge of forgery is made specifically in respect of *The Rosie Crucian Secrets* and also in respect of another MS, also in the Harleian Collection, namely No. 6486, the title of which is HERMETIS TRISMEGISTI: SPONSALIA CELEBERRIMA. *The Famous Nuptials of the Thrice-Greatest Hermes, allegorically describing the Mystical Union and Communion of Christ with every Regenerate Soul. Composed by C.·.R.·., a German of the Order of the Rosie Cross about 255 years past, and from the Latin MS faithfully translated into English by Peter Smart, Master of Arts, 1714.* On the reverse of the title, and by the same hand, it is said that in the margin are brief notes by the late Dr Rudd, explaining some hard words and sentences.

I will revert to this MS shortly, but the mention of Dr Rudd involves some consideration of the following Harleian MSS, said to be by Rudd and copied by Smart, namely No. 6481, *The Miraculous Decensions and Ascensions of Spirits*; No. 6482, *Tabula Sancta Cum Tabulis Enochi*; No. 6483, *Liber Malorum Spirituum, Seu Goëtia*; and No. 6484, *The Talismanic Sculpture of the Persians*. There are two more Rudd MSS not mentioned by Mr Waite, namely Harleian 6479 and 6480. Of these the former is *A defence of Jewes and other Eastern Men* and the latter *A Hebrew Grammar*.

As far as I can ascertain, these are the only known works attributed to Dr Rudd, and by innuendo it is suggested that he is merely Smart's *alter ego*. Alternatively it is claimed that despite Smart's several allusions to ancient manuscripts of the late Dr Rudd, the latter cannot have written later than the close of the seventeenth century, 'some of his materials coming from Vaughan and Heydon.'[14]

It is important to consider these charges as, if proved, they would be valuable evidence as to the character of Peter Smart and would tend to confirm the suggestion that *The Rosie Crucian Secrets* came in the same category.

As regards any materials that may be found in Heydon, this is, indeed, no proof as to date or illegitimate borrowings, for in an age admittedly lax as to literary honesty Heydon stands out as *facile princeps* among the plagiarists[15] so that not only are the materials involved all older than the date suggested[16] but the ultimate source is also an open question.[17]

Thomas Vaughan is not in the same category and I cannot remember anyone casting any doubt upon his literary integrity. But in any event only one case can be adduced where there seems to have been direct borrowing from him by Rudd, and that is the opening vision in the *Decensions and Ascensions of Spirits*. This particular vision, it is to be observed, was also borrowed by Heydon. All three versions vary fairly considerably, though there are passages in each which are to all intents and purposes identical and the very nature of the discrepancies and coincidences seems to suggest a common origin outside all three. I hope, however, that confirmation of this idea will be found when I develop my argument as to the possible origin and authorship of *The Rosie Crucian Secrets*. For the present I will content myself with remarking that no one who has studied the literature with any care would dream of suggesting that the main elements in these MSS of Dr Rudd were original or that they were written with any intention of being published. My submission is that they were private compilations by a student of these subjects.

As to Rudd himself, we have no positive information, but there was a Thomas Rudd (1583-1656), a mathematician and a Captain of Engineers, who in 1651 published the first six books of Euclid with a preface by John Dee.[18] This is not the date of the first publication of this preface, for it had appeared before H. Billingsley's translation of *Euclid's Elements* in 1570. It may well be, however, that Thomas Rudd knew Dr Dee (he was twenty-five years old at the time of Dee's death) and for that reason made use of his preface. It is unlikely that he was the mysterious Dr Rudd himself, although the name is uncommon and in those days the mathematician, the astrologer and the student of occult mysteries were much akin; but he may have been a relation. In this case he was presumably the younger man, for although there is no proof of the supposition, it is not unreasonable to imagine that the Dr R. mentioned in a marginal note at the end of the fiftieth sheet of Dr Dee in *The Rosie Crucian Secrets*[19] as having sent him by letter on October 19th 1605 'A Process upon the Philosophic Vitriol' is the Dr Rudd of the MSS in question.

One more point in connection with Dr Rudd remains to be mentioned, namely the marginal notes to the *Sponsalia Celeberrima Hermetis Trismegisti*.[20] Mr Waite is emphatic regarding these, stating that the translation is not by Smart, who, he says, used the English version by E. Foxcroft published in 1690 and that the notes are 'the marginalia of the English rendering and these derive in turn from the

German text.' Mr Waite is also positive that there never was a Latin original.[21]

Now in the first place the authorship of this work, the *Nuptiae Chemicae* or *The Chemical Marriage* as it is usually called, is by no means certain. It is the third and most striking of the original Rosicrucian documents, and was first printed in German in Strasbourg in 1616, the authorship being attributed to Christian Rosenkreutz under the date 1459. Modern opinion rather inclines to assign it to Johannes Valentinus Andreae on the strength of a statement made in his autobiography, which was written late in life. He claims — and it must be remembered that he writes as an opponent of the Fraternity — to have written it in 1601 or 1602 as a jest, though at that time he could only have been fifteen or sixteen years of age. Personally I confess to finding this incredible[22] but the reader must judge for himself.[23] It is a matter of some importance, for if not by Andreae, there may well have been a Latin original of an earlier date, of which the so-called High Dutch 'original' is a translation, and it is interesting to note that Latin is the language of most of the marginal notes.[24] But to return to the statement regarding Rudd's alleged notes. A comparison will at once show that while the Latin notes of Smart's version vary slightly from those of Foxcroft, there are many additional notes in English, which do not appear in the latter, which are, therefore, either those of Rudd or Smart or borrowed by one or other of them from some unknown source. The alternatives are not in themselves important, but it is quite clear that Mr Waite is in error in stating that all the marginal notes in Smart's copy are to be found in Foxcroft.

I do not suggest that the English translation is actually by Smart, through the fact that it is to all intents and purposes identical with that of Foxcroft cannot be taken as positive proof, but I would suggest that it is quite possible that neither of these gentlemen was responsible for the labour involved, but both used an earlier version that had been in circulation in a manner which I shall suggest later, in which case the copy which passed into the hands of Smart may well have had annotations additional to those in the copy which came to Foxcroft, being those of Rudd. Admittedly this does not redound to the credit of Peter Smart, but at the same time it seems obvious that his various MSS were not intended for publication and his claim to be the actual translator from the Latin may be ascribed to the same personal vanity which probably led to the statement in two of the MSS that they were 'methodised' by him.

It may appear to be a long digression, but the character of our copyist is of some importance, seeing that it has been suggested that he was not merely a gratuitous liar but a worse plagiarist than Heydon and that he is guilty of having forged *The Rosie Crucian Secrets*.

It is with the last of these statements that we are really concerned, and it would appear that in making a charge of forgery, especially in this particular case, a very material point has been overlooked, namely that it is the purpose of a forgery to deceive; for it seems obvious that at the time in question, namely in 1713, there could have been little hope of achieving such a result.[25] This, I maintain, is proved by the bulk of the contents themselves. *Elharvareuna* was published in 1665, the letter of Helvetius, published in 1667, deals with events which occurred in 1666,[26] fifty-eight years after's Dee's death, and an English translation of Maier's *Themis Aurea* had appeared in 1656. I suggest that no forger would have been so clumsy as to weld together these various, comparatively recent and presumably still familiar elements with any hope of passing them off as the work of Dee. Possibly Mr Waite had these facts in mind when he said as long ago as 1893[27] that 'it is, in fact, a very curious forgery, rendered the more difficult to account for by its want of assignable motive.'

Having indicated some of the chief weaknesses of the argument against Smart either as an incorrigible plagiarist or as the forger of the Rudd MSS and more particularly of *The Rosie Crucian Secrets*, it now remains to be seen from what source Smart could have obtained the MS which appears under that title. At the end of Harleian MS No. 6483, *Liber Malorum Spirituum*, there is a note by Smart indicating that what followed was *The Rosie Crucian Secrets*, and stating: 'This Manuscript of Dr Dee was given me by Dr John Gadbury in Anno 1686.' This introduces a new character to the scene in the person of the well-known astrologer and astronomer,[28] who was born in 1627 and died in 1704. Among his friends was John Heydon — for whom, on more than one occasion, he wrote laudatory verses to be prefaced to his books[29] — and he was evidently a student of alchemy and the Rosicrucian literature. I have no evidence to show how the alleged Dee MS may have come into his possession, though I have, I maintain, a reasonable explanation, but in the absence of anything to the contrary, there seems to be no reason why Smart's statement should not be accepted. For the moment I am not even concerned with the question of authorship, but merely to show that there is a high degree of probability in favour of the hypothesis that Smart only figures in the history of this mysterious manuscript as a copyist.[30]

Before I come to any consideration of the possible history of *The Rosie Crucian Secrets*, however, it would be as well to examine in a little more detail the nature of its contents. As has already been admitted, approximately the first third of Part I is almost identical with Heydon's *Elharvareuna*[31] except that the latter is written as a dialogue supposed to take place between Eugenius Theodidactus[32] and Eugenius Philalethes.[33] Many considerable passages are taken verbatim from the works of Thomas Vaughan[34] and it is remarkable that in every case, without a solitary exception, Vaughan's words are put into the mouth of Heydon himself. This transcends the limits of ordinary plagiarism to such an extent — Heydon having, on his own showing, a list of two hundred and sixty authors on whom he drew[35] — that it seems hardly credible. As will appear I incline rather to the idea that Heydon, having found a suitable MS, re-wrote it in dialogue form. His acquaintance with Gadbury would easily account for the way in which he could have got his material. I am further confirmed in this opinion by the fact that the literary style of *Elharvareuna* changes very markedly after page 190 — at which point it breaks away from our MS — the remaining eighteen pages being, presumably, Heydon's sole contribution to this volume. Incidentally the style of the *Holy Guide* and his other works differs very radically from *Elharvareuna*, but the whole of *The Rosie Crucian Secrets*, allowing for certain variations in some of the formulae where there is redundancy, is obviously by the same hand.[36] There is, to be accurate, one exception to this statement, namely a short and very curious section[37] which is very distinctly reminiscent of certain of the communications in Dee's *True and Faithful Relation*.

I am aware that if my suggestion is correct it would seem that a charge of unacknowledged borrowing must also be laid against Thomas Vaughan, whose reputation for literary honesty has so far not been assailed. I feel, however, that the evidence is only circumstantial and that where he made use of portions of this MS, the probability is that, as in other cases, he did so with permission, but was debarred from mentioning his source for reasons which I shall hope to make clear. These reasons are, in fact, closely involved in my theory as to the possible origin of *The Rosie Crucian Secrets*, and to this I must now devote some attention.

In the first place, as far as the alleged Dee authorship is concerned, there is the vexed question as to the possible antiquity of the Rosicrucian Fraternity, as it is now commonly called. In this connection, as so often happens, the ill-considered writings of those who seek to maintain the original as given, or even to ascribe to it the 'time immemorial' description, do more to bring such theories into disrepute than all the reasoning of the critics. I do not propose, therefore, to go into the large number of stories, many of them fantastic, that have been circulated as fact, nor even to lay further stress on the dates given by Maier.[38]

There seems, however, to be unexpected corroboration[39] of John Yarker's statement that the original Rosicrucians were initiated by 'Moslem sectaries' independent of the traditional visit of C∴R∴C∴ to Damcar, Damascus and Fez, which is rejected by the critical historians.[40] This evidence is supplied in an interesting pamphlet recently published, entitled *Die Praxis der Alten Türkischen Friemauerei*, by Rudolf Freiherr von Sebottendorf, who indicates a definite alchemical practice based on the I.A.O., which is commonly recognized as being in use among Rosicrucians.[41] There is a further link indicating that this actual practice was known to certain alchemical adepti in Germany at an early epoch to be found in Sebottendorf's interpretation of the mysterious 'zodiacal paragraph' in the ninth of the *Twelve Keys* of Basil Valentine; for although there is great uncertainty as to his date, it is, according to Mr Waite, fairly safe to place him at the end of the fifteenth and beginning of the sixteenth centuries.[42] It is, perhaps, worthy of note that this treatise was of such interest to Maier (whose connection with the Fraternity is almost beyond dispute) that he included it in his *Golden Tripod*; and it is at least interesting to note that another work of Valentine, *Azoth or the Secret Aureliae of the Philosophers* was published in 1613 in an edition described as 'Interpreted by M. Georgius Beatus.' Vaughan quotes a long and singularly fine extract from this work, which he definitely states is by 'one of the Rosy Brothers, whose testimony is equivalent to the best of these, but his instruction far more excellent.'[43] It is, of course, impossible to say whether Vaughan was alluding to Beatus or Valentine when he made this remark, but the balance of probability would seem to point to the latter. In any event his silence should be borne in mind when considering the theory regarding the origin of *The Rosie Crucian Secrets* as I shall later put it forward.

I must confess that I have always found considerable difficulty in grasping the reasons put forward for suggesting that whatever its origin may be, the account given in the *Fama* and *Confessio* is definitely untrue. This whole hypothesis appears to rest on the alleged Lutheran and definitely anti-papal tone of these documents, coupled, perhaps, with a somewhat naïve-seeming enthusiasm on the part of the authors, that might even be described as boastful or bombastic in certain places. There is, of course, the fact that we do not know of any city of Damcar in Arabia, and that the ingenuity of critical scholars has revealed what appear at first sight to be minor discrepancies in the story itself. In justice to the anonymous authors, however, it is only fair to state that these latter are very largely exaggerated, even, in certain cases, being fabricated or imagined, as a careful examination of the actual text of the *Fama* will show.[44]

For this reason, while I must agree with Mr Pryse[45] that the story of C∴R∴C∴ cannot be accepted as strict history, I find his reasons, which would appear to be the seeming anachronisms in the story,[46] weak. I admit that the narrative is, like much else that passes for accepted history, lacking in evidential corroboration, as is only to be expected when one remembers that it deals with a secret Fraternity, and I am glad to observe that Mr Pryse does not suggest that there is absolutely no historical basis for the story of the foundation of the society and the finding of the tomb, and places the date of the *Fama* as 1610, 'perhaps a year or two earlier'.[47] He even finds evidence of the existence of a group of individuals with agents as far apart as Danzig and Amsterdam, in whom 'we may recognise the germ of the Fraternitas R∴C∴'[48] and after mentioning Maier and Fludd, very pertinently asks why Andrew Libavius, who in 1615 violently attacked the Order, in the following year exhorted his readers to join it.

Mr Waite himself is in favour of an earlier origin[49] for the Fraternity than 1610, seeing the beginnings of it in the Militia Crucifera Evangelica and the *Naometria* of Simon Studion, which was published in 1604, the year of the alleged finding of the tomb of C∴R∴C∴. The date, however, of the writing of *Naometria* is unknown, but we are given to understand that Studion was born *circa* 1543, graduated at Tubingen in 1565 and seems to have been present at the memorable meeting of the Militia Crucifera Evangelica at Lüneburg in 1586.

This theory of the origin of the Fraternity is, of course, purely speculative. It is, however, interesting to note that in *Naometria* is to be found a diagram uniting the symbolism of Rose and Cross, which makes it possible that Studion was connected with a society or group using this emblem before *Naometria* was written. That there had been such associations in England, France, Germany and Italy at least as far back as the early part of the fifteenth century and probably earlier seems beyond doubt. Indeed documentary evidence for the existence of some of them (though unnamed) is available,[50] but the fact that they were, from their very nature — whether the advancement of science or the liberation of religion — secret, supplies a more than cogent reason for our almost total absence of information concerning them.

I do not suppose that it will be disputed that Dr Dee is in every way the type of individual that one would expect to have belonged to some such body. There can, of course, be no certainty on this point, but there is at least evidence that the circulation of MSS by him to various individuals under conditions of secrecy is credible seeing that we have it in his own hand that he gave to Mr Richard Cavendish 'a copy of Paracelsus, twelve lettres, written in French with my own hand, and he promised me before my wife never to disclose to any that he hath it.'

That he was associated with students abroad is beyond dispute, and it is noticeable that at Bremen he was visited by Heinrich Khunrath of Hamburg, all of whose books were published after this conference with Dee.[51]

This suggestion cannot, of course, be stretched too far, and is, in any event, purely a speculative hypothesis — as are those of all serious writers on this subject — but a likely list of names occurs to one in this connection, such as Dee, Christopher Heydon, Khunrath, Maier, Fludd, Dr Rudd and Thomas Rudd, Ashmole, Vaughan,[52] Gadbury and John Heydon.

In the foregoing list the Rudds, or at least Dr Rudd, form a connecting link between one generation, as it were, and another, and would account for any MSS in circulation among the members reaching Gadbury and thus, finally, our copyist, Peter Smart. And although proof, in the historical sense, is lacking, I would suggest that more than one of these individuals was in all probability a member of the Rosicrucian Fraternity. For example Robert Fludd and Maier give every indication of writing from within. Then there is Ashmole himself, about whom there is a very strong tradition and some grounds for accepting it.[53] Lastly there is Vaughan, whose acquaintance with the Brethren seems to have been more intimate than he was willing to admit. These are perhaps the more obvious names, but Khunrath, the great contemporary of Maier, also comes within the range of possibility, and many have held his *Amphitheatrum Sapientiae Eternae* to contain Rosicrucian emblems. Mr Waite has stated[54] that he considers the doctrine of the ninth diagram to be 'so much in consonance with the theosophy of the Rosy Cross that it might have appeared in Fludd's vast treatise on the Macrocosm'. Not merely is this the case, but in the first figure, according to Sebottendorf[55] the signs of the three vowels, I. A. O. are plainly illustrated.[56]

Within such a group it is quite natural to suppose that many, if not all, of the MSS were by the members; hence the *Rosie Crucian Secrets* may well have been by Dee himself, though I do not insist upon this.[57] The alternative explanation is that a manuscript book belonging to Dee in as much as it was in his handwriting, but to the group in so far as it was not his personal possession, came into the hands of Gadbury, who added certain other relevant matter which interested him, namely the letter of Helvetius, the alchemical lexicon and the copy of Maier's *Themis Aurea*, but without being careful to name his sources, there being no particular reason why he should do so. When, therefore, this book came into the possession of Peter Smart, the latter, in making his own copy, failed to observe, or at least to comment upon, the fact that the work was a compilation and not a homogeneous whole and annotated his pages with the Dee folios.

The circulation of such MSS among the members of a secret group, presumably bound by certain obligations of secrecy, would account for the finding of various passages used without due acknowledgement by a scrupulous writer like Thomas Vaughan, seeing that acknowledgement would have been virtually impossible.[58] It would also account for the amazing impertinence which occurs in *Elvharvareuna* already mentioned, where sections previously used by Vaughan are put into the mouth of Heydon himself by that blatant plagiarist; and we note that this particular work was not published till 1665, the year of Vaughan's death.

That Vaughan denied, at least by implication,[59] his connection with the Fraternity of R.·.C.·., must, of course, be admitted; but so did Maier and Fludd; nor is it a matter for surprise, seeing that the policy of the Order was to keep itself secret and not to disclose the names of its members. It seems, therefore, only logical to suppose that although apologists came forward to defend the Brethren and their *Fama* and *Confessio*, they should either remain anonymous or conceal their real connection, of which the latter alternative was infinitely preferable, the anonymous writer being always suspect.

To sum up my contentions, I submit that in the first place there is really no evidence worth considering for the suggestion that *The Rosie Crucian Secrets* is a late forgery by Peter Smart, who, in my opinion, figures simply as a copyist; that there is a mass of evidence in favour of the supposition that as early as Dee's time there was in existence a secret fraternity, probably with membership both in this country and abroad, to which he belonged, among whom circulated certain private MSS; that this society may even have been, and probably was, a branch of the Rosicrucian Brotherhood; that there is a very obvious and probable line of descent by which the MS we are considering could have come into the hands of Peter Smart; and finally that the attribution by him of the whole MS to Dee is a simple and understandable error.

E. J. Langford Garstin
London
January 16th 1935

INTRODUCTION

As the underlying basis of the major portion of this book is Qabalistic, it would seem advisable very briefly to provide the reader who is unfamiliar with this tradition with sufficient information to enable him to appreciate the frequent allusions thereto that he will find in both the text and my notes. What follows is, therefore, in no way to be regarded as an essay on Qabalistic alchemy, but is merely a more or less tabular outline of the fundamental notions with which he should be familiar, arranged as far as possible in such a manner as to be easy of reference.

The Qabalah postulates that before all manifestation the Deity existed negatively under the three forms of *Ain*, the negatively existent One, *Ain Soph*, the Limitless and *Ain Soph Aur*, the illimitable Light. These three forms of the unknowable and nameless One are, of course, completely beyond all human comprehension, existing in the mind as ideas only and obviously incapable of definition. They are known as the three veils of the negative existence and they formulate within themselves the hidden ideas of what are to be the ten Emanations of Sephiroth.

With the Sephiroth themselves we come to the stage of manifest existence, though not necessarily to an existence apprehendable or comprehensible by man, for he inhabits the lowest of the four Worlds into which the Universe is divided and only in this world and that which precedes it is form to be found, the two higher worlds transcending everything that is perceptible and nearly everything that may be imagined conceptually.

For the purpose of this Introduction it is not necessary to investigate these ideas at any length, but merely to point out that the Sephiroth are arranged in the manner illustrated in the accompanying diagram (fig. 1), which is called the Tree of Life, in which they themselves are known as the first ten Paths, while those lines shown as joining them

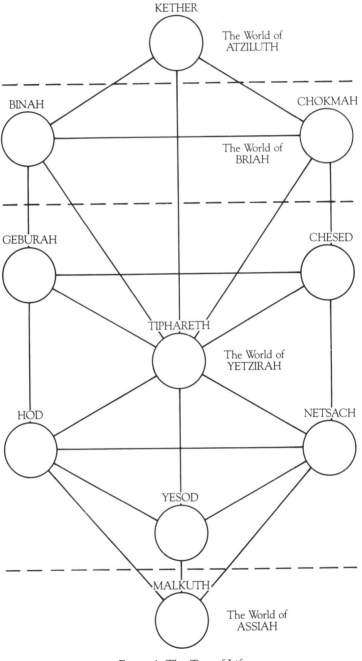

Figure 1. The Tree of Life

are the twenty-two connecting Paths, the whole forming the thirty-two Paths of the *Sepher Yetzirah* or *Book of Formation*. The dotted lines indicate the division of this scheme into the four Worlds previously mentioned, which are known as Atziluth, Briah, Yetzirah and Assiah and are respectively Archetypal or pure Deity, Archangelic or Creative, Angelic or Formative, and Material. Each World is regarded as having its own ten Sephiroth and corresponding thereto are allotted the appropriate Divine and other Names. It will be seen from Table I that in Assiah the names are not those of entities, but of elements acted upon.

Now according to the *Zohar*, the great treasure-house of Qabalistic teaching, man is the microcosm and is created on the same pattern as the greater universe, namely on the plan of the Sephirothic System. I am not here concerned with his body but with what is generally termed his Soul, and the Qabalah regards the Soul as being divided into three principal parts of which the highest is termed Neshamah, corresponding to the two highest of the four Worlds, Atziluth and Briah, the Deific and the Creative; the second is the Ruach, which may be translated Spirit, corresponding to the third, the Yetziratic or Formative World, while the third is the Nephesch, the Lower Soul or Self, corresponding to Assiah, the Material World of sense.

Now Neshamah itself, which corresponds to the two highest Worlds and thus to the first three Sephiroth, is also divided into three parts corresponding therewith, namely Yechidah, Chiah and Neshamah respectively, so that the first of these conveys the illimitable and transcendental idea of the Great, Absolute and Incomprehensible One in the Soul. This is linked by Chiah, which suggests the idea of Essential Being, with Neshamah, and these two together represent Wisdom and Understanding, the higher, governing, creative idea, the aspiration to the Ineffable One in the Soul. Neshamah in turn links these Supernals with the Ruach or Spirit, which is here the Mind, the Reasoning Power, that which possesses the knowledge of good and evil. It should be carefully and especially noted that this is the rational or discursive mind and not the higher mind, which is represented by Neshamah. Lastly we have the Nephesch, which is that power in the Soul which represents the passions and physical appetites. To this last corresponds the body of man on which his spirit acts through the Nephesch, just as his Neshamah can only act on the Nephesch through the Ruach, and then only when the former has been equilibrated by the action of the latter. These ideas form the basis of Theurgy or Spiritual Alchemy.

On the physical side — and it must be remembered that the two departments of the Art, namely the spiritual and the material, are so closely parallel and so nearly allied that they are not wholly to be separated — the Tree of Life again appears, having the various philosophical principles and metals referred to the Sephiroth in two principal ways. *Aesch Mezareph*, cap.i, instructs the aspiring artist on this point as follows:

> But know that the Mysteries of this Wisdom differ not from the superior Mysteries of the Qabalah. For such as is the consideration of the Predicaments in Holiness, the same is also in Impurity; and the same are in Assiah, yea the same in that Kingdom which is commonly called the Mineral Kingdom, although their Excellency is always greater upon the spiritual plane. Therefore the Metallic Root here possesseth the place of Kether, which hath an occult Nature, involved in great obscurity, and from which all Metals have their Origin, even as the Nature of Kether is hidden and the other Sephiroth flow forth from thence.
>
> Lead hath the place of Chokmah, because Chokmah immediately proceeds from Kether, as it immediately comes from the Metallic Root; and in Ænigmatic similes it is called the Father of the following Natures.
>
> Tin possesseth the place of Binah, showing Age by its greyness and shadowing forth Severity and Judicial Rigour by its crackling.
>
> Silver is placed under the Classis of Chesed by all the Masters of the Qabalah, chiefly for its Colour and Use.
>
> Thus far the White Natures. Now follow the Red.
>
> Gold is placed under Geburah, according to the most common opinion of the Qabalists; Job in *cap.* xxxvii, 22, also tells us that gold cometh from the North, not only for its colour, but for the sake of its Heat and Sulphur.
>
> Iron is referred to Tiphereth, for he is like a Man of War, according to *Exod.*, xv, 2, and hath the Name of 'Seir Anpin', from his swift Anger, according to *Psalm* ii, 12, 'Kiss the Son lest he be angry.'
>
> Netzach and Hod are the two Median places of the Body and the Seminal Receptacles and refer to the Hermaphroditic Brass. So also the two Pillars of the Temple of Solomon (referring to these two Sephiroth) were made of Brass, *I Kings*, vii, 15.
>
> Jesod is Argent Vive. For to this the name of 'Living' is Characteristically given; and this Living Water is in every case the Foundation of all Nature and of the Metallic Art.
>
> But the true Medicine of Metals is referred to Malkuth for many Reasons; because it represents the rest of the Natures under the Metamorphoses of Gold and Silver, right and left, Judgement and Mercy, concerning which we will speak more largely elsewhere.
>
> Thus I have delivered to thee the Key to unlock many Secret Gates and have opened the door to the inmost adyta of Nature. But if anyone hath placed those things in another order, I shall not contend with him,

inasmuch as all systems tend to the one truth.

For it may be said, the Three Supernals are the Three Fountains of Metallic things. The thick water (Mercury) is Kether, Salt is Chokmah and Sulphur is Binah, for known reasons. And so the Seven Inferior will represent the Seven Metals, *viz.*, Gedulah and Geburah, Silver and Gold; Tiphereth, Iron; Netzach and Hod, Tin and Copper; Jesod, Lead; and Malkuth will be the Metallic Woman and the Luna of the Wise Men and the Field into which the Seeds of secret Minerals ought to be cast, that is the Water of God, as this Name (Mezahab) occurs, *Genesis*, xxxvi, 39.

But know, my Son, that such Mysteries are hid in these things as no Tongue may be permitted to utter. But I will not offend any more with my Tongue, but will keep my Mouth *with a Bridle, Psalm*, xxxix, 2.

In considering the above the reader should remember that although the metals are referred to the planets, they are not attributed to the Sephiroth in the same way, as a comparison between Tables I and III will show.

Considerable importance attaches in the Qabalah to the Hebrew alphabet itself, which is composed of twenty-two letters, corresponding to the twenty-two connecting Paths of the Tree of Life. These letters are divided into classes as follows, namely three mother letters, referred to the three Elements of Air, Water and Fire; seven double letters, referred to the seven planets; and twelve simple letters, referred to the twelve Signs of the Zodiac. A further point of importance lies in the fact that every Hebrew Letter is a number, so that every word is a number, from which arises the system of exegesis known as Gemmatria, which deals with numerical values.

In addition to the purely Qabalistic allusions which occur in the text and notes, it will be found that the author attaches importance to certain Astrological and Geomantic considerations and I have, therefore, appended Tables showing the names of the various Angels, Intelligences and Spirits involved, together with their Sigils where relevant.

Table I.

The Ten Sephiroth	Meaning of the Names	Elements acted upon in Assiah	Meaning of the Names
1. Kether	Crown	Rashith Ha-Galgalim	Primum Mobile
2. Chokmah	Wisdom	Masloth	Zodiac
3. Binah	Understanding	Shabbathai	Saturn

The Ten Sephiroth	Meaning of the Names	Elements acted upon in Assiah	Meaning of the Names
4. Chesed	Mercy	Tzedeq	Jupiter
5. Geburah	Severity	Madim	Mars
6. Tiphareth	Beauty	Shemesh	Sun
7. Netzach	Victory	Nogah	Venus
8. Hod	Glory	Kokab	Mercury
9. Yesod	Foundation	Levanah	Luna
10. Malkuth	Kingdom	Cholom Yesodoth	Elements

Table II.

The Ten Sephiroth		The Four Worlds	The Parts of the Soul	
1. Kether		Archetypal	Yechidah	
2. Chokmah	Atziluth		Chiah	Neshamah
3. Binah				
4. Chesed				
5. Geburah	Briah	Creative		
6. Tiphareth				
7. Netzach				
8. Hod	Yetzirah	Formative	Ruach	
9. Yesod				
10. Malkuth	Assiah	Material	Nephesch	

Table III. The Two Forms of the Alchemic Sephiroth

The Ten Sephiroth	Attributes 1st Form	Attributes 2nd Form
1. Kether	Metallic Root	Mercury
2. Chokmah	Lead	Salt
3. Binah	Tin	Sulphur
4. Chesed	Silver	Silver
5. Geburah	Gold	Gold
6. Tiphareth	Iron	Iron
7. Netzach	Brass	Tin
8. Hod	Brass	Copper
9. Yesod	Argent Vive	Lead
10. Malkuth	Medicine of Metals	The Metallic Woman, Luna Philosophorum

Table IV.

Planet	*Angel*	*Intelligence*	*Spirit*	*Houses*
♄	Cassiel	Agiel	Zazel	♑ ♒
♃	Sachiel	Yophiel	Hismael	♐ ♓
♂	Samael	Graphael	Barzabel	♈ ♏
☉	Michael	Nakhiel	Sorath	♌
♀	Anael	Hagiel	Kedemel	☿ ♎
☿	Raphael	Tiriel	Taphthartharath	π ♍
☽	Gabriel	Malka-Be-Tharshisim-Ve-Od-Ruachoth-Schechalim	Chasmodai	♋

Table V.

Geomantic Figure	*Name*	*Ruler*	*Sigil*	*Genius*	*Sigil*	*Sign*	*Planet*
	Puer	Bartzabel		Malchidael		♈	♂
	Amissio	Qedemel		Asmodel		♉	♀
	Albus	Taphthar-tharath		Ambriel		♊	☿
	Populus	Chasmodai		Muriel		♋	☽
	Fortuna Major	Sorath		Verchiel		♌	☉
	Conjunctio	Taphthat-tharath		Hamaliel		♍	☿
	Puella	Qedemel		Zuriel		♎	♀
	Rubeus	Bartzabel		Barchiel		♏	♂
	Acquisitio	Hismael		Advachiel		♐	♃
	Carcer	Zazel		Hanael		♑	♄
	Tristitia	Zazel		Cambiel		♒	♄
	Laetitia	Hismael		Amnixiel		♓	♃
	Cauda Draconis	Zazel & Barzabel		Zazel & Barzabel		☋	♄ ♂ ☋
	Via	Chasmodai		Muriel		♋	☽
	Caput Draconis	Hismael & Qedemel		Hismael & Qedemel		☊	♃ ♀ ☊

Editor's Note

In transcribing this MS I have been careful throughout to do so fully and exactly. In the few cases where I have thought it desirable to alter a word or phrase, I have indicated the MS reading in a footnote. Any additions that I have made to facilitate reading are clearly shown by the use of square brackets, [ ], round brackets, ( ), being those of the original.

Apart from these modifications I have done nothing except to modernize the spelling in places.

PART I

Qui vult secreta scire, debet secreta secrete custodire.

The Rosie Crucian Secrets
Their Excellent Method of Making Medicines of Mettals. Also their Lawes and Mysteries.

The Preface[60]

The Contemplative Order of the Rosie Cross have presented to the world Angels, Spirits, Planets and Metals, with the times in Astromancy and Geomancy to prepare and unite them telesmatically. The Water is not extracted by the hands of men, but it is made by nature a Spermatick, Viscous Composition of water, earth, air and fire, all those four natures united in one crystalline, coagulated mass. By Mercury I understand not Quicksilver, but Saturn philosophical, which devours the Moon and keeps her always in his belly. By Gold I mean the Spermatick Green Gold,[61] not the adored lump which is dead and ineffectual.[62] This is the substance which at present is[63] our study. [It] is the child of the Sun and Moon,[64] placed between two fires, and in the darkest night receives a light from the stars and retains it. The Angels or Intelligences are attracted by an horrible emptiness[65] and attend the Astrolasme for ever. He hath in him a thick fire by which he captivates the thin Genii. At first the Telesma is neither metal nor matter, neither solid nor fluid, but a substance without all form but what is universal.[66] He is visible and a fume of Mercury, not crude but cocted. This fume utterly destroys the first form of Gold, introducing a second and a more noble one. He hath no certain colour, for Camelion like, he puts on all colours, and there is nothing in the world hath the same figure with him when he is purged from his accidents. He is a water coloured with fire, deep to the sight and, as it were, hollow and he hath something in him that resembles a commotion. In a vaporous heat he opens his belly and discovers an airy heaven, tinged with a milky white light; within this *Coelum* he hides a little Sun, a most powerful red fire sparkling like a Carbuncle, which is the red Gold of the Rosie Crucians.

That you may know the Rosie Crucian philosophy, endeavour to know God Himself, the worker of all things, and to pass into Him by a whole image of likeness (as by an essential contract and bond), whereby we may be transformed and made as God, as the Lord spake

First Sheet

concerning Moses, saying, I have made thee the God of Pharaoh.[67] This is the true Rosie Crucian philosophy of wonderful works, that they understood not, the Key whereof is Intellect.[68] For by how much the higher things we understand, with so much the sublimer virtues are we endowed, and so much greater things do work and the more easily and efficaciously. But an Intellect being included in the corruptible flesh, unless it shall exceed the way of the flesh and obtain a proper nature, cannot be united to those virtues (for like to like) and is, in searching into the Rosie Crucian secrets of God and nature, altogether inefficacious. For it is no easy thing for us to ascend to the Heavens, for how shall he that hath lost himself in mortal dust and ashes find God? How shall he apprehend spiritual things that is swallowed up in flesh and blood? Can man see God and live? What fruit shall a grain of corn bear if it be not first dead; for we must die to the world, to the flesh and [to] all [the] senses and to the whole man animal, who would[69] enter into the closest of secrets, not because the body is separated from the Soul, but because the Soul leaves the body, of which death St Paul wrote to the Collossians, Ye are not dead and your life is hid with Christ.[70] And elsewhere he speaks more clearly of himself, I know a man, whether in the body or out of the body I cannot tell, God knows, caught up into the third Heaven,[71] etc. I say by this death, precious in the sight of God, we must die, which happens to few, and not always, for very few whom God loves and are virtuous are made so happy. And first those that are born not of flesh and blood but of God; secondly those that are dignified by the blessed assistance of Angels and Genii, the power of Nature, [the] influence of the planets and the heavens and [the] virtues of the figures and Ideas at their birth.[72]

BEHOLD THE ROSIE CRUCIAN CROWNE

This Crown[73] is set with seven Angels, seven Planets, twelve Signs, seven Rulers, twelve Ideas and sixteen Figures.[74]

Observe this harmony. The seven Angels guide the seven Planets, the seven Planets move continuously in the twelve Signs, the seven Rulers run in the twelve Ideas over the face of the Earth, and with the Elements project sixteen Figures. These have their influence upon the seven metals which you must prepare for the Diseases of mankind, as for example, if Mars cause the disease, Venus and Kedemel will cure it and you must make your Medicine of Copper.

If Saturn and Zazel cause the disease, Jupiter and Hismael in Tin prepared will lend you their influence to cure the party.[75] If Saturn cause the disease the Sun and prepared Gold will cure the disease.

Now I will demonstrate in what thing, of what thing or by what thing is the Medicine or Multiplication of Metals to be made. It is even in the nature, of the nature and by the nature of metals, for it is a principle of all philosophers that Nature cannot be bettered but in his own nature.[76]

Trevisan saith: Every Substance hath his own proper and principal seed of which it is made. A pear tree bringeth forth a pear and an apple tree an apple, and God said in the beginning, let everything bring forth his fruit and let the seed be multiplied in itself. And Arnoldus de Villa Nova saith: Every seed is correspondent to his seed and every shrub bringeth forth his proper fruit, according to his kind, for nothing but man is engendered of man, nor of the animals but their like; whereupon Paracelsus concludeth thus: True Alchemy, which only alone teacheth the Art to make Sol and Luna of five metals, will not admit any other receipt because[77] that which is thus (and it is truly spoken): perfect metals are made only of metals, in metals, by metals and with metals for in some metals is Luna and in other metals is Sol. If this be true that in Metals are their seed whereby they may be multiplied, how is it then that the philosophers say their Gold and Silver are not common Gold and Silver, for common Gold and Silver are dead but their Gold and Silver liveth. To this I answer, common Gold and Silver are dead except they be revived by art, i.e., except their seeds, which are naturally included in them, be projected into their natural earth, by which means they are mortified and revived like as the grain of wheat that is dead and unapt to increase, except by art and industry of man it is in due season sown in his kindly earth and there putrefied and again revived and multiplied. For which cause Trevisan hath written that the vulgar bodies that Nature only hath perfected in the mine are dead and cannot perfect the imperfect bodies. But if we take them and reiterate perfection upon them seven, ten or twelve times,[78] then will they tinge infinitely, for then are they entering, tincting and more than perfect and quick in regard of that which they were before.

Paracelsus likewise affirmeth metallic spirits are dead and lie still so that they cannot work, unless by art they be revived, which thing Arnoldus verifies. Gold and Silver, therefore, simple and absolute in their bodily and metallic form, are dead, but by art they are revived and made Gold and Silver of the Philosophers. And they are revived and brought to yield their seed by reducing them into their first matter, which is called *prima materia metallorum*,[79] for it is impossible for the species or forms of metals to be transmuted but by reducing them into their first matter.

Second Sheet

Now the first matter of metals is Argent vive, i.e., Quicksilver,[80] as all philosophers verify. For the first matter of anything is the self same thing into which it is resolved as snow and ice are resolved into water, which is the proper and first matter, and so metals are dissolved into Argent vive. Therefore Argent vive or Mercury is the first matter of metals.[81] Therefore metals of necessity must be reduced into Mercury and not into cloud water as the philosophers affirm, but into a viscous water[82] which is the first matter of metals, for it is the opinion of Paracelsus, Arnoldus and Trevisan that labour is lost which is spent in the Separation of the Elements, for nature will be severed by human distinction, but hath her own separation in itself. Therefore metals should not be reduced into cloud water but into a viscous water.

Albertus Magnus saith the first matter of metals is Argent vive, which is a viscous, incombustible moisture commixed in a strong and wonderful mixture with a subtle earthliness in the mineral caves of the earth, which continually moveth and floweth because successively one part hath rule over another. As the cause of flowing and moving is by moisture bearing the chief rule, so[83] terrestrial dryness bearing chief rule over the action of moisture is the cause it will not stick to that which it toucheth nor moisten [it].

Trevisan saith that is the nearest matter of metals whose viscous moisture is mixed with his subtile earthliness.

And Geber saith, we could never yet find anything permanent in the fire but this viscous matter or moisture which is the self same note[84] of all metals, and all the other moistures[85] do easily fly from the fire by evaporation and separation of one element from another, as water by fire, one part going into smoke, another into water, another into earth remaining in the bottom of the vessel; but the viscous moistness, that is to say Mercury, is never consumed in it nor separated from his earth nor from any other his element; for either they remain altogether or vanish altogether, so that no part of the weight may perish.

Geber thus describeth the nature of Quicksilver:[86] Argent vive, which the Alchemists call Mercury, is nothing else but a viscous water in the bowels of the earth, of a moist and subtile substance of white earth united altogether by a moist, temperate heat by the least parts, until the moist be temperated by the dry and the dry by the moist, so that being thus both equally united and mixed, neither of them may be separated nor taken from one another by the fire. And in this Argent vive, the mother of all metals, is only the whole perfection, for it hath in its composition sulphury parts dry, the which tinge and colour[87] [the] whiteness in act and redness in power, and therefore this is the true Sulphur which perfecteth, formeth, coagulateth, coloureth and fixeth by his action. But this incombustible, hidden and unknown Sulphur which is in power in Argent vive, cannot bring itself forth into act but by due decoction, wherefore you may now perceive that neither nature in the veins of the earth nor we above ground, have any[88] other matter to work upon but only pure Mercurial Form[89] wherein Sulphur is enclosed, that is to say fire and air, which indeed is the internal and essential part of the Mercury itself; but it doth not dominate therein but by the means of heat, the which is caused by the reflexion of the fiery sphere which encloseth the air, and also by[90] the continual and equal motion of the heavenly bodies, which do stir so lent an heat as that it can hardly be perceived or imagined. And thus by most perfect decoction, and also by continual proportional digestion in long success of time is introduced in art and made manifest in the end of the operation of Nature that aforesaid unknown and incombustible Sulphur, which is the true form and ferment of Gold. And thus mayest thou see that metalline form[s] take their original only of pure mercurial substance, the which is the mother of all metals and coupleth and is united with her male, that is with the said Sulphur, the father of metals, the which causeth the diversity of metals according to the different degrees of decoction and alteration caused in Mercury by his own natural heat of inward Sulphur.

The philosophers do agree that there are[91] in the nature and original of metals two sperms or seeds, the one masculine and agent, which they call Sulphur, the other feminine and patient, which they name Mercury; and these two have the natural conjunction and operation one with another in the womb of the earth, whereby they engender metals of diverse form and quality according to the difference and diversity of their degree of digestion and concoction.

Now I will briefly discover the difference between Sulphur and Mercury, and the beginning and natural generation of them, and then show how they have their natural operation, the one with the other, in the bowels of the earth to be made metals perfect and imperfect.

Sulphur is double in every metal save only in Gold, that is to say external, burning and internal, not burning, which [latter] is of the substantial composition of Argent vive. The Mercury or Quicksilver spoken of is engendered or compounded in the bowels of the earth of clear, viscous water by a most temperate heat, united by the least parts, indissoluble, with an earthly substance, incombustible Sulphur, white, most subtile in art, without the which the substance of Argent vive cannot subsist, which coloureth it naturally with a white colour, but in our magistery it maketh it white and red as we will by governing the nature of it; wherefore Argent vive is the total material

Fourth Sheet

cause and total substance of the Philosophers' Medicine, containing in itself that internal Sulphur, being a simple fire, lively, quickening, the which indeed is the true masculine agent that before we spake of, the which, by perfect and due digestion and proportional decoction, congluteth, coloureth, formeth and fixeth his own Argent vive into Gold according to nature and to art in the philosophical medicine. But when that Argent vive is by nature thus fixed and made perfect by most high digestion into Gold only by his own proper and inward Sulphur, which is the true ferment, then the external, combustible Sulphurs cannot enter in nor be mixed with him, but they are[92] parted clear away as the corruptible from the permanent; wherefore they enter[93] not into Gold and therefore cannot be the matter or form, or any part of the matter or form of the Philosophers' Medicine. And thus you may understand the difference between the true Sulphur and Mercury, for when it appeareth simple it is flowing and is called Mercury, and is volatile, carrying or holding his proper incombustible Sulphur or ferment hidden in power. But when in the end of the aforesaid decoction that hidden Sulphur is brought wholly into act, whereby the whole is manifest and doth show the nature of Sulphur, then it is called Sulphur, which doth coagulate, reduce and fix his Argent vive to his proper nature, which is to be made Gold. Wherefore this is the only tincting Sulphur of the philosophers, the which is unknown to the common people. But the compound of them is called the Mixed Medicine, perfect and sound, and in the commixtion they are made all one as wax, and so in truth you may now see that these two spermatic matters are of one root, substance and essence, that is to say of the only essence of pure Argent vive. But the diversity of the sundry shapes, forms and bodies of metals, the which is the cause of the perfection or imperfection of them, is according to the diverse and several degrees of alteration caused by their decoction and digestion. For the Mercury, [which] is Argent vive running in the veins of the earth, conjoineth and is mixed with the aforesaid external Sulphur, and being so mingled and conjoined together by the sundry and different degrees of the decoctions of the internal Sulphur caused by the motions of the heavenly bodies, there is engendered the sundry shapes and forms and bodies of the metals in the entrails of the earth.[94] For first in the first degree of natural operation and digestion, the heat of the internal Sulphur working and somewhat prevailing in the humidity of his Mercury, beginneth somewhat to fix and coagulate the mercurial humour and giveth it the form of Lead. And by further digestion and decoction, the Sulphur yet somewhat more prevailing over his Mercury, the Mercury is somewhat more fixed and receiveth the form of Tin.

Then doth the heat dominate more and maketh Copper and then Iron, and further proceeding in their digestion, the internal Sulphur yet more subduing the moist[ure] and cold of his Mercury by a temperate heat, and attaining by his concoction purity and perfection of whiteness, it more firmly fixeth his body and giveth it the form and fixation and tincture of Silver. And now the essence that was in power is brought forth into act, whereby the external, earthly Sulphur, which gave a transitory form to the undigested metals, is almost utterly expoliated and separated by reason of his perfect form introduced by the means of our digestion and proportional decoction.

And yet in the Silver there are some small parts of the external Sulphur, the which are by the last and most temperate, complete digestion of nature wholly and thoroughly expoliated. And then by nature is accomplished the most perfect, simple and pure substantial form of Gold, which Gold in the perfection of his metalline nature is pure fire, digested by the said Sulphur existing in Mercury, whereby his Mercury, that is to say his whole substance, is converted into the nature of his pure Sulphur and made permanent and triumphant in the force and violence of the fire. And by the separation of the external Sulphur, the metals are made perfect according to the[95] divers degrees of their decoction, digestion and alteration, wherein they separate themselves from the earthly and combustible Sulphur and attain their true, complete, pure form and fixation.

But whereas the philosophers do seem to set down by degrees first Saturn, then Jupiter, then Luna, then Venus, then Mars and then Sol, they had a further meaning therein which is not to be understood according to the letter; for indeed Venus and Mars are placed after Luna, not that it should be believed that Luna doth turn or go into an imperfect body as Venus and Mars, but in truth they are placed after Luna for two causes, first because of the over great and excessive burning of the filthy and fixed, earthly, external Sulphur, which is joined with their Mercury and is outwardly by too much intemperate and an overgreat, superfluous, drying, combustible heat, coagulated and decocted with the Argent vive to a corruptible body, while the other cause is philosophically to be understood in the order and degrees of the colours[96] in the working of the Philosophers' Medicine, which is a similitude and analogy, and this over great quantity of burning, gross, earthly, external Sulphur is the cause of the hard melting of Mars. But so soon as nature by a temperate, complete digestion hath introduced into act the internal, pure Sulphur, then are separated all those external Sulphurs from the Mercury and a perfect form is introduced. [An] example [of this is to be seen] in the projection of the Philosophers'

Fifth Sheet

Medicine, which, being cast upon imperfect metals molten, doth only by virtue of the most pure, temperate, high and mighty digestion fix and give a true, natural form to the Mercury of the bodies, whereby is expoliated away all external Sulphur and they are perfected into fine Gold. And you must also know that nature doth not always [proceed by means] of these degrees in passing through the dispositions and paths[97] of the metals, or any one of them, but doth oftentimes engender perfect Sol as the aforesaid beginning by a most temperate and due decoction in the bowels of the earth. The reason hereof, the knowledge of the countries and mines will make manifest unto you.[98]

And thus have I made plain the very operation and work of nature in the earth, as all the philosophers deciphered it. And this operation of nature are we to imitate and follow as near as possible in our art, according to the earnest precepts and prescriptions of all the philosophers in this behalf.

Now I shall show how and in what manner our art must imitate the operation of nature; but first I will resolve, wherefore do the philosophers call Mercury or Quicksilver the First Matter of Metals, when there is another matter or sperm, as we have declared, which must be joined with it before metals can be engendered.

The philosophers do truly call Mercury the First Matter of Metals, being so indeed, for the Sulphur which is the masculine sperm, is of her, and she is the root of him and his coagulation, as Hermes said. And also the same man saith, this water coagulateth when it is congealed and running water is the mother of that which is congealed and coagulated and so it was ever. For which cause the philosophers call the feminine sperm the patient, or matter which suffereth the action of her agent, and taketh the impression of his forms in her substance; and therefore the philosophers said truly that Sulphur giveth the form and beginning of being more than matter, when as that it is his act and matter power and form; for according to the truth of forms, they are named the substance of things, but matter may after another sort be called more the substance in as much as it is the beginning to everything, and from it are extracted all forms.

If, therefore, any man would like to know the form of Gold, he must of necessity know the matter of Gold, the which is Argent vive. It springeth flowing, liquid, flying, bright and suffereth coagulation, and is, therefore, truly called the First Matter of Metals, because all metals have their first matter or substance from her, their mother, the forms of the metals being affected by the moving of the active elements, fiery and airy, of Mercury, that is to say, Sulphur,[99] the which moveth Argent vive, as this proper matter for generation into metals, according to the degrees of his motions.

Now we proceed to apply the operation of an art to the operation of nature, and show what is the first work of art.

Learn to know what is the first work of art by the first work of nature, always provided that it be that first work of nature that art is able to perform. But because the first work of nature was to make the two sperms of nature, which art cannot do, therefore the second work of nature, which is the conjunction of the two sperms in one, must of necessity be the first work of art, and the creation or making of the two sperms must be only referred to nature, who hath provided and prepared to art the matter that art is to work upon. According to the saying of the philosopher, art of itself cannot create the sperms, but when nature hath created them, then doth art, joined with that natural heat which is in the sperms already created, mix them as the instrument of nature, for it is plain that art doth add neither form, nor matter, nor virtue, but only aiding the thing existing, to bring it to perfection. And again, nature hath created a matter unto art, unto which art neither addeth anything nor taketh anything away, but removeth such things as are superfluous; likewise nature hath provided for us one Stone and one matter and one medicine, unto the which we, by our art, add no foreign thing, nor in any point diminish it, but in removing that which is superfluous in the preparation,[100] and this is done in the purification which is effected by solution. By these words it plainly appeareth that nature hath prepared the matter wherein art is to work, and art by no means can make the same matter; but the only work of art is to cleanse and purify that which nature hath left impure, and make that perfect which nature hath left imperfect, as is verified by this last saying of Arnoldus, and that first of Trevisan.

Sixth Sheet

Now, therefore, it follows that the first work of Art, wherein art doth imitate nature, must of necessity be that which is the second work of nature, (*viz.*) as the second work of nature after she had created the sperm was to join these two sperms of nature together, whereby to make the First Matter of Metals, so the first work of art must be to conjoin the sperms of metals together, whereby we must make the First Matter of one pure Medicine, that may bring the impure and imperfect metals into the purity and perfection of nature. And this can no otherwise be done but by reduction of them into their First Matter, as is before said, by which means we may have (as Arnoldus saith) the same sperms of the metals above earth that nature did work in under the earth. And this reduction is nothing else but the dissolution in which they are dissolved into the natural Mercury and Sulphur again, but more pure than they were before by reason that they are in their dissolution separated and purified from the fex and impurity of their nature and made more pure and perfect whereby to engender a more pure and perfect matter than nature could do; and for this cause hath the philosopher written this conference in the lamentation of nature between nature and art, 'Without me, which do yield the matter, thou shalt never effect anything, and without thee also, which dost minister unto me, I cannot alone finish this work.'

It is the chiefest and highest secret of the philosophers to know out of which of the metals must we have these sperms. I ought not to disclose the same in plain terms, but in dark speeches and figures as they have done. Notwithstanding, mark that which shall follow and I will discover to thee the secrets of the philosophers in hope that thou wilt hide them in thy heart and commit the papers to the fire. Now first and chiefly thou must call to remembrance the words of the philosophers before named, who say that in some metals is Sol and in some metals Luna. That is to say, in some metals is the masculine sperm and in some is the feminine sperm. In some of the metals is the tincture of Gold and in some of the metals is the tincture of Silver. Some of them are masculine and some are feminine. For that these words are true in their expositions, the words of Hermes do very well prove, who said Red Sol is his father and White Luna his mother.[101] If, therefore, Sol be the father and Luna the mother, and in some of the metals be Sol and in some Luna, what is this but to say that some of the metals are masculine and some of them feminine, or in some of them is the masculine sperm and in some of them is the feminine sperm. Now, therefore, consider which of them are the masculine bodies, and out of which the masculine sperms are to be had, and then we shall more perfectly discern the feminine bodies whence the feminine sperms are to be fetched.

Note that the philosophers do diversely name these two sperms. The masculine they call agent, the Sulphur or rennet, the body or ferment, the poison or flower of Gold, the tincture or inward fire and the form. The feminine sperm they call the patient, Mercury, the Spirit volatile, Argent vive, *menstruum*, water, azoth and the matter and by many other names they name them both. But this *caveat* in the discerning of them I give thee for three causes especially. The one is because thou shouldest in reading of the philosophers not mistake any one of them for the other; the second cause, that thou shouldest by these names know which of the metals are masculine by the quality of the names; and the third cause is that thou shouldest thereby gather and understand that the two sperms, being of two several natures and qualities, can by no means be fetched from one body, as divers have misconstrued, no more than both the sperms of man and woman are in man alone. But they are to be had of two substances of one root, as Trevisan, Arnoldus and the rest of the philosophers affirm.

But I will give thee this secret note, that the two sperms must be had out of two several bodies, yea two bodies in one only root, which is the same Hermaphrodite of the philosophers, which they often write of,[102] or their Adam,[103] as in due place shall be disclosed; but in all the reading of the philosophers keep well this *caveat* in thy mind, of the several names and natures of the two sperms.

Seventh Sheet

But now I shall proceed to prove by the philosophers which are the masculine bodies, and how a question shall arise whether is that which giveth the form or tincture the masculine sperm or the feminine. You need not to doubt that among the metals Sol and Luna are both agents and masculine sperms,[104] for they both give form and tincture severally, the one to the white work, the other to the red work, according to the sayings of the philosophers.

For Arnoldus in his *Rosary* saith Gold is more precious than all other metals and is the tincture of redness tincting and transforming every body, but Silver is the tincture of whiteness, tincting all other bodies with a perfect whiteness; and therefore he which knoweth to tinct Argent vive with Sol and Luna cometh into the secret. Likewise in another place he saith thus. The first work is to sublime Mercury and to dissolve it, that it may return into the First Matter. Then let the clean bodies be put into this clean Mercury, but mix not the white body with the red, nor the red with the white, but dissolve every one severally apart, because the white water is to whiten and the red water is to make red, therefore mix not the water of the one medicine with the water of the other, because thou shalt greatly err and be blinded if thou do otherwise. By those two sentences of Arnoldus it appeareth not only that Sol and Luna are agents, the one giving form to the red work, the other to the white, but also there is another body that is to be dissolved into Mercury, which is the patient of these two, for as much as those two are to be put into the same; yet it is not the patient to them both together, but each of them severally and assunder, which proveth them plainly to be both masculine and agent, and none of them patient to any other, nor by any means to be mixed one with another, but a third thing to be patient to them both, that is to say the same Mercury or Argent vive that they before spake of where they said that he which knoweth how to tinct Argent vive with Sol and Luna cometh to a secret.[105] Likewise the noble Trevisanus saith, Our medicine is made of two things, being of one essence, to wit of the union mercurially of fixed and not fixed, spiritual and corporeal, cold and moist, hot and dry, and of no other thing can [it] be made. By those words it is manifest that the two Mercuries whereof our medicine is to be made are both of one root but of contrary qualities; that is to say, the one is a Mercury fixed, the other not fixed; the one a corporeal, the other a spiritual; the one hot and dry, the other cold and moist; which several Mercuries are contrary, and contrary matters cannot be included in Sol or Luna. For they, as Agents, are only hot and dry, corporeal and fixed, but they are not, as patients, cold and moist, volatile or spiritual[106] and unfixed, and therefore in them may be the masculine sperm, but in no wise the feminine; and therefore, saith *Turba* [*Philoso*]*phorum*, a tincture proceeding from the fountain of Sol and Luna giveth perfection to imperfect metals, upon which considerations they have also set down this most excellent canon and principle, (*viz*.) the secret of all secrets is to know that Mercury is the matter and *menstruum*, and the matter of perfect bodies is the form. What is this but as who should say, seeing the Mercury drawn from the perfect bodies is the form or agent sperm of our medicine, then Mercury of an imperfect body must needs be the matter or feminine sperm;[107] to the confirmation whereof Paracelsus saith thus: Philosophical Mercury that is of Sol, is in the conjunction compared unto the corporeal spirit of Mercury, as is the husband to his wife whereas they are both one, and the self same root and original, although the body of Sol remains fixed in the fire but the metallic woman unfixed. Notwithstanding *that*, compared to *this*, is no otherwise than the seeds to the field or earth.

Eighth Sheet By these words of Paracelsus it is evident that the difference between the metallic man and the metallic woman is that the metallic man is fixed and the metallic woman unfixed; by which means it is plain that this metallic woman cannot be Silver or the Spirit of Silver, as some do fondly surmise, and as the most do take it, but of some imperfect body that is unfixed. For who is so simple but knoweth that Luna is fixed and permanent in the fire and inseparably united with his pure white Sulphur.

Then it is proved the two perfect bodies are the agents, giving the forms and tinctures, and so, consequently to be the masculine sperm[108] and no less proving that the feminine sperm is to be had from an unfixed body, of which nature neither of them is, and therefore we must yield to the apparent reasons and authority of the philosophers.

I shall now expound by some of the philosophers the saying of Hermes that his father is Sol and Luna his mother.

These words of Hermes, though they be so full of truth and have no deceit in them, yet a great number have been deceived thereby. The cause of their error is because they do not consider the nature of Luna, which they take to be meant of Hermes to be the mother of our matter. For if they did either consider the masculine property of Silver or perused the philosophers touching their construction of this point, they should well perceive that Luna is not the Silver[109] that Hermes meaneth, but a certain unfixed matter or Mercury, of the nature and quality of the Celestial Luna,[110] as in the *Canons of the Philosophers* appeareth, and in the *Turba [Philoso]phorum* by these words: It is a thing worthy to be noted that Luna or Silver is not the mother of common Silver, but it is a certain Mercury endued with the nature and quality of the Celestial Moon, which is the same Mercury or woman before spoken of, that is not fixed as Silver is, but is of the nature of the Celestial Moon in respect of her moist, unmixed[111] and watery quality, having her fixation, form and tincture of her Sulphur as the Celestial Moon taketh light of the Sun. Therefore out of doubt it must be drawn from a body of the same nature, and not from a body of a contrary quality; for what can be more absurd than to think that an unfixed matter can be in a fixed metal or a fixed nature in an unfixed body. Consequently what can be more evident and manifest, seeing the philosophers do all affirm that the metallic man is fixed and the metallic woman unfixed, than that the fixed sperm must be had of a fixed metal and the unfixed and volatile nature out of an unfixed substance, and, therefore, by no means had from Luna, because of her fixed and masculine nature, which all the philosophers in plain terms confirm to be true, as in their *Canons*, by a question demanded and answered in this manner. The question amongst wise men is, whether the Mercury of Luna joined with the Mercury of Sol may be had instead of the philosophical *menstruum*. They[y] answer, Mercury of Luna doth hold the nature of the male or masculine, but two males cannot engender no more than two females. Likewise in another place thus, the Sulphurs Sol and Luna are the two sperms or masculine seeds of the Medicine. And in the *Turb[a]* thus, metallic Lunes are of a masculine nature. Thus I have proved that the two perfect metals are the two masculine bodies, from which we are to fetch our two masculine sperms or forms or tinctures, i.e., both of the red and white, which, seeing they are fixed and perfect bodies, the form and tincture and agents of our matter, they have sufficient reason of themselves to persuade that they can be no other than the masculine sperms, except we will, contrary to all rule of reason and nature, have one thing both the agent and the patient.

Now I will demonstrate which are the feminine bodies, and out of which the feminine sperms of our matter is to be fetched.

This secret of both these secrets is the greatest and requireth of itself to be kept as secretly in the hearts of all wise men hereafter as it hath been of all ancient philosophers heretofore.

Understand the secret by this figure 3, which number indeed it doth contain in itself, and is the very figure of the Trinity in the Deity.

Ninth Sheet — First I will show the reasons as the marks and tokens whereby thou shalt understand and know that this 3 is the same feminine body where is the feminine sperm of our blessed matter, which I will prove by the authority of the philosophers in this manner. First the philosophers do all agree that the metallic man in our matter is fixed and the metallic woman unfixed. If, therefore, I prove our matter 3 to be unfixed, it is a great argument and probability that our 3 is the same woman.

The second mark and token whereby she is known is that the philosophers agree that their Mercury or water which reduceth their Gold or Sulphur into his First Matter is the same that abideth and is permanent with it as Trevisanus declareth.[112] There is required in our natural solution the permanency of both, viz., of the water dissolving and of the dissolved body; and in another place, no water dissolveth the metallic essence with a natural reduction but that water which is abiding therein in matter and form, which water also, the metals themselves being dissolved, are able to congeal. And Arnoldus saith, the nature of the dissolved body and the dissolving water is all one, but only that the nature of the body is complete, digested and fixed, but the nature of the water is incomplete, undigested and volatile until it be fixed by the body. And in Paracelsus our woman dissolveth her man and the man fixeth the woman. By these words it is plain that the water which dissolveth the body is the same that is permanent with them,[113] that is to say, the woman or feminine sperm that is to be joined with the man or masculine.

Paracelsus saith plainly, speaking in the person of the figure 3, my spirit is the water, dissolving the congealed bodies of my brethren and Raymund Lullius saith in his *Epistle to the King*, Our water, you know, is extracted from a certain stinking *menstruum*, which is compounded of four things, and is stronger than all the water of the world, and it is mortal, whose spirit multiplieth the tincture of the ferment. And in another place he saith, all alchemical Gold is made of corrosives and of an incorruptible quintessence, which is fixed with ferment, but such quintessence is a certain spirit reviving and mortifying the mineral medicine. And *Turba* [*Philoso*]*phorum* saith, take the black spirit and with it dissolve bodies and divide them. Now consider the nature of our figure 3, and judge if this be that water or no. It must needs be the same, for the words fit the nature of our figure 3 and no other of the imperfect bodies but her, for all the philosophers agree that she is earthly, dark, cold and stinking, and Paracelsus nameth her plainly, the water dissolving her brethren.

Consider yet another note or mark whereby she is known, as the ancient and modern philosophers do affirm that their Gold must be sown in his own proper earth, as also in the *Turb[a]*, let our Gold be sown in his own proper earth.

Arnoldus in his *New Light* saith, with my own hands, my eyes being witnesses I have made the Elixir that converted Saturn into Sol, which matter truly I have now named, and it is the philosophers Magnesia, out of which they found[114] quicksilver of quicksilver and Sulphur of Sulphur. To construe these words rightly, what is our figure 3 but Mercury of Mercury, and what is our Gold but Sulphur of Sulphur. I will yet impart a greater secret.

It is written by good philosophers and found true infallibly by daily experience, that the figure 3 is never found simple or pure by himself in the mine, but is ever mixed with Gold or Silver, whose grains or seeds in him are plainly to be seen to the eyes; by which means it appeareth that there is no mine of himself, but he is the mine of them and so their very natural earth.

Consider these words following from Flammellus,[115] and thou shalt yet hear a greater secret than these. Mercury being never so little congealed in the veins of the earth, there is straightways fixed in it the grain of Gold which, of the two sperms, do bring forth true springs and branch of Mercury as we may see in the caves of Saturn, wherein there is no mine in any of which the true grain of the fixed may not be contained manifestly, that is the grain of Gold or Silver. For the first congelation of Mercury is the mine of Saturn in which it is put by nature. This may truly be multiplied into his perfections without fail or error, being, notwithstanding, in his Mercury not separated from his mine. For the metal consisting in his mine is Mercury, from which if the grain be separated it will be an unripe apple plucked from his tree, which is altogether destroyed. The fixed grain is the apple and Mercury is the tree; therefore the fruit is not to be separated from the tree, because it cannot elsewhere receive nourishment than from his Mercury. It is as great a folly to put Gold or Silver into Mercury as to fasten an apple again to the tree from whence it was taken. Therefore, that this business might be duly accomplished, the tree together with his fruit must be taken, that again it might be planted, without taking away the fruit, into a more fertile and new soil, which will give more nourishment in one day than the first field would have yielded in an hundred years, for the continual agitation of the winds. Go up, therefore, into the Mountain that thou mayest see the vegetable, Saturnian, royal and mineral herb,[116] for let the juice be taken pure, the feces being

Tenth Sheet

cast away, for thereof thou mayest effect the greatest part of thy work. This is the true Mercury of the Philosophers.

Trevisan confirms the matter thus. Our work is made of one root and two substances Mercurial, taken crude, drawn out of the mine clean and pure, conjoined by fire of amity as the matter requireth it, cocted continually until that of two be made one; and in this one, when the two are mixed, the body is made spirit and the spirit is made body. Paracelsus likewise speaking plainly in the name of our figure 3 saith: It would be profitable to the lesser world[117] if he did know or at least believe what lay hid within me, and what I could effect, for he that doth discourse upon the art of Alchemy would more profitably understand that which I can do if he would use that only which is in me, and that which by me may be done. And in another place, under an enigma, he notably discovereth this our blessed matter where he saith: Whatsoever staineth into a white colour hath the nature of life and the power and property of light, which causally[118] effecteth life; and contrariwise, whatsoever staineth into blackness or maketh black hath the nature common with death and the property of darkness and the strong power of death. The coagulation and fixation of such manner of corruption is the earth with her coldness. The house is always dead, but the inhabitant of the same liveth, and if thou canst find forth the example thereof thou hast prevailed.

By these words it appeareth that as the tincture of whiteness is the cause of life, which is the spirit of generation, so the blackness, which is the spirit of corruption, is death; and these two tinctures are in our blessed herb. The natural blackness whereof, that is to say our figure 3, is the spirit of the corruption or mortification, which is the same earth which he here noteth with his coldness. The same dead house within the artificial digestion is the death and mortification and putrefaction of the matter, and our Silver and Gold, which is naturally included in the same, is the tincture in his first artificial operation according to the philosophers, who say there is no Gold, but first was Silver before it was Gold. This tincture of whiteness is the same inhabitant which liveth in the same dead house, according to the saying before, the house is dead but they live which inhabit it; by which means it is plain that this is the same example which he speaketh of when he saith, the example whereof, if thou be able to find out, thou hast thy purpose.

Arnoldus noteth in his *Rosary*. This we see, that in the calculation of our figure 3, that first [it] is converted into black powder, next into white, then into a more yellow or red, which words very well discover his enigma written of this matter. Elsewhere he saith thus. The thing that hath both a red head, white foot and black eyes is the *materia*. Likewise it appeareth by the enigma of Hermes,[119] The falcon is always on top of the mountain crying I am the white of the black and the red of the citron. Now I will show how there is in our figure 3 that [which] I before spake of; the other thing [is] to show how it is the Hermaphrodite or Adam of the philosophers.[120]

In our mineral herb is the number of 3 thus. First therein is our figure 3. Secondly there is our Sulphur, i.e., our Gold or Silver which is naturally mixed with him. Thirdly there is the root of these two, that is to say Mercury or Quicksilver, whereof they were engendered, and whereunto they must be reduced, in respect of which trinity in unity it representeth the Figure of the Deity. Now of our Hermaphrodite or Adam therein. What else is our mineral herb[121] but one root of two substances, wherein is both our man or woman, that is to say our Gold is our Man, or sperm masculine, or Silver according to his natural mine, which is also the Sulphur, the tincture, the ferment and form before spoken of, having the perfect and fixed nature of the man, and the two agent elements of fire and air in them, and our woman is our figure 3, i.e., which is the feminine sperm, the patient, the *aqua* the *menstruum*, the matter, the Spirit volatile and the undigested[122] or unfixed body, having in her the two patient elements of water and earth.

Eleventh Sheet

Thus you see that Sol and Luna are the masculine sperms in our matter or figure 3, which is also the natural woman, water and earth of them both, where by nature they are planted and spring. That is to say the matter of our red work is our figure 3 joined with Sol and the matter of our white work is our figure 3 joined with Luna,[123] which matters are first to be had for more surety and security of art even in nature itself called *fex plumbi* or *Quehaeli Hispanica*. And thus dost thou see in our blessed matter, 4. 3. 2. and 1., yea and one only thing according to the words of all philosophers, [and] that you may not in the least doubt of the truth hereof, I have truly laid it open. The root of the operation of art in the matter shall hereafter be at large declared.

Commending, for this great and gracious mystery and secret of nature, to the Godhead all eternal glory, to Whom it is due.

The Lord illuminate my heart with His light and truth so long as my spirit remains in me, for His light is very delightful and good for the eye of my soul to see by; for so shall the night be enlightened to me as the day, neither shall the clouds shadow it. It shall not be like the light of the Sun by day because it shall not be clouded, nor like the light of the Moon by night, because it shall never be diminished as her light is.

The sun was made to rule the day and not to give light to it only, as appears *Gen.* i. And the Moon was made to rule the night and not to give light to it only, because she hath no light to give. Also God made the whole Host of Heaven, the fixed stars and planets, and gave them virtues together with the luminaries, but these virtues are not so great as the virtues of the luminaries, neither is the virtue of the Moon so great as the virtue of the Sun, because she borrows her light from the Sun. Also the whole Host of Heaven, that is the fixed stars, move all in the same sphere, and therefore their distance is always the same, but it is not so with the planets, for their course is various and so is their distance the one from the other, and so is their latitude. For some times they are upon the ecliptic, sometimes North from it and sometimes South, sometimes retrograde, sometimes direct, sometimes in conjunction with one another, sometimes in opposition, sometimes in other aspects. The reason of this is because the sphere of one is lower than the sphere of the other and the lower the sphere is, the sooner they make their revolution.

The nearest to the earth of all the planets is the Moon, and therefore her course is swiftest; and besides her difference in longitude or latitude there happen other accidents to her, which are not visible to other planets; for sometimes she increaseth and sometimes decreaseth, and sometimes she is invisible or faileth in light. The reason why the planets are not seen horned as the Moon is because their distance is greater from us. All the planets are seen biggest when they are at their greatest distance from the Sun, or when they are nearest to the earth according to Copernicus. Also sometimes the Moon is eclipsed, but not in the same manner as the Sun, for the Sun never loseth his light but is only shadowed from a particular people or place by the body of the Moon, but the Moon, eclipsed totally, loseth her light and the reason is the Sun's light is his own, but the Moon['s] is a borrowed light. This being premised, I consider all things under the Moon universally, whether men, beasts or planets, are changed and never remain in the same state, neither are their thoughts and their deeds the same. Take council of your head and it will certify you of the truth hereof; and they are varied according to the various course and disposition of the planets. Look upon your own genesis and you shall find your thoughts moved to choler so often as the Moon transits the place where the body or aspect of Mars was in your genesis; and to melancholy when she doth the like to Saturn. The reason is because the Moon is assimilated to the body of man, whose virtue as well as her light increaseth and diminisheth, for she brings down the virtue of the planets to the creatures and to man if he lives upon earth.

The Sun causeth heat and cold, day and night, winter and summer. When he arrives to the house of his honour or exaltation, to wit Aries, then the trees spring, living creatures are comforted, the birds sing, the whole of creation rejoiceth and sicknesses in the body show themselves in their colours. Also when he arrives at his Fall, to wit Libra, the leaves of the trees fall, all creatures are lumpish and mourn like the trees in October. Another notable Rosie Crucian experiment. Usually sick people are something eased from midnight to noon, because the Sun is in the ascending part of the heaven, but they are most troubled when the sun descends, that is from noon to midnight. The course of the Moon is to be observed in many operations both in the sea and rivers, vegetables, minerals, shellfish, as also in the bones and marrow of men and of all creatures. Also seed sown in the wane of the Moon grows either not at all or to no purpose.

The Rosie Crucians have experiences of many virtues of the stars, and have left them to posterity, and have found the changes and terminations of diseases by the course of the Moon. Wherefore the 7th, 14th, 20th or 21st, 27th, 28th or 29th days of the sickness are called critical days, which cannot be known but by the course of the Moon. But rest not in the number of the days, because the Moon is sometimes swifter, sometimes slower. As for such diseases as do not terminate in a month (I mean a lunar month, the time when the Moon moveth round the zodiac, which is in 27 days, some odd hours and minutes), you must judge of these by the course of the Sun.

The day is called critical because the Moon comes to the quartile of the place she was in at the decumbiture, sometimes a day sooner or later.

When she comes to opposition of the place she was in at the day of the decumbiture, she makes a second crisis; the third when she comes to the second quartile, and the fourth when she comes to the place she was in at the decumbiture, and then is the danger.

The reason of the difference of the Moon's motion is the difference of her distance from the earth, for when the centre of her circle is nearest to the centre of the earth, she is swift in motion; and hence it comes to pass that sometimes she moves more than 15 degrees in 24 hours, sometimes less than 12. Therefore if she be swift in motion she comes to her own quartile in six days, if slow, not in seven; therefore must you judge according to the motion of the Moon, and not according to the number of days.

Upon a critical day, if the Moon be well aspected with good planets, it goes well with the sick; if by ill planets it goes ill. You must be resolved in one particular which is, if the crisis depend upon the motion of the Moon and her aspect to the planets, what is the reason if two men be taken sick at one and the same time, that yet the crisis of the one falls out well and not so in the other. I answer, the virtue working is changed according to the diversity of the virtue receiving.[124] For you all know the Sun makes the clay hard and the wax soft; it makes the cloth white and the face black; so then if one be a child whose nature is hot and moist, the other a young man and the third an old man, the crisis works diversely in them all because their ages are different. Secondly the time of year carries a great stroke in this business. If it be in the spring time, diseases are most obnoxious to a child because his nature is hot and moist; a disease works most violently with a choleric man in summer; with a phlegmatic man by reason of age or complexion in winter.

If the Moon be strong when she comes to the quartile or opposition of the place she was in at the decumbiture, viz. in her house of exaltation, the sick recovers if she be aspected to no planet.

Judge the like of the Sun in chronical diseases, but judge the contrary if either of them be in detriment or fall. If the Moon be void of course at the beginning of a disease, the sign is neither good nor bad. Look then to the sign ascending at the beginning of a disease and let the Moon alone for a time.

Thirteenth Sheet

Observe the following directions how to prepare all the seven metals. If Mars cause the disease, Venus helps more than Jupiter, that is a medicine of Venus cures. If Saturn, then Jupiter more than Venus, i.e., prepared Jupiter cures.

Whatsoever is said of the Moon in acute diseases will hold as true of the Sun in chronical diseases.

What diseases every planet signifies and the diseases that are under the twelve signs, with the parts of the body every planet rules, the cure of those diseases by Rosie Crucian physic, by the seven metalic preparations, shall in his proper place be handled at large.

To unlock this grand Rosie Crucian mystery of the ASTROBOLISMES of metals, the miraculous saphiric medicines of the Sun and Moon, the ASTROBOLISMES of Saturn, Jupiter, Mars, Venus, Mercury.

Seriously consider the system or fabric of this world;[125] it is a certain series *a non gradu ad non gradum*, from that which is beneath all apprehension to that which is above all apprehension. That which is beneath all degrees of sense is a certain horrible, inexpressible darkness. The magicians call it *tenebrae activae*,[126] and the effect of it in nature is cold etc. For darkness is *vultus frigoris*,[127] the complexion, body and matrix of cold, as light is the face, principle and fountain of heat. That which is above all degree of intelligence is a certain infinite, inaccessible fire or light. Dionysius calls it *Caligo Divina*,[128] because it is invisible and incomprehensible. The Jew styles it Ein,[129] that is *nihil* or nothing, but in a relative sense or, as the schoolmen express it, *quoad nos*.[130] In plain terms it is *Deitas nuda, sine indumento.*[131] The middle substance or chain between these two is that which we commonly call nature. This is the *Scala* of the great Chaldee which doth reach[132] from the subternatural[133] darkness to the supernatural fire. These middle natures came out of a certain water, which was the sperm or First Matter of the great world. And now we will begin to describe it: *capiat qui capere potest.*[134]

It is in plain terms Χὔτὸν ϰαι Ρὔτὸν ὑδωρ,[135] or rather it is Η χυτὴ,[136] that is Ταια χυματώδης, ϰαι τὸ χεισεται της γῆς,[137] an exceedingly soft, moist, fusible, flowing earth, an earth of wax that is capable of all forms and impressions. It is Ὑδραμένος γηγενέτης, *terrae filius aqua mixtus* (Son of the Earth mixed with Water), and, to speak as the nature of the thing requires, Τεωμίγὴς ϰαι γῆς γάμος.[139] The learned alchemist defines it as Θεῖον ἀργύριον ζωτιϰὸν, ἕνωσις τῶν πνευματῶν ἐν σῶμα.[140] It is a divine animated mass, of complexion somewhat like Silver, the union of masculine and feminine spirits.

The quintessence of four, the ternary of two and the tetract of one. These are his generations, physical and metaphysical. The thing in itself is a world without form, neither mere power nor perfect action, but a weak virgin substance, a certain soft, prolific Venus, the very love and seed, the mixture and moisture of heaven and earth. This moisture is the mother of all things in the world; and the masculine, sulphureous fire of the earth is their father.

Now the Rosie Crucians,[141] who without controversy were the wisest of people, when they discourse of the generation of metals tell us it is performed in this manner. The Mercury or mineral liquor, they say, is altogether cold and passive, and it lies in certain earthy, subterraneous caverns. But when the Sun ascends in the East his beams and heat, falling on this hemisphere, stir up and fortify the inward heat of the earth. Thus we see in winter weather that the outward heat of the Sun excites the inward, natural warmth of our bodies and cherisheth the blood when it is almost cold and frozen. Now then, the central heat of the earth, being stirred and seconded by the circumferential heat of the Sun, works upon the Mercury and sublimes it in a thin vapour to the top of its cell or cavern. But towards night, when the Sun sets in the West, the heat of the earth — because of the absence of that great luminary — grows weak and the cold prevails, so that the vapours of the Mercury, which were formerly sublimed, are now condensed and distil in drops to the bottom of the cavern. But the night being spent, the Sun again comes about to the East and sublimes the moisture as formerly. This sublimation and condensation continue so long till the Mercury takes up the subtle, sulphureous parts of the earth and is incorporated therewith, so that this Sulphur coagulates the Mercury and fixes him at last, that he will not sublime but lies still in a ponderous lump and is concocted to a perfect metal.[142]

Fourteenth Sheet

Take notice then that our Mercury cannot be coagulated without our Sulphur, for *Draco non moritur sine suo compare*, the Dragon dieth not apart from his fellow. It is water that dissolves and putrefies earth, and earth that thickens and putrefies water. You must therefore take two principles to produce a third agent, according to that dark receipt of Hali the Arabian. *Accipe canem masculum Corascenum et catellam Armeniae: conjunge et parient tibi catulum coloris coeli.* Take, saith he, the Corascene dog and the bitch of Armenia. Put them both together and they will bring thee a sky-coloured whelp. This sky-coloured whelp is that sovereign, admired and famous Mercury, known by the name of the philosopher's Mercury. Now for my part I advise thee to take two living Mercuries; plant them in a purified, mineral Saturn; wash them and feed them with water of salt vegetable;[143] and thou shalt see that speech of the Adepts verified: *Pariet mater florem germinalem, quem ubere suo viscoso nutriet, et se totam ei in cibum vertet, fovente patre.*[144] But the process or receipt is no part of my design, wherefore I will return to the First Matter; and I say it is no kind of water whatsoever. If thou wilt attain to the truth, rely upon my words, for I speak the truth. The mother or First Matter of metals is a certain watery substance, neither very water nor very earth, but a third thing compounded of both and retaining the complexion of neither. To this agrees the learned Valentine in his apposite and genuine description of our sperm. *Materia prima*, saith he, *set aquosa substantia, sicca repeta et nulli materiae comparabilis.* The First Matter is a waterish substance found dry, or of such a complexion that wets not the hand, and nothing like to any other matter whatsoever. Another excellent and well-experienced philosopher defines it thus. *Est terrena aqua et aquosa terra, in terrae ventre terra commixta, cum qua se commiscet spiritus et coelestis comparabilis.* It is, saith he, an earthy water and a watery earth, mingled with earth in the belly of the earth; and the spirit and influences of heaven commix themselves therewith. Indeed it cannot be denied but some authors have named this substance by the names of all ordinary waters, not to deceive the simple but to hide it from the ranting, ill-disposed crew. On the contrary, some have expressly and faithfully informed us it is no common water, and especially the reverend *Turba*.

Ignari, said Agadmon,[145] *cum audiunt nomen aquae putant aquam nubis esse, quod si libros nostros intelligerent, scirent esse aquam permanentum, quae absque suo compari cum quo facta est unum permanens esse non possit.* The ignorant, saith he, when they hear us name water, think it is water of the clouds; but if they understood our books they should know it to be a permanent or fixed water which, without its companion, to which it hath been united, cannot be permanent. The noble and knowing Sendivogius tells us the very same thing. *Aqua nostra est aqua coelestis, mon madefaciens manus, non vulgi, sed pluvialis.* Our water is a heavenly water, which wets not the hands, not that of common water, but almost, as it were, pluvial. We must therefore consider the several analogies and similitudes of things, or we shall never be able to understand the philosophers.

This water then wets not the hands, which is notion enough to persuade us it can be no common water.

It is a metalline, bitter, saltish liquor. It hath a true mineral complexion. *Habet*, saith Raimund Lullis, *speciem solis et lunae, et in tali aqua nobis apparuit, non in aqua fontis aut pluviae.*[146] But in another place he describes it more fully. *Est aqua sicca,* saith he, *non aqua nubis aut phlegmatica, sed aqua cholerica, igne calidior.* It is a dry water, not water of the clouds or phlegmatic water, but a choleric water, more hot than fire. It is, moreover, greenish[147] to the sight, and the same Lully tells you so. *Habet colorem lacertae viridis.* It looks, saith he, like a green lizard. But the most prevalent colour in it is a certain inexpressible azure, like the body of heaven in a clear day. It looks in truth like the belly of a snake, especially near the neck, where the scales have a deep blue tincture; and this is why the philosophers call it their serpent or dragon. The predominant element in it is a certain fiery, subtle earth, and from this prevalent part the best philosophers have denominated the whole compound. Paracelsus names it openly but in one place, and he calls it *viscum terrae,*[148] the slime or viscous part of the earth. Raymund Lully describeth the crisis or constitution of it in these words: *Substantia lapidis, nostri,* saith he, *est tota pinguis, et igne impregnata.* The substance of our Stone is altogether fat or viscous and impregnated with fire — in which respect he calls it elsewhere not water but earth. *Capias terram nostram,* saith he, *impregnatam a sole, quia lapidem est honoratus, repertus in hospitiis, et est intus inclusum velut magnum secretum et thesaurus incantatus.* Take our earth which is impregnated or with child by the sun; for it is our precious Stone which is found in desolate houses, and there is shut up in it a great secret and treasure enchanted. And again, in a certain place, he delivers himself thus: *Prima materia, Fili, est terra subtilis sulphurea, et haec nobilis terra dictum est subjectum*

Fifteenth Sheet

mercuriale. My son, he saith, the First Matter is a subtle, sulphureous earth, and this noble earth is called a mercurial subject. Know then for certain that this slimy, moist sperm or earth must be dissolved into water, and this is the Water of the Philosophers, not any common water whatsoever. This is the grand secret of the Art, and Lully discovers it with a great deal of honesty and charity. *Argentum vivum nostrum*, saith he, *non est argentum vivum vulgare: imo argentum vivum nostrum est aqua alterius naturae, quae reperiri non potest supra terram, cum in actionem venire non possit per naturam, absque adjutorio ingenii et humanorum manuum operationibus*. Our Mercury is not common Mercury or Quicksilver. But our Mercury is a water which cannot be found on earth, for it is not made or manifested by the ordinary course of nature, but by the art and manual operations of man. Seek not then for that in nature which is an effect beyond her ordinary process; you must help her, that she may exceed her common course, or all is to no purpose. In a word, you must make this water before you can find it. In the interim you must permit the philosophers to call their subject or chaos a water, for there is no proper name for it, unless we call it a sperm, which is a watery substance but certainly no water. Let it suffice that you are not cheated, for they tell you what it is and what it is not, which is all that man can do. If I ask you by what name you call the sperm of a chick you will tell me it is the white of an egg, and truly so is the shell as well as the sperm that is within it. But if you call it earth or water you know well enough it is neither; and yet you cannot find a third name. Judge then as you should be judged, for this is the very case of the philosophers. Certainly you must be very unreasonable if you expect that language from men which God hath not given them.

Now that we may confirm this our theory and discourse of the sperm not only by experience but by reason, it is necessary that we consider the qualities and temperament of the sperm. It is then a slimy, slippery, diffusive moisture. But if we consider any perfect products, they are firm, compacted, figurated bodies; and hence it follows they must be made of something that is not firm, not compacted, not figurated, but a weak, quivering, altering substance. Questionless thus it must be, unless we make the sperm to be of the same complexion with the body; and then it must follow that generation is no alteration. Again, it is evident to all the world that nothing is so passive as moisture. The least heat turns water to a vapour and the least cold turns that vapour to water. Now let us consider what degree of heat it is that acts in all generations, for by the agent we may guess at the nature of the patient. We know the sun is so remote from us that the heat of it, as daily experience tells us, is very faint and remiss. I desire then to know what subject there is in all nature that can be altered with such a weak heat but moisture. Certainly none at all; for all hard bodies, as salts, stones and metals, preserve and retain their complexions in the most violent, excessive fires. How then can we expect that they should be altered by a gentle and almost insensible warmth? It is plain then, and that by infallible inference from the proportion and power of the agent, that moisture must needs be the patient. For that degree of heat which nature makes use of in her generations is so remiss and weal it is impossible for it to alter anything but what is moist and waterish. This truth appears in the animal family, where we know well enough that sperms are moist. Indeed in vegetables the seeds are dry, but then nature generates nothing out of them till they are first macerated or moistened with water. And here the Peripaptetic philosophers are quite gone with their *pura potentia*,[149] that fanatic chaos of the son of Nichomacus.

Sixteenth Sheet

But I must advise my chemists to beware of any common moisture, for that will never be altered otherwise than to a vapour. See, therefore, that thy moisture be well tempered with earth; otherwise thou hast nothing to dissolve and nothing to coagulate. Remember the practice and magic of the Almighty God in His creation, as it is manifested to thee by Moses. *In principio*, saith he, *creavit Deus coelum et terram*.[150] But the original, if it be truly and rationally rendered, speaks thus: *In principio Deus miscuit rarum et densum*. In the beginning God mingled or tempered together the thin and the thick. For heaven and earth in this text signify the Virgin Mercury and the Virgin Sulphur. This I will prove out of the text itself, and that by the vulgar, received translation, which runs thus: In the beginning God created the heaven and the earth. And the earth was without form and void; and darkness was upon the face of the abyss. And the Spirit of God moved upon the face of the waters. In the first part of this text Moses mentions two created principles,[151] not a perfect world, as we shall prove hereafter, and this he doth in these general terms, heaven and earth. In the latter part of it he describes each of these principles in more particular terms and he begins with the earth. And the earth, saith he, was without form and void. Hence I infer that the earth he speaks of was a mere rudiment or principle of this earth which I now see;[152] for this present earth is neither void nor without form. I conclude then that the Mosaical earth was the Virgin Sulphur, which is an earth without form, for it hath no determinated figure. It is a laxative, unstable, incomposed substance, of a porous, empty, *crasis*, like sponge or soot. In a word, I have seen it, but it is impossible to describe it. After this he proceeds to the description of his heaven or second principle in these subsequent words: And the Spirit of God moved upon the face of the waters. Here he calls an abyss and waters what he previously called heaven. It was indeed the heavenly water or chaos, out of which the separated heaven or habitation of the stars was afterwards made. This is very clear from the original, for *Hamaim* and *Hashamaim* are the same words like *Aqua* and *Ibi Aqua*, and they signify one and the same substance, namely water.[153] The text then being rendered according to the primitive natural truth and the undoubted sense of the author speaks thus: In the beginning — or, according to the Jerusalem Targum, *in wisdom*[154] — God made the water and the earth. And the earth was without form and void; and there was darkness upon the face of the deep. And the Spirit of God moved upon the face of the waters. Here you should observe that God created two principles, earth and water, and of these two He compounded a third, namely the sperm or chaos. Upon the water, or moist part of this sperm, the Spirit of God did move; and, saith the Scripture, there was darkness upon the face of the deep. This is a very great secret; neither is it lawful to publish it expressly and as the nature of the thing requires; but in the magical work it is to be seen, and I have been an eye-witness of it myself.

To conclude: remember that our subject is no common water, but a thick, slimy, fat earth. This earth must be dissolved into water and that water must be coagulated again into earth. This is done by a certain natural agent which the philosophers call their Secret Fire. For if you work with common fire it will dry your sperm and bring it to an unprofitable red dust, of the colour of wild poppy. Their Fire then is the Key of the Art,[155] for it is a natural agent but acts not naturally without the sun. I must confess it is a knotty mystery, but we shall make it plain if you be not very dim and dull. It requires indeed a quick, clear apprehension. Behold[156] our 7 Bramaah[157] and their wonderful mysteries, for by them you may cure all diseases, young or old, but know first our fire and use in the work.

Seventeenth Sheet

Fire, notwithstanding the diversities of it in this sub-lunary kitchen of the elements, is but one thing from one root. The effects of it are various, according to the distance and nature of the subject wherein it resides, for that makes it vital or violent. It sleeps in most things, as in flints, where it is silent and invisible. It is a kind of *perdue*, lies close like a spider in the cabinet of his web, to surprise all that comes within his lines. He never appears without his prey in his foot. Where he finds aught that's combustible there he discovers himself; for if we speak properly, he is not generated, but manifested. Some men are of opinion that he breeds nothing but devours all things and is therefore called *Ignis quasi ingignens*.[158] This is a grammatical whim, for there is nothing in the world generated without fire. What a fine philosopher then was Aristotle, who tells us this agent breeds nothing but his *pyrausta*, a certain fly which he found in his candle but could never be seen afterwards. Indeed too much heat burns and destroys; and if we descend to other natures, too much water drowns, too much earth buries and chokes the seed, that it cannot come up. And verily at this rate there is nothing in the world that generates. What an owl was he then that could not distinguish, with all his logic, between excess and measure, between violent and vital degrees of heat, but concluded the fire did breed nothing because it consumed something. But let the mule pass, for so Plato called him, and let us prosecute our Secret Fire. This Fire is at the root and about the root — I mean about the centre — of all things, both visible and invisible. It is in water, earth and air; it is in minerals, herbs and beasts; it is in men, stars and angels. But originally it is in God Himself, for He is the Fountain of heat and fire, and from Him it is derived to the rest of the creatures in a certain stream or sunshine.

Now the Rosie Crucians[159] afford us but two notions whereby we may know their fire. It is, as they describe it, moist and invisible. Hence they have called it their *venter equi*[160] and *fimus equinus*[161], but this is only by way of analogy, for there is in horse-dung a moist heat but no fire that is visible. Now let us compare the common Vulcan with this philosophical Vesta, that we may see wherein they are different. First, then, the philosopher's fire is moist, and truly so is that of the kitchen too. We see that flames contract and extend themselves; now they are short, now they are long, which cannot be without moisture to maintain the flux and continuity of their parts. I know Aristotle makes the fire to be simply dry, perhaps because the effects of it are so. He did not indeed consider that in all complexions there are other qualities besides the predominant one. Surely then this dry stuff is that element of his wherein he found his *pyrausta*. But if our natural fire were simply dry the flames of it could not flow and diffuse themselves as they do: they would rather fall to dust or turn, like their fuel, to ashes. The common fire is excessively hot, but moist in a far inferior degree, and therefore destructive, for it preys on the moisture of other things. On the contrary, the warmth and moisture of the magical agent are equal; the one tempers and satisfies the other. It is a humid, tepid fire, or, as we commonly express ourselves, blood-warm. This is their first and greatest difference in relation to our desired effect: we will now consider their second. The kitchen fire, as we all know, is visible, but the philosopher's fire is invisible, and therefore no kitchen fire. This Almadir expressly tells us in these words: *Solas radios invisibilis ignis nostri sufficere.* Our work, saith he, can be performed by nothing but the invisible beams of our fire. And again: *Ignis noster corrosivus est ignis, qui supra nostrum vas nubem obducit, in qua nube radii hujus ignis occulti sunt.* Our fire is a corrosive fire which brings a cloud about our glass or vessel, in which cloud the beams of our fire are hidden. To be short: the philosophers call this agent their bath, because it is moist as baths are; but in very truth it is no kind of bath, neither *maris* nor *roris*,[162] but a most subtle fire, and purely natural; but the excitation of it is artificial. This excitation or preparation is a very trivial, slight, ridiculous thing. Nevertheless all the secrets of corruption and generation are therein contained. Lastly, I think it just to inform thee that many authors have falsely described this fire, and that of purpose, to seduce their readers. For my own part I have neither added nor diminished. Thou hast here the true, entire secret, in which all the easterns agree, Alfid, Almadir, Belen, Gieberim, Hali, Salmanazar and Zadich, with the three famous Jews, Abraham, Artephius and Kalid. Now I will tell thee how to use it.

Eighteenth Sheet

Take our two serpents, which are to be found everywhere on the face of the earth. They are a living male and a living female.[163] Tie them both in a love-knot and shut them up in the Arabian *Caraha*.[164] This is thy first labour, but thy next is more difficult. Thou must encamp against them with the fire of nature, and be sure that thou dost bring thy line about. Circle them in and stop all avenues, that they find no relief. Continue this siege patiently; and they will turn into an ugly black toad, which will be transformed to a horrible devouring Dragon, creeping and weltering in the bottom of her cave, without wings. Touch her not by any means, not so much as with thy hands, for there is not upon earth such a violent, transcendent poison. As thou hast begun so proceed, and this Dragon will turn to a Swan, but more white than the hovering, virgin snow when it is not yet sullied with the earth. Henceforth I will allow thee to fortify thy fire till the Phoenix appears. It is a red bird of a most deep colour, with a shining, fiery hue. Feed this bird with the fire of his father and the ether of his mother;[165] for the first is meat and the second is drink, and without this last he attains not to his full glory. Be sure to understand this secret, for fire feeds not well unless it first be fed. It is of itself dry and choleric; but a proper moisture tempers it, gives it a heavenly complexion and brings it to the desired exaltation. Feed thy bird then as I have told thee, and he will move in his nest and rise like a star of the firmament. Do this and thou hast placed nature *in horizonte aeternitatis.*[166] Thou hast performed the command of the Kabalist: *Fige finem in principio, sicut flammam prunae conjunctam, quia Dominus superlative unus et non tenet secundum*. Unite the end to the beginning, like a flame to a coal; for God, saith he, is superlatively one and He hath no second.[167] Consider then what you seek: you seek an indissoluble, miraculous, transmuting, uniting union; but such a tie cannot be without the First Unity. *Creare enim*, saith one, *atque intrinsecus transmutare absque violentia, munus est proprium duntaxat Primae Potentiae, Primae Sapientiae, Primi Amoris.* To create and transmute essentially and naturally, or without any violence, is the only proper office of the first Power, the first Wisdom and the first Love. Without this love the elements will never be married; they will never inwardly and essentially unite, which is the end and perfection of magic. Study then to understand this, and when thou hast performed I will allow thee that test of the *Mekkubalim: Intellexisti in sapientiam et sapuisti in intelligentia; statuisti rem super puritates suas, et Creatorem in Throno Suo collocasti.*[168]

To close this section, I say it is impossible to generate in the patient without a vital, generating agent. This agent is the philosophical fire, a certain moist, heavenly, invisible heat. But let us hear Raymund Lully describe it: *Quando dicimus*, saith he, *quod lapis per ignem generatur, non vident alium ignem, nec alium credunt, nisi ignem communem; nec aliud Sulphur, nec aliud Argentum Vivum, nisi sit vulgare. Ideo manent decepti per eorum caecas estimationes, inferentes quod causa sumus suae deceptionis et quod dedimus illis intelligere rem unam pro alia. Sed non est verum salva eorum pace, sicut probabimus per illa quae philosophi posuerunt in scriptis. Solem enim appellamus ignem, et vicarium suum vocamus calorem naturalem. Nam illud quod agit calor solis in mineris metallorum per mille annos, ipse calor naturalis facit in una hora supra terram. Nos vero et multi alii vocamus eum Filium Solis, nam primo per solis influentiam fuit generatus per naturam, sive adjutorium scientiae vel artis.* When we say the Stone is generated by fire, men neither see, neither do they believe there is any other fire but the common fire, nor any other Sulphur and Mercury but the common Sulphur and Mercury. Thus are they deceived by their own opinions, saying that we are the cause of their error, having made them to mistake one thing for another. But, by their leave, it is not so, as we shall prove by the doctrine of the philosophers. For we call the sun a fire and the natural heat we call his substitute or deputy. For that which the heat of the sun performs in a thousand years in the mines, the heat of nature performs above the earth in one hour. But we and many other philosophers have called this heat the Child of the Sun, for at first it was generated naturally by the influence of the sun without the help of our Art or knowledge. Thus Lully: but one thing I must tell thee, and be sure, Reader, thou dost remember it. This very natural heat

Nineteenth Sheet

must be applied in the just degree and not too much fortified; for the sun itself doth not generate but burn and scorch where it is too hot. *Si cum igne magno operatus fueris*, saith the same Lully, *proprietas nostri spiritus, quae inter vitam et mortem participet, separabit se et anima recedet in regionem sphaerae suae.* If thou shalt work with too strong a fire, the propriety of our spirit, which is indifferent as yet to life or death, will separate itself from the body, and the soul will depart to the region of her own sphere.

Take therefore along with thee this short but wholesome advice of the same author: *Facias ergo, Fili, quod if loco generationis aut conversionis sit talis potentia coelestis quae possit transformare humidum ex natura terrestri, in formam et speciem transparentem et finissimam.* My son, saith he, let the heavenly power or agent be such in the place of generation or mutation that it may alter the spermatic humidity from its earthly complexion to a most fine, transparent form or species.

See here now the solution of the slimy, fat earth to a transparent, glorious Mercury! This Mercury is the water which we look after, but not any common water whatsoever. There is nothing now behind but that which the philosophers call *Secretum Artis*,[169] a thing that was never published and without which you will never perform, though you know both fire and matter. An instance hereof we have in Flamel, who knew the Matter well enough and had both fire and furnace painted to him by Abraham the Jew; but notwithstanding he erred for three years because he knew not the secret. Henry Madathan, a most noble philosopher, practised upon the subject for five years together but knew not the right method and therefore found nothing. At last, saith he, *Post sextum annum clavis potentiae per arcanam revelationem ab omnipotente Deo mihi concredita est*; after the sixth year I was entrusted with the Key of Power by secret revelation from the Almighty God. This Key of Power or third secret was never put to paper by any philosopher whatsoever. Paracelsus indeed hath touched upon it, but so obscurely it is no more to the purpose than if he had said nothing.

And now I have done enough for the discovery and regimen of the fire, and more than any one author hath performed. Search it then, for he that finds this fire will attain to the true temperament; he will make a noble, deserving philosopher and, to speak in the phrase of our Spaniard, *Dignus erit poni ad mensam duodecim parium*.[170]

And now I will teach you how to make the DRAMAAH into Medicine mixed with the metals. And first

OF MERCURY

The Rosie Crucians describe unto us the Mount of God and His

Mystical, philosophical Geomancy, which is nothing else but the highest and purest part of the earth; for from Tetragrammaton He shines upon the Orders and they carry His power to the planets, so you see the superior, secret portion of this element is holy ground; it is the seed plot of the eternal nature. And the Chaos was divided into eight parts; the eight[171] was deadly, but first of the seven; the matter was the body of the lapsed Angels.[172] After light began to appear,[173] the centre[174] was red, an ash colour blush; the circumference blue. The second division green, fiery red and purple. In the third division the centre was fiery, the inferior waters purple and the superior white. The fourth division was azure blush, the Sun and Moon then appearing pale blush. In the fifth division the earth was red and the centre fiery, the waters blush azure, the Sun and Moon ash colour. The sixth division of the earth was a red blush, and centre fiery. The seventh apparition is the immediate vessel and recipient of heaven, whence all minerals have their life and by which the animal monarchy is maintained.

Twentieth Sheet

This philosophical black Saturn mortifies and coagulates the invisible Mercury of the Stars and, on the contrary, the Mercury kills and dissolves the Saturn; and out of the corruption of both, the Central and Circumferential Suns disgenerate new bodies, the Green Lion in a blush circle; the Green Lion swallowed to the hinderparts; the virtues in a purple vessel of Nature, half Moon made; the vegetable, animal mineral in a blush; calcination of fiery and blue earth; sublimation fiery, airy and azure; solution black, white and azure; the Spirit descends. The masculine and feminine Mercury generated there will appear azure, purple, ash colour, yellow and red. In putrefaction our matter is black and azure; the Spirit descends. In conception our *Astrum Solis* is a bloody, fiery, spirited earth; the Spirit descends and the superfinals [are] azure. In impregnation the *Astrum Solis* ascends from a muddy water and the Spirit with it. In fermentation the black, shabby toad lies sultering in his vessel, and the Spirit in azure descending appears in separation of fire, air, water and earth. The toad lies in the earth black, the earth ash colour, the water green, the air blue, the fire blood-red and the aether a liquid white fire; the Spirit ascends. In conjunction of elements the fire is red, air blue, water green and earth dark ash and the Spirit descends in a clear sky. In separation of earth, fire, air and water, the earth lies in the bottom dark, the fire flaming upon it, breaking through the air to the water, and disposeth itself in conjunction of water in air; the Spirit descends in a clear sky to that blue composition; the air in the water is green, the fire red and the earth ashy. In the separation of fire, water, air in water, earth, the earth is dark, muddy, the air in water blue, the water transparent and the fire flaming red and white, and the Spirit ascends in an azure sky.

In conjunction of air in fire, fire in water, water in air, earth, the earth is dark and heavy, the water in air blue, the fire in water green, the air in fire a blush red; the Spirit descends in a clear sky. In separation air, water, fire in air, earth, the earth is ash colour, fire in air blood red, flaming through the azure water and air; the Spirit ascends. In conjunction fire in air, water in fire, air in water, earth, the earth is black, the air in water is green, the water in fire is like the sunbeams in a mist, the fire above all lies in the air blue, flaming; the Spirit descends. The next separation is flames of fire breaking out in all the elements, the earth only lies of a darker colour. The unnatural fire stands thus, air water, fire earth, the earth covered with a blue flame, the fire ascending to the central colour, water and air; the Spirit descends. The rising of the Rosie Crucian Medicines. The earth *cineri coloris,* a white star and moon appearing in a star; the power and Spirit ascends in a clear sky. In fermentation a dark star lies in the earth and the Spirit descends to it in a clear sky. In purgation the earth is black and the Spirit descends clear. In this separation there appears water in air, fire in water, turned upwards; below is a blue space, then the earth in fire is red, air in earth ash colour.

[In] this conjunction of air in fire, water in earth, fire in air, earth in water; the earth in water is dark, the fire in air red, but not violent, the water in earth green, the air in fire blue; the Spirit descends. And [in] this conjunction of earth in air, water in fire, and fire in earth; here in the bottom the earth is animated with a secret fire, invisible, occult, the water shadows a mild fire, the air in water above these is green and glorious, the earth in air is a bluish white; the Spirit descends.

In this exaltation of the Quintessence the Pelican is in the bottom; next above is azure; then two circles; of the first the upper is blue, the lower a white fire; the next is a green and red sea of fire environing the white matter, and this exaltation of the Quintessence is azure, a globe [which] in the bottom [is] divided in four quarters; from the East to the South is blue, from the South to the West green, from the West to the North white, from the North to the East red, and all the upper part of it azure. Above this globe the fire flames upon both sides. In fixation the branches of fire spread both ways round the white and azure globe; this projection is upon a blue and white powder, the perspect in Multiplication runs down the vessel through the azure to the matter in the bottom.

One and Twentieth Sheet

In imbibition the Serpent lies at the bottom of the matter; in sublimation a strong fire drives the azure part to the top; in coagulation the azure binds or weighs down the fire to the bottom; in conjunction the fire star lies in the bottom; in the[175] exaltation the double circled fire arises, and in the[176] quintessence appears an Angel amidst the ascending globes of fire; and in fixation all is circled with purple and red fire and in the middle stands an Angel in a star, doubled, with his wings spread and holding the glorious Crown of the Rosie Cross in his hands.

1. Of the Preparation of the Gold, Mercury or Argent Vive. 2. Purification. 3. Sublimation. 4. Calcination. 5. Exuberation. 6. Solution. 7. Separation. 8. Conjunction. 9. Putrefaction into Sulphur. 10. Fermentation. 11. Multiplication in virtue. 12. Multiplication in quantity.[177]

1. He that can make the medicine of Argent Vive or Mercury alone is the greatest searcher out of Art and Nature because there is all that in Mercury which wise men seek. For Quicksilver is the Mother and Sperm of all metals and their nearest matter, and it is not only a spirit but a body; it is also a middle nature and also a Sulphur; it is a lingering Mercury; it dieth and riseth again and is fixed with its own proper elements; wherefore it is first necessary that it be purged from its impurities.

2. The Purgation or Purification is on this wise. Grind it upon a marble with a mullet, or a wooden pestle in a wooden mortar, with common salt and a little vinegar sprinkled thereupon till the salt be black; then wash it well with vinegar and dry it easily at the fire or at the sun; then strain it through a double cloth or a new skin of a sheep till it be dry and the vinegar clear taken away and be of a white colour and clear.

3. Grind it upon a marble with a little Mercury Sublimate and let it mortify and incorporate with it; then grind it with its equal weight of Saltpeter and green Copperas till it be like a paste; then put all into a subliming glass and in ashes sublime all the mercury that it be white and clean as snow in the head of the limbeck; sublime it again three times or oftener, and it will be pure Mercury and[178] Sublimate.

4. Put a pound of this Mercury Sublimate into two pounds of common *Aqua Fortis* by little and little at once till all be dissolved like sugar in wine; then shut the glass and set it *in Balneo* to dissolve the space of ten days; then distil away the *Aqua Fortis* in a lent heat *in Balneo* and the Mercury will remain in the bottom like butter, of a white colour and calcined by Corrosive Water.

5. Put this calcined Mercury into an earthen body with a limbeck and in ashes sublime the whole dissolved substance three times, which will all be very white, and then it is called Mercury Exuberate.

When you have three or four pound of this, receive[179] the third part and fix it by often sublimation till it remain in a hard mass and ascend no more but remain fixed, which is called the Glue of the Eagle or the prepared body permanent and the volatile made fixed, which is to be reserved for the earth of the Stone.

6. Dissolve the other two parts *in Balneo* or in a cold cellar or put it in a bladder and hang it over fuming hot water till it be all come to water.

Take this water thus made and digest it in a Circulatory, well closed, the space of nine days, then put it in a body with a head and receiver well luted and in ashes or [*in*] *Balneo* distil the water of a white colour, or milky white, which is called *Lac Virginis*, dissolving all metals, and so you have separated the Spirit of the Stone, which is also called the lingering Spirit and the white tincture of the white Stone of Mercury.

7. Take the third part which before you reserved and fixed, called the Glue of the Eagle, as much of it as you please, and add thereto equal weight of its Spirit or *Lac Virginis*[180] and stop up the glass and so you have joined the man and the woman, Mercury with her own earth, the Spirit with the body.

8. Set your *Lac Virginis* thus joined with his own, each *in Balneo* to putrefy 150 days and there let it stand unmoved. After 40 days it will be black and it is then called the Head of the Crow; then it will be of a green colour, after that the Peacock's Tail and many false colours, for between this and white it will appear red; but at last you shall see it white and then increase your fire and it will stick to the sides of the glass like fishes eyes,[181] then you have each in the nature of Sulphur.

Take of this Sulphur as much as you please and weigh it and add thereto two parts of the white tincture or *Lac Virginis* and set it *in Balneo* to dissolve the space of six days; then distil away the *Lac Virginis* or tincture, and the Sulphur will remain in the form of liquor, for it is the liquor of the white Sulphur of Mercury which is to be joined with the liquor of the Sulphur of Luna or Silver.

9. The Sulphur of the white luminary, or Silver, or Luna, is made as the other, whereof we shall speak more in the next branch. This liquor of the Sulphur is the Soul, which is joined with the Spirit and body, which quickeneth the whole Stone. The other conjunction before was only the union of the Spirit and the body, but this is a threefold copulation, viz., the uniting of the Soul, Spirit and Body.[182] Add equal

weight of these two liquors of Sulphur, that is to say the liquor of the Sulphur of Mercury and of Silver or Luna and close well the glass and set it in ashes till it be white, for it will be all colours again and at last white; and then it is the perfect Stone converting all metals into Silver.

10. This Medicine or Elixir is thus multiplied in virtue. Dissolve it in *Lac Virginis* and distil it away and dry it and dissolve it again etc. And let it be so often dissolved and dried till it will dry no more but remain an incombustible oil, and is then Elixir of the third order.

11. Take one part of this Elixir and project it upon 100 or 1,000 parts of melted silver (according to the goodness and virtue thereof) and it will turn the Silver into a brittle mass or substance, which beat to a powder in an iron or brass mortar, or upon a marble and project one part of this powder upon 100 parts of Mercury purged, made hot, and it will be perfect Medicine whereof one part turneth 100 or 1,000 parts of the bodies into good silver. And this way is your Medicine multiplied in quantity. Here followeth the Mercurial Medicine prepared after we have taught you to make the Medicine of the Moon.

12. It remaineth now that we speak of the Medicine of the Elixir of Life, which is called Potable Silver. But although the liquor of Silver may be made potable Silver if it be corroborated[183] before by digestion *in Balneo* seven days with the Spirit of Wine, and then distil away the Spirit of Wine that the oil of the Silver may remain in the bottom, which may easily be given for medicine, yet the philosophers would have us do otherwise; for they teach us to bring the metals first into their Quintessence before they be taken inwardly, and that there are[184] no other Quintessences but those that are of a Second Nature according to the old saying:

Elixir de te est res secunda
De quo sunt facta corpora munda.

That is to say the four Elements are destroyed and by putrefaction a new body [is] created and made into a Stone, which is the Quintessence as Lully would have it. But I do boldly and constantly affirm that there is no true Silver or Potable Silver nor Quintessence unless it be first Elixir, and that is done in a quarter of an hour by projection of the Elixir upon Silver or pure Gold, molten, according as the Elixir was red or white. If, therefore, you desire after the first composition of the Elixir to make the Arcanum of *Argentum* or *Aurum Potabile*, project the Elixir or Medicine according to his quality or property upon pure Silver or Gold, molten, and then it is made brittle and frangible, and grind it to powder and take thereof so much as you please and dissolve it in distilled Vinegar (or rather in Spirit of Wine) the space of nine days. Then distil away the Vinegar or Spirit of Wine [and] that which remaineth in the bottom is the true Medicine, Quintessence, Elixir of Life, Ferment of Ferments and Incombustible Oil converting metals and man's body into perfect health from all diseases of man's body which proceed from Mercury or Luna. And thus is the true Potable Silver made, curing the vertigo, syncope, epilepsy, madness, phrensy, leprosy etc.

Three and Twentieth Sheet

And this is the right way of making the Stone of Mercury alone; but the Elixir cannot be made without the addition of Silver to the white and of Gold to the red.

To each this work, consider eight principles:

1. Luna. 2. Pure Silver. 3. Calcination. 4. Solution. 5. Putrefaction. 6. The Sulphur. 7. The Liquor of the Sulphur. 8. White Ferment.

Hermes saith the Elixir is nothing else but Mercury, Sol and Luna. By Mercury nothing is understood but the Sulphur of Nature, which is called the true Mercury of the philosophers, and that Sulphur gotten by putrefaction by the conjunction of the Spirit and the body of imperfect bodies and metals.

By Sol is meant Gold, by Luna, Silver; both of them are to be joined to imperfect bodies, that is to say, white Sulphur and Red, whence the same Hermes, in his seven[th] treatise of Sol, saith there happeneth a conjunction of two bodies, and it is necessary in our maistry. And if one of those bodies only were not in our Medicine, it would never by any means give any tincture. Upon which Morienus saith: For the Ferment prepareth the imperfect body and converteth it to its own nature and there is no Ferment but Sol and Luna, that is Gold and Silver. Of which Rosinus [saith]: Sol and Luna prepared (that is to say their Sulphurs) are the ferments of metals in colour.

But this is made more evident by Raymund in his *Apertory*, where he saith there is no Ferment except Sol and Luna, for the Ferment of the Medicine to white is Silver and to the red Gold, as the philosophers do demonstrate, because without Ferment there doth proceed neither Gold nor Silver nor anything else that is of its kind or nature, therefore join the Ferment with its Sulphur that it may beget its like, because the Ferment draweth the Sulphur to its own colour and nature also, and weight and sound,[185] because every like begetteth its like. Because the Ferment, even as Sol, tingeth and changeth his Sulphur into a permanent and piercing Medicine, therefore the philosopher saith: He that knoweth how to tinge Sulphur and Mercury with Sol and Luna shall attain to the greatest secret. And for this reason it is necessary that Sol and Luna be the tincture and ferment thereof.

2. And so also Arnoldus saith in his *Rosary*, there is no body more noble and pure than Sol or his shadow, that is to say Silver, without which no tingeing Mercury is generated. He that endeavoureth to give colour without this Gold or Silver goeth blindly to work, like an ass to a harp, for Gold giveth a golden and Silver an argentive colour; therefore he that knoweth how to tinge Mercury with Sol and Luna cometh or reacheth to the secret which is called white Sulphur, the best to Silver, which, when it be made red, will be red Sulphur, to Gold best.

3. Take pure Luna, that is to say Silver. That is best which is beaten into leaves; and bring it into calx with Mercury, and it is then called water Silver; then is the Luna well prepared for calcination.

4. When you have your Silver thus prepared, take four or six ounces thereof and put it in double proportions of *Lac Virginis* mixed with equal quantity of corrosive water to dissolve in an egg glass. After it hath dissolved so much as it can in the cold, set [it] *in Balneo* and there let it stand nine days till the whole substance of the silver be dissolved into a green water. Then let the *Balneum*[186] cool and take it out and put the dissolution into the body and set thereon a head and distil off the water from the matter remaining, which is the oil of Silver, calcined not into a calx but [into] a liquor, because this *Lac Virginis*, if it be mixed or joined with common *Aqua Fortis* or alone without it (as it pleaseth the operator) is so strong that the very Diamond cannot resist it but is dissolved. Therefore this water is called the Water of Hell and is the only miracle of miracles of the world, because it containeth such a fiery nature in itself and propriety of burning of all bodies into liquor, whereas the elemental fire prevaileth no further than to reduce metals into calx or ashes. But to return from whence I digressed, I now come to the third operation.

5. To the end, therefore, that this liquor or oil of Silver may be more perfectly dissolved, and that all the imperfection of adustion[187] may be taken away, which by the ancients is called the corroborating of the le[a]st humidity, put the oil or liquor into another egg glass like the former, pour thereupon so much Spirit [of Wine] above it [as shall reach to a depth of] four fingers, then close well the glass and set it *in Balneo* to digest seven or ten days and you shall find the oil or liquor turned into a thin or rare water [or] oil. Put this water into a still and *in Balneo* draw away the spirit of wine till none of the Spirit of Wine

Four and Twentieth Sheet

remain with the Silver dissolved, and thus you have your Silver prepared for putrefaction.

Observe the power of the Moon and her Angel [upon] Hasmodai,[188] Muriel, Populus, Via and Silver. Practice and prepare after this manner. This Medicine cures all the diseases of the neck and breast etc. It must be Silver purely refined.

Geomancy the Harmony in this Preparation.[189]

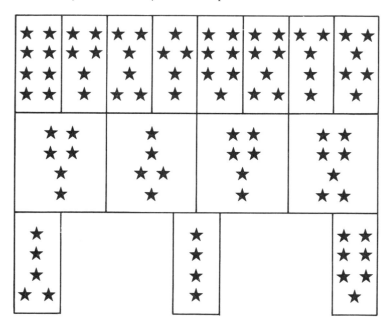

6. This liquor of Silver is potable, but not the Quintessence. Put this water into a fit putrefying glass and seal it up and set it to putrefy *in Balneo* till the time of putrefaction be past, which is about one hundred and fifty days, and when you see the first sign of putrefaction, which is called the head of the Crow, increase your fire a little till all the colours begin to appear and you see it begin to be white.

When you see it white, increase your fire yet more and it will rise up and stick to the sides of the glass, most transparent, like the eyes of fishes,[190] which is Sulphur of Nature or Salt, or the putrefied body of the white luminary, viz., Luna, which yet is not so hard as a body nor so soft as a Spirit, but of a mean hardness between a Spirit and a body, and is called the Philosophers' Mercury and the Key and means of joining Tinctures.

7. But to come to the liquor of the white Luminary. This body being brought into Quintessence is prepared for dissolution like the Sulphur of the imperfect body; but whereas that is done by virtue of the white tincture or *Lac Virginis*, I rather do it by virtue of the fire natural, which is the Spirit of Wine; and after the drawing away thereof it remaineth in a liquor.

Now this liquor of Luna dissolved is the Quintessence, which then is the liquor of the white luminary and the soul[191] (as Eximandrus saith) quickening the whole Medicine, without which it is dead and will never give form nor colour.

8. Therefore the fourth part of the liquor of the white luminary is to be joined to three parts of the former liquor of the Sulphur of Mercury, and after to be kept in a lent fire of ashes, well closed, till it pass through all colours and at last come to its former colour of whiteness; and so the Medicine is fermented[192] and turned into the white Elixir.

The residue of the foresaid dissolved Sulphur keep diligently, and therewith ferment the white Sulphur of other imperfect bodies or stones into Elixirs, which, when they are thrice dissolved and again congealed and remain in a liquid, then they are called incombustible oils and Elixirs of the third order.[193]

And thus the Medicine is made of Mercury alone as followeth by this example. Having spoken of the white Medicine it now resteth that we speak of the making of the Red Elixir, whereof there are two processes, the first whereof is from the Radix, i.e., the long way; the other an accurtation that is much shorter and more excellent. And this way the Elixir may be made in eighty days, and excels all other accurtations; neither is there found therein any diminution of the virtue, but a plentiful and perfect fullness of power and virtue, having all the properties which the Elixir ought to have.

THE OPERATION UNDER THOSE HEADS

1. Vivum.[194] 2. Sublimation. 3. Calcination. 4. Precipitation. 5. Solution. 6. Fixed Oil. 7. Incertation.[195] 8. Dessication. 9. Contrition. 10. Fermentation. 11. The Red Elixir. 12. The Third Table.

1. Purgation of Mercury I shall omit because it was spoken of before.

2. The Sublimation is to be done otherwise than in the former work, for that which is called Sublimation here is not done with Vitriol and Saltpeter, but is only the distillation of the Mercury in an earthen body with a limbeck, and that without any additament.

Five and Twentieth Sheet

3. When the Mercury is once sublimed in ashes wholly into the head of the limbeck, having a retainer joined thereto, take off the head and with a feather gather the sublimed matter and you shall find your Mercury of a black colour, having lost his fairness, and like a dust or powder sticking to his body.

4. Put it again into the body and sublime it as before, and reiterate this work seven or nine times until you have a sufficient quantity of this powder, a pound or more and this is the Calcination.

5. When you see your Mercury will ascend no more, but remain[s] in the bottom of a black colour, and that it is dead and brought perfectly into calx, let it cool and remove your body into sand till it be turned into a red colour. And this is the perfect Precipitation, [to] prove[196] [which], without the help of any corrosive water, take a little of this powder upon a hot Iron plate. If it fume, dry it longer; if not it is well.

6. Take of this red powder as much as you will dissolve and put thereupon at least his double weight of *Lac Virginis* and set *in Balneo* till you see your *Lac Virginis* stained a yellow or red colour; then filter it from its feces and keep it by itself in a glass well stopped and dry the matter that remaineth in ashes and pour thereon new *Lac Virginis* and do as before, till you have drawn out all the tincture and your Mercury is dissolved.

7. Put these solutions into a body, luting to a head and *in Balneo* distil away the *Lac Virginis* and the red oil precipitate will remain, which is fixed and needeth no distillation, but is the tingeing oil of red Mercury, and the red tincture of the red Medicine of Mercury, and the Soul and Spirit of the Medicine joined as for example.

8. Take part of the white Sulphur reserved in the first Table, and rubify it in ashes till it be red. Then imbibe it with equal weight of the oil of the tincture of this red Mercury and set it to dissolve *in Balneo*; and when you see it is dissolved into a liquid substance, take it out.

9. Then set it in ashes, or under the fire, to fix till the matter, being dried, remain fusible and fixed, standing in a mean heat, not over-hot, which try upon a hot iron plate; and if it fume not it is well; if it do, increase your fire till it be totally fixed and dry.

10. If this matter be imbibed again with its oil till it drink up as much as it will, and again dissolved *in Balneo* and then dried in ashes, it will show many colours and lastly appear red.[197] And then it is the Stone, penetrating and fusible, apt for form.

11. Join this imbibed matter (or Medicine) with the fourth part of the liquor or oil of the red Sulphur of Gold or the red Ferment, and dissolve it *in Balneo* and dry it again; and again dissolve it in a glass hanged in the fume of hot water or *Balneum* and congest it again till it stand like honey. Then it is the perfect Red Elixir of Mercury.

12. The Multiplication or Augmentation of the virtue and quantity is showed in the preparation before of the White Elixir.

OF GOLD
SOL

1. The Preparation of Gold, Sol. 2. Purged Gold. 3. Calcination. 4. Solution. 5. Putrefaction. 6. *Filius Solis Coelestis*. 7. *Filia Lunae Coelestis*.

1. The Putrefaction or Purgation of Gold is done as the Goldsmiths use to do by melting it with Antimony, that the Gold may remain in the bottom pure and clear from the metals, which they call *Regulus*.

2. Take 4 or 5 ounces of this refined Gold leaf or filings and dissolve it in *Lac Virginis* mixed with equal weight of *Aqua Fortis*, wherein Salt Armoniack sublimed is dissolved, and when it is dissolved into a red liquor, or deep yellow, then it is well calcined.

3. The Solution and Putrefaction is done as before you did with Silver in the preparation of the White Ferment.

4. When you have your white Sulphur of Nature (after Putrefaction) sticking to the sides of the glass,[198] let it cool and take out of the glass and set it in ashes and increase your fire, but not too much, lest your matter vitrify, and let your ashes be no hotter than you can hold your hand therein, and so let it stand till the Sulphur be of a perfect deep red colour. Then have you the red Sulphur of the red luminary as for example —

Twenty-Sixth Sheet

Observe the Harmony of Geomancy in the Preparation. (See diagram on page 74).

Behold the power of the Sun and his Angel upon Sorath, Verchiel, Fortuna Major and Minor in Gold and of his Medicine, which, being thus prepared, hath performed incredible, extraordinary cures upon the bodies of Princes and Peers in Europe.

5. If you resolve this red Sulphur in Spirit of Wine or distilled Vinegar into an oil, it is then the liquor of the red luminary and *Aurum Potabile* curing all infirmities if the Spirit of Wine or Vinegar be distilled from

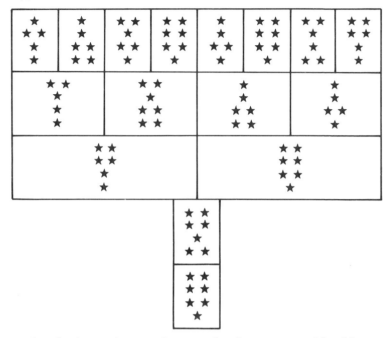

it; but for this work it were better to dissolve it in our red *Lac Virginis*, distil away the *Lac* from the Sulphur in ashes, and the Sulphur remaining in an oil is the Ferment of all stones to the red.

6. The Augmentation of this red Elixir in virtue is with his red Tincture as before in the white Tincture. The Augmentation in quantity is by projection upon the body of Gold molten, and that brittle matter of Gold upon Mercury; and if it be powdered and resolved with Spirit of Wine in an oil, as was said before of Silver, then it is the Quintessence of Gold and the Great Elixir of Life and the Spiritual Ferment for the transmutation of metals and for the health of man's body.

Although Raymund, writing to the King, was pleased to say that every accurtation diminisheth the perfection, because Medicines which are made by accurtation have less effect of transmutation — which I also assent to with him for a great truth, if the work be begun from the first fountain — yet because this work has its beginnings from those things, which before were brought to a perfect degree of perfection, therefore in this there is no diminution of the perfection.[199]

Therefore it ought to be declared unto thee that if they be both well prepared (and that thou begin with them) thou wilt do a wonderful work without any great labour sooner than if thou should begin with one thing alone. Therefore, my son, begin thy work of two things together as I showed thee in the greater Medicines, when we spoke of the two-fold custody of the actions which are caused by the bodies and spirits. Thus far Raymund. By that which is caused by the bodies and Spirits he means nothing else but Sulphur, willing that we should begin with Sulphur, to which I do so well agree that I begin this my accurtation with this Sulphur alone, and I add no other body to this Elixir, but only the Sulphur of Mercury, alone created of his own body and Spirit.

Take, therefore, two ounces of the white Sulphur described at the beginning of this treatise, and set it in ashes to rubify. In thirty days it will be turned into red Sulphur which when you have done, dissolve that Sulphur in the red Tincture of Mercury; when it is dissolved draw away the Tincture; in the bottom remaineth the Liquor of Sulphur.

To which, if you add a due proportion of the liquor of the red luminary, it will be perfect Ferment, which, if you dissolve and congeal as before is showed, it is then Elixir of very great virtue to the red work, and no man can make a shorter abbreviation in the world; and when the Sulphur of any body is prepared, it may this way very speedily be converted into Elixir by adding the liquor of the Ferment.

Now I will lay down instructions concerning:

1. The Body. 2. The Spirit. 3. The Lion. 4. The Eagle. 5. The Philosophers' Lead. 6. Antimony. 7. Antimony Mercury. 8. The Glue of the Eagle. 9. Solution of the red Lion into Blood. 10. Solution of the Glue of the Eagle. 11. Solution of the Blood of the red Lion. 12. Conjunction. 13. Putrefaction. 14. Fermentation. 15. In the Trinity of the Physical and Alchemical Tincture of the Soul. 16. Is the Unity of the Medicine.

1. Take Antimony, calcined, so much as you please and grind it to a subtile powder; then take twice so much *Lac Virginis* and put your powder of Antimony therein and set it *in Balneo* seven days; then put it into a body and set it in sand or ashes till the *Lac* be turned red, which draw off and pour on more, and so let it stand. When that is coloured red, pour it to the other and thus do till you have drawn out all the Tincture. Set all this water *in Balneo* or lent ashes to distil with a limbeck, and distil it with a lent fire; and first of all the *Lac* will ascend, [and] then you shall see a stupendous miracle because you shall see through the nose of the Limbeck as it were a thousand veins of the liquor of this blessed Mineral to descend in red drops, just like blood, which, when you have got, thou hast a thing whereunto all the treasure in the world is not equal. Now you have the Blood of the Lion according

Twenty-Seventh Sheet

to Rupecissa. I will now speak of the Glue of the Eagle, of which Paracelsus thus saith.

2. Reduce Mercury so far by sublimation till it be a fixed crystal. This is his preparation of Mercury and his way of reducing it into the Glue of the Eagle; but above all I require that that way be used which is described by me before or that hereafter set down after this.

3. Then, saith the aforesaid author, go on to resolution and coagulation, and I again will give you to observe the same manner of solution showed at first.

4. Now let us come to conjunction. After the solution of these two, take equal weight of them and put them in a vessel well shot.[200]

5. After you have thus joined them together, set your glass in your furnace to putrefy and after the space of certain days.[201] Therefore Paracelsus saith: Then at length and presently after your Lily[202] is made hot in your glass, it appeareth in wonderful manners (or demonstration) blacker than the Crow. After that, in process of time, whiter than the Swan, and then passing by yellow to be more red than blood.

6. This being putrefied and turned into red, is to be taken for the Medicine, and then it is time to be fermented.

7. Of which fermentation[203] Paracelsus thus speaketh: one part thereof is to be projected upon 1,000 parts of molten Gold and then the Medicine is prepared, and this is the fermentation of it. But if the half or one part of the liquor of the Sulphur of Gold before described be added to it, then it would be spiritual Ferment and would be much more penetrating in fortitude and fusible, as Paracelsus doth testify in his *Aurora*, where he would have us to join the Star of the Sun or the oil of Sol to this Pantarva.[204] And thus the physical, alchemical Tincture is performed in a short time, for curing all manner of infirmities and human diseases (which is also the Great Elixir for metals so courtly concealed by the ancients) which Hermes Trismegistus the Aegyptian, Osces the Graecian, Haly an Arabian and Albertus Magnus a German, with many others have sought and prosecuted, everyone after his own method, and one in one subject another in another, so much desired by the philosophers only for prolongation of life.

8. In this composition Mercury is made a fixed and dissolved body, the Blood or Spirit of the Red Lion is the Ferment or Soul, and so of trinity is made unity, which is called the physical and alchemical tincture, never before that I know of collected or writ in one work,

and I had not done this except that otherwise the composition of this blessed Medicine had been soon forgot.

A SHORTER WAY TO MAKE THE GLUE OF THE EAGLE

If you desire to make the Glue of the Eagle in a briefer way, take part of the red precipitate produced[205] as it is taught before in Mercury, and dissolve it in distilled Vinegar and the Vinegar will be coloured into a yellow or delightful golden colour; and after you have distilled away the Vinegar, there will remain in the bottom a white substance of the Mercury fixed and fair, which is to be joined to the oil of the Lion; and this work is much shorter and less laborious.

THE CALCINATION OF ANTIMONY INTO THE RED LION

Take Antimony, well ground, so much as you please and melt it in naked fire with Salt Armoniack; and when it is melted, cast it suddenly into a vessel almost full of distilled Vinegar, wherein Salt Armoniack hath been dissolved; and thus melt it and cast it three times. Then pour off the Vinegar from the calx of the Antimony and dry it well and grind it small and dissolve it as before is taught, and so have you the Red Lion of the philosophers' Lead or Antimony.

Twenty-Eighth Sheet

THE ROSIE CRUCIAN MEDICINE OR ELIXIR OF COPPER

I will make plain the 1. Elixir. 2. Conjunction. 3. Separation. 4. The Medicine. 5. Fermentation. 6. The Earth. 7. Spirit Oil, Blood of the Lamb.[206] 8. Distillation. 9. Resolution. 10. Putrefaction. 11. Solution. 12. Vitriol. 13. Calcination. 14. Copper.

Now many have sought the way of the Mineral Pantarva in Vitriol or green Copperas, but they were altogether deceived, which common Vitriol by the philosophers is called the Green Lion of Fools. But this our noble Red Lion taketh its original from the metallic body of Copper.

Although I am not ignorant how to draw an oil out of Roman Vitriol of a more sweet smell and delightful taste than any balsams if the tincture be taken out of the calcined Vitriol in Spirit of Wine; yet the philosophers' will is to command that it doth consist of a metallic virtue, wherewith the transmutation of metals is to be effected. Therefore they say it is to be made of bodies and not of Spirits, as of Vitriol, Sulphur as well and the like. Whence I find it written in the Philosophers' *Turba*, and in the first exercitation: But the philosophers' Medicine is a metallic matter, converting substances and forms of imperfect metals, and it is concluded by all the philosophers that the conversion is not made except by its like. Therefore it is necessary that the *Presoria* be made of a metallic matter, yet [207] if any be made of Spirits; yet it would be better and much more philosophical and more near to a metallic nature to be made of bodies than of Spirits. But if by art the body should be turned into a Spirit, then the same body would be both body and Spirit, and not to be [regarded as] doubled, but the Medicine might be made of such a body or Spirit. But let me return to our purpose. It being granted that this our Vitriol is such a body according to which Paracelsus testifieth in his *Aurora Philosophorum* under this enigma or secret of the ancient philosophers:

Visitabis Interiora Terrae Rectificando Invenies Occultum Lapidem Voram Medicinam.

Out of the first letter of every word of this enigma is gathered this word VITRIOLUM, by which is meant that thereof the Medicine is made.

3. Therefore Paracelsus saith the inward parts of the earth are to be visited; not only the earth, which is Vitriol, but the inward parts of the earth. He meaneth the sweetness and redness, because there lieth hid in the inward parts of the Vitriol a subtile, noble and fragrant juice, a pure oil.

4. And this is especially to be noted: the production of this Copper into Vitriol is not to be done neither by calcination of the fire nor distillation of the matter, lest it be deprived of its grossness, which being lost it wants both power and strength.

5. Paracelsus speaks not one word of the preparation of this Vitriol, by whose silence many have erred; therefore I determined to leave him here a little and to prosecute and follow the order of the Table, wherefore I begin with the calcination of the metal. And note that this calcination of Copper is made that it may be turned into Vitriol, and not the calcination of Vitriol made of Copper.

6. Take therefore as much Copper as you please and dissolve it and calcine it in *Aqua Fortis* to a fair green water; then set it three or four days to digest till the matter be clear, which pour out into a limbeck and *in Balneo* draw away the corrosive water so that the matter remain dry, for then it is calcined.

7. Then upon every two pound of this calcined matter pour a gallon of distilled Vinegar and lute it up in a glass and set it *in Balneo*, almost

boiling, the space of seven days. when it is cold put it into a limbeck to distil away all the Vinegar *in Balneo,* and in the bottom of the alembick you shall have your Vitriol very well congealed, far fairer than Roman Vitriol, which is corporeal and metallic Vitriol.

8. Which Vitriol I do not dissolve in rain water like the Paracelsians, but rather with *Lac Virginis* as before is taught, or in Raymund's Calcination Water; and after its dissolution and perfect digestion, that is to say fifteen days, I put it into a limbeck and [*in*] *Balneo* draw off the *Lac Virginis,* which being done you shall find an oily water, green and clear, upon which pour the Spirit of Wine; and after it hath been digested seven days, and the Spirit of Wine distilled away *in Balneo,* you shall find your green water perfectly rectified, made pure, subtile and spiritual, and fit for putrefaction; for if it be not well dissolved and rarified it will not putrefy.

Twenty-Ninth Sheet

9. But now that I may join with Paracelsus in the manner of putrefaction, I return to him and say with him, commanding to digest in a warm heat in a glass well closed the space of some months, and so long till divers colours appear and be at length red, which showeth the termination of its putrefaction.

But yet in this process this redness is not sufficiently fixed, but is to be more fully purgated from its feces in this manner.

Resolve it or rectify it in distilled Vinegar till the Vinegar be coloured, then filter it from its feces. This is its true tincture and best resolution and rectification, out of which a blessed oil is to be drawn.

This tincture, being thus resolved and rectified is to be put into a body with a limbeck, and *in Balneo* distil the Vinegar gently away.

10. Then in sand or ashes lift up the Spirit gently and temperately, and when you see a fume ascend into the glass and red drops begin to fall out of the nose of the limbeck into the receiver, then the red oil beginneth to distil. Continue your distillation till all be come over. When it is done you shall have the oil in the receiver lifted up and separated from its earth, more delightful and sweet than any balsam or aromatick, without any sharpness at all, which oil is called the Blood of the Lamb.[208] In the bottom of the body you shall find a white, shining earth, like snow, which keep well from dust, and so you have the clear earth separated from its oil.

Take this white earth and put it in a glass viol and put thereto equal weight of the oil or Soul and body,[209] which will receive it and embrace it in a moment.[210]

But that it may be turned into a Medicine when you have joined these two together, set it into our furnace the space of forty days and you shall have an absolute oil of wonderful perfection, wherewith Mercury and other imperfect metals are turned into Gold as Paracelsus was pleased to say.[211]

11. The Medicine being thus made, I now come to the fermentation, without which it is not possible to give a form to it; neither will I adhere to the opinion of one man alone contrary to all philosophers, that is to say Paracelsus, repugnant to the rest of the philosophers, because they all of them of necessity have decreed to give form to the Medicine by ferment and union, that is to say of an imperfect body, and by how much the ferment is more spiritual the Medicine will be of so much more penetration and transmutation.

12. These things being promised, I do not think it fit that you should proceed to projection upon Mercury instead of fermentation as Paracelsus teacheth, or that the Pantarva should be fermented his way with Gold, either corporeal or spiritual, which Gold will be the foundation of the first projection.

But what do the philosophers command us to do? That projection, that is to say fermentation, be made of a perfect foundation, and that upon imperfect bodies that Medicines may be made with foundation of the Pantarva or Elixir is not [commanded] except it be only the white or red ferment, in respect of which both Gold and Silver are said to be imperfect bodies. Therefore the Pantarva is to be fermented before it is projected upon the corporeal foundation, or imperfect, that is to say corporeal, Gold.

13. Therefore join this oil to the fourth part of the oil of the Sulphur of Gold, and this is the true fermentation or conversion into the Elixir.

14. Then augment it in virtue by solution and coagulation, and in quantity by projection, first upon its corporeal foundation, that is to say Gold, then that upon purified Mercury and that Medicine upon other bodies which are most fit for projection, that is to say most fusible, as Lead or Tin, which, after they are purified, are most apt by reason of their easy melting.

Thirtieth Sheet
And thus the inward parts of the earth are visited and by reflection the hidden Medicine is found, the true Medicine out of the Green Lion of the philosophers, and not of fools, and out of corporeal and metallic Vitriol, not terrestrial and mineral Copperas.

THE AUGMENTATION AND PROJECTION OF THE MEDICINES OF METALS ROSY CRUCIAN

First I will treat of the augmentation of the virtue or quantity of which

Raymund saith:[212] The augmentation in quality and goodness is by solution and coagulation of the tincture, that is to say by imbibing it with our Mercury and drying it. But let us hear Arnoldus more attentively. Take one part of your prepared tincture and dissolve it in three parts of our Mercury; then put it in a glass and seal it up and set it in ashes till it be dry and come to a powder; then open the glass and imbibe it again and dry it again; and the oftener you do thus, so much shall you gain more tincture.

And also as it is found in *Clangor Buccinae*. Dissolve it in the Water of Mercury of which the Medicine was made till it be clear; then congeal it by light decoction and imbibe it with its own oil upon the fire till it flow, by virtue whereof it will be doubled in tincture with all its perfections as you will see in projection, because the weight which was before projected upon a thousand is now to be projected upon ten thousand, and there is no great labour in this multiplication. Again the Medicine is multiplied two manner of ways. By solution of calidity and solution of rarity. By solution of calidity is that you take the Medicine, put [it] in a glass vessel and bury it in our moist fire seven days or more till the Medicine be dissolved into water without any turbulency.

By solution of rarity, is that you take your glass vessel with your Medicine and hang it in a new brass pot full of water that boileth, and close up the mouth of the pot that the Medicine may dissolve in the vapour of the boiling water. But note that the boiling water must not touch the glass wherein the Medicine is to hang above it three fingers, and this solution will be in two or three days. After your Medicine is dissolved, take it from the fire to cool, fix and congeal and be hard and dry. This do often, and how much the more the Medicine be dissolved it will be so much more perfect; and such a solution is the sublimation of the Medicine and its virtual sublimation,[213] which the oftener it is reiterated, so much more abundantly and more parts it tingeth.

Whence Rasis[214] saith the goodness of the multiplication consisteth in the reiteration and fixation of the Medicine, and by how much more this order is repeated, it worketh so much more and is augmented; for so often as you sublime your Medicine and dissolve it, you shall gain so much every time in projection one upon a thousand; and if the first fall upon a thousand, [the second upon ten thousand] the third upon a hundred thousand, the fourth upon a million and so infinitely. For Morienus the philosopher saith: Know for certain that the oftener our Pantarva is dissolved and congealed, the Spirit and Soul is joined more to the body and is retained by it, and in every time the tincture is multiplied. Whence we thus read in *Scala Philosophorum* [that] which also the philosophers say. Dissolve and congeal. So without doubt it is understood of the Solution of the body and Soul with the Spirit into water, and congelation makes the Soul and Spirit mix with the body; and if with one solution and simple coagulation the Soul and Spirit would be perfectly joined to the body, the philosophers would not say dissolve again and congeal and again dissolve and congeal, that the tincture of the Pantarva may grow if it could be done with one congelation only.

The Medicine is another way multiplied by fermentation; and the ferment to the white is pure Silver and the ferment to the red is pure Gold. Therefore project one part of the Medicine upon two of the ferment (but I say three parts of the Medicine upon one of the ferment) and all will be Medicine, which put in a glass upon the fire and close it so that no air go in nor out, and keep it there till it be subtiliated as you did with the first Medicine, and one part of the second Medicine will have as much virtue as one part of the first Medicine had. (But here again *Clangor Buccinae* hath erred, for it should be writ thus: One part of the second Medicine will have as much virtue as ten parts of the first Medicine had.) And thus by solution and fermentation the Medicine may be multiplied infinitely.

We have spoken enough of this multiplication; we now come to the other way of augmentation, which is called corporeal multiplication, and according to Raymund is thus defined: Augmentation is the addition of quantity; whence Avicen writeth: It is hard to project upon a million and to predicate it incontinently. Wherefore I will reveal one great secret unto you; one part is to be mixed with a thousand parts of its nearest in kind (I call that nearest that is the body of the same metal whereof the Medicine was made or perfected). But to return again to Avicen: Close all this firmly in a fit vessel and set it in a furnace of fusion three days till it be wholly joined together, and the manner of the work is thus projected, one part of the aforesaid Medicine upon a hundred parts of molten Gold, and it makes it brittle and will all be Medicine, whereof one part projected on a hundred of any molten metal converteth it to pure Gold; and if you project it upon Silver in like manner, it converteth all bodies into Silver.

In *Scala Philosophorum* all sorts of projection is set thus down in few words. You must know that first it is said project, that is one upon one hundred etc. Yet it is better to project *nunc dimittis* upon *fundamenta* and *fundamenta* upon *verba mea* and *verba mea* upon *diligam te domine* and *diligam te* [*domine*] upon *attendite*. This brief enigma is thus expounded; it is nothing else but the words and opinion of the former author concealed under the enigma. Therefore let us repeat the words of the enigma or oracle:

> *Nunc dimittis super fundamenta,*
> *Fundamenta super verba mea,*
> *Verba mea super diligam te,*
> *Diligam te super attendite.*

These are trifles for the hiding and concealing [of] the perfection of the art, if the expert could be diverted with such simple words, which, though they are at first [obscure] to [the] young artist, yet they are thus explained. We therefore begin with the first sentence.

Nunc dimittis super fundamenta

This is here allegorically taken for the last action almost of the work, which is called the Medicine or Pantarva, which Medicine is to be projected upon the ferment, that is to say upon the oil of Sol or Luna, which are the ferments or foundations of the art in spiritual augmentation (as before was said) upon molten Gold or Silver. And that spiritual ferment converted into Medicine is to be projected upon molten Gold and Silver, which are corporeal ferments in corporeal augmentation and the corporeal fundaments of the art upon Quicksilver.

Fundamenta super verba mea

This is spoken also allegorically, because in the adage it is said words are wind, as if a word were nothing else but the motion of the lips and exaltation of the lungs, which no sooner arise from motion but fly away and are turned to air, so likewise Quicksilver or Mercury goeth out of the bodies of the other metals and is so volatile in the fire or heat as words in the air. And therefore Mercury is likened to words upon which the fundaments are to be projected.

Verba mea (viz. Mercury) *super diligam te*

That is to say upon other metals which have most affinity with Quicksilver and [are] easy of fusion, as Saturn and Jupiter, that is to say Lead and Tin, which by this concord and love are easily by the penetration and aimiableness of the Medicine converted into Medicine. And one part of this Medicine converteth other parts of metals into Gold and Silver according to the force and power of the Elixir; which other metals, because they are the substance of the former bodies whereof the Medicines were made, they are the attendants of these Medicines whereof the philosopher commandeth that *diligam te* be projected upon *attendite*, that the second Medicine, or the last, projected upon metal, especially that whereof the Medicine (that is to say the Pantarva) was made, should turn that metal into Gold or Silver according to the property[215] and quality of the Medicine.

But to put an end to this projection, take it according to the opinion of Arnoldus, gathered out of his thirty-first chapter: Who willeth to project one part of the Elixir upon one hundred of Mercury purged, and all will be Medicine, afterwards project one part of this Medicine last congealed upon one hundred parts of Mercury washed, and all will be Gold or Silver according as the Elixir is white or red. Lastly that I may briefly rehearse the absolute manner of projection. First the Medicine is to be projected upon Gold or Silver molten, then upon Quicksilver purged, so long till it turns it into Medicine, and lastly upon metals most near, that they may be converted into pure Gold or Silver according to the properties and quality of the Medicine.

Because we have said something of the propinquity of metals, that is to say that the Elixir is to be projected upon that imperfect body out of which its Mercury and Sulphur was first extracted, therefore it will not be unnecessary to set down one example, that is to say, if the Medicine was made of Mercury, then it is to be projected upon Quicksilver[216] for making Gold or Silver, because Quicksilver is a near body to Mercury, and so of the rest. Yet it is to be noted that all Elixirs may and ought to be projected upon Quicksilver, because Quicksilver is the mother and sperm of all metals; therefore Quicksilver made and turned into Medicine is to be projected upon a body most near to it, which is Lead or Tin,[217] upon which the Medicine is always to be projected, whether white or red, for the making and transmuting of metals; but both the Quicksilver and Lead are first to be purged that they may be purified and deprived of their filth. Enough hath been said before of the purgation and putrefaction of Mercury.

Two and Thirtieth Sheet

OF THE PUTREFACTION OF LEAD

Melt your lead in a crucible, and when it is melted let it stand in the fire a quarter of an hour, and put therein a little Salt Armoniack, and let it stand a while in the fire and stir it well with an iron spatula till all the Salt Armoniack be gone away in fume; then scrape the skin away out of the crucible that is upon the Lead and let it stand to cool and it will be much whiter and fairer. And thus you must purify your Lead or Tin before projection, because no other bodies are so fusible and apt to melt. Wherefore every Elixir ought to be projected upon Quicksilver and upon Lead or Tin for [the] making or transmuting of metals. But to the end [that] the manner of projection may be yet more plain, I will set down two rules which must be carefully observed.

The first whereof is that the first Medicine, that is to say the Pantarva, be projected upon the ferment always, three parts of the Medicine upon one of the ferment, and one part of this upon ten or one hundred of pure molten Gold, and one part of this Medicine thus made upon 100 parts of an imperfect body, that is to say of Mercury for Medicine.

The latter is that you must always consider the fortitude and debility of your Medicine, for it is to be projected so often upon Quicksilver as it bringeth it into a brittle Medicine, and when it falleth, then project one part thereof upon Lead or Tin for making transmutation according to the order and form of the Elixir.

These being remembered you may easily conceive the order of augmentation in virtue and quantity.

The[se] things being ended, the other three which follow are set down in order because we have spoken before of *Aurum Potabile, Argentum Potabile*, or potable Gold or Silver. It is therefore necessary after we have made an end of projection to set down another method of the Elixir of Life in the next place, and after speak of its virtue and power as we find [it] among all the ancient and modern philosophers.

But that we may come at last to the thing intended,[218] observe this manuduction.

You know that no artificer can build, but the earth must be the foundation to his building; for without this groundwork his brick and mortar cannot stand. In the Creation, when God did build, there was no such place to build upon. I ask then, where did He rest His matter and upon what? Certainly He built and founded Nature upon His own supernatural centre. He is in her and through her and with His Eternal Spirit doth He support heaven and earth, as our bodies are supported with our Spirits. This is confirmed by that oracle of the Apostle, *Omnia portat verbo virtutis suae*, He beareth up all things with the word of His power.[219] From this power is He justly styled, απ ιροδυναμις και πανταδυναμις δυναμο παος,[220] The infinitely powerful and the all-powerful power-making power.[221]

I say, then, that fire[222] and Spirit are the Pillars of Nature, the props on which the whole fabric rests and without which it could not stand one minute. This fire[223] is the Throne of the Quintessential Light,[224] from whence He dilates[225] himself to generation as we see in the effusion of the sunbeams in the great world. In this dilation of the Light consist the joy or pleasure of the Passive Spirit, and in its contraction His melancholy or sorrow. We see in the great body of Nature that in turbulent weather, when the Sun is shut up and clouded, the air is thick and dull and our own Spirits, by secret compassion with the Spirit of the Air, are dull too. On the contrary, in clear, strong sunshine, the air is quick and then the Spirits of all animals are of the same rarified and active temper.

It is plain, then, that our joys and sorrows proceed from the dilation and contraction of our inward Quintessential Light. This is apparent in despairing lovers, who are subject to a certain violent, extraordinary panting of the heart, a timorous trembling of the pulse, which proceeds from the apprehension and fear of the Spirit in relation to his miscarriage. Notwithstanding he desires to be dilated, as it appears by his pulse or sally wherein he doth discharge himself, but his despair checks him again and brings him to a sudden retreat or contraction. Hence it comes to pass that we are subject to sighs, which are occasioned by the sudden pause of the Spirit. For when he stops, the breath stops, but when he loseth himself to an outward motion, we deliver two or three breaths, that have been formerly omitted, in one long expiration, and this we call a sigh.

Three and Thirtieth Sheet

This passion hath carried many brave men to sad extremities. It is originally occasioned by the Spirit of the Mistress or affected party, for her Spirit ferments or leavens the Spirit of the lover, so that it desires an union as far as Nature will permit. This makes us resent even smiles and frowns like fortunes and misfortunes. Our thoughts are never at home according to that well grounded observation, *Animus est ubi amat, non ubi animat*, the Soul dwells not where she lives but where she loves. We are employed in a continual[226] contemplation of the absent beauty; our very joys and woes are in her power; she can set us to what humour she will.[227] This and many more miraculous sympathies proceed from the attractive nature of the fire; it is a Spirit that can do wonders. And now let us see if there be any possibility to come at him. Suppose then we should dilapidate or discompose some artificial building stone by stone; there is no question but we come at last to the earth whereupon it is founded. It is just so in Magick; if we open any natural body and separate all the parts thereof one from another,[228] we shall come at last to the fire,[229] which is the candle and secret Light of God. We shall know the Hidden Intelligence and see the Inexpressible Face, which gives the outward figure to the body. This is the syllogism we should look after, for he that hath once passed the Aquaster enter the fireworld and sees what is both invisible and incredible to the common man.[230] He shall discover to the eye the miraculous conspiracy between the fire and the Sun. He shall know the secret love of the heaven and earth and the sense of that deep Cabalism, *Non est planta hic inferiora cui non est stella in firmamento superius, et ferit eam stella, et dicit ei: Cresce*. There is not an herb here below, but he hath a star in heaven above, and the star strikes him with her beams and says to him: Grow. He shall know how the fire-Spirit hath his root in the spiritual fire-earth and received from it a secret influx upon which he feeds as herbs feed on that juice and liquor which they receive at their roots from this common earth. This is it which our Saviour tells us, Man lives not by bread alone, but by every word that comes out of the mouth of God.[231] He meant not by ink and paper or the dead letter. It is a mystery, and St Paul hath partly expounded it. He tells the Athenians that God made man to the end that he should seek the Lord if haply he might feel after Him and find Him.[232] Here is a strange expression you will say, that a man should feel after God and seek him with his hands. But he goes on and tells you where you shall find Him. He is not far (saith he) from every one of us, in Him we live and move and have our being.[233] For the better understanding of this place I wish you to read Paracelsus, his *Philosophia ad Athenienses*.[234] Again, he that enters the centre shall know why all influx of fire descends against the nature of fire, and comes from heaven downwards. He shall also know why the same fire, having found a body, ascends again towards heaven and goes upwards.[235]

To conclude, I say the grand, supreme Mystery of Magic is to multiply[236] the fire and place him in the most serene[237] Aether, which God hath purposely created to qualify the fire. For I would have thee know that this Spirit[238] may be so chafed, and that in most temperate bodies, as to undo thee upon a sudden. This thou mayest guess thyself by the χρυσοκεραυνὸς, or Thundering Gold[239] as the chemist calls it. Place him as God hath placed the stars in the condensed Aether of his Chaos, for there he will shine, not burn; he will be vital and calm, not furious and choleric. This, I confess, transcends the common people.

Now I will teach the blessed Pantarva Rosie Crucian, their *Aurum Potabile* or the Elixir of Life and also the way of making malleable glass.

1. Elixir of Life. 2. Gold dissolved. 3. Silver dissolved. 4. Gold melted. 5. Melted Silver. 6. Projection of the Red Medicine. 7. Projection of the White Medicine.

I have now fully discovered to you the principles of our Chaos.[240] In the next place I will show you how you are to use them. You must unite them to a new life and they will be regenerated by water and the Spirit. These two are in all things; they are placed [there] by God Himself according to that speech of Trismegistus: *Unumquodque habet in se semen sua regenerationis.*[241] Proceed then patiently but not manually. The work is performed by an invisible artist, for there is a secret incubation of the Spirit of God upon Nature. You must only see that

Four and Thirtieth Sheet

the outward heat fails not, but with the subject itself you have no more to do than the mother hath with the child that is in her womb. The two former principles perform all; the Spirit makes use of the water to purge and wash his body, and he will bring it at last to a celestial, immortal constitution. Do not thou think this is impossible. Remember that in the incarnation of Christ Jesus the *quaternarius*, or four elements as men call them, were united to their Eternal Unity and *Ternarius*.[242] Three and four make seven. This septenary is the true Sabbaoth, the rest into which the creature shall enter. This is the best and greatest manuduction that I can give you. In a word, salvation itself is nothing else but transmutation.[243] Behold (saith the Apostle) I show you a Mystery: we shall not all die, but we shall be changed in a moment, in the twinkling of an eye, at the sound of the last Trumpet.[244] God of His great mercy prepare us for it, that from hard, stubborn flints of this world, we may prove crysolites and jaspers in the new, eternal foundation, that we may ascend from this present distressed Church, which is in captivity with her children, to the free Jerusalem from above, which is the mother of us all.

Hermes, speaking of fermentation, bids us to take the Sun and his shadow.[245] By the shadow he meaneth the Moon, because in respect of dignity, lustre and power she is much more weak and inferior than the Sun. And the Moon followeth the Sun as a shadow doth the body, and is not illuminated except by the light of the Sun. We will first speak of the body, that is to say of Gold, and after come to the shadow, of which Gold it is written in a book of chemical art in this manner: The Rosie Crucian Pantarva is made of Gold alone and only by Nature, and is more sublime than them which the philosophers affirm cureth all infirmities. According to the opinion of this philosopher, I purpose to begin with Gold alone and the Medicine, which is a new and sole nature and ancient and sound Quintessence.

2. But to the end this Gold may be better and more pure, it may be purged two manner of ways, that is to say by Antimony and by disollution and in corrosive waters with which copper plates are mixed as goldsmiths use to do, which is called Water Gold. When you have thus prepared your gold, project one part of your Red Medicine (or Red Elixir) upon 100 parts thereof, when your Medicine is augmented in virtue and all that weight of molten Gold will be converted into a red, brittle mass, which grind upon a marble to an impalpable powder.

Then dissolve these hundred parts, or so much thereof as you please, in distilled Vinegar or in Spirit of Wine, and set it to digest *in Balneo* the space of a day or two. Then distil the Spirit of Wine *in Balneo* and in the bottom will remain the fixed and pure oil of the Gold, which is then true *Aurum Potabile* and spiritual Elixir of Life. If you will give to anyone of this powder presently before it be converted into oil, warm a little white or Rhenish wine and dissolve in either or them so much of the red powder, and the wine so tinctured will be *Aurum Potabile*, but it would be better and more penetrating if it were tinctured with the aforesaid oil.[246]

In like manner is the White Medicine to be projected after the purification of the Silver in a corrosive water as is before declared.

And so the melted Silver will be converted into a brittle powder and white mass, which likewise is to be dissolved and turned into oil, and then the white Elixir or Life is made and potable Silver, curing and healing, so far as it is able in human diseases, for it cannot be supposed that the Elixir of Luna hath so great virtue as the Elixir of Sol hath, or *Aurum Potabile*.

Now whereas among the vulgar and [also the] philosophers Gold hath this report, that being in his first disposition that it cureth the leprosy and [hath] many other virtues, this is not except by [247] its complete digestion, because the excellency of the fire acting in it consumeth all evil humours that are in sick bodies as well in hot as cold causes. But Silver cannot do this because it hath not so much superfluity of fire and is not so much digested and decocted with natural maturity; yet notwithstanding this, it hath a fieriness occultly and virtually in it, but not so fully, because the fire causeth not such elemental qualities as in Gold. And therefore Silver, being in his first disposition, doth not cure leprosy so potently unless it be first digested by art until it have the chief degrees of Gold in all maturity. Wherefore other sick metallic bodies more weakly cure infirmities according as they differ more from them[248] in perfection and maturity. Some differ more, some less, which is by reason of the Sulphur, infected and burning, of which they were made at the beginning in their generation and coagulation, and therefore they cure not, whereas the fire in them is burning, and so infected with the elemental feces [and] the mixtures of other elemental qualities.

Five and Thirtieth Sheet

4.[249] Seeing, therefore, that Gold is of such vigour amongst the vulgar, and that being in his first disposition, what wonder is it if it, being brought into Medicine (as is experienced) by art and his virtue be[ing] subtiliated by digestion of decoction and purgation of the qualities, but it may then cure more, nay infinite, of all diseases.

It makes an old man young, as our Rosie Crucian *Aurum Potabile* will do; it preserveth health, strengtheneth nature and expelleth all sickness of the body. It driveth poison away from the heart, it moisteneth the arteries and, briefly, preserveth the whole body sound. The manner of using this Medicine according to all the philosophers is thus: If you will use to eat of this Medicine, then take the weight of two Florence ducats of our *Aurum Potabile* and one pound of any confection, and eat of that confection the quantity of one dram in the winter. And if you do thus it driveth away all bodily infirmities from what cause soever they proceed, whether hot or cold, and conserveth the health and youth in a man and maketh an old man young and maketh grey hairs to fall; it also presently cureth leprosy and diseases of phlegm, mundifieth the blood; it sharpeneth the sight and all the senses after a most wonderful manner, above all the medicines of the Philosophers.

5. To which purpose we thus find in the *Rosary* of the philosophers. In this (that is to say in this *Aurum Potabile*) is completed the precious gift of God, which is the Arcanum of all sciences in the world and the incomparable treasure (for as Plato saith) he that hath the gift of God hath the dominion of the world (that is to say of the Microcosm) because he attaineth to the end of riches and hath broke the bonds of Nature, not only for that he hath power to convert all imperfect metals into pure medicine and [250] preserve both man and every animal in perfect health.

To this purpose speaketh Geberhim, Hermes, Arnoldus, Raymundus Lullius, Ripley, Senotus, Augurellus, Aegidius, Valescus, Roger Bacon, Scotus, Laurentius, Ventura and divers uncertain authors.

Lastly, I now come to the general consent of all the philosophers and repeat what is found in their writings in the book *De Aurora Consurgens*[251] and in *Clangor Buccinae*. It is to be noted that the ancient philosophers have found four principal effects or virtues in the glorious repository of their treasure:

(1) First it is said to cure man's body of all infirmities.
(2) To cure imperfect metals.
(3) Thirdly to transmute base stones into precious gems.
(4) To make glass malleable.

6. Of the first. All philosophers have consented that when the Elixir is perfectly rubified, it doth not only work miracles in solid bodies, but also in man's body, of which there is no doubt; for being taken inwardly it cureth all infirmities. It cureth outwardly by unction. The philosophers also say if it be given to any in water or wine first warmed, it cureth them of the Phrensy, Dropsy and Leprosy and all kinds of

fevers are cured by the Tincture, and [it] taketh away whatsoever is in a weak stomach; in bindeth and consumeth the flux of peccant humours being taken fasting; it driveth away the melancholy and sadness of the mind; it cureth the infirmities of the eyes and dryeth up their moisture and blearedness; it helpeth the purblind, red or bloodshot eyes and all other incident diseases are easily cured by the philosophical Medicine of the Rosie Crucians.

It comforteth the heart and spiritual parts by taking [it] inwardly; it mitigateth the pain of the head by anointing the temples therewith; maketh the deaf to hear and succoureth all pains of the ears; it rectifieth the contracted nerves by unction; it restoreth rotten teeth by washing; also all kinds of imposthumes[252] are cured by it, by ointments or emplaisters or injecting the dry powder therein.

It cureth ulcers, wounds, cancers, fistulas, *noli me tangere*[253] and such like diseases, and generateth new flesh. If it be mixed with corrupt and sour lime it restores it; it expelleth poison, being taken inwardly; it also killeth worms if it be given in powder; it taketh away wrinkles and spots in the face by anointing therewith and maketh the face seem young; it helpeth women in travail being taken inwardly, and bringeth out the dead child by emplaister. It provoketh urine and helpeth generation. It preventeth drunkenness, helpeth memory and augmenteth the radical moisture; it strenghteneth nature and also administereth many other good things to the body.

Six and Thirtieth Sheet

2. Of the second[254] it is written that it transmuteth all imperfect metals in colour, substance, lasting, weight, ductibility, melting, hardness and softness.

3. Of the third, that is to say of transmuting base and ignoble stones into precious.

4. Of the fourth it is writ that it maketh glass malleable by mixture (that is to say, of the powder of the white corporeal Elixir) when the glass is melted.

Thus far *Aurora Consurgens* and *Clangor Buccinae*.

Now if you desire to make pure and malleable glass, beware of what glass you make your metal; for you must not take glass of flint, wherewith glass of windows are made, but such as your Venice glass is made of, and that is to be chosen out of the first metal of the glass which hath stood molten in the fire in the glass-maker's furnace the space of a night, and then it will be without spots and pure. Therefore take as much of the said glass out of the furnace with your iron rod as you have a desire to convert, and when it is cold weigh it and melt it by itself in a pot; and when it is molten, project your white corporeal Elixir upon it and it will be converted into malleable metal and fit and apt glass for all goldsmith's operations. And thus is glass made malleable and prepared for any use; but if this were done with the red Elixir it would be much more during, for there is nothing more precious.

To perfect the Great Work which all philosophers have concealed, observe my direction which by experience I have found true. To calcine, dissolve and separate the elements. After join them together, putrefy them or reduce them into Sulphur; ferment, project, augment in virtue and quantity. This is the work of the philosophers.

This subject[255] I call *Limus Coelestis*[256] and the Middle Nature. The philosophers call it the venerable nature, but amongst all pretenders I have not yet found one that could tell me why. This chaos hath in it the four elements, which of themselves are contrary natures, but the wisdom of God hath so placed them with their very order reconciles them.

For example air and earth are adversaries, for one is hot and moist, the other cold and dry. Now to reconcile these two God placed the water between them, which is a middle nature, or of a mean complexion between both extremes. For she is cold and moist, and as she is cold she partakes of the nature of the earth, which is cold and dry; but as she is moist she partakes of the nature of air which is hot and moist. Hence it is that the air and earth, which are contraries in themselves, agree and embrace one another in water, as in a middle nature, which is proportionate to them both and tempers their extremities.

But verily this *salvo* makes not up the breach; for though the water reconcileth the two elements, like a friendly third, yet she herself fights with a fourth, namely with the fire. For the fire is hot and dry, but the water is cold and moist, which are contraries.

To prevent the distemper of the two, God placed the air between them, which is a substance hot and moist; and as it is hot it agrees with the fire, which is hot and dry; but as it is moist it agrees with the water which is cold and moist, so that by mediation of the air the other two extremes, namely fire and water, are made friends and reconciled. Thus you see, as I told you at first, that contrary elements are united by that order and texture wherein the wise God hath placed them. Now I tell you that this agreement of friendship is but partial, a very weak love, cold and skittish; for whereas those principles agree in one quality, they differ in two as you may easily compute. Much need, therefore, have they of a more strong and powerful[257] mediator to confirm and preserve their weak unity; for upon it depends the very eternity and incorruption of the creature.[258] This blessed cement and balsam is the Spirit of the Living God, which some ignorant scribblers have called Quintessence, for this very Spirit is in the Chaos, and, to speak plainly, the fire is[259] His Throne,[260] for in the fire is He seated. This was the reason why the Magi called the First Matter their Venerable Nature and their Blessed Stone. This Blessed Spirit fortifies and perfects that weak disposition which the elements already have to union and pace (for God works with Nature and not against her) and brings them at last to a beauteous, specifical fabric. Now if you will ask me, where is the Soul, or as the schoolmen abuse her, the form, all this while? What doth she do? To this I answer that she is as all instrumentals ought to be, subject and obedient to the will of God, expecting the perfection of the body. For it is God that united her to the body and the body to her.

Soul and body are the works of God, the one as well as the other. The Soul is not the artificer of the house, for that which can make a body can also repair it, and hinder death; but the Soul cannot do this, it is the power and wisdom of God. In a word, to say that the Soul formed the body, because she is in the body is to say that the jewel made the cabinet or that the Sun made the world and cherisheth every part thereof. Learn, therefore, to distinguish between Agents and their instruments, for if you attribute that to the creature which belongs to the Creator, you bring yourselves in danger of hell fire, for God is a jealous God and will not give the glory to another. *Seven and Thirtieth Sheet*

If thou dost know the First Matter, know also for certain thou hast discovered the Sanctuary of Nature. There is nothing between thee and her treasures but the door; that indeed must be opened. If thy desire lead thee on to the practice, consider well with thyself what manner of man thou art, and what it is that thou wouldst do; for it is no small matter. Thou hast resolved with thyself to a be co-operator with the Spirit of the Living God and to minister to Him in His work of generation. Have a care, therefore, that thou dost not hinder His work; for if thy heat exceeds the natural proportion, thou hast stirred the wrath of the moist natures and they will stand up against the central fire and [the central fire] against them and there will be a terrible division in the Chaos; but the sweet Spirit of Peace, the true eternal Quintessence, will depart from the elements leaving both them and thee to confusion; neither will He apply Himself to that Matter as long as it is in thy violent, destroying hands.

I will now lay down plain instructions concerning:

1. The Elixir of Saturn. 2. Putrefaction into Sulphur. 3. The Oil, of the Sulphur. 4. Of the Conjunction. 5. Of the Salt. 6. Of Oil of the Spirit. 7. Of Salt of Saturn, which containeth the Oil or Soul of the *Menstruum*. 8. Of White Mercury. 9. Of Red Water of Paradise. 10. Resolution. 11. Solution. 12. Distillation. 13. Hyle. 14. Purgation. 15. Resolution. 16. Of Sericon. 17. Of the Gum. 18. Of Sericon. 19. Of the Solution. 20. Of Minium Or[e]. 21. Adrop. 22. Of Calcination. 23. Of Minium. 24. Adrop. 25. Of Red Lead. 26. Of Calcination of Lead. 27. Of *Aqua Fortis*.

Now [261] see which way the philosophers move. They commend their secret water and I admire the tears of *Beata Pulchra*.[262] I will tell you truly what she is; she is not any known water whatsoever, but a secret spermatic moisture, or rather the Venus, that yields that moisture. Therefore do not you imagine that she is any crude, phlegmatic, thin water, for she is a fat, thick, heavy, slimy humidity. But lest ye should think I am grown jealous and would not trust you with my mistress, Arnoldus de Villa Nova shall speak for me. Hear him. *Amplius tibi dico, quod nullo modo invenire potuimus, nec similiter invenire potuerunt philosophi, aliquam rem perseverantem in igne, nisi solam unctuosam humiditatem. Aqueam humiditatem videmus de facili evaporare, arida remanet, et ideo separantur, quia non sunt naturales. Si autem eas humiditates consideremus, quae difficulter separantur ab his quae sunt naturales, non invenimus aliquas nisi unctuosas et vi scosas.* I tell thee further (saith he) that we could not possibly find, neither could the philosophers find before us, anything that would persist in the fire, but only the unctuous humidity. A watery humidity, we see, will easily vapour away, and the earth remain behind, and the parts are, therefore, separated, because their composition is not natural. But if we consider those humidities which are hardly separated from those parts which are natural to them, we find not any such but the unctuous, viscous humidities.

This vicous humidity[263] is Water of Silver, which some have called Water of the Moon; but it is Mercury of the Sun and partly of Saturn, for it is extracted from these three metals and without them it can never be made.[264]

Very many have written of Saturn or Lead, but none that I know of have written fully thereof in any particular treatise. Therefore I do not only here set down what I have gathered from them most briefly and truly, but also those things which I have found and proved by my own experience, which I have annexed to them that the work may be absolute and complete.

Of which, as they say, Mary the prophetess, the sister of Moses, in her *Books of the Work of Saturn* is said to write: Make your water running like the water of the two Zaibeth[265] and fix it upon the Heart of Saturn. And in another place: Marry the Gum with the true Matrimonial Gum and you shall make it like running water; of which process of Mary, George Ripley hath these verses:

> Maria mira sonat
> Quae nobis talia donat
> Gummis cum binis
> Fugitivem fugit in imis
> Horis in trinis
> Tria vinclet fortia finis
> Filia plutonis
> Confortia jungit Amoris.

Eight and Thirtieth Sheet

The Heart of Saturn, you shall find why is his body white and clear; the work is briefly thus described. That a water be made out of the body of Saturn like the water Zaibeth, and that water fixed upon the Heart of Saturn. The direction for drawing out the water of Zaibeth and the way of making the Heart of Saturn is hereafter at large declared, with reduction of the body of Saturn into his Heart or Salt.

Note the power of Saturn and his Angel upon earth, Cambiel, Hanael, Cancer, Tristitia, and Lead thus prepared for Medicines and Telesmas. You see here the wonderful power of God, how he rules heaven and earth by ten names, ten Sephiroth, ten orders of blessed Souls, ten Angels in their ten Spheres, seven Angels that carry their power to seven planets and the earth; and here we teach you knowledge of the seven metals and the miraculous Medicines of the Rosie Crucians.

Having thus described the work, I now come to the explanation and say that the calcination of the body is two-fold, for the calcination thereof in the shorter work for extracting the Heart of Saturn is done on this wise by *Aqua Fortis*.

Take eight or ten ounces of Lead in filings and dissolve it in *Aqua Fortis* in double proportion and justified with Salt Armoniack in an earthen vessel with a narrow neck and set in ashes till it be totally dissolved; and there will remain a white matter in the bottom like grains of white Salt, which is a figure of perfect solution. Then pour your matter that is dissolved in the water into a body and set thereon a limbeck and *in Balneo*, draw away the corrosive water till there remain a dry subtance in the bottom, and so you have the body converted white by calcination with corrosive water out of which the Heart of Saturn is to be drawn.

7. The way to wash away and purge the corrosive water from the body. Pour warm water upon the substance in the limbeck and pour it often off till it have no sharpness at all upon the tongue and then the body is prepared for drawing out the Salt.

8. When your matter is well dried, dissolve it again in distilled Vinegar and distil the Vinegar twice or thrice from it and in the bottom you shall have a lucid, clear and white, shining Salt, which is called the Heart of Saturn.

9. Now I come to the practice of the other greater work, that the verity of the Medicine may be found, of which many have made mention in their books, as Raimundus, who called it the Vegetable, Mineral and Animal Medicine. Geber saith there groweth a Saturnian Herb on the top of a hill or mountain, whose blood, if it be extracted, cureth all infirmities.[266]

10. Ripley writ a whole book called his *Practical Compendium*, of the practice of the Vegetable Medicine, teaching the manner and form of operation; but because he neither set down the solution plainly nor perfectly, he hath been the cause of much error and hath not only deceived me, but all those that followed him, until after a long time I found a way to dissolve Saturn, so that it could never after by distillation be turned into Lead again, which is the choicest and greatest secret of the Vegetable Medicine.

11. But let us hear the words of Mary the prophetess and Ripley taken from her: The Radix of our Matter is a clear and white body, which putrefieth not but congealeth[267] Mercury or Quicksilver with its odour, makes its water like the running water of the two Zabieth (or Zubech) and fix[eth] it upon the fixed Heart of Saturn. Which words do most aptly agree with the properties of Lead, for if anyone be short or wounded with a bullet and the bullet remain in the body, it will never putrefy.

12. And also if Quicksilver be hanged in a pot over the fume of molten Lead, so as the fumes of the Lead touch the Quicksilver, it will congeal it.

Nine and Thirtieth Sheet

13. Thus far of the preparation of Lead. We now come to its denomination. They bid us fix the water [of] Zabieth upon the fixed body of the Heart of Saturn. Now for the exposition of the body for the name of Saturn. Ripley called it Adrop,[268] of which that is made which the Masters call Sericon,[269] the water of Sericon they call their *Menstruum*. The two Zabrieths joined together in one water[270] are the two Mercuries, that is to say white and red, contained in one

Menstruum, that is to say of the water and oil of the fixed body or Heart of Saturn.

14. Isaacus also writ a treatise of Lead. He worketh chiefly according to the doctrine of Mary the prophetess and laboureth much to fix the earth of Saturn and after to dissolve the body in distilled Vinegar, that by the addition of corroding the sharp things his red oil may be distilled, which he called the Water of Paradise, that he may imbibe his fixed earth therewith: which way is much shorter than Ripley's, but the rubification and fixation of the earth is long and uncertain; wherefore I have both forsaken Isaacus and Ripley in making the earth, instead of which I have given the fixed Heart of Saturn.

15. But that the body may be prepared according to this Table and after my intention and the desire of Ripley, we both will that the pil or Water of Paradise be drawn out of the Gum of Sericon (whose father is Adrop). Sericon is made of red Lead; therefore it is first necessary to show the way of making Minium of Lead. Take the description as followeth and therewith the composition of the Gum of Sericon.

16. Take ten or twelve pounds of Lead and melt it in a great iron vessel as plumbers use to do; and when it is molten, stir it still with an iron spatula till the Lead be turned to powder, which powder will be of a green colour. When you see it thus, take it from the fire and let it get cool and grind that powder upon a marble till it be impalpable, moistening the powder with a little common Vinegar till it be like thick honey, which put into a broad earthen vessel and set it on a trevet over a lent fire to vapour away the Vinegar and dry the powder and it will be of a yellow colour. Grind it again and do as before, till the powder be so red as red Lead, which is called Adrop. And thus is Saturn calcined into red Lead or Minium.

17. Take a pound of red Lead and dissolve it in a gallon of Vinegar and stir it with a stick three or four times in a day. Then take your earthen vessel and set it *in Balneo* twenty-four hours then let it cool and filter the liquor three times; and when it is clear put it in a bottom [and distil away the Vinegar when] the Gum of Sericon will remain like thick honey, which set apart and dissolve now more Lead as before for more Gum till you have ten or twelve pound thereof.

18. Now give careful attention, for we now come to the point and period of Ripley's error; for if you put four pounds of this Sericon to distil in a limbeck, and from thence would draw as *Menstruum* as Ripley

teacheth, perhaps you would have scarce one ounce of this oil, and some part of a black earth will remain in the bottom and most of the Gum melted again into Lead, by which you may know that the Sericon is not well dissolved, nor as yet sufficiently prepared that a Chaos may be made thereof fit for distillation because it is not yet well dissolved. Therefore in Isaacus there is found a way, resolving this Gum with distilled Vinegar, acuated with calcined Tartar and Salt Armoniack; wherefore, saith he, if thou be wise resolve the Gum. But I like not this acuation of the Vinegar as I may call it. I rather choose to resolve the Sericon in Raymund's Calcination Water, which is a compound water of Vegetable Mercury, or fire natural, with the fire against nature, as Ripley testifieth; and it is more verified by Raymund in his books of Mercury, where he teacheth how to dissolve bodies with his Calcinative Water.

19. I will reveal unto you this water, which is almost unknown. Note, therefore, that the Vegetable Mercury is the Spirit of Wine (instead of which we may sometimes use distilled Vinegar) and that the Fire against Nature is a corrosive water made of Vitriol and Saltpeter.

20. Therefore take which you will, either Spirit of Wine rectified (or *Aqua Vitae*) or distilled Vinegar four pounds and two pounds of corrosive water and mix them together.

In this water thus compounded, resolve half a pound of Gum of Sericom in a circulatory and set it *in Balneo* four or five days, and the Gum will be totally dissolved into the form of water or oil of a duskish red colour.

Fortieth Sheet

21. Then distil away the water *in Balneo* and there will remain an oil in the bottom which is the Chaos out of which you may draw a *Menstruum* containing two elements, and this is the true resolution of the Gum of Sericon. In this water you may resolve so much Gum as you please by reiteration.

22. Take two pound of this Chathodical substance and prepare it for distillation in naked fire or sand, and lift up the clear red oil, wherein both the Spirit and Soul doth secretly lie hid, which Isaacus calleth the Water of Paradise, which, when you have [it], you may rejoice, for you have gone through all the gross work and come to the philosophic work.

Therefore proceed to conjunction and join the white Heart of Saturn with the red oil as it is found in the *Rosary, candida succinto jacet uxor nupta marito*, that is to say the red Mercury to the Salt if you proceed to the red work.

23. Therefore take four ounces of the Salt or Heart of Saturn and as much of the red oil or Water of Paradise, and seal them up in a philosophers' egg; and so soon as they shall feel the heat of the *Balneum*, the Salt will dissolve and be made all one with the oil so as you shall not know which was the Salt nor which was the oil.

Set your glass *in Balneo* and there let it stand in an equal degree of fire till all your matter be turned white and stick to the sides of the glass and shine like fishes eyes[271] and then it is white Sulphur of Nature. But if you proceed to the red work, then divide your white Sulphur into equal parts, reserving one part for the white work, and go on with the other part, and in a new glass, well sealed up, set it in ashes till it is turned into a red colour.

24. When your Sulphur is thus converted, imbibe it again with equal weight of its Soul, dissolving and congealing till it remain in an oil and it will congeal no more, but remain fixed and flowing.

This then is to be fermented with the fourth part of the Oil of Gold.

We have set down already before of the augmentation in quantity and quality, therefore it is not necessary to repeat it here.

We will now return to the white Sulphur before reserved, that we may set down the manner of the white work.

When you have your red oil or Soul, if you desire to make the white Elixir, set part of the said oil in a glass *in Balneo* to digest. Then take it out and put it into a body and in a lent fire distil away the Spirit or white Mercury, which you must try and know whether it arise pure without water or not, as you do when you try the spirit of wine. For if it burn all up it is well; if it do not, rectify it so often till it be without any waterings at all; then have you rectified your Spirit, wherewith dissolve your white Sulphur till it remain fixed and flowing as you did before in the red work. Then ferment it and augment it with the fourth part of the oil of the white Luminary or Luna, as you did the red, and it will be the white Elixir, converting imperfect bodies into perfect Silver.

25. Ripley divided the scope of this work into four operations, whereof the first is the dissolution of the body; the second the extraction of the *Menstruum* and the separation of the elements; the third is not necessary in our work, because we cast away the earth after every distillation, instead of which we use our Salt or Heart of Saturn; the fourth is that there be a conjunction of our Salt as is before described.

HERE FOLLOWETH THE ACCURTATION OF THE WORK OF SATURN

The way of extracting Quicksilver out of Saturn found in Isaacus, of which I know how to make a special accurtation with his Water of Paradise, which I gathered partly from the foresaid writer and others. Ripley made his accurtation with Quicksilver precipitated with Gold and imbibition with corrosive water, which I like not, because the Elixir so made will be the greatest poison, as himself confesseth that it were better for a man to eat the eyes of a Basilisk than taste that Elixir.

26. But because I desire to set down this accurtation of Lead alone with his elements, that no strange body may be added to our Elixir, and also that it may be made a Medicine for all uses, I have found out the way of making [it] alone with the Mercury of Saturn and his own proper Tincture; for I make a body of one thing, which is a Spirit, and make that Medicine with its own proper Spirit. Read all the philosophers and you shall never find a word of this process, nor none of the ancients will teach how to make the Mercury of Saturn.

OF THE MEDICINE, ELIXIR, FERMENTATION IMBIBITION, PRECIPITATION, QUICKSILVER, SATURN, LEAD, THE TOAD

One and Fortieth Sheet

Sir Christopher Heydon saith in a manuscript of his; *Levi enim arte norunt Alchemistae Mercurium currentem conficere ex plumbo.* The Alchemists know how by an easy art to make current Mercury out of Lead. But what art that was no author of the ancients hath showed unto us. *Quaevite, quaevite,* saith the first alchemist[272] (so Paracelsus was pleased to say in imitation of him) *et invenietis, pulsate et operietur vobis.* I tried many experiments, although they were repugnant to doctrine and philosophy; I almost despaired of that art; yet because nothing is difficult to the industrious, by often knocking at last I found it apart, by which means I attained to the art of such a felicity, that is to say of making Quicksilver of[273] Lead. This art revealed is a great secret. The instruments necessary in this work are[274] a furnace, a crucible and a pair of tongs. Let the furnace be filled with coals, whereunto put fire, and when the coals are well burnt, so that they give a clear flame and fire, take your crucible, well annealed so that it break not with the sudden heat, and put therein three ounces of filed Lead, having twelve ounces of Mercury sublimate well ground, and Salt Armoniack six ounces, mixed together, which put upon the filings of Lead in the crucible, and when the fire is strong and glowing hot, take your tongs and presently take up your crucible and put it into the hole in the top of the furnace till you hear a great noise and buzzing; then so soon as you can (lest the Quicksilver fly away with the Spirits) take away the crucible with the matter therein and set it in an earthen dish filled with ashes to cool; and when it is cold, strike the lower part of the crucible so that the matter of the Lead may fall into an earthen dish, and you shall find your Lead converted into Quicksilver.

Take of this Quicksilver so much as you please and put it to precipitate in a round glass, well luted; and set it in ashes to the top of the glass. Yet let us stay here a little while [that] the understanding may be more enlightened.

Therefore understand that the intention of this work is to fix the Spirit, which may sooner be done with the Spirit of a fixed body, which before was homogeneal with the body, and which of its own nature desireth to join again with its body.

Therefore Nature requireth that she may be helped by art in this work, to which the artist consenting, he administereth thereto the pure and desired metal, which it delighteth to adhere unto, which metal is Gold, which is thus prepared that it be sooner parted by the Quicksilver and stick thereunto.

Take as much pure Gold as you please and dissolve it in *Aqua Regis* mixed with equal part of *Acetum acerrimum* or *Lac Virginis*. Then set it to digest the space of a day; then put your dissolution into an alembick and set it *in Balneo*. So distil away the water as dry as you can and do thus three times and the third time distil it in ashes that the Salt Armoniack may sublime. Then put distilled Vinegar upon the matter remaining, and after it hath stood three days *in Balneo*, distil the Vinegar away in ashes that all the substance of the Salt Armoniack may sublime, and do thus three times, always putting in new Vinegar, until the oil of the dissolved Gold remain in the bottom. Then take of your Quicksilver three times so much as your Gold and pour it upon the solution of the Gold that they may mix together and be united. Then put your Quicksilver with the solution in a round glass, stopped only with a piece of cotton, and with a stick put it down every day as it doth ascend; and keep your glass in ashes for a month till your Quicksilver be turned into a red precipitate. Then again dissolve it in new distilled Vinegar till the whole substance of the Quicksilver be dissolved and the Vinegar be coloured into a golden colour; then distil away the Vinegar in ashes and again precipitate the Quicksilver, which is in the bottom of a gold colour, into a red and fixed body, and so have you the Mercury precipitate of Saturn.

It remaineth now that the body be imbibed with its Soul, that thus being from a Spirit reduced into a body [it] may again imbibe its Soul that it may be dissolved therewith. Therefore put it into a glass and add thereto equal proportion of its Soul or Water of Paradise, and shut your glass well the space of five days till the body be dissolved with the Soul.

Then dry it in ashes till it penetrate and flow; and when it is dried, try it upon a hot iron plate if it be fixed and melt, if not, imbibe it again with half the weight of its water and do so till you make it fusible and piercing by imbibing and drying. And when it will melt in the fire and penetrate, it is then the Medicine and fit for fermentation. And after the fermentation it will be the Elixir.

Forty Second Sheet

Then it is to be augmented and projected as is before declared, and thus the work of Saturn is accurtated, of which George Ripley saith: Adrop is the father of the Medicine, Sericon his brother, Lympha his sister, the earth its mother.

But if you desire to know all the secret of Saturn or Lead, I will set you down one process out of Paracelsus: When you have well prepared the Heart of Saturn, saith he, take two or three ounces of that Heart and grind it small with double [the] weight of Saltpeter and put it in a subliming glass with a head well luted to sublime, increasing the fire by little and little as long as anything will ascend or sublime. Thus far Paracelsus. Now if you would find this true, Ripley will tell you what you shall do in these words.

When by the violence of the fire in the distillation of the Gum of the Sericon, a certain white matter shall ascend sticking to the head of the limbeck, like ice, keep the matter, which hath the property of Sulphur, not burning, and is fit matter for receiving form. You shall give it form after this manner by rectifying it in ashes; and when it is red Sulphur, give it of its Soul until it pierce and flow, then ferment it.

Here I have delivered unto you all the ways and manners of Saturn which are found in any of the philosophers' books. To the end, therefore, that the work may be completed with a demonstration of this word *Plumbum Philosophorum* as appears in the *Practical Compendium* of Ripley, I say that the philosophers' Lead is not taken for Antimony but for Adrop, being converted into the Gum of Sericon.

The influence of Jupiter and his Angel upon Hismael, Advachiel, Aquisitio, Letitia and Tin, by art and nature fitted for man's use. Jupiter followeth Saturn's steps, for he is the offspring of Saturn and naturally born from him.

♃ *presentat Stannum sub quo aliquando Mercurius Sublimatus et Sal Ammoniarum intelligitur. Cineritius ille probus justus Jupiter influentiam suam habet in terrestrem Jovem, qui post preparationem suam, se claro* aërio suavi cum sale Sulphureque lunari ostentat, et mortalibus virtutes suas presentat. Habet quoque specialem suam influentiam bonus ille Jupiter in Jecur, sanat propterea illud, omnesque affectus qui inde oriuntur.

TO MAKE THE ELIXIR OF IRON

Observe in this work 1. Calcination. 2. Solution. 3. Separation. 4. Conjunction. 5. Putrefaction. 6. Sulphur. 7. Fermentation. 8. Elixir.

Mars being most earthly of all the planets or bodies, it is not to be doubted but that it may easily be reduced into a body with little labour and therefore most easily converted into Salt, which is done by Calcination; therefore I will first show his conversion into Salt. Understand therefore that hence ariseth a two-fold consideration, that is to say that it be calcined one way into its body or Salt, the other way that the body be prepared for solution by calcination.

The practice differs but a little, for whether you calcine Iron for its Salt or *Menstruum*, one only manner of preparation[275] sufficeth.

That is to say, that you take filings of Iron or Steel, as much as you please, and mix these with equal weight of Sulphur in an earthen body with a limbeck well luted thereto; then set it in ashes to sublime till all the Sulphur be sublimed from it; then dissolve the filings which remain in the bottom in *Aqua Regis* and it will be converted into Salt, which will be cleansed from the said water if you put thereon distilled Vinegar and distil it away. Do thus three times with new Vinegar and you shall have a yellowish-red Salt in the bottom, which then is a body to be joined to the Soul, which keep in warm ashes till you use it.

Now for the practice of Iron for dissolution. Take filings of Iron or Steel, so much as you please, and put it in an iron dish filled with Vinegar and set it in the flaming fire the space of three hours; then take it out and let it cool. Reiterate this work four or five times, then calcine it with Sulphur as you did before.

When it is thus calcined, set it to dissolve in a corrosive water by adding equal weight of our *Acetum acerrimum*, and let it stand till it have dissolved so much as it can in the cold; then set it in hot ashes and let it stand there the space of four or five days. Pour off the water and dry [that] which is not dissolved, and again calcine it and dissolve it; and when it is dissolved, so as the water be coloured red, pour it out into a body and keep it till you have dissolved as much calcinated Iron as you please.

Then take[276] all your dissolution, and with an alembick distil away the water *in Balneo* and put distilled Vinegar upon the matter remaining

Forty Third Sheet

in the bottom and let it stand upon it *in Balneo* the space of seven days; then take out your glass and filter the dissolution and then again *in Balneo* distil off the Vinegar and in the bottom will remain a thick oil of Iron or[277] Steel. But if it be not dissolved to your mind, reiterate your solution in Raymund's Calcination Water, but it would be better if it were edulcorated[278] with *Aqua Vitae*, drawing it away again in *in Balneo*, and so you have Iron dissolved into a liquor.

Therefore proceed to distillation, that there may be a separation, and distil it in an earthen vessel in a strong fire increasing the fire as much as you can and receive the oil or Soul or red tincture of Mars, separated from the remaining feces by the nose of the limbeck, which oil is the most permanent tincture for colouring Sulphur for the red work or for exaltation of all Elixirs in colour, for it makes it tinge and colour higher.

When you have thus prepared the tincture, then proceed to conjunction and work with the Salt before reserved, taking three or four ounces of the Salt and equal weight of the Soul.

Then seal it up and set it to putrefy *in Balneo*, and keep it there till it pass through all colours and be white, and then it is Sulphur of Nature.

The nature of Mars and his Angel upon Barzabel, Malchidael, Barchiel, Puer, Rubeus and Iron, with the mixtion of elements. The Medicine must be made when Mars ascends in Aries or Scorpio in the hour of Mars, Puer projected in the Ascendent.

Then take out your glass and set it in ashes in a greater degree of heat till it be red; then dissolving the red Sulphur with its own Soul and again dissolve and fix it; dissolving it *in Balneo*, fixing it under the fire, and so it is prepared for fermentation.

The fermentation is, as hath often been spoke of before, with the resolved oil of the Sulphur of Gold in a four-fold proportion to the Medicine, that by the addition of the ferment it may be made Elixir transmuting all bodies.

And note that the Elixir of Iron excelleth all other Elixirs, for it rubifieth more and tingeth higher and is better for man's body, for it prevaileth against the spleen, constringeth the belly and cureth wounds; it knitteth broken bones together and stoppeth the superfluous flux of the courses etc.

I WILL NOW SHOW THE OPERATION OF THE PHYSICAL AND ALCHEMICAL TINCTURE OF THE RED LION AND GLUE OF THE EAGLE

It is chiefly to be remembered how I taught you to dissolve Antimony with our *Acetum acerrimum*, which may be also well done if you dissolve it in our Calcination Water; and after that Antimony is calcined, which hereafter shall be at large treated of, also of the Glue of the Eagle. You must understand that we attribute no other beginning to this accur[t]ation except that where before we took the Blood of the Red Lion and the Glue of the Eagle when they were both destroyed, we now join them sound and not hurt together, that they, living, may mortify and dissolve themselves, which I have fitly called Corporeal Matrimony or the Union, for in this wedlock they die together that they may be vivified in the Celestial Antimony. It is not to be wondered if this [work] differ from the other, for this pertaineth to the handling of Spirits, the other way to teacheth the manner of making the Elixir of bodies.

That I may plainly reveal all things unto you, take Antimony well ground, half a pound, and as much Mercury Sublimate likewise ground, and grind them both together upon a marble till you cannot know them one from another; then set them in a cold place that the matter dissolving may drop into a glass set underneath, for when the matters are well mixed together, then [I] say that they will both shortly be dissolved; when the water is perfectly dissolved it will be of a greenish colour and loathsome smell.

Forty-Fourth Sheet

Put this water with the thick part within into a glass, and let it stand the space of three days in a fixatory under the fire, and in [a] short time you shall have your dissolvedness of a brownish black colour, and after, that is to say in the foresaid time, it will be red, something higher than red Lead.

Dissolve this calcined matter in Raymund's Calcinative Water, and when you have dissolved it all into a red liquor, or deep yellow, then is your matter brought well into its Chaos.

Put this liquor into a fit body with an alembick and receiver, and by distillation separate the red oil or the red Mercury from the white body which remaineth in the earth, and if any matter ascend into the head of the alembick, despise it not, but try if it [be] fixed; and if it be not fixed enough, sublime it till it be fixed.

Whereunto join equal weight of its Soul, for the Celestial Matrimony, and always leave out the earth in the bottom if you have any sublimate fixed; if not, take the white earth remaining in the bottom, with which proceed as before is said, and join the white body with the Soul. When they are thus joined or married, set them to impregnate and revivify *in Balneo* till it pass through all colours and at last be converted into red, which then is Medicine.

The manner of fermentation [and] augmentation, both in quantity, quality and projection, is spoken already.

And thus I have opened many choice secrets of the ancient philosophers, and also have amended many things in them. Their writings were rather published to conceal the art than to make it manifest or teach it. Although it pleaseth Hermes Trismegistus, the first writer of this art, both to say and protest that he had never revealed, taught nor prophesied anything of this art to any, except fearing the Day of Judgement or the damnation of his Soul for shunning the danger thereof, even as he received the gift of faith from the Author of faith, so he left it to the faithful. Yet when you read his writings either in his *Smaragdine Tablet* or in his *Apocaled* or his *Twelve Golden Gates* and shall find nothing plain, what shall ye think of such an author? Believe me, all the ancients have concealed the secret of their preparations in the gross work, although they writ most famously of the philosophic operation; therefore I have used my endeavour to try, for out of their writings I found that the Elixir might be made of the planets or metals, and also of mean minerals, which came near to a metallic nature. Then, reading more, I found a certain method amongst them all, as it were with one consent or voice on this wise.

First and principally that bodies should be made incorporeal, that is to say discorporated or discompounded, which then is called Hyle or Chaos. Secondly that out of the Chaodical substance, which is one thing, three elements should be separated and purified.

[Thirdly] that the separated and purified elements should be joined, the man and the woman, the body and the Soul, heaven and earth, with infinite other names so called that the ignorant might think they were divers, which only were nothing else but water and Salt, or the Body and Spirit or Soul, that is to say white Mercury and Red, which they joined together that a new and pure body might be created in putrefaction and a Microcosmical infant might be created in imitation of the Creation, that is to say, Sulphur of Nature.[279]

Fourthly that it should be fed with Milk, that is to say that its own proper tincture, and after[wards] nourished by fermentation, that it may grow to its perfect strength.

Having learned these I began to practise, and in the practice of every body and Spirit I found divers errors; but reading more and trying more, at last I found the manner and true way of dissolving all bodies, separating and conjoining them, finding the composition of their secret of secrets, that is to say *Lac Virginis* or *Acetum acerrimum*, and Raymund's Calcining Water, wherewith I dissolved all bodies at pleasure and perfected the gross work. Wherefore I purposed, contrary to[280] the customs of the philosophers, [to] reveal the whole work lest I, being envious, should be the author of errors like themselves. Therefore I have added their secrets to my own experiments and inventions, which are plainly and truly writ.

Alchemy revealeth and openeth unto us four other secrets.

The first is the Composition of Pearls, far greater and fairer than natural ones, which cannot be perfectly done without the help of the Elixir.

The second is the manner of making precious stones out of ignoble ones, by the same art as we made malleable glass.

The third is the manner of making artificial Carbuncles in imitation of natural ones, which few or none have spoken of.

The fourth is the manner of making Mineral Amber, of which Paracelsus hath only writ in his *Book of Vexations of Philosophers*[281] and in the last edition of his work in the sixth[282] [book of] his Archidoxes; but because they cannot be made without the help of the Elixirs, therefore they deserve a place among the Elixirs, where I shall discover the virtue or rather the vice of making Amber.

Forty-Fifth Sheet

THE OPERATION OF MAKING PEARLS CONSISTETH OF THESE PARTS. VIZ:

Lac Virginis
Dissolved Pearls[283]
Quicksilver and
The White Elixir.

Take *Lac Virginis* or *Acetum acerrimum*, so much as you think sufficient for dissolving the Pearls, as in double proportion to the Pearls, as if there be three ounces of the Pearls let there be six ounces of *Lac Virginis*, wherein dissolve the Pearls and set the glass *in Balneo* to digest the space of a day. Then pour out the solution and distil it *in Balneo*, and in the bottom of the glass you shall find the thick oil of the Pearls, whereunto add so much of your white corporeal Elixir as sufficeth to make the matter like paste, and put thereto equal weight of the pearls of Quicksilver. If the matter be too thin, put more powder of the Elixir; if it be too thick, add more *Lac Virginis* or Quicksilver, till it be like liver. Grind this mass upon a stone till it be brought to a fit thickness.

Then make it up in what form you please, [and] therefore it is necessary that you have a pair of brass or iron moulds in readiness (but it would be better if they were of silver) of what form you will, and fill them with the matter while it is soft; then pierce them through with a needle or such like thing, and put as many of them in a glass as you will (but first hang them upon a thread) and close well the glass and bury it with the pearls therein two foot under the earth and let it stand there the space of six months till they be congealed with the cold into a shining and clear substance like natural Margarites. These Pearls made and compounded in this manner are no less than natural ones, but much greater and more excellent by reason of the white Elixir.

THE OPERATION OF THE MAGISTERY OF CARBUNCLES

Carbuncles have their birth and origin in the pits and golden mines of the earth, of the Spirit of Gold and mineral Salt, indurated and corporeal, being decocted and disgested into the hardness of stone by the Archaeus[284] of Nature, as well by the heat of the climate as by the great heat of the Sun; for they arise from the Spirit of the *minere* of Sol or Gold under the earth, by whose influence they shine as also from [whom] the[y are] hardened into the nature of the stone; whence the philosopher intendeth and endeavoureth as he can to imitate nature by art and to make and compound artificial Carbuncles above the earth with the same materials which nature formeth them of under the earth; therefore he useth the same principles, operating with the Spirit and Soul of Sol undivided, and the most hard Salt of the earth, whereof Venice glass is made, which two are the material organs. For [the] manual [operation] there things are required, that is to say a glass maker furnace,[285] a flaming fire and a crucible.

We now come to the materials, which are two and are to be joined together; the first giveth the form, the other receiveth it. That which giveth the form is the Spirit and Soul of Sol or Gold, joined together in the Red Elixir and is the agent and, as it were, the man. That which receiveth the form is the hardest salt of the earth contained in glass, and is the power of heaven impregnating the earth; the patient is the power of the earth retaining the impression of the heaven.

Having thus demonstrated the theory we now lay the foundation[s] of the practice, which are two, whereof the first is the preparation of the Elixir, the other of the glass. Therefore your red corporeal Elixir is to be dissolved with the oil or tincture of Mars or Iron, because it has the greatest virtue above all other bodies, by whose celestial power the earth, that is to say the glass, is to be brought to the hardness of a stone and converted into stone. And so the Elixir is prepared for projection upon glass; but for the preparation of glass there is no more required but that it be made of the same matter that Venice glass is made of, the composition of which, if ye know not, take as much Venice glass as you please and weigh it exactly, upon which [to] project your Elixir. When you have done so, put your glass in the crucible to melt, and when it is well molten then take your corporeal red Elixir dissolved as before (or if you will, undissolved) as much as sufficeth to tinge the molten glass, and put it tied up in a paper in the glass, stirring it a little with a rod, and there let it stand the space of an hour. Then take out the crucible and pour the matter into an ingot, and it will be malleable but as hard as glass and stone-like to the sight; and you may either cut it like stone or work it with a hammer. This Carbuncle stone or metal hath the property of a Carbuncle in shining and glistring above all natural Carbuncles; and if you touch a Toad or Spider, they presently die, because it taketh virtue from the Elixir against all poisons. And if the sick carry this Carbuncle about with him, so that it doth touch the region of his heart, it taketh away the cardiac passion and diminisheth the strength of the disease.

Forth-Sixth Sheet

OF THE COMPOSITION OF THE MINERAL ELECTRUM OF[286] AMBER AS WELL NATURAL AS ARTIFICIAL AND OF THE BELL MADE OF AMBER USED BY TRITHEMIUS

Having finished these two secrets we now come to the Electrum, but whether it is to be reckoned amongst stones or amongst bodies it may be doubted because in the West Indies it is found writ in the Spanish Decads of the virtue thereof, for it is affirmed to be the greatest antidote against all poison and far more noble than Gold; but if it be a metal it must necessarily be the chief and supreme of all metals, for other metals have their origin from Sulphur and Mercury, but this metal consisteth of seven metals and is the best of all those which grow by the Ideas of the earth. For where Gold is taken for the most noble of all metals by reason of its perfect digestion and colour, this hath a greater degree of digestion and colour having a higher colour, that is to say, clear red, approaching nearer to the true colour of the Sun. For as Gold is the Sun of other metals, so this Electrum is to Gold as the heaven [is] to the Sun, wherein nature, as it were, in heaven hath created certain stars shining with clear beams of a silver colour, showing plain to the eye that it consisteth of red and white metals mixed in the highest degree of digestion.

On the contrary it may be objected:

Object. 1. That there are only six metallic bodies, amongst which this is not to be found, [287] therefore it is rather a Spirit than a body.

Also that:

Object. 2. The *minere* of every body or metal is converted into metal by fusion, but the *minere* of Electrum in melting always remaineth, therefore it is no metal.

Object. 3. There is nothing generated in the earth but stones, Spirits, metals or mean minerals. But Electrum is none of these, therefore it seems to be no mineral.

1. To the first objection it is thus answered. We say that it is not apparent out of the books of any of the ancient philosophers that they even dreamed of this natural and mineral Electrum. But more to the purpose: those are called Spirits which fly from the fire; but the Electrum flieth not from the fire; therefore it is no Spirit as Quicksilver and the rest and also mean minerals.

2. We now come to the next. We grant that the *minere* of every metal is converted into metal by the fire, which consists of Mercury and Sulphur. This axiom is evident in those metals which are imperfect and fly from the fire either in their *minere* or in themselves after they be reduced to metal; and also the Gold *minere*, although before melting it fly from the fire, before the Gold be molten and converted into metal, yet because Gold never flieth after it be molten, but is fixed in all probation, therefore it is accounted the worthiest of all metals which consist of Sulphur and Mercury.

3. Now the third. I say that I think it rather is of a stony and metallic nature joined together, by which mixture it differs from a stone and also from metal; but because it consisteth of Mercury, earthly Salt and Sulphur mixed, therefore it gets unto it a mixed nature of them, so that it is half stone, half metal.[288]

Wherefore it is to be judged that it consisteth of three natures mixed together; that is to say mineral, metallic and stony, and is the best of all those which grow in the Ideas of the earth, for it exceeds mean minerals in fixation and constancy, because they pass away in fume by long melting and vanish to nothing, or else they melt easily in moisture as Salts etc. But this Electrum or [289] Amber remaineth fixed and constant as well in the fire as water.

It exceeds metals in digestion, colour and dignity. In digestion because it is endowed with the sign of greater and more perfect digestion. For as gold is more yellow by reason of his greater heat and more perfect digestion, so the Electrum, because it hath a higher colour than Gold hath, therefore it is more digested in colour; for as Gold exceeds other metals in colour, so Electrum exceeds Gold; for Gold is yellow but Electrum is red, which is a higher colour than yellow. And as Silver is the Luna of white metals, so Gold is the Sol of red metals: so Electrum is to Gold as the heaven is to Sol in dignity and value. For by how much more Gold is more noble than Silver, so much this Electrum is more noble than Gold.

Lastly it exceeds stones in shining and virtue; in shining because these shine by reason of their hardness; so this Electrum showeth many sparks,[290] not by reason of its hardness, but by reason of this completeness. And as the heaven is adorned with stars, so this Electrum [is] with sparkling, because it hath the clearness and brightness of all metals. And as the heaven containeth all the stars and planets, so this Electrum, which is the heaven of metals, containeth the Sun and Moon and the rest of the planets in itself, Gold and Silver as it were the greater luminaries, the other bodies or metals as the rest of the planets, mean minerals as stars in virtue.

For although many stones have singular properties and virtues, so that some help the sight, others the spleen, some the heart, some stop blood, some hinder abortiveness, some hasten childbirth, some resist poison, yet there is no one found which takes away all infirmities, as Electrum does more than all mean minerals, metals or[291] stones, according to the three-fold conjunction, that is to mineral, metallic and lapifidic.[292]

Therefore, whatsoever others please to think of this natural Electrum, this seemeth most probable to me, that it is not simply a metal, but of a nature exceeding metal; for whereas stones, mean minerals and metals are generated of Salt, Sulphur and Mercury, this Electrum takes his original from stones, minerals and metals. From stones it takes Salt, from minerals Mercury and from Metals Sulphur.[293] These three being brought into one by the Ideas of Nature are its elements, from a greater virtue and power of nature; which elements have formed a higher degree of perfection than in any other stone, mineral or metal, as it were by the command of God, nature should ascribe a crown of virtue and dignity above all minerals.

But however it be, it is taken two manner of ways among the later Magicians [and] Rosie Crucians, and that is to say, that which is made naturally and [that which is made] artificially. Naturally is that which groweth in the natural Ideas of the earth; the artificial is that which is made by art above the earth in imitation of nature.

Whence Paracelsus, a worthy Master in Magic, seeing fully the nature and the utility of Alchemy, commanding to make the Elixir thereof, when as its natural body cannot anywhere be had, in his *Book of the Vexations of Philosophers*[294] and the sixth of his *Magical Archidoxes*,[295] teacheth to compound an Artificial Electrum that the Elixir must be made thereof, as appears more at large in the said books, which I like not at all. He teacheth how to make the Elixir out of Electrum; I contrarily, the Electrum out of Elixir; he would make the Elixir out of the virtue of the Elixir. I leave his way to his own followers, but I desire mine not to weary and vex themselves in such a weak, but [in] a more strong principle.

I make two kinds of Electrum one way, the first whereof is spiritual, the other corporeal. First of the former. After you have made your red corporeal Elixir by projection, in the same crucible melt one ounce of Lead and likewise another of Tin; and when they are hot, take the crucible from the fire and pass therein one ounce of Silver melted in another crucible. And when these three white metals begin to be cold, take two ounces of Mercury well purged and put these two ounces of Quicksilver upon the molten metal by drops, then increase the fire gently so that too much of the Mercury do not fume away.[296] Then in three other several crucibles melt Iron, Copper and Gold, of each one ounce, which you must have in readiness molten. And first put your molten Gold into the crucible where your four white metals stand molten, and pour upon them[297] the Copper and last of all your Iron, stirring the whole mass with a stick, that is may mix together, and let it stand in a melting heat the space of an hour. Then take all out that it may mix together and let it stand in melting in the crucible and consider well the weight of it and according to the goodness of the Elixir make projection for Medicine. And then you have created and compounded spiritual Electrum of the weight of seven ounces, consisting of seven metals, which metals so converted into Medicine, will be the Elixir of Electrum and an universal Medicine, for you need not after regard upon what body (or metal) you project it. It is also the choicest of Medicine for man's body; for although three or four of all the diseases of the Microcosm were united together, yet they may be cured with this one Medicine. If you dissolve part of this in Spirit of Wine and distil away the same Spirit *in Balneo* and the oil of the Medicine of Elixir[298] remain in the bottom, you shall have a most noble Rosie Crucian Medicine of Life.

Note that if your Iron melt not well, then dissolve your Electrum in the oil or tincture of Mars, dissolving and congealing until it have imbibed a sufficient quantity.

But if you desire to make corporeal Electrum, when your Medicine beginneth to fail to convert metals any more into Medicine, then in like manner project your Medicine upon your melted metals or bodies and they will be converted into corporeal Electrum, metallic and malleable. Of the abuse of this Electrum Paracelsus writeth that Virgil Hispanus[299] and Trithemius made a diabolical bell of this Artificial

Forty-Eighth Sheet

Electrum, upon which, when they would invocate Spirits (which they called by a more decent name of Intelligences) they writ the character of what Spirit they desired and at the third ring of the bell the Spirits obeyed their desires so long as they desired to talk with them; and when they would talk no more, they hid the character, and by the reverse ringing of the bell the Spirits departed. This supernatural Magic is altogether infamous and unlawful.[300]

Before I come to the *Particularia*, or the preparations of the seven metals, I will discover some Arcanums belonging to Vitriol, Sulphur and [the] Magnet.

There is a subterranean mineral Salt called Vitriol, which for dyeing of cloths and many other uses we cannot want. It is distinguished from other Salts in its sharpness and quality in eating through. The mineral of this Salt is strange [and] of a very hot and fiery quality as [is] apparent in its Spirit, the like [of which is] not found in other Salts. It is white and red and hath an extraordinary medicinal quality. This Salt containeth a combustible Sulphur, which is not in other Salts. Therefore in metalline affairs, touching their transmutation, it performeth more than others. It not only opens some, but helpeth the generation of others by reason of its innate heat. When Vitriol is separated by fire, then its Spirit at first comes in a white form; after that there comes from its earth a Spirit of a red condition. Staying in the earth, the Salt, being united with its expelled Mercury and Sulphur, can sharpen them; the remainder that stayeth behind is a dead earth of no efficacy. Consider well this now kindled Ternary, for as you find in Vitriol's body three distinct things, as Spirit,[301] Oil[302] and Salt, even so you may expect from its own Spirit again (which without the mingling of its oil is driven from its matter) three distinct things as you did formerly from the body of Vitriol, which well deserveth the name of *Speculum Sapientiae Physicae*. Separate this Spirit of Vitriol as it ought, then that affords again unto you three principles, out of which only, without any addition, since the beginning of the world the Philosophers' Stone hath been made. From that you have to expect again a Spirit of a white form, an oil of a red quality [and] after these two a crystalline Salt. These three being duly joined in their perfection generate no less than the Philosophers' great Stone, for that white Spirit is merely the Philosophers' Mercury and the red oil is the Soul[303] and the Salt is the true Magnetic Body. As from the Spirit of Vitriol is brought to light the red and white tinctures, so from its oil there is made Venus, her tincture, and in the centre they are much distinct assunder, though they dwell in one body. In this knowledge lieth hid an irrecoverable error; worldly wit cannot conceive of it that the Spirit of Vitriol and the remaining oil should be of so great distinction in their virtue. Touching their properties, the Spirit being well dissolved and brought into its three principles, Gold and Silver only can be made of it, and out of its oil only Copper, which will be apparent in a proof made.

Forty-Ninth Sheet

The condition of the Spirit of Vitriol and its remaining oil is this, that where there is Copper and Iron, the Solar Seed is not far from it commonly; and again where there is Seed of Gold at hand, Copper and Iron are not far from it, by reason of its attractive magnetic quality and love, which they, as tingeing Spirits in a visible manner continually bear one to another. Therefore Venus and Mars are penetrated and tinged with the superabounding tincture of Gold, and in them there is found much more the root of the red tincture than in Gold itself, unto which there belongeth also the *minera* of Vitriol, which goeth beyond these in many degrees, because its Spirit is mere Gold and *rubedo*,[304] a crude, indigested tincture, and in very truth is not found out otherwise.

But this Spirit must be divided into certain distinct parts, as into Spirit, Soul and Body. The Spirit is the Philosophic Water, which, though visibly parted assunder, yet can never be separated radically (because of their unavoidable affinity they bear and have one to another) as it appeareth plainly when afterward they are joined, [for] the one, in their mixture, embraceth the other, even as a magnet draweth Iron, but in a meliorated essence better than they had before their dissolution. This Spirit (I can prove) is the essence of Vitriol, because this Spirit and oil do differ so much and were never united radically; [and] because the oil cometh after the Spirit, each can be received apart. This fiery Spirit may rather and more fitly be called an[305] essence, Sulphur and substance of Gold, and it is so, though it lieth lurking in Vitriol as a Spirit.

This golden Water, or Spirit drawn from Vitriol, contains again a Sulphur and a Magnet; its Sulphur is the *anima*, an incombustible fire; the Magnet is its own Salt, which in the conjunction attracteth its Sulphur and Mercury, uniteth with the same and are inseparable companions. First in a gentle heat is dissolved the undigested Mercurial Spirit; by this is further extracted after a magnetic way by the Mercurial Spirit,[306] so still the one is a Magnet unto the other, bearing magnetic love one to another, as such things whether the last together with the medium is drawn forth by the first, and are thereby generated and thus take their beginning. In this separation and dissolution the Spirit or Mercury is the first Magnet, showing its magnetic virtue towards the Sulphur and Soul which it, *quasi magnes*, attracteth. This Spirit, *per modem distillationis*, being absolved and freed, showeth again its magnetic power towards the Salt, which it attracteth from the dead earth; after the Spirit is separated from it, then the Salt appeareth in its purity. If that process be further followed, and after a true order and measure the conjunction be undertaken and the Spirit and Salt be set together into the philosophic furnace, then it appears again how the heavenly Spirit striveth in a magnetic way to attract its own Salt, [for] it dissolveth the same within forty days, bringeth it to an uniform water with itself, even as the Salt hath been before its coagulation. In that destruction and dissolution appeareth the highest blackness and eclipse and darkness of the earth that ever was seen. But in the exchange thereof a bright, glittering whiteness appearing, then the case is altered and the dissolved, fluid, waterish Salt turns into a Magnet; for in that dissolution it layeth hold on its own Spirit, which is the Spirit of Mercury, attracteth the same powerfully like a Magnet, hiding it under a form of a dry, clear body, bringing the same by way of uniting into a deep coagulation and firm fixedness by means of a continued fire and the certain degrees thereof.

Note that from all metals, especially from Mars and Venus, which are very hard and almost fixed metals, of each a part can be made Vitriol. This is the reduction of a metal into its mineral. For minerals grow to metals and metals were at first minerals, and so minerals are *proxima materia* of metals, but not *prima*. From these Vitriols may be made other reductions, namely a Spirit is drawn from them by the virtue of the fire.

This Spirit being driven over, then there is again a reduction of a mineral into its spiritual essence, and each Spirit in its reduction keepeth a metalline property; but this Spirit is not the *prima materia*.

OF THE SULPHUR AND FERMENT OF THE PHILOSOPHERS

I have formerly told you plainly how the Philosophers' Sulphur is made; [in] *loco masculi* pour this Spirit upon purged and fined Gold. Let it dissolve and putrefy fourteen days, *in Balneo Mariae* distil it and pour the water again on the Gold calx, and cohobate this until the Gold pours over with the water; set this again to distil, abstract the water gently, leave a third part of it in the bottom, then set it into a cellar; let it coagulate and crystallise, wash these crystals with distilled water, amalgamate them with Mercury vive, evaporate the Mercury gently, then you have a subtile powder; put it in a glass, lute it, reverberate it for three days and nights, do[ing] it gently; thus is the philosophers' Sulphur well prepared for your work and this is the Purple Mantle or Philosophic Gold; keep it safe in a glass for your conjunction.

Fiftieth Sheet

OF THE PHILOSOPHIC VITRIOL

After the philosophers' Sulphur is made, which [in] *loco masculi* is to make the King or man, now you must have the female or wife, which is the Mercury of the Philosophers or the *materia prima lapidis*, which must be made artificially; for our Azoth is not common Vinegar, but is extracted with the common Azoth, and there is a Salt made of *materia prima* or Mercury of the Philosophers, which is coagulated in the belly of the earth. When this matter is brought to light it is not clear and it is found everywhere; it is ponderous and hath a scent of a dead body. Take this matter, distil, calcine, sublime [and] reduce it to ashes, for if an artist want ashes, how can he make a Salt, and he that hath not a metalline Salt, how can he make the philosophers' Mercury?

Therefore if you have calcined the matter, then extract its Salt, rectify it well, let it shoot into the Vitriol, which must be sweet without any corrosiveness or sharpness of Salt. Then you get the philosophers' Vitriol or Philosophic Oil. Make further of it a mercurial water. Thus you have performed an artificial work. This is called the philosophers' Azoth, which purgeth Laton[307] that[308] is not yet washed. For Azoth washeth Laton, as the ancient philosophers have told two or three thousand years agone. For the philosophical Salt or Laton must with its own humidity, or its own mercurial water be purged, dissolved, distilled, attract its Magnet and stay with it. And this is the philosophers' Mercury or *Mercurius duplicatus*, and it consists of[309] two Spirits, or a Spirit and a water of the Salt of Metals. Then this water beareth the name of *Succus Lunaris*,[310] *Aqua Coelestis, Acetum Philosophorum, Aqua Sulphuris, Aqua Permanens, Aqua Benedicta*. Take eight or ten parts of this water and one part of the Ferment or Sulphur of Sol; set it in the philosophers' egg, lute it well; put it in the athanor, into that vaprous yet dry fire; govern it to the appearance of a black, white and red colour; then you get the Philosophers' Stone.

OF THE PHILOSOPHIC MAGNET

Hermes, the father of the philosophers, had this art and was the first that wrote of it and prepared the Stone out of Mercury, Sol and Luna of the philosophers, whom some hundred laborators have imitated. I do assure you for a truth that the philosophers' Stone is composed of two bodies; the beginning and ending of it must be with philosophic Mercury.

And this is now *prima materia* and is coagulated in the entrails of the earth, first into Mercury, then into Lead, then into Tin and Copper, then into Iron etc. Thus the coagulated Mercury must by art be turned into its *prima materia* or water, that is mercurial water.

This is a stone and no stone,[311] of which is made a volatile fire in [the] form of a water, which drowneth and dissolveth its fixed father and its volatile mother. Mettaline Salt is an imperfect body which turneth to philosophic Mercury, that is a permanent or blessed water, and is the philosophers' Magnet, which loveth its philosophic Mars, sucketh unto him and abideth with him. Thus our Sol hath a Magnet also, which Magnet is the first root and matter of our Stone. If you conceive of and understand my saying and what Hermes saith, three things are required for the work; first a volatile or mercurial water, *aqua coelestis*, then *Leo viridis*, which is the philosophic Lune, thirdly *oes Hermetis*, Sol or Ferment.

Lastly note philosophers had two ways, a wet one, which I made use of, and a dry one. Herein you must proceed philosophically; you must purge well the philosophers' Mercury and make Mercury with Mercury, adding the philosophic Salt, Ferment or Sulphur of philosophers and then you have [firstly] the philosophers' magnet, that is the philosophers' Mercury, secondly the metalline Salt or philosophic Salt, thirdly *oes Hermetis* or philosophic Sulphur.

A PROCESS UPON THE PHILOSOPHIC WORK OF VITRIOL[312]

Take ten pound of Vitriol dissolved in distilled rain water; being warmed let it stand for a day and a night. At that time many feces were settled. I filtered the matter, evaporated it gently *ad cuticulum usque*. I set it in a cool place to crystallise. This onshot[313] Vitriol I exiccated, dissolved it again in distilled rain water, let it shoot again, which work I iterated so till the Vitriol got a celestial green colour, having no more any feces about it, and lost all his corrosiveness and was of a very pleasant taste.

This highly putrefied Vitriol, thus crude and not calcined. I put into a coated retort, distilled it in open fire, drove it over in twelve hours space by an exact government of fire in a white fume. When no more of these fumes came and the red corrosive oil began to come, then I let the fire go out. The next morning, all being cold, I took off the receiver, poured the gift in the receiver into a body, and some of the lute being fallen in too, I filtered it and had a fair menstrual water, which had some phlegm because I took that Vitriol uncalcined, which I abstracted *in Balneo*, not leaving one drop.

I found my Chaos in the bottom of a dark redness, very ponderous, which I poured into a viol, sealed it *hermeticé*, set it on a three-foot

One and Fiftieth Sheet

into a wooden globe into a vaprous bath made of water, where I left it so long till all was dissolved. After some weeks it separated into two parts, into a bright, transparent water and into an earth, which settled to the bottom of the glass in [the form of] a thick, black corrosive like pitch.

I separated the white spirit from it and the fluid black matter I set in again to be dissolved. The white Spirit which was dissolved [out] of it I separated again. This work I reiterated, leaving nothing in the bottom save a dry, red earth. After that I purged my white Spirit *per distillationem* very exactly; it was as pure as the tear that falls from the eye. The remaining earth I exiccated under a muffle; it was porous and as dry as dust. On this I poured again my white Spirit [and] set it in a digestion. This Spirit extracted the Sulphur or philosophic Gold and was tinged of a red yellow. I canted it off from the matter and in a body I abstracted the Spirit from the Sulphur. That Sulphur stayed behind in [the] form of an oil, very fiery, nothing [being] like unto its heat, as red as Ruby. The[314] abstracted white Spirit I poured on the earth again, extracted further in Sulphur and put it to the former. After this that *corpus terrae* looked of a paler colour, which I calcined for some hours under a muffle [and] put it into a body; on it I poured my white Spirit [and] extracted its pure, white, fixed Salt. The remaining earth was very porous, [and] good for nothing, which I flung away; thus these three principles were fully and perfectly separated.

After this I took my astral, clarified Salt, which weighed half an ounce after the weight at Strasbourg in Germany, and of the white Spirit, which weighed four ounces, of Mercury one ounce and a quarter of an ounce. These I divided into two parts, whose quantity was half an ounce and one dram. I put this Salt to one part of the other in a viol and nipped it [and] set it in digestion; there I saw perfectly how the Salt dissolved itself again in this Spirit, therefore I poured to it the other part, which was half an ounce and one dram. No sooner this was put to it than presently the body, together with the Spirit, turned as black as coal, ascended to the end of the glass, and having no room to go any further, it moved to and fro. Sometimes it settled to the bottom; by and by it rose to the middle; then it rose higher. Thus it moved from the fourth of July to the seventh of August, namely thirty-four days, which wonderful work I beheld with admiration. At last these were[315] united and turned to a black powder staying on the bottom and was dry. Seeing that it was so I increased my fire in one degree, took it out of the wet and set it in ashes; after ten days the matter on the bottom began to look somewhat white, at which I rejoiced heartily. This degree of fire I continued till the matter above and below became as white as the glittering snow. But it was not yet fix[ed as I discovered upon] making trial of it, [so I] set it in again [and] increased my fire one degree higher; then the matter began to ascend and descend, moved on high, stayed in the middle of the glass, not touching the bottom of it. This lasted thirty-eight days and nights, [and] I beheld them as well as formerly, at the thirty days, a variety of colours which I am not able to express.

At last this powder fell to the bottom [and] became fix[ed]. [I] made projection with it, putting one grain of it to one and a quarter ounce of Mercury, transmuting the same into very good Lune. Now it was time to restore unto this white tincture her true *anima*, and imbibe it, to bring it from its whiteness unto redness and to its perfect virtue.

Thereupon I took the third principle, namely the *anima*, which hitherto I had reserved, (in quantity it was one ounce and one dram) poured it to my reserved Spirit of Mercury, (whose quantity was one ounce and a quarter of an ounce) [and] drew it over several times *per alembicum* so that they in the end united together. I then divided[316] them into seven equal parts; one part I poured on my clarified earth or tincture, which greedily embraced its *anima*, together with its Spirit, and turned to a ruddiness in twelve days and nights, but had no tingeing quality as yet, saving [that] Mercury vive and Saturn it transmuted into Lune, which Lune at the separating yielded three grains of Gold. I proceeded futher with my imbibition and carried all the seven parts of the *anima* into [my tincture]; at the fourth imbibition one part of my work tinged ten parts of Copper into Gold; at the fifth imbibition one part of my work tinged ten parts of Copper into Gold; at the fifth imbibition one part tinged an hundred parts; at the sixth it tinged a thousand parts; at the seventh it tinged ten thousand parts. At this time I got of the true Medicine four ounces, half an ounce and one dram.

Two and Fiftieth Sheet

OF THE PREPARATION OF THE SEVEN METALS. AND FIRST OF THE SULPHUR OF SOL, WHEREBY LUNA IS TINGED INTO GOOD GOLD

Take of pure Gold, which is three times cast through Antimony, and of well purged Mercury vive, being pressed through leather, six parts; make of it an *Amalgama*; to the quantity of this *Amalgama* grind twice as much of common Sulphur; let it evaporate on a broad pan in a gentle heat under a muffle, stirring it well with an Iron hook; let the fire be modified that the matter do not melt together. This Gold calx must be brought to the colour of a Marigold flower, then it is right.

Then take one part of Saltpeter, one part of Sal Armoniack, half a part of grinded pebbles[317] [and] draw a water from it. Note this water must be drawn warily and exactly; to draw it after the common way will not do; he that is used to chemic preparations knows what he hath to do. And note you must have a strong stone retort, which must be coated, to hold the Spirit closely; its upper part must have a pipe upward of half a span's length; its wideness must bear two fingers breadth; it must be set first in a distilling furnace, which must be open above that the upper pipe may stand out directly; apply a large receiver [and] lute it well; let your first fire be gentle, then increase it that the retort look glowing hot; put a spoonful of this ground matter in at the pipe suddenly with a wet clout [and] the Spirits come rushingly into the receiver. These Spirits being settled, then carry in another spoonful; in this manner you proceed till you have distilled all. At last give time to the Spirits to be settled [and] to turn into water. This water is a hellish, dissolving, strong one, which dissolveth instantly prepared Gold Calx and laminated Gold into a thick solution. This is that water which dissolves not only Gold but bringeth it to a volatility, carrying it over the helmet, whose *anima* may afterwards be drawn from its torn body.

Note the Spirit of common Salt effecteth the same if drawn in that manner which I shall mention afterwards. If three parts of this Salt Spirit be taken, and one part of *Spiritus Nitri*, it is stronger than Sal Armoniack water, and is better because it is not so corrosive, dissolveth Gold the sooner, carrieth it over the helmet, [and] maketh it volatile and fit to part with its Soul. You have your choice to use which you think best and may easier be prepared thus: Take one part of the prepared Gold calx and three parts of the water which you make choice of. Put it into a deep body, lute a helmet of it, set it in warm ashes [and] let it dissolve; that which is not dissolved, pour three times as much water upon, that all dissolve. Let it cool, separate the feces, put the solution into a body, lute a helmet to it [and] let it stand in a gentle heat day and night *in Balneo Marine*. If more feces be settled separate them, digest them again *in Balneo* nine days and nights, then abstract the water gently to a spissitude like unto an oil in the bottom. This abstracted water must be poured on that spissitude [and] this must be iterated again and often that it grow weary and weak; remember to lute well at all times. To the oleity on the bottom pour fresh water which was not yet used; digest day and night, firmly closed, then set it in a sand cupel [and] distil the water from it [till it be reduced] to a thickness; make the abstracted water warm, put it in a body, lute it, abstract it, iterate this work and make all the Gold come over the helmet.

Note, at the next drawing always the fire must have one degree more. The Gold being come over into the water, abstract the water gently from it in the Balney to the oleity [and] set the glass into a cool place; there will shoot transparent crystals; these are the Vitriol of Gold. Pour the water from it, distil it again unto an oleity [and] sat it by for shooting; more crystals will shoot; iterate it as long as any do shoot. Dissolve these crystals in distilled water, put to it of purged Mercury three times as much, shake it about, many colours will appear, an *Amalgama* falls to the ground [and] the water cleareth up. Evaporate the *Amalgama* gently under a muffle, stirring it still with a wire; at last you get a purple coloured powder, scarlet like; it dissolveth in Vinegar into a blood redness. Extract its *anima* with prepared Spirit of Wine mixed with the Spirit of common Salt, entered together into a sweetness. This tincture of Sol is like a transparent Ruby, leaving a white body behind.

Note that without information you cannot attain unto the Spirit of Salt; if it be not sweet it hath no attractive power; to the attaining hereof observe these following manuals: Take good Spirit of Salt, dephlegmed exactly, driven forth in that manner as ye shall hear anon. Take one part of it, add half a part to it of the best Spirit of Wine, which must not have any phlegm, but be a mere Sulphur of Wine and must be prepared in that manner as I shall tell you anon. Lute a helmet to it, draw it over strongly, leave nothing behind. To the abstracted [part] put more Spirit of Wine, draw it over somewhat stronger than you did the first time, weigh it, put a third time more [Spirit of Wine] to it [and] draw it over again well luted; putrefy this for half a month, or so long as it be sweet, and it is done in Balney very gently. Thus the Spirit of Wine and Salt is prepared, loses[318] its corrosity and is fit for extracting.

Three and Fiftieth Sheet

Take the Ruby-red prepared Gold powder, put of this prepared Spirit of Salt and Wine so much that it stand two fingers breadth over it, set it in a gentle heat [and] the Spirit will be red tinged; this Spirit must be canted off. Pour a new Spirit on that which remaineth on the bottom, set it luted into a gentle heat, let it be tinged deeply, then cant it off; this work must be iterated [till] that the body of Sol remain on the bottom like Calx vive, which keep, for therein sticketh yet more Salt of Gold, which is effectual in ways of Medicine, as shall be showed anon.

Those tinged Spirits put together, abstract them gently *in Balneo* [and] there will be left a red subtile powder in the bottom, which is the true tincture animated, or Sulphur of Gold. Dulcify it with distilled rain water [and] it will be very subtile, tender and fair. Take this extracted Sulphur of Sol as you were taught, and as much of the Sulphur of

Mars, as you shall hear anon when I treat of Mars. Grind them together, put it in a pure glass, pour on it so much of Spirit of Mercury — let it stand over it two fingers breadth — that the matter may be dissolved; see to it that all dissolve into a Ruby-like Gold water, jointly drive it over, then is it one and were at first of one stem. Keep it well, that nothing of it evaporate; put it in separated Silver calx, being precipitated with pure Salt and afterwards well edulcorated and dried; fix it together in a fiery fixation that it sublime no more; then take it and melt it in a wind-oven; let it stream well; then you have united Bride and Bridegroom and brought them unto Gold of a high degree. Be thankful to God for it as long as you shall live.

I shall hereafter at large set forth how this extracted Soul of Sol may be made potable. I will now set forth how the white solar body shall further be anatomised, and that by art its Mercury vive and its Salt may be obtained. The process of it is thus.

Take the white body of Sol, from which you have drawn its *anima*, reverberate it gently for half an hour, let it become corporeal, then pour on it well rectified honey-water, which is corrosive [and] extract its Salt in a gentle heat. It is done in ten days space. The Salt being all extracted, abstract the water from it *in Balneo*, edulcorate the Salt with iterated distillings with common distilled water, clarify it with Spirits of Wine, then you have *Sol auri*, of which you shall hear more in its due place [and] of the good qualities in hath by way of medicine upon man. On the remaining matter pour Spirit of Tartar, of which elsewhere because it belongeth unto medicinals. Digest these for a month's time, drive it through a glass retort into cold water, then you have quick Mercury of Sol; many strive to get it but in vain.

There is one mystery more in Nature, that the white solar body, having once lost its *anima*, may be tinged again and brought to be pure Gold, which mystery is revealed to very few. I shall briefly declare it, as also about the universal Stone of [the] Philosophers, how it resteth merely upon the white Spirit of Vitriol, and how that all three principles are found only in this Spirit and how you are to proceed in and to bring each into its certain state and order.

Take the philosophic Sulphur, which in order is the second principle and is extracted with the Spirit of Mercury; pour it on the white body of the King,[319] digest it for a month in a gentle Balny, then fix it in ashes and at last in sand, that the brown powder may appear; then melt it with a fluxing powder made of Saturn; then it will be malleable and fair Gold as it was formerly, in colour and virtue nothing defective. But note, the Salt must not be taken from the Solar body.

There may be prepared yet in another manner a transparent Vitriol from Gold in the following manner.

Take good *Aqua Regis* made with Sal Armoniack one pound, *id est* dissolve four ounces of Sal Armoniack in *Aqua Fortis*, then you have a strong *Aqua Regis*. Distil and rectify it often over the helmet, let no feces remain behind; let all that ascends be transparent. Then take thinly beaten Gold rolls, cast formerly through Antimony, put them into a body, pour on it *Aqua Regis*, let it dissolve as much as it will or as you can dissolve in it. Having dissolved all the Gold, pour into it some oil of Tartar or Salt of Tartar dissolved in fountain water till it begins to hiss. Having done hissing, then pour in again of the oil. Do it so long till all the dissolved Gold fallen to the bottom and nothing more of it precipitate, and the *Aqua Regis* clear up. This being done, then cant off the *Aqua Regis* from the Gold calx, edulcorate it with common water eight, ten or twelve times. The Gold calx being well settled, cant off that water and dry the Gold calx in the air where the Sun doth not shine. Do it not over a fire, for as soon as it feeleth the least heat in kindleth and great damage is done, for it would fly away forcibly that no man could stay it. This powder being ready also, then take strong Vinegar, pour it on, boil it continually, over [the fire] in a good quantity of Vinegar, still stirring it that it may not stick unto the bottom, for twenty-four hours together, then the fulminating quality is taken from it; be careful you do not endanger yourself; cant off the Vinegar, dulcify the powder, and dry it. This powder may be driven *per Alembicum* without any corrosive, blood-red, transparent and fair, which is strange and uniteth unwillingly with the Spirit of Wine and by means of coagulation may be brought to a solar body.

Do not speak much of it to the vulgar. If you receive any benefit by my plain and open information, keep these mysteries secret to thy dying day. I will impart unto thee this arcanum also and entrust thee on thy conscience with it.

Take good Spirit of Wine, being brought to the highest degree, let fall into it some drops of Spirit of Tartar; then take thy Gold powder, put to it three times as much of the best and subtilest common Flowers of Sulphur, grind these together, set it on a flat pan under a muffle, give to it a gentle fire, let the Gold powder be in a glowing heat, put it thus glowing into the Spirit of Wine, cant off the Spirit of Wine [and] dry the powder against a heat. It will be porous being dried. Then add to it again three parts of *Flores Sulphurii* let them evaporate under a muffle, neal the remaining powder in a strong heat and put it in Spirit of Wine; iterate this work six times [and] at last this Gold powder will be so soft and porous as firm butter; dry it gently, because it melteth easily. Then take a coated body, which in its hinder part hath a pipe;

Fifty-Fourth Sheet

lute a helmet to it, apply a receiver, set it freely in a strong capel; let your first fire be gentle, then increase it; let the body be almost in a glowing heat, then put in the softened, well dried Gold powder, being made warm, behind at the hollow pipe. Shoot it in nimbly. There come instantly red drops into the helmet. Keep the fire in this degree so long till nothing more ascendeth and no more drops fall into the receiver. Note, in the receiver there must be of the best Spirit of Wine into which the drops of Gold are to fall.

Then take this Spirit of Wine, into which the Gold drops did fall, put it in a pelican, seal it *hermeticé* [and] circulate it for a month; it turneth then to a blood red Stone, which melteth in the fire like wax. Beat it small, grind among it lunar calx [and] melt it. Then you find [as] much good Gold as the Gold powder and the spirit of wine together with the moiety of[320] the added lunar calx did weigh, but one moiety of the lunar calx is not tinged and[321] is as good as it was to be used. If you hit this rightly, then be thankful to God. If not, do not blame me; I could not make it plainer.

Now if you will make this Vitriol, then take the powder formerly made, boiled in Vinegar; pour on it good Spirit of common Salt, mingled with Saltpeter water and the Spirit of Salt of Nitre. This Saltpeter water is made as *Aqua Tartaris* is made, using[322] Saltpeter. Gold is dissolved in this water, which being done then abstract the water to a thickness [and] set in a cellar; then there shooteth a pure Vitriol of Sol. The water which stayeth with the Vitriol must be canted off, [then] distil it again to a spissitude, set it in the cellar [and] more of the Vitriol will shoot. Iterate this work as long as the Vitriol shooteth. If you are minded to make the Philosophers' Stone out of solar Vitriol, as some fantastic men endeavour in that way, then be first acquainted and ask counsel of thy purse and prepare ten or twelve pounds of this Vitriol, then you may perform the work very well, and the Hungarian Vitriol and others digged out of the mines will permit thee to do it. You may extract from this Vitriol also its Sulphur and Salt with spirit of wine, which is all easy work.

THE PARTICULAR OF LUNE AND OF THE EXTRACTION OF ITS SULPHUR AND SALTS

Take of Calx vive and common Salt and,[323] neal them together in a wind oven; then extract the Salt purely from the Calx with warm water: coagulate it again, put to it an equal quantity of new Calx, neal it, extract the Salt from it, iterate it three times, then is the Salt prepared.

Then take the prepared Lunar Calx, stratify the Calx with prepared Salt in a glass viol, pour strong water on it, made of equal quantities of Vitriol and Saltpeter, abstract the *aqua fort* from it, iterate this three times,[324] at last drive it strongly, let the matter melt well in the glass, then take it forth [and] your Lune is transparent and blueish like an Ultramarine. Having brought Lune thus far, then pour on it strong distilled Vinegar [and] set it in a warm place, the Vinegar is tinged with a transparent blue, like a Saphire and attracteth the tincture of Lune, being separated from the Salt [and] all which comes from Lune goeth again into the Vinegar, which must be done by edulcoration; then you will find the Sulphur of Lune fair and clear. Take one part of this Sulphur of Lune, one half part of the extracted Sulphur of Sol [and] six parts of the Spirit of Mercury; join all these in a body, lute it well [and] set it in a gentle heat in digestion; that liquor will turn to a red-brown colour, having all driven over the helmet, and nothing [will] stand in the bottom; then pour it on the water[325] remaining of the Silver you drew your Sulphur from, lute it well, set it in ashes for to coagulate and to fix it eleven days and nights, or when you see the lunar body be quite dry, brown and nothing of it doth any more rise or fume; then it will melt quickly with a sudden flux [at the] fire before the blast; cast it forth; then you [will have] transmuted[326] the whole substance of Silver into the best, most malleable Gold.

Fifty-Fifth Sheet

I formerly told you that the Spirit of Salt can destroy Lune, so that a potable Lune can be made of it, of which potable Lune shall hereafter be set forth as to the preparation and the use thereof in medicine.

When you perceive that the Sulphur of Lune is wholly extracted and the Vinegar take no more tincture from her nor the Vinegar doth taste any more of Salt, then dry the remaining calx of Silver, put it into a glass, pour on it corrosive Honey water as you did to the Gold,[327] yet it must be clear and without any feces; set it in warmth for four or five days, extract Lune's Salt, which you may perceive when the water groweth white. The Salt being all out of it, then abstract the Honey water, edulcorate the corrosiveness by distilling and clarify the Salt with Spirit of Wine. The remaining matter must be edulcorated and dried; pour upon it the Spirit of Tartar, digest it for half a month, then proceed as you did with the Gold. Then you have Mercury of Lune. The said Sal[328] of Lune hath excellent virtues upon man's body. The efficacy of its Salt and Sulphur may be learned by the following process.

Take of the sky-coloured Sulphur, which you extracted from Lune and is rectified with Spirit of Wine, put it in a glass, pour on it twice as much of Spirit of Mercury, which is made of the white Spirit of Vitriol. In like manner take of the extracted and clarified Salt of Silver, put to it three times as much of Spirit of Mercury. Lute well both glasses [and] set them in a gentle Balney for eight days and nights. Look to it that the Sulphur and Salt lose nothing, but keep their quantity as they were driven out of the Silver. Having stood these eight days and nights, then put them together into a glass, seal it *Hermeticé*, set it in gentle ashes, let all be dissolved and let it be brought again into a clear and white coagulation. At last fix them by the degrees of fire, then the matter will be white as snow. Thus you have the white tincture, which with the volatile dissolved *anima* of Sol you may animate, fix, bring to the deepest redness and at last ferment and augment the same *ad infinitum*, the Spirit of Mercury being added thereunto. And note that upon Gold a process is to be ordered with its Sulphur and Salt.

If you understood how their *primum mobile*[329] is to be known, then is it needless in this manner and to that purpose to destroy metals; but you may prepare everything from or of the first essence and bring them to their full perfection.

OF THE PARTICULARS OF MARS TOGETHER WITH THE EXTRACTION OF ITS *ANIMA* AND SALT

Take of red Vitriol oil or oil of Sulphur one part and two parts of ordinary well water. Put these together [and] dissolve therein filings of Steel. This dissolution must be filtered. Being warmed, let it gently evaporate a third part of it, then set the glass in a cool place [and] there will shoot crystals as sweet as sugar, which is the true Vitriol of Mars. Cant off that water, let it evaporate more, set it again in a cold place [and] more crystals will shoot. Neal them gently under a muffle, stirring it still with an Iron wire; then you get a fair, purple coloured powder. On this powder cast distilled Vinegar, extract the *anima* of Mars in a gentle Balney, abstract again the Vinegar and dulcorate the *anima*. This is the *anima* of Mars, which, being added to the Spirit of Mercury and united with the *anima* of Sol, tingeth Lune into Sol as you heard about the Gold.

OF THE PARTICULAR OF VENUS WHAT MYSTERIES THERE ARE HID THEREIN AND OF THE EXTRACTION OF ITS SULPHUR AND SALT

Fifty-Sixth Sheet

Take as much of Venus as you will and make Vitriol of it, after the usual and common practice; or take good Verdigris sold in shops — it effecteth the same; grind it very small, pour on it good distilled Vinegar [and] set it in a warmth; the Vinegar will be [coloured a] transparent green, cant it off [and] pour on the remaining matter on the bottom new Vinegar; iterate this work as long as the Vinegar taketh out any tincture and the matter of the Verdigris on the bottom lieth very black. Put the tinged Vinegar together, distil the Vinegar from it to a dryness, else a black Vitriol will shoot, thus you get a purified Verdigris. Grind it small, pour on it the juice of immature grapes [and] let it stand in a gentle heat; this juice maketh the transparent tincture as green as a Smaragd and attracteth the red tincture of Venus, which affords an excellent colour for painters, limners and others for their several uses.

When the juice extracts no more of the tincture, then put all the extraction together, abstract the moiety of this juice gently, set it into a cool place [and] there shooteth a very fair Vitriol. If you have enough of that, then you have matter enough to reduce the same and to make of it the Philosopher's Stone, in case you should make a doubt to perform this great mystery by any other Vitriol. The common Azoth is not the matter of our Stone, but our Azoth or *materia prima* is extracted with the common Azoth and with the wine, which is the outpressed juice of unripe grapes, and with other waters also must be prepared. These are the waters wherewith the body of Venus must be broken and be made into Vitriol, which you must observe very well, then you may free yourselves from many troubles and perplexities.

But especially note that it may be done with great profit if you drive forth the red oil of Vitriol and dissolve Mars in it and crystallise the solution as you were told when I treated of Mars. For in this dissolution and coagulation Venus and Mars are united. This Vitriol must be nealed under a muffle unto a pure red powder and must be extracted further with distilled Vinegar as long as there is any redness in it. Then you get the *anima* of Mars and Venus doubled. Of[330] this doubled virtue, after the addition of the *anima* of Sol, which you made in the before quoted quantity, take twice as much of Silver Calx and fix it. But note that there must be twice as much of the Spirit of Mercury than there was allowed in that place but in the rest the process is alike. The Salt of Venus must be extracted when the juice taketh no more of the green tincture; then take the remaining matter, dry it, pour Honey Water upon it, then that Salt goeth in that heat for five or six days and clarify it with Spirit of Wine; then is the Salt ready for your Medicine.

OF THE PARTICULAR OF SATURN TOGETHER WITH THE EXTRACTION OF ITS SOUL AND SALT

Saturn, the highest of the Celestial Planets, hath the meanest authority in our Magistery, yet is the chiefest key in the whole art. Saturn is not to be slighted by reason of its external despicable form; if he be wrought in a due process after the philosophers' way, he is able to requite all the labourer's pains bestowed upon him, for the great virtues of it in Medicine for man's health and for meliorating of metals.[331] The preparation of it is thus:

Take red Minium or Ceruse, laminate it thinly, hang these lamens in a large glass filled with strong Vinegar, in which is dissolved a like quantity of the best Sal armoniack, sublimed thrice with common Salt. Stop the glass' mouth very closely that nothing evaporate, set the glass in ashes of a gentle heat, otherwise the Spirits of the Vinegar and Sal armoniack ascend and touch the Saturnal lamens. At the tenth or twelfth day you will spy a subtile Ceruse hanging on those lamens; brush them off with a hare's foot [and] go on and get enough of this Cerus. Take a quantity of it [and] put it in a body; pour strong Vinegar on it, which several times hath been rectified and was fortified at the last rectification with a sixteenth part of Spirit of vulgar Salt, dephlegmed and drawn over. Spot the body well, or, which is better, lute a blind head to it, set the body in ashes to be digested, swing it often about and in a few days the Vinegar begins to look yellow and sweet at the first. Iterate three times;[332] it is sufficient.

The remnant of the Ceruse stayeth in the body's bottom, unshapely; filter the tinged Vinegar clearly, that is of a transparent yellowness, put all the tinged Vinegar together, abstract two parts of it *in Balneo Mariae*, [but] let the third part stay behind. This third part is of a reasonable *rubedo*. Set the glass in cold water, then the crystals will shoot off the sooner; being shot, take them out with a wooden spoon [and] lay them on a paper for to dry; these are as sweet as sugar and are of great energy against inflamed symptoms. Abstract the Vinegar further *in Balneo*, in which the crystals did shoot, set that distillation aside for the shooting of more crystals and proceed with these as you did formerly.

Fifty-Seventh Sheet

Now take all these crystals together; they in their appearance are like unto clarified sugar or Saltpeter; beat them in a mortar of glass or Iron, or grind them on a marble unto unpalpableness, reverberate it in a gentle heat to a bloodlike redness. Provided[333] they do not turn to blackness. Having them in a scarlet colour, put [them] in a glass, pour on them a good Spirit of Juniper abstracted from its oil and rectified several time into a fair, white, bright manner; lute the glass above, set it in a gentle heat [and] let the Spirit of Juniper be tinged with a transparent redness like blood; then cant it off neatly from the feces into a pure glass, with that proviso that no impure thing run therewith;

on the feces pour over Spirit of Juniper [and] extract still as long as any Spirit taketh the tincture. Keep the feces; they contain the Salt.

Take all these tinged Spirits together, filter them, abstract them gently in *Balneo* [and] there remaineth in the bottom a neat Carnation powder, which is the *anima* of Saturn. Pour on it rain water, often distilled; distil it strongly several times to get off that which stayed with the Spirit of Juniper, and so this subtle powder will be edulcorated delicately. Keep it in a strong boiling, cant it off, then let it go off neatly. Let it dry gently; for safety's sake reverberate it again gently for its better exiccation; let all impurity evaporate, let it grow cold, put it in a viol, put twice as much of Spirit of Mercury to it, seal it *hermeticé*; set it in a vaprous bath called the philosophers' *fimus equinus*, let it stand in the mystical furnace for a month, then the *anima* of Saturn closeth daily with the Spirit of Mercury and both become inseparable, making up a fair, transparent, deeply tinged, red oil. Look to the government of the fire; be not too high with it, else you put the Spirit of Mercury as a volatile Spirit to betake himself to his wings, forcing him to the breaking of the glass. But if these be well united, then no such fear look for, for one nature embraceth and holdeth up the other.

Then take this oil or dissolved *anima* of Saturn out of the viol. It is of a gallant fragrancy. Put it into a body, apply a helmet to it, lute it well, drive it over, then Soul and Spirit are united together and fit to transmute Mercury precipitated into Sol.

The precipitation of Mercury is done thus: Take one part of the Spirit of Salt Nitre and three parts of oil of Vitriol; put these together, cast into half a part of quick Mercury, being very well purged, set it in sand, put a reasonable strong fire to it, so that the Spirits may not fly away [and] let it stand a whole day and night; then abstract all this Spirit, then you find in the bottom a precipitated Mercury, somewhat red. Pour the Spirit on it again, let it stand day and night, abstract it again and then your precipitate is at the highest *rubedo*; dulcify it with distilled water [and] let it strongly be exiccated. Then take two parts of this precipitated Mercury, one part of the dissolved Saturnal oil, put these together, set it in ashes [and] let all be fixed; not one drop must stick anywhere to the glass. Then it must be melted with due additionals of Lead; they close together and afford Gold, which afterward, at the casting through Antimony, may be exalted.

Note that Mercury must not be precipitated unless with pure oil of Vitriol or oil of Venus, with the addition of the Spirit of Salt Nitre. Albeit such Mercury cannot be brought to its highest fixation by way of precipitating but its fixed coagulation is found in Saturn.

Beat the above said Mercury small, grind it on a stone, put it in a viol, pour on it the Saturnal dissolved oil [and] it entereth instantly, if so be you proceeded aright in the precipitation. Seal the viol *hermeticé*, fix it in ashes [and] at [the] last in sand, to its highest fixation. Then you have bound Mercury with a true knot and brought him into a fix[ed] coagulation, which brought its form and substance into a melioration with an abundance of riches. If you carry it on a white precipitate, then you get only Silver, which holds but little Gold.

One thing more I must tell thee about this process, that there is yet a better way to deal upon Saturn with more profit. Take two parts of the above said dissolved oil, or oil of the Saturnal Soul, one part of *Astrum Solis* and of Antimonial Sulphur, whose preparation followeth afterwards, two parts, half as much of Salt of Mars as all those are, weigh them together, put them into a glass viol and let the third part of it be empty; set them in together to be fixed, then the Salt of Mars openeth in this compound, is fermented by it and the matter begins to incline to blackness. For ten or twelve days it is eclipsed, then the Salt returns to its coagulation, laying hold in its operation on the whole compound. Coagulate it first into a deep brown mass, let it stand thus unstirred in a continual heat [and] it turneth to a blood-red body; increase the fire that you may see the *Astrum Solis* to be predominant, which appeareth in a greenish colour, like unto a Rainbow; keep this fire continually, let all these colours vanish [and] it turneth to a transparent red stone, very ponderous, needless to be projected upon Mercury, but [which] tingeth after its perfection and fixation all white metals into the purest Gold. Then take of the prepared, fixed, red Stone or of the powder, one part and four parts of the white metal. First let the metal melt half an hour and let it be well clarified; then project the powder upon it [and] let it drive well so that it be entered into the metal and the metal begin to congeal; then is it transmuted into Gold. Beat the pot in pieces [and] take it out; if it hath any slacks[334] drive them with Saturn, then it is pure and malleable. If you carry it on Lune, then put more of the powder on it than you do upon Jupiter and Saturn, as half an ounce of the powder tingeth five ounces of Lune into Sol. Let this be a miracle. Fool not thy Soul with imparting this mystery unto others that are unworthy of it. Proceed with Salt of Saturn as you were informed about Mars and Venus, only [note that] distilled Vinegar performeth that which Honey Water did by the others and clarify it with Spirit of Wine.

OF THE PARTICULAR OF JUPITER WITH THE EXTRACTION OF ITS *ANIMA* AND SALT

Take pumice stones sold in shops, neal them, quench them in old good wine, neal them again and quench them as you did formerly [and] let this nealing be iterated a third time; the stronger the wine is you quench withal, the better it is. After that dry them gently; thus are they prepared for that purpose. Pulverise these pumice stones subtilly, then take good Tin, laminate it, stratify it in a cementing way, in a reverberating furnace reverberate this matter for five days and nights in a flaming fire [till] it draweth the tincture of the metal. Then grind it small, first scraping the Tin lamens; put it in a glass body, pour on it good distilled Vinegar and set it in digestion [when] the Vinegar draweth the tincture, which is red-yellow. Abstract the Vinegar *in Balneo*, edulcorate the *anima* of Jupiter with distilled water, exiccate gently and proceed in the rest as you did with the *anima* of Saturn, viz., dissolve radically in or with the Spirit of Mercury, drive them over, pour that upon two parts of red Mercury precipitated; being precipitated with this Venerean, sanguine quality, then coagulate and fix; if done successfully you may acknowledge Jupiter's bounty that gave leave to transmute this precipitate into Gold, which will be apparent at their melting. It performeth this also, it transmuteth ten parts of Lune into Gold, if other Sulphurs be added thereunto; force no more upon Jupiter, it is all he is able to do; being of a peaceable disposition he told all what he could do.

The process about this Salt is to extract it with distilled rain water, clarified with Spirit of Wine.

OF THE PARTICULAR OF MERCURY VIVE AND OF ITS SULPHUR AND SALT

Take of quick Mercury, sublimed several times, half a pound, [335] grind it very small, pour on it a good quantity of sharp Vinegar, boil it on the fire for an hour or upward, stirring the matter with a wooden spatula, [then] take it from the fire and let it be cold, [when] the Mercury settleth to the bottom and the Vinegar cleareth up. If it be slow in the clearing, let some drops of Spirit of Vitriol fall into the Vinegar; it doth precipitate the other, for Vitriol precipitateth Mercury Vive, Salt of Tarter precipitateth Sol, Venus and common Salt doth precipitate Lune and Mars does the like to Venus; a lixivium[336] of Beech ashes doth it to Vitriol and Vinegar is for common Sulphur, and Mars for Tartar and Saltpeter for Antimony. Cant off the Vinegar from the precipitate [and] you will find the Mercury like a pure washed sand. Pour on it Vinegar, iterate this work a third time, then edulcorate the matter [and] let it dry gently.

Take two ounces of *anima* of Mars, one ounce of *anima* of Saturn, one ounce of *anima* of Jupiter, dissolve these in six ounces of Mercurial Spirit [and] let all be dissolved; then drive it over, leaving nothing behind [and] it will be a golden water like a transparent dissolution of Sol; your prepared and edulcorated Mercury must be warmed in a strong viol, pass this warmed water gently upon [the other],[337] a hissing[338] will be, stop the viol and then the hissing[338] is gone; then seal it *hermeticé*, set it in a gentle Balney [and] in ten days the Mercury is dissolved into a grass-green oil. Set the viol in ashes for a day and a night [and] rule the fire gently; this green colour [then] turneth into a yellow oil; in this colour is hid the *rubedo*; keep it in this fire and let the matter turn to a yellow powder like unto Orpiment; when no more comes over, then set the glass in sand for a day and a night; give a strong fire to it, let the fairest ruby *rubedo* appear, melt it to a fixedness with a fluxing powder made of Saturn [and] it comes now to a malleableness; one pound of it containeth two ounces of good Gold, as deep as ever Nature produced any.

AN OIL MADE OF MERCURY AND ITS SALT

Take quick Mercury, often sublimed and rectified with Calx Vive, put it in a body, dissolve it in a heat in strong nitrous water, [and] abstract the water from it; the corrosiveness which stayeth there must be extracted with good Vinegar well boiled in it. At last abstract the Vinegar, [when] the remainder of it must be dulcified with distilled water and then exiccated. Afterward on each pound must be poured one pound of the best Spirit of Wine. Let it stand luted in putrefaction, then drive over what may be driven, first gently, then more strongly. From that which is come over abstract the Spirit of Wine *per Balneum* [and] there stayeth behind a fragrant[339] oil, which is *Astrum Mercurii*, an excellent remedy against venereal diseases.

Seeing the Salt and *Astrum* of Mercury is of the same medicinal operation, I hold it needful to write of each in particular and will join their operation into one and declare of it in the last part about the Salt of Mercury, because they are of one effect in medicinal operations. Take the made oil or *Astrum Mercurii*, which by reason of its great heat keeps its own body in a perpetual running, casting it on the next standing earth, from which you formerly drew the oil; set it in a low heat [and] and the oil draweth its own Salt. That being done, put to it a reasonable quantity of Spirit of Wine [and] abstract it again; the Salt stayeth behind, dissolved in the fresh Spirit of Wine, being dulcified by cohobation. Then is the Mercurial Salt ready and prepared for the

Medicine. Mercury is able to do no more, neither *particulariter* nor *universaliter*, because he is far off from philosophers' Mercury, although many are deceived in their fancies to the contrary.

OF THE PARTICULAR OF ANTIMONY TOGETHER WITH THE EXTRACTION OF ITS SULPHUR AND SALT

Take good Hungarian Antimony, pulverise it subtilly to a meal, calcine it over a gentle heat, stirring it still with an Iron wire, and let it be albified and [become so] that at last it may be able to hold out in a strong fire. Then put it into a melting pot, melt it, cast it forth, turn it to a transparent glass, beat that glass, grind it subtilly, put it in a glass body of a broad, flat bottom, pour on it distilled Vinegar [and] let it stand luted in a gentle heat for a good while. The Vinegar extracteth the antimonial tincture, which is of a deep redness; abstract the Vinegar [and] there remaineth a sweet, yellow, subtile powder, which must be edulcorated with distilled water. All acidity must be taken off. Exiccate it, pour on it the best graduated Spirit of Wine [and] set it in a gentle heat. You have a new extraction, which is fair and yellow; cant it off, pour on other Spirit, let it extract as long as it can, then abstract the Spirit of Wine. Exiccate [and] you find a tender, deep yellow, subtile powder of an admirable medicinal operation, [which] is nothing inferior unto potable Sol.

Take two parts of this powder [and] one part of Solar Sulphur; grind these small, then take three parts of Sulphur of Mars, pour on it six parts of Spirit of Mercury, set it in digestion, well luted, let the Sulphur of Mars be dissolved totally, then carry in a fourth part of the ground matter of the Sulphur of Antimony and of Sol. Lute and digest. Let all be dissolved, then carry in more of your ground Sulphur [and] proceed as formerly, iterating it so long till all be dissolved; then the matter becomes a thick, brown oil. Drive all over jointly into one, leave nothing behind in the bottom; then pour it on a purely separated Lunary Calx, fix it by degrees of fire, then melt it into a body, separate it with an *aqua fort* [and] six times as much [more] of Sol is precipitated than did enter by weight into the ponderosity of the above compound.[340] The remainder of Lune serveth for such works as you please to put it unto.

The Antimonial tincture being extracted totally from its *vitrum*, and [when] no Vinegar takes more hold of any tincture, then exiccate the remaining powder, which is of a black colour; put it into a melting pot, lute it, let it stand in a reasonable heat [and] let all the Sulphurous part burn away; grind the remaining matter, pour on it new distilled Vinegar, extract its Salt, abstract the Vinegar, edulcorate the acidity by cohobation [and] clarify it so long that the water be white and clear.

Sixtieth Sheet lIf you have proceeded well in your manuals, then the lesser time will be required to extract the antimonial Salt as you shall hear of it, whereby you may observe that the antimonial Sulphur is extracted in the following manner and is of the same medicinal operation, but is of a quicker and speedier work, worthy to be observed.

A SHORT WAY TO MAKE ANTIMONIAL SULPHUR AND SALT

Take good Vitriol, common Salt and unslaked Lime, of each one pound, [and] four ounces of Sal Armoniack. Beat them small, put them in a glass body, pour on it three pound[s] of common Vinegar [and] let it stand in digestion, stopped, for a day. Put it afterwards into a retort, apply a receiver to it [and] distil it as usually an *aqua fort* is distilled. Take of the off-drawn liquor and of common Salt one pound of each, rectify them once more; let no muddiness come over with it; all must come clear. Then take one pound of pulverised antimonial glass, pour this Spirit on it, lute it well, digest and let all be dissolved. Then abstract the water *in Balneo Mariae* [and] there remains in the bottom a black, thick, fluid matter, but somewhat dry. Lay it on a glass table [and] set it in a cellar [and] a red oil floweth from it, leaving some feces behind. Coagulate this red oil gently upon ashes, let it be exiccated there, then pour the best Spirit of Wine on it [and] it extracteth a tincture which is blood-red. Cant off that which is tinged, pour other Spirit of Wine on the remainder and [by iteration] let all redness be extracted. Thus you have the tincture of antimonial Sulphur, which is of a wonderful medicinal efficacy and is equivalent unto potable gold as you were told before.[341] This black matter which stayed behind after the extraction of the Sulphur must be well exiccated. Extract its snow-white Salt with distilled Vinegar, edulcorate it, clarify it with Spirit of Wine and observe its virtues in medicine.

I have mentioned and demonstrated that all things are made and compounded of three essences, viz., of Mercury, Sulphur and Salt. But know this that the Stone is made of one, two, three, four and five.[342]

Of five, that is the quintessence of its matter; of four are understood the four elements; of three are the three principles of all things; of two, for that is the double mercurial substance; of one, that is the *Ens Primum* of all things, which flowed from the *fiat* of the first creation.[343]

Many well-minded artists may be doubtful, by all these sayings, to attain the foundation and discovery thereof. Therefore I shall first very briefly speak of Mercury, secondly of Sulphur, thirdly of Salt; for these are essences of our matter of the Stone.

First know that no common Argent Vive is made of the best metal by the Spagyric Art,[344] [but one that is] pure, subtile, clear, splendent as a fountain, transparent as crystal, without any impurity. Of this make a water or incombustible oil,[345] for Mercury was at the first water, as all the philosophers agree.

In this mercurial oil dissolve its proper Mercury, out of which the water was made, and precipitate that Mercury with its proper oil; then have you a double mercurial substance. And know that your Gold must first be dissolved in a certain water after its purification and must be reduced into a subtile Calx as hereafter shall be declared at large. And then the said Calx must be sublimed by Spirit of Salt and precipitated again and by reverberation reduced into a subtile powder; then its own proper Sulphur will the more easily enter into its own substance and be in amity with it, for they wonderfully love each other. So have you two substances in one and [it] is called the Mercury of the Philosophers and yet it is but one substance, that is, the first Ferment.

Your Sulphur you must seek in the like metal, then you must know how to extract it out of the body of the metal by purification and destruction of its form and reverberation without any corrosive. Then dissolve this Sulphur in its own proper blood, whereof it was made before its fixation, according to its due weight; then have you nourished and dissolved the true Lion[346] with the blood of the Green Lion;[347] for the fixed blood of the Red Lion is made out of the volatile blood of the Green Lion, therefore are they of one nature. And the volatile blood maketh the fixed blood volatile, and the fixed likewise maketh the volatile blood fixed as it was before its solution. Then set them together in a gentle heat until the whole Sulphur be dissolved; then have you the Second Ferment, nourishing the fixed Sulphur with the volatile as all philosophers agree with me herein. This afterwards is driven over with Spirit of Wine, red as blood, and is called *Aurum Potabile*, whereof there is no reduction to a body.

OF THE SALT OF THE PHILOSOPHERS

Salt maketh fixed and volatile according as in its degree it is ordered and prepared. For the Spirit of Salt of Tartar, if it be drawn per se and without addition, maketh all metals volatile by resolution and putrefaction and resolveth them into a true vive or current Mercury, as my practice declares.

Sixty-First Sheet

Salt of Tartar *per se* fixeth most firmly, especially if the heat of Calx vive be incorporated with it, for both then have a singular degree of fixing.

So also the vegetable Salt of Wine both fixeth and maketh volatile according to the divers[e] preparation thereof, as its use requireth, which certainly is a great Mystery of Nature and a wonder of the philosophic Art.

If a man drink Wine and out of his urine a clear Salt be made, that is volatile and maketh other fixed things volatile and carrieth them[348] over the helmet with it, but it fixeth them[348] not, and although the man drink nothing but Wine, out of whose urine the Salt was made, yet it hath another property than the Salt of Tartar or of the feces of Wine. For there is made a transmutation in the body of man, so that out of a vegetable, that is out of a Spirit of Wine, an animal Spirit of Salt is made. Horses, by the corroboration of their natural virtue, do transmute oats, hay and such like and convert it into fat and flesh; so doth the bee make honey out of the best of flowers and herbs. So understand of other things. This key and cause consisteth only in putrefaction, from whence such a separation and transmutation taketh its original.

The Spirit of common Salt, which is drawn after a peculiar manner, maketh Gold and Silver volatile; if a small quantity of the Spirit of Dragon[349] be added to it, it dissolveth it and carrieth it over with it *per alembicum*, as also doth the Eagle with the Dragon's Spirit, which dwelleth in stony places; but if anything be melted with Salt before the Spirit be separated from its body, it fixeth much more than it volatiliseth.

If the Spirit of common Salt be united with Spirit of Wine and both be three times distilled over together, then it waxeth sweet and loseth its acrimony. This prepared Spirit doth not corporeally dissolve Gold, but if it be poured on a prepared Calx of Gold it extracteth its highest tincture and redness, which, if it be rightly done, it reduceth pure and white Luna into the same colour, whereof its[350] body was before it[351] was extracted. Also the old body[352] will again attain its colour by the love of enticing Venus, being descended from the same original, state and blood.[353]

Know also [that] the Spirit of Salt destroyeth Luna and reduceth it into a spiritual essence, from whence afterwards *Luna potabile* may be prepared, which Spirit of Luna is appropriated to the Spirit of Sol as man and wife by the copulation and conjunction of the Spirit of Mercury or its oil.

The Spirit lieth in Mercury; seek the tincture in Sulphur[354] and the coagulation in Salt;³⁵⁵ then have you three matters, which may again produce some perfect thing, that is the Spirit of³⁵⁶ Gold fermented with its own proper oil. Sulphur is plentifully found in the propriety of most precious Venus, which inflameth the fixed blood gotten of her. The Spirit of the philosophic Salt gives victory to coagulation, although the Spirit of Tartar and Spirit of Urine, together with the true *acetum*, may do much; for the Spirit of Vinegar is cold and the Spirit of Calx vive is very hot, therefore are they esteemed and found to be of contrary nature. This I faithfully declare. Seek your matter in a metalline substance, make thereof Mercury, which ferment with Mercury; then a Sulphur, which ferment with its proper Sulphur, and with Salt reduce it into order;³⁵⁷ distil them together [and] conjoin them all according to their due proportion, then will it become one thing, which before came from one; coagulate and fix it by a continual heat, then multiply and ferment it three times.

The Key of the process discovering the Tincture is thus. When the Medicine and Stone of the philosophers is made and perfectly prepared out of the true *Lac Virginis*, take thereof one part, of the best and purest Gold, melted and purged by Antimony, three parts and reduce it into as thin plates as possibly you can; put these together into a crucible wherein you use to melt metals. First give a gentle fire for twelve hours, then let it stand three days and nights continually in a melting fire; then are the pure Gold and the Stone made a mere Medicine of a subtile, a spiritual and penetrating quality. For without the ferment of Gold the Stone cannot operate or exercise its tingeing quality, being too subtile and penetrative; but being fermented and united with its like ferment, the prepared tincture obtaineth an ingress in operating upon other bodies. Then take of the prepared ferment one part to a thousand parts of melted metal, if you will tinge it, then know for a very certain truth that it shall be transmuted into good and fixed Gold; for one body embraceth the other, although they be not alike, yet by the force and power added to it, it is made like unto it, like having its origin from its like.

Note well that out of Black Saturn and friendly Jove a Spirit may be extracted, which is afterwards reduced into a sweet oil as its noblest part, which Medicine, *particulariter*, doth most absolutely take way the nimble, running quality from common Mercury and bringeth him to a melioration.

Sixty-Second Sheet

Having thus attained the matter, nothing remains but that you look well to the fire, that you observe its regimen, for herein is the highest concernment and the end of the work. For our fire is a common fire and our furnace is a common furnace, although some philosophers, to conceal the art, write the contrary.[358] The fire of the lamp with the Spirit of Wine is unprofitable; the expense thereof would be incredible. *Fimus Equinus* spoileth it, for it cannot perfect the work by the right degree of fire.

Many and various furnaces are not convenient, for in our threefold furnace only the degrees of heat are proportionately observed. And as our furnace is common so is our fire common and as our matter is common, so is our Glass likened to the Globe of the Earth.

OF MERCURY

There are several sorts of Mercury. Mercury of animals and vegetables is merely a fume of an incomprehensible being unless it be caught and reduced to an oil; then it is for use. But Mercury of metals is of another condition, as [is] that also of minerals, though the same, also, may be compared with a fume, yet is it comprehensible and running. One Mercury is better and nobler than the other, for the Solar Mercury is the best of them all. Next unto that is the Lunar Mercury and so forth. There is a difference, also, among Salts and Sulphurs. Among the mineral Salts that carrieth away the bell which is made of Antimony and that Sulphur which is drawn from Vitriol is preferred before all others. Mercury of metals is hot and dry, cold and moist; it containeth the four qualities.

There are medicaments prepared of it of a wonderful efficacy, of several sorts and forms, which is the reason why there is such a variety of virtues therein. In Mercury lieth the highest arcanum for man's health, but [it] is not to be used crude, but must first be prepared into its essence. It is sublimed with Copper water and is further reduced into an oil. There is an oil made of it *per se*, without any corrosiveness, which is pleasant and fragrant. Several sorts of oils, with additionals, can be made of it, good for many things. It is prepared also with Gold, being first made into an *Amalgama*; there is made a precipitate of it in water, wherein it dissolveth green, like unto a Smaragd or Chrysolite. The volatile Mercury serveth for outward use, if a separation is made by some means and [if it] is brought into [a] subtile, clear liquor and then to a red-brown powder and its received corrosiveness is separated, then it may do well for other uses.

The mixed Mercury serveth for inward use. Mercury, being purged, is precipitated with the blood of Venus, is well digested with distilled Vinegar, and thus his corroding quality is taken off. Have a care what quantity you minister; if it is[359] given in a true dose, then it does its part very well. But for its operation it is not equally sublimed unto the fixed, its coagulation is found in Saturn, his malleableness is apparent when he is robbed of his life; he containeth his own tincture upon white and red, being brought in his fixed coagulation unto a white body, is tinged again by Vitriol water and being reduced to Gold is graduated by Antimony. Though that bloodthirsty Iron Captain with his spear assaulteth Mercury very much, yet he alone cannot conquer him unless cold Saturn come in to hide him and Jupiter command the peace with his sceptre. Such process being finished, when[360] the Angel Gabriel, the Strength of the Lord, and Uriel, the Light of the Lord, hath showed Mercury unto humble Michael, then Raphael can make right use of the highest Medicine.[361]

OF ANTIMONY[362]

It is very difficult to find out all the mysteries that are hid therein. Its virtue is miraculous; its power is great; its colour, hidden therein, is various; its crude body is poisonous; yet its essence is an antidote against poison [and] is like unto Quicksilver, which ignorant physicians can neither comprehend nor find, but the knowing physician believeth it to be true, having made many experiments with it.

This mineral containeth much of Mercury, much of Sulphur and little of Salt, which is the cause why it is so brittle and appliable; for there is no malleableness in it by reason of the small quantity of Salt. The most amity it beareth unto Saturn is by reason of Mercury, for philosophers' Lead is made out of it and is affected unto Gold by reason of its Sulphur; for it purgeth Gold, leaving no impurity in it. There is an equal operation in it with Gold if well prepared and [ad]ministered to man medicinally. It flieth out of the fire or[363] keeps firmly in the fire if it be prepared accordingly. Its volatile Spirit is poisonous, purgeth grievously [and] not without damage unto the body. Its remaining, fixed redness purgeth also, but not in that manner as the former did, provoketh not to stool but seeketh merely the disease wherever it is, penetrateth all the body and the members thereof, suffers no evil to abide there, expels it and brings the body to a better condition. In brief Antimony is the Lord in medicinals. There is made out of it a *Regulus* out of Tartar and Salt; if at the meeting of Antimony some Iron filings be added, by a manual used there cometh forth a wonderful Star, which philosophers before me called the Signet Star.[364] This Star being several times melted with cold earth Salt, it groweth then yellowish, is of a fiery quality and of a wonderful efficacy. This Salt afterwards affords a liquor, which further is brought to a fix[ed], incombustible oil, which serveth for several uses.

Sixty-Third Sheet

Besides there are made of common Regulus of Antimony curious flowers, either red or yellow or white, according as the fire hath been governed. These flowers being extracted and the extract, without any addition, *per se* being driven into an oil, have an admirable efficacy. This extraction may be made also with Vinegar of crude Antimony or of its *Regulus*, but it requireth a longer time, neither is it so good as the former preparation.

And being reduced into a *Philistea* there is a glass made of it *per se*, which [if it] is extracted also, [and] then abstracted, there remaineth a powder of incredible operation, which may safely be used after it hath been edulcorated. This powder, being dissolved, healeth wounds, sores etc., causing no pains. This powder being extracted once more with Spirit of Wine, or driven through the helmet with some other matter, affords a sweet oil.

Antimony is melted also with cold earth Salt, dissolved and digested for a time in Spirit of Wine. It [then] affords a white fixed powder [which] is effectual against *Morbus Gallicus* [and] breaks inward imposthumes. It hath several virtues besides.

There is made an oil also of Antimony, the Flying Dragon[365] being added thereunto, which, being rectified thrice, then it is prepared. Though a cancer were never so bad and the wolf[366] never so biting, yet they, with all their fellows, be they fistulas or old ulcers, must fly and be gone. The little powder of the Flying Dragon prepared with the Lion's Blood, must be [ad]ministered also, three or four grains for a dose according to the party's age and complexion.

A further process may be made with this oil with the addition of a water made of stone serpents[367] and other necessary spices, not those that are transported from the Indies. This powder is of that efficacy that it radically cureth many chronical diseases. There is made a red oil of Antimony, Calx vive, Sal armoniack and common Sulphur, which hath done great cures in old ulcers; with stone Salt or with common Salt there is forced from Antimony a red oil which is admirable good for outward symptoms.

There is made a sublimate of Antimony with Spirit of Tartar and Salmiac,[368] being digested for a time, which by means of Mars is turned into quick Mercury. This antimonial Mercury hath been sought of many but few have gotten it, which is the reason why his praise is not divulged, much less is his operative quantity[369] known. If you know how to precipitate it well, then your arrow will hit the mark to perform great matters; its qualities ought not to be made common [knowledge]. It is needless to describe its combustible Sulphur, how that is made out of Antimony; it is easy and known; but that which is fixed is a secret and hidden from many. If an oil be made of it in which its own Sulphur be dissolved and these be fixed together, then you have a Medicine of rare qualities, in virtue, operation and ability far beyond vegetables.

Quicksilver being imbibed with Quicksilver melted with Antimony for some hours in a wind oven, the Salt of the remainder being extracted with distilled Vinegar, then you have the philosophers' Salt, which cureth all manner of agues.

There is an *acetum* made of Antimony, of an acidity as other *acetums* are; if its own Salt be dissolved in this *acetum* and distilled over, then this *acetum* is sharpened, which is an excellent cooler in hot swellings and other inflamed symptoms about wounds, especially if there be made an unguent of it together with *anima* of Saturn.

There is a quintessence of Antimony, which is the highest Medicine, the noblest and subtilest found in it and [it] is the fourth part of an Universal Medicine. Let the preparation of it be still a mystery. Its quantity or dose is three grains. There belong four instruments to the making of it; the furnace is the fifth, in which Vulcan dwelleth; the manuals and the government of the fire afford the ordering of it.

Sixty-Fourth Sheet

OF COPPER-WATER

Copper is a mineral whose Salt is set forth in the highest manner, whose[370] great and good qualities are of the transcendency that reason is not able to comprehend or to conceive of them. It went generally by the name of Copper-water to make the meaning and sense of it plain. And be thus informed that Vitriol containeth two Spirits, a white and a red one; the white is the white Sulphur upon white, the red Spirit is the Red Sulphur upon red.

Observe it diligently. The white Spirit is sour, causeth an appetite and a good digestion in a man's stomach; the red Spirit is yet sourer and is more ponderous than the white; in its distilling a longer fire must be continued because it is more fixed[371] in its degree. Of the white, by distilling with[372] Sulphur of Lune, is made *Argentum potabile*. In the like manner the Gold,[373] being destroyed in the Spirit of common Salt and made spiritual by distilling and its Sulphur taken away from it and joined with a red Spirit in a due dose, that it may be dissolved and then for a time putrefied in Spirit of Wine, to be further digested and often abstracted that nothing remain in the bottom, then you have made an *Aurum potabile* of which great volumes have been written, but very few of their processes were right.

Note that the red Spirit must be rectified from its acidity and brought into a sweetness subtily penetrating, of a pleasant taste and sweet fragrancy.

The sweet Spirit is made of Sulphur of Vitriol, which is combustible like other Sulphur before it is destroyed. For the Sulphur of the philosophers is not combustible. Note this well. The preparation is easy [and] requireth no great pains nor great expenses to get a combustible Sulphur out of Vitriol. This sweet oil is the essence of Vitriol and is such a Medicine which is worthy the name of the Third Pillar of the Universal Medicine. The Salt is drawn from Colchotar[374] and is dissolved in the red or white oil or in both and is distilled again; if it be fermented with Venus it performeth its office very well, for it affords such a Medicine which at the melting tingeth pure Iron into pure Copper.

Colchotar of Sulphur affords true fundamentals unto [the] healing of perished wounds, which otherwise are hardly brought to any healing, and such sores which by reason of a long continued white redness will admit of no healing. Colchotar affords an ingress thereunto, setting a new foundation that quality and virtue are not in the Colchotar, but the Spirit, together with the Salt, are the matters which dwell therein.

There is made of Copper and Verdigris a Vitriol of a high degree, which[375] is far spread in its tincture. There is a Vitriol made of Iron also, which is of a strange quality; for Iron and Copper are very nigh kind[376] one to another, belong[ing] together as man and wife. This mystery I would have concealed.

[When] Vitriol [is] corroded with Sal Armoniack in its sublimation, there ariseth a combustible Sulphur together with its Mercury, of which there is but little because it hath most of Sulphur. If the same Sulphur be set at liberty again by the Eagle[377] with Spirit of Wine, there can be made a Medicine of it, as I told you before, though there be a nearer way to make combustible Sulphur out of Vitriol, as of its precipitation upon a precedent dissolution by the Salt or Liquor of Tartar, as also by a common *lixivium* made of Beech-ashes; yet this is the best reason, because the body of Vitriol is better and more opened with the Key of the Eagle.[377] There is not found in its nature either cold or moist quality, but [it] is of a hot and dry, substantial quality and [this] is the reason why, by its superabounding calidity, it heateth other things, digesteth them and at last it bringeth them to a full maturity, the fire being continued for a certain time.

OF COMMON SULPHUR

The usual common Sulphur is not so perfectly exalted in its degree and brought unto maturity as [when] it is found in Antimony and Vitriol. There is made of it *per se* an oil against putrid, stinking wounds, destroying such worms which grow in them, especially if the little Salt in it be dissolved from its Sulphur.

There is made of it a balsam with Sallet oil[378] or oil of Juniper, in like manner with the white Spirit of Turpentine, and [it] is of a red colour [and] is made thus. Take of Flowers of Sulphur made with Colchotar of Vitriol and digest them for a time in horse-dung. This balsam may safely be used for such that are in a consumption of the lungs, especially [if it] be rectified several times with Spirit of Wine, drawn over and separated, that it be blood red. This balsam is a preservative against corruption and rottenness.

The quintessence of Sulphur is [found] in a mineral where a sulphureous flint is generated. Thus [let] beaten pebbles [be] put in a glass and on it be poured a strong *aqua fort*, made of Vitriol and Saltpeter, and let dissolve what may be dissolved, [then] abstract the water; the remainder must be well dulcified and reverberated to a rednes; pour on that Spirit of Wine, extract its tincture [and] afterwards circulate for a time in the Pelican; let all the essence of Sulphur be separated, it stayeth below the Spirit of Wine like [a] fat Sallet oil, by reason of its ponderousness; its dose of six grains is found to work sufficiently. If you digest in this essence of Sulphur, Myrrh, Aloes and other Spirits, it extracts their virtues and makes them[379] into a balsam, which suffers no flesh or other parts that are subject to putrefaction to fall into rottenness, for which reason the ancients have put this name to it, *Balsamus mortuorum*. There may be made an oil of it[380] which is found very useful. The Sulphur may be sublimed in a high instrument with a good heat, which sublimation in a long time changeth [it] into a liquor or oil [if left] standing in a humid place.

Sixty-Fifth Sheet

There may be cocted a Liver out of common Sulphur, which is turned into milk, and it may also be changed into a red oil. Many other Medicinals may be made out of Sulphur. Its Flowers, Essence and Oil are preferred before the rest, together with the white and red fixed Cinnabar[381] which are made of it, because in them is found a mighty virtue.

OF CALX VIVE

The secrets of Quicklime are known to few men and few there are which attained to a perfect knowledge of its qualities. But though Lime is contemptible, yet there lieth great matters therein and [it] requireth an understanding master to take out of it what lieth buried in it. [By this] I mean to expel its pure Spirit, which colaterally stands in affinity with minerals, is able to bind and help to make fix[ed] the volatile Spirits of minerals, for it is of a fiery essence [and] heateth, concocteth and bringeth [them] unto maturity in a short time, when in many years they could not [otherwise] be brought to it. The gross, earthly body of it doth not do the feat, but its Spirit doth it, which is drawn out of it. This Spirit is of that ability that he bindeth and fixeth other volatile Spirits.

For note, the Spirit dissolveth *Occuli cancròrum*,[382] dissolveth crystals into a liquor. These two being duly brought into an unity *per modum distillationis* (I will say nothing now of Diamonds and such-like stones) that water dissolveth and breaketh the stones in the bladder and the gouty Tartar settled into the joints of hands and feet [and] suffers not any gout to take root in those parts. This is a rare secret. Quick Lime is strengthened and made more fiety and hot by a pure and unsophisticated Spirit of Wine, which is often [to be] poured on it and abstractd again; then the white Salt of Tartar must be grinded with it, together with its additionals which must be dead and contain nothing, then you will draw a very hellish Spirit, in which great mysteries lie hid.

OF ARSENICK

Arsenick is in the kindred of Mercury and Antimony as a bastard in a family may be. Its whole substance is poisonous and volatile, even as the former two; in its external colour to the eye it is white, yellow and red, but inwardly it is adorned with all manner of colours, like to its metals, which it was fain to forsake, being forced thereunto by fire. It is sublimed *per se* without additions and also in its subliming there are added several other matters as occasion requireth. If it be sublimed with Salt and Mars, then it looks like a transparent crystal, but its poison stayeth still with it, unfit to be joined or added to metals [and it] hath very little efficacy to transmute any metals.

The subterranean Serpent bindeth it in the union of fire, but cannot quite force it that it might serve for a Medicine for man and beast. If it be further mixed with the Salt of a Vegetable Stone,[383] which is with Tartar,[384] and is made like unto an oil, it is of great efficacy in wounds which are of an hard healing. It can make a coat for deceitful Venus, to trim her handsomely, that the inconstancy of her false heart may [not?] be disclosed by her wavering servants, without gain, with her prejudice and damage. When Antimony and Mars are made my companions [saith Arsenick], and [I] am exalted by then to the top of Olympus, then I afford a Ruby in transparence and colour [like un]to that which cometh from [the] Orient and I am not to be esteemed less than it. If I am proved by affliction, then I fall off like a flower which is cut off and withers, therefore nothing can be made of me to fix any metal or tinge it to any profit.

OF SALT PETER

Two elements are predominant in me, as fire and air; the lesser quantity is water and earth. I am fiery, burning and volatile. There is in me a subtile Spirit, I am altogether like unto Mercury, hot in the inside[385] and cold in the outside. [I] am slippery and very nimble at the expelling of my enemies. My greatest enemy is common Sulphur and yet is [he] my best friend also, for being purged by him and clarified in the fire, then am I able to allay all heats of the body within and without and am one of the best Medicaments to expel and keep off the poisonous plague.

Sixty-Sixth Sheet

I am a greater cooler outwardly than Saturn, but my Spirit is more hot than any. I cool and burn according as men will make use of me and according as I am prepared. When metals are to be broken I must be a help, else no victory can be obtained, be the understandings great or small. Before I am destroyed I am a mere ice, but when I am anatomised, then am I an hellish fire.

OF SAL-ARMONIACK

Sal-armoniack is none of the meanest Keys to open metals thereby, therefore the ancients have compared it with a volatile Bird. It must be prepared, else you can do no feats with it, for if it be not prepared it doth more hurt than good unto metals [and] carrieth them away out of the chimney hole. It can elevate and sublime with its swift wings the tincture of minerals and of some metals to the very mountains, where store of snow is found usually, even at the greatest heat of summer. If it be sublimed with common Salt, then it purgeth and cleareth and may be used safely.

He that supposeth to transmute metals with this Salt, which is so volatile, surely he doth not hit the nail on the head, for it hath no such power; but to destroy the metals and make them fit for transmutation, in that respect it hath sufficient power, for no metal can be transmuted unless it be first prepared thereunto.

OF TARTAR

This Salt is not set down in the book of minerals but is generated of a vegetable seed,[386] but its Creator hath put such virtue into it that it beareth a wonderful love and friendship unto metals, making them malleable. It purgeth Lune unto a whiteness and incorporateth into her such additionals which are convenient for her; being digested for a time with minerals or metals and then sublimed and vilified,[387] they all come into a quick Mercury, which to do there is not any vegetable Salt besides it. Many mysteries lie hid in it. It is a good remedy either outwardly or inwardly in Medicine; its Salt being made spiritual and sweet it dissolveth and reaketh the stone in the bladder and dissolveth the coagulated Tartar of the gout settled into the joints or anywhere else besides. Its ordinary Spirit, which is used for [the] opening of metals, being used and applied outwardly, layeth a foundation for healing such ulcers which admit hardly any healing, as fistulas, cancers, wolves and such-like.

OF VINEGAR

In Alchemy and Medicine nothing, almost, can be prepared but Vinegar must set a helping hand to it. In Alchemy it is used to set metals and minerals into putrefaction. It is used also for to extract their essences and tinctures, being first prepared thereunto even as the Spirit of Wine is usual to extract the tinctures from vegetables.

In Physic it deserveth its praise also, for it taketh the pure from [the] impure and is a separator and taketh from the mineral Medicaments their sharpness and corrosiveness, fixeth that which is volatile and is a great defender against poison. Vinegar is used inwardly also and both men and beasts are benefited thereby. Outwardly it is applied to hot inflammations and swellings for a cooler. Spirit of Wine and Vinegar are of great use both in Alchemy and Physic. Both have their descent from the Urine [and] are of one substance, but differ in the quality by reason of [the] putrefaction the Vinegar got there. But this is not the philosophers' Vinegar. Our Vinegar or *Acetum* is another liquor, namely a matter itself[388] for the Stone of [the] Philosophers is made out of the Azot of [the] Philosophers, which must be prepared with ordinary distilled Azot, with Spirit of Wine and with other waters besides and must be reduced unto a certain order.

Note this for a memorandum. If distilled, pure Vinegar be poured upon destroyed Saturn and is kept warm in Mary's Bath, it looseth its acidity altogether [and] is as sweet as sugar; then abstract two or three parts of that Vinegar, set it in a cellar [and] then you will find white, transparent stones like unto crystals. These are an excellent cooler and healer of all adust[389] and inflamed symptoms.

If these crystals are reduced into a red oil and poured upon Mercury precipitated by Venus and proceeded in further as it ought; if that [I say] be done[390] rightly, then neither Sol nor Lune will hinder thee from getting riches.

OF WINE

The true Vegetable Stone is found in Wine, which is the noblest of all vegetables. It containeth three sorts of Salt, three sorts of Mercury and three sorts of Sulphur.

The first Salt sticketh in the wood of the Wine, which, if [it be] burnt to ashes and a *lixivium* made of it [is able to] have its Salt drawn forth, which must be coagulated. This is the first Salt.

Sixty-Seventh Sheet

The second Salt is found in Tartar, if that be incinerated; then draw its Salt forth, dissolve and coagulate it several times and let it be sufficiently clarified.

The third Salt is this. When the Wine is distilled it leaveth feces behind, which are [to be] made to powder; its Salt can [then] be drawn out with warm water.

Each of these Salts hath a special property. In their centre they stand in a harmony, because they descend from one root.

It hath three sorts of Mercury and three sorts of Sulphur. The first oil is made of the steam, the second oil is made out of crude Tartar, the third is the oil of Wine.

There is a strange property in the Spirit of Wine, for without it there cannot be extracted any true tincture of Sol, nor can there be made without it any true *Aurum Potabile*; but few men know how a true Spirit of Wine is made, much less can its property be found out wholly. Several ways have been tried to draw and to get the Spirit of Wine without sophistication, as by several instruments and distillings with metalline Serpents and other strange inventions, of sponges, papers and the like. Some caused a rectified *Aqua vitae* [to] be frozen in the greatest frost, expecting the phlegm thereof should turn to ice [and] the spirit thereof to keep liquid, but nothing was done to any purpose.

TO MAKE A TRUE SPIRIT OF WINE

Take *Vinum Adustum*[391] and put it into a strong Vessel, which will endure the fire; light it with a match of Brimstone and put quickly a head of Iron or Copper upon it and the true, fiery Spirit will be resolved into a water in the receiver, which must be large. This is the true aerial, fiery Spirit of Wine. It must be subtile, penetrating, without any phlegm, pure, aerial and volatile, so that air in a magnetic quality may attract it; therefore it had need to be kept close in. It is of a penetrating and effectual operation.

There are three which are the noblest creatures in the world; these three have a wonderful affection one to another.[392] Among animals it is man, out of whose Mummy is made an Animal Stone, in which [the] Microcosm is contained. Among minerals Gold is the noblest, whose fixedness is a sufficient testimony of its noble offspring[393] and kindred. Among vegetables there lieth hid a Vegetable Stone.[394] Man loveth Gold and Wine above all other creatures, which may be beheld with the eyes. Gold loveth Man and Wine, because it lets go its noble part if Spirit of Wine be put to it, being made potable, which giveth strength to Man and prolongeth his life in health. Wine beareth affection to Man also and to Gold, because it easily uniteth with the tincture of Sol, expelleth melancholy and sadness [and] refresheth and rejoiceth Man's heart. These Stones renew men and beasts, cure leprous metals and cause barreness to become fruitful with a new birth.

THE TRUE PREPARATION OF AURUM POTABILE WITHOUT SOPHISTICATION

First [I will describe] what is that true and highest *Aurum potabile* and Universal Medicine. After this in order there followeth another *Aurum potabile* made of the fixed red Sulphur or Soul of the corporeal Gold, most highly purged, and [it] is prepared with the conjunction of the Universal Spirit of Mercury. After this there followeth another particular Medicine, which is half an *Aurum potabile*, showing its efficacy and power in many trials. Then I will add thereunto a description of *Aurum potabile*, because it traceth the steps of Gold and it showeth wonderfully its great energy and virtues.

The highest and chiefest *Aurum potabile* which the Lord god hath laid into Nature is the excocted, prepared and fixed substance of our Stone before it is fermented. A higher, greater and more excellent Universal Medicine and *Aurum potabile* cannot be found nor had in the circumference of the whole world; for it is a heavenly balsam because its first principles and original cometh from heaven, made formal in earth or under ground, and is afterwards, being exactly prepared, brought into a *plusquam* perfection, of which first principle and nativity of this heavenly substance I have already writ sufficiently.

Now as this excocted and perfect substance is the highest, chiefest and greatest Universal Medicine unto man, even so, on the other side, the same matter, after its fermentation, is a tincture also and the chiefest, greatest and most powerful Universal Medicine upon all metals whatsoever and thereby [they] may be transmuted into their highest melioration and health, namely into the purest Gold.

This is the first, chiefest and greatest *Aurum potabile* and Universal Medicine of the whole world, of which alone great volumes could be writ, whose preparation is already written.

Now I will declare the true and full process how a true *Aurum potabile* is to be made.

How true *Aurum potabile* is to be had and prepared from Gold, which in the best manner is exactly putrefied. Take the extracted Soul of Gold, draw[n] forth with the sweet Spirit of common Salt, as I informed you about the Particular of Gold,[395] where the body of Gold appeared very white; abstract the Spirit of Salt from it; edulcorate the *anima* of Sol ten or twelve times [and] at last let it be exiccated. Weigh it; pour on it four times as much of Spirit of Mercury; lute it well; set it in the Vaprous bath [and] putrefy it gently. Let the *anima* of Sol be quite dissolved and be turned into water or its *prima materia*. Both will turn into a blood-red liquor, fair and transparent, no Ruby on the earth [being] comparable unto it.

Sixty-Eighth Sheet

But note, when the *anima* of Sol begins to be dissolved and brought into its *prima materia*, that at the first, on the side round the glass where the matter lieth there [will] be seen a green circle, on it a blue, then a yellow. Afterwards all the colours of the rainbow join and make appearance, which do but last a little while.[396] The *anima* of Sol being wholly dissolved into the Mercurial Spirit, and [when] nothing is seen in the bottom, then pour to it twice as much of the best rectified Spirit of Wine, brought to its highest degree. The glass must be luted exactly. Digest and putrefy gently for twelve or fifteen days together, then abstract *per alembicum*, [when] the matter cometh over in a blood-red, transparent colour. This abstracting must be iterated; nothing must be left in the bottom which is corporeal; then you have the true *Aurum potabile*, which can never be reduced into a body.

But note, the Gold, before its destruction and [the] extraction of its Soul, must be purged in the highest degree. There is made another *Aurum potabile* and [one that is] artificially prepared, which, though it cannot be said or set down in writing to be the full and true potable Gold, yet is it [counted] more than half an *Aurum potabile* because it is transcending effectual in many diseases in which Nature might have stood in great doubts. This half *Aurum potabile* is made in a twofold manner, where the latter is better and more effectual than the former and asketh more pains and time than the former.

Take this extracted Soul of Gold drawn forth with the sweet Spirit of common Salt, edulcorate it most purely and exactly [and] at last exiccate it [and] put it in a spacious viol or body of glass. Pour on it red oil of Vitriol, which was dephlegmed and rectified *per retortam* that it be transparent, clear and white and you may see that it seizeth on the Gold and dissolveth it and is tinged deeply red. Put so much of this oil to it that in it may be dissolved [the] Sulphur or the Soul of Gold. Let it putrefy in *Balneo Mariae*[and] put a reasonable fire to it, that you may see that the Soul of Gold is quite dissolved in the oil of Vitriol. The feces which it hath settled must be separated from it; then put twice as much of the best rectified Spirit of Wine to it, which rectification you shall be further informed of, seal the glass, let no Spirits of Wine evaporate [and] set it again in putrefaction in the *balneum*; let it be there for a month, then the sharpness of the Vitriol is mitigated by the Spirit of Wine and loseth its acidity and sharpness [and] both together make an excellent Medicine; drive both over [and] let nothing stay behind in the bottom, then you get more than half an *Aurum potabile*, in form and colour of a deep yellow liquor.

Note that some metals in this manner may be proceeded withal. First a Vitriol may be gotten out of the metal, then a Spirit is further driven from it and joined in this manner with the Soul [and] dissolved and further digested with Spirit of Wine. All must enter into a Medicine as I formerly said, which [Medicines] have their special efficacy.

The second way to prepare this half *Aurum potabile*, which though it be but half an *Aurum potabile*, yet in virtue and efficacy, is far preferred before the other now spoken of, is done as followeth.[397]

Take the extracted solar Soul spoken of above, put it into a viol [and] pour on it the extracted philosophic Sulphur, which is the second principle, which is drawn with Spirit of Mercury from the philosophers' earth and Mercury, or Spirit of Mercury, unto an oleity, which now is Sulphur again and must be abstracted gently *per modum distillationis*.

Of this philosophic Sulphur pour on it as much that the solar Soul may be dissolved. Let it stand in a gentle bath, let the dissolution be made, then pour more of the best Spirit of Wine to it, digest gently, draw these over, let nothing stay behind in the bottom [and] then you have a Medicine that shall not want above two grains of the right and true *Aurum potabile*.

Those are the chiefest ways to make the corporeal *Aurum potabile*. This I close and proceed further with a short but true process how the Silver, which is the next to Gold concerning perfection, is made potable also. This process must be done in the following manner.

Take the sky-coloured Sulphur or Spirit of Lune, which was extracted with distilled Vinegar as I informed you in the particular of Lune,[398] edulcorate it, rectify it with Spirit of Wine, exiccate it, put it in a viol, pour to it three times as much of Spirit of Mercury, which is prepared from the white Spirit of Vitriol as I taught you before, lute the glass firmly, set it in putrefaction in the vaprous bath [and] let all be dissolved and nothing more see in the bottom. Then put to it an equal quantity of the best Spirit of Wine, set it in digestion for half a month, drive all over, let nothing stay behind [and] then you have the true potable Luna which in its efficiency is admirable and doth wonders when it is used.

A DESCRIPTION OF THE FIERY TARTAR

Distil of good Wine a Spirit of Wine, rectify it with white calcined Tartar, let all come over [and] put that which is distilled over into a viol. Pour four ounces of well sublimed Sal-armoniack to one quart of Spirit of Wine, set a helmet upon [it], set a great receiver into cold water [and] drive the volatile Spirits into [it] gently *in Balneo Mariae*. Leave but a little quantity of it behind. Note the alembick must always be cooled with wet cloths, then the Spirits will be dissolved and turn into a liquor. Thus is prepared this hot Spirit of Wine.

OF THE SALT OF TARTAR

First you must note that the philosopher's Tartar is not the vulgar Tartar, wherewith the lock is opened, but it is a Salt which cometh from root[399] and is the only mystical Key for all metals and is prepared thus: Make a sharp *lixivium* of the ashes of Sarments[400] or twigs of the vine,[401] boil away all its moisture [and] there stayeth behind a ruddy matter, which must be reverberated for three hours in a flaming fire. Stirring it still, let it come to a whiteness, which white matter must be dissolved in distilled rain water; let the feces of its settle [and] filter and coagulate them in a glass, that the matter in it be dry, which dry matter is the Salt of Tartar from which the true Spirit is driven.[402]

Note. As precious stones have many rare virtues and qualities, so there are many despicable and ignoble stones, which have great virtues, [as] for example the Limestone, Calx vive, which in men's judgements is held of no great value and lieth contemptibly in obscurity; however there is a might virtue and efficacy in it which appeareth if application be made of it to the most heaviest diseases, seeing that its triumphant and transcendent efficacy is almost unknown for the generality; therefore for the good of such which are inquisitive into natural and supernatural mysteries I will discover this mystery concerning Calx vive and show how its Spirit is driven from it, which work, indeed, requireth an expert artist who is well informed aforehand of its preparation.

Take unslaked Lime as much as you will; beat and grind it on a well dried stone to an impalpable powder [and] put on it so much of Spirit of Wine as the pulverised Calx is able to drink. There must not stand any of that Spirit upon it. Apply a helmet to it and lute it well and put a receiver before it [and] abstract the Spirit from it gently *in Balneo*; this abstracting must be iterated eight or ten times. This Spirit of Wine strengtheneth the Spirit of Calx mightily and [it] is made more fiery hot. Take the remaining Calx out of the body, grind it very small and put to it a tenth part of Salt of Tartar, which is pure, not containing any feces.

As much as this matter weigheth together, add as much of the additional of Salt of Tartar thereunto, namely the remaining matter from which was extracted the Salt of Tartar, and it must be well exiccated. All this must be mingled together and put in a well coated retort. Three parts of the retort must be empty. Lute[403] a great receiver or body to it very strongly. Note [that] the body into which the retort's nose is put must have a pipe of a finger's breadth unto which may be applied another body and a quantity of Spirit of Wine in it. Then give a gentle fire to it. At first there comes over some of the phlegm, which falls into the first applied body. The phlegm being all come over, then increase the fire [and] there cometh a white Spirit to the upper part of the body, like unto the white Spirit of Vitriol, which doth not fall among the phlegm but slideth through the pipe into the other body [and] draweth itself into the Spirit of Wine, embracing the same as one fire doth join with the other. Note [that] if the Spirit of Calx be not prepared first by the Spirit of Wine and drawn off and on as I told, then he does not so, but falleth among the phlegm where he is quenched [and] loseth also all his efficacy. Thus difficult a matter is it to search Nature th[o]roughly, [she] reserving [as she does] many things unto herself. This Spirit being fully entered into the Spirit of Wine, then take off the body [and] put away the phlegm, but keep carefully the Spirit of Wine and Spirit of Calx.

Note both these Spirits are hardly separated because they embrace closely one another and being distilled they come over jointly.

Seventieth Sheet Therefore take these mixed and united Spirits, put them into a jar-glass [and] kindle it; the Spirit of Wine burneth away, [but] the Spirit of Calx stayeth in the glass; keep it carefully. This is a great arcanum; few of other Spirits go beyond its efficacy if you know how to make good use of it. This Spirit dissolves *occuli cancrorum*[404] [and] the hardest crystals. These three being driven over together and often iterated in that distilling, three drops of that liquor being ministered in warm wine break and dissolve any gravel and stone in man's body, expelling their very roots [and] not putting the patient to any pain.

This Spirit of Calx at the beginning looks bluish [but] being gently rectified [it] looks white, transparent and clear, leaving few feces behind. This Spirit dissolveth the most fixed jewels and precious stones. On the other side he fixeth all volatile Spirits with his transcendent heat.

This Spirit conquereth all manner of podagrical[405] symptoms, be they never so nodose[406] and tartarous; [it] dissolves them and expels them radically.

OF VITRIOL AND ITS PREPARATION AS ALSO OF ITS POWER AND VIRTUE

Take good Hungarian Vitriol, calcine it till it be of a yellowish colour and no higher; grind this calcined Vitriol very small, put it into a distilling vessel with a long neck, well luted, *luto sapientiae*. Put thereto a large receiver and begin to distil day and night with a very gentle fire, that gives not a stronger heat than the Sun doth in a hot day. Afterwards increase the fire by degrees, forcing at last the Spirits with the strongest fire, till red, visible drops do come over, which work hath taken up three days and nights. This being done take that which is left in the distilling vessel, commonly called *Caput Mortuum*, and grind it small. Pour on it clean rain water, first distilled, and boil therein the Cholcotar and the Salt of Vitriol will go into the water. The water being settled and clear, filter it that the feces may be separated. Let the water vapour away in some glass vessel till the Salt be dry, [then] dissolve the Salt again in rain water, first distilled and let it vapour away again to dryness. Repeat this operation the third time and the Salt of Vitriol will be very fair, clean and clear. Put this dry Salt into a crucible of glass and pour on it the above made Spirit of Vitriol; lute the glass *luto sapientiae* and set it in digestion for some days. This being done, open the glass and put the materials together into a retort of glass and distil them [at] first gently; and when it ceaseth to drop, increase the fire and force it over till nothing will come more. Let it become cold and then take the Spirit out of the receiver, which must be somewhat large and strong. Put the Spirit into a glass body and rectify it by distillation till it be freed from the phlegm and the matter in the glass body appear to be of a red-deep-brown colour.

Then take the glass body and set it with the said matter in a cellar and there will shoot from it very clear, white, transparent crystals. Put these transparent crystals into a large phial with a very large and long neck and pour on them the first white Spirit of Turpentine and it will boil up and foam; therefore you must be careful and not over hasty in doing this. The crystals will dissolve and the Spirit of Turpentine will grow transparent [and] as red as blood. This being done, pour on it three times the weight of common Spirit of Wine freed fully from its phlegm, so that it stand two fingers high above it. Then put a little head of glass upon the neck of the phial, luting it well, join it to a receiver and distil very gently the Spirit of Wine *in Balneo Mariae* and the tincture of Vitriol comes over very pleasant[ly] with the Spirit of Wine and that which is corrosive remains behind with the oily parts of the Spirit of Turpentine. The Spirit of Wine being come with the tincture, put it together into another phial and pour on it some fresh Spirit of Wine and distil again gently *in Balneo Mariae* as you did before; if any corrosive be come over with the fire it will now stay behind. Repeat this operation the third time and the work is done and perfect. Put this fair, red, transparent Spirit of Vitriol into a Pelican, add to it at once half an ounce of well pulverised Unicorn's horn[407] and let it stand in circulation in a gentle heat a whole month. Then pour it off very clear from the feces and the tincture of Vitriol is prepared for the Medicine, of a very pleasant taste, and is to be used after this manner following, to wit: Let him that is troubled with the falling sickness[408] take half a dram of it in a spoonful of *Lillum Convallium* water when the fit is coming upon him. Thus let him use it three times and the Medicine will cure him by the help of God. He that is mad and distracted should take it likewise in Wine for the space of eight days and he will have reason to give God thanks for it. Moreover if it be taken in wine it doth resolve any hardness settled in the nerves and if it be constantly used for some time, even the gout itself is consumed and cured thereby.

Seventy-First Sheet

Likewise it maketh those who are melancholy and troubled with sadness, if it be used as before, very cheerful and light-hearted; it dispelleth all sadness and breedeth good and pure blood. It hath been found very excellent in swimmings and giddiness in the head; it comforteth the brain and preserveth the memory. If it be administered in consumptions of the lungs and any other coughs in the manner aforesaid, it will cure those distempers and is very useful for many other things.

AN ADDITION

Take Sal Armoniack, dissolve a considerable quantity of it in the strongest Vinegar and add to it filings of Copper. Let it putrefy in heat till the filings are all grown friable so that they may be grinded into powder and you will have a yellow powder, which edulcorate well.

Having done so, dry the powder and pour on it the red *Aqua Vitae*

Vitrioli, which hath been distilled over with its proper Salt, so that it cover it all over. Set it thus in heat and the powder of the Copper will be dissolved in the oil, but there must be some fair water be mixed with it. Then draw it off in sand to dryness and the phlegm comes over. The remainder force out of a retort in an open fire and you will find an *Oleum Veneris*, green [and] transparent like an Emerald. Put again into this *Oleum* some of the powder of Copper and it will be dissolved in it. Then coagulate to dryness and you have a powder, half an ounce whereof will transmute a whole pound of Iron, being in flux, into very good Copper.

OF THE SWEET ESSENCE OF VITRIOL

The sweet Essence of Vitriol, whereby many wonderful cures may be wrought, is only prepared out of its Sulphur, which burneth like other Brimstone. To obtain this proceed after this manner. Take of the best Vitriol you can get [and] dissolve it in fair fountain water; after this take Pot-ashes, such as dyers use for their dyeing [and] these dissolve likewise in fair fountain water; let it settle well and then pour off the clear from the dregs and add it to the solution of Vitriol and one will enflame the other and cause a separation. For the Sulphur of Vitriol doth separate itself by precipitation. Make a considerable quantity of it and edulcorate it from all impurity. Afterwards dry the same Sulphur, which will burn like other Sulphur, being cast upon glowing coals.

Take now this Sulphur and sublime it by itself without any addition and there will remain some feces, which separate and put away. Then take the Sulphur and grind together with it half its weight of common Salt of Tartar and distil them together through a retort and there will come over a reddish oil. Pour to this oil some distilled Vinegar and there will precipitate a brown powder and the Spirit of Tartar remaineth in the water. Edulcorate the same powder very well, for therein is the treasure to be looked after. This work being done, pour some Spirit of Wine on the said powder and let it circulate in heat for eight days. Thus the excellent sweet Essence of the Sulphur of Vitriol goeth into the Spirit of Wine and swimmeth upon the top, *in forma olei*, like an oil of cinnamon. Then separate the essence from the Spirit of Wine by means of a separating glass and keep it very carefully for use, it being a great treasure.

THE USE OF THIS MEDICINE

This Essence of Sulphur, four grains of it being taken in Balm water, drieth up the bad humours of the blood, strengtheneth and incites men and women to copulation, cleanseth the womb, hindreth the rising of the mother and breedeth good seed for the procreation of children.

The same quantity being taken in parsley water and continued for a fortnight, doth consume all phlegmatic humours of the whole body cures the dropsy radically, drives out the putrefied blood [and] openeth imposthumes, yea you will find it do wonderful cures if you will be industrious and careful in the preparation thereof; but you must never whilst you live forget God your Creator, to call upon Him for a blessing and to render to Him thanks for all His fatherly benefits He hath bestowed upon you.

THE PREPARATION OF THE STONE *IGNIS*[409]

Now I will teach you the chiefest preparation of Antimony and the use of it in Medicine. In this Antimony are hidden and found so many wonderful mysteries that there is none too old to learn and to search to find them out. I will instruct you to make some preparations which are also required to other things.

Take pure mineral Antimony, which is brought from Hungary, grind it very small and wash it very clean, that the earth may be separated from it. Take then a pound of it, mix with it as much of fluxing powder and melt it once again and then the *Regulus* will be clean and pure.

Add to this *Regulus* its weight of Nitre and melt it down. Pour it out together and beat off the *Scoriae* and put again to the *Regulus* its weight of Nitre and melt it.

Seventy-Second Sheet

Repeat this till all is gone into *Scoriae*, which you must carefully keep; they will burn upon the tongue like fire. This being done, take the matter so gathered, grind it small and edulcorate the Salt-peter from it and there remaineth a brown-yellow powder, which dry and keep; it looketh like grinded glass. Take now a common *Regulus* of Antimony made with Salt-peter and Tartar, grind it small and put it into a round glass, which must not be too high, and fasten a head to it. Sublime your *Regulus* in sand by itself without any addition, sweep the sublimate with a feather again into the glass and sublime it again. Repeat this so long till nothing do rise, but [the matter] remain red and fixed in the bottom. Then take this fixed Antimony and put it upon a stone in a cellar and in time it will be dissolved into water, which distil *in Balneo Mariae* until the sixth part only of the water do remain in the glass. Set this in a cold place and there will shoot reddish crystals, which dissolve in rain water. Filter it and draw off the phlegm to a thickness, set it to dry as before and the crystals will shoot white and very pure, like unti Salt peter. This is the Salt of Antimony.

Take these crystals and pour upon them pure distilled Vinegar and they will dissolve in the Vinegar. Then distil the Vinegar, the glass being very close luted, forcing at last the Spirits into the Vinegar and then the Vinegar is prepared. Take this Vinegar and pour it on the prepared brown-yellow powder and set it in some warm place and the Vinegar will draw out the tincture of Antimony, altogether red, within half or quarter of an hour. Pour off this extraction together and set it to digest twenty-eight days *in Balneo Mariae*.

Afterwards distil from it the Vinegar through an Alembick in sand, forcing in the end the oil into another glass, which comes over with many strange and wonderful veins. Rectify this oil in ashes and the rest of the Vinegar, if any be left, will come off and the oil remaineth very sweet and of a pleasant red colour like a Ruby. Thus have you joined the Sulphur with the Salt of Antimony and brought it over like an *Aqua Vitae*, which keep very carefully. Furthermore take again a common *Regulus* of Antimony made with Salt-peter and Tartar and beat it to [a] powder. Then take of strong distilled Vinegar four quarts and a half. Put into it of Sal Armoniack [and] of Salt of Tartar likewise eight ounces (I shall teach how to make it at the end of the directions). Digest this to the evaporation of the Vinegar and mingle with the Salts three parts of Venice Tripoli and distil the Spirit, which is of a singular nature and property.

Pour this Spirit on the pulverised *Regulus* of Antimony and having the glass well luted let it stand in digestion sixteen days; then distil the Spirit from the matter to a dryness and grind four times the weight of filings of steel with the same. Put it into a retort and putting thereto a large receiver full of water, distil it, forcing at last with a strong fire, and the Mercury comes over in fumes and is quickened in the water, which is the true Mercury of Antimony.

Take common Spirit of Vitriol, add a little common water to it and put your filings of steel into it. Let it stand till the filings are dissolved, then pour it off clean and put away the feces. Afterwards distil the Spirit in ashes to a thickness and set the glass in a cold place and there will shoot good Vitriol of Iron, which take, and having first vapoured away the phlegm mingle with it three parts of the powder made of burned potsherds of broken pots, put into a retort, draw off the phlegm first, then force the Spirit with a strong fire into a proper glass, which rectify to the height and there will remain an oil in the bottom. Pour this oil upon the Mercury made before and draw off the phlegm in hot ashes and the tincture of the *Aqua vitae* remains behind and doth precipitate the Mercury into a fair, high-coloured powder of very great virtues in curing old running sores.

THE CONJUNCTION OF THE THREE PRINCIPLES SULPHUR, SALT AND MERCURY OF ANTIMONY

Take of this precipitate, well edulcorated with Spirit of Wine, one part and pour on it of the above mentioned sweet oil, three parts, in a phial, so that the phial be not above one half full.

Then seal it hermetically and place it in a philosophical furnace and the precipitate will be dissolved in that continual heat. Open then the glass and continue a strong fire till the matter become a fixed powder and do fix and then the Stone *Ignis* is prepared of which I have written. This Stone is a particular tincture in men's bodies as well as in those of metal[s]. This may be used in many hard and dangerous distempers. Take of this Stone or particular tincture half an ounce, cast it upon twelve ounces and a half of pure Silver or upon as much Pewter or Lead, let it flow very well for four and twenty hours, then drive it off clean and quart[410] it as tryers and refiners do and you will find in the Silver two ounces and a half of very good Gold and in the Pewter or Lead one ounce upon the cupel.

ANOTHER MEDICINE MADE OUT OF ANTIMONY AND MERCURY AND OF ITS EFFECTS IN OUTWARD SORES

Take Hungrian Antimony and sublimed Mercury and grind them well together and distil them through an earthen retort, forcing them at last with the strongest fire imaginable and you will obtain an oil, which separate and keep apart. Put away the quick Mercury, if so there be any, and the Cinnabar you will find in the neck of the retort. But as for the *Caput Mortuum*, grind it small and put it into a new retort and having poured on it the oil, first made warm, distil it again from it. Repeat so often till the *Caput Mortuum* remain behind like ashes and then your oil is prepared.

After this take so much fresh Antimony as first of all the *Caput Mortuum* did weigh, grind it small and put on it the oil, first warmed, and so many times distil[411] as before till the oil be come over as red as a Ruby and the *Caput Mortuum* likewise remain like ashes in the bottom of the glass and then the oil is prepared.

THE PREPARATION OF THE SUBLIMATE FOR THIS WORK

Take one pound and a half of Hungarian Vitriol, one pound of common Salt and four ounces of Salt-peter; grind this together and put [with(?)]

one pound of Quicksilver into the bottom of a glass body; place it in sand so that the sand do not come above the matter in the glass; put a head thereupon and give it a convenient fire and the sublimate will stick to the sides of the glass, which is to be used in your work.

Take the above prepared *Aqua vitae*[412] and add to eight ounces of it three ounces of Salt-peter water and distil it out of a coated, glass retort and you will have an ounce of the *Aqua vitae*[412] remain behind fixed. Then put again to the *Aqua vitae*[412] one ounce of fresh Salt-peter water into a retort and distil as before and there will stay more behind. This addition of fresh Salt-peter water to the *Aqua vitae*[412] and[413] distillation out of a coated retort, as has been said before, repeat so often till all remains fixed in the retort.

THE SALT-PETER WATER IS MADE THUS

Take unburned potsherds grinded small and with three parts of the same grind one part of purified Salt-peter. Put into the receiver half a pound of water to one pound of Salt-peter and force the Spirits over into it. That which is fixed with this water,[414] put into a glass body and pour upon it the common *Aqua vitae Vitrioli* so that it be four fingers high upon it. Then distil it till the matter become dry. Take out this matter and dry it yet more that the rest of those corrosive Spirits may evaporate, then edulcorate it well with Spirit of Wine and the Medicine is prepared.

THE USE

Three or four grains of this Medicine being taken in some good treacle for some days cureth the French pox; there [be] no sore so old and festered but is cured infallibly by it. I have cured with it likewise many spreading, old, running ulcers, as fistulas, cancers, the wolf[415] and the like. The Name of the Lord be praised therefore.

THE PREPARATION OF A MEDICINE OUT OF COMMON SULPHUR

Take common Sulphur and grind it small, then grind with it three parts of calcined Vitriol, put it together into a high cucurbite and sublime it in sand till nothing will sublime more. Take then these flowers, put them into a glass and pour on them a common *Aqua vitae Tartari*, which hath been dissolved in a cellar, so that it swim on the top of its a hand's breadth. Place it in a convenient heat and the Sulphur will open itself in [a] few hours and become transparent red like a Ruby.

This being done pour off the extraction into another glass and put to it very good distilled Vinegar and the Sulphur falls to the bottom with a great stink.

Pour off the *Aqua vitae* and edulcorate well the Sulphur and dry it gently. Put this Sulphur again into another glass cucurbite and pour upon it Spirit of Wine, which is prepared with philosophical Tartar, set it in heat for three days and the Spirit of Wine imbibeth again that excellent tincture of the Sulphur. Then pour off the extraction and draw off the Spirit of Wine with a pretty strong fire in sand and there will come over with it a pleasant, sweet smelling *Aqua vitae*. Having done so, rectify the oil *in Balneo Mariae* and draw off the Spirit of Wine gently and the *Aqua vitae Sulphuris* remaineth in the bottom.

THE USE OF THIS MEDICINE

Six or eight drops of this oil being taken in a spoonful of Wine are good for those that are in a consumption. It is good likewise for coughs, openeth the breast and ulcers of the breast, likewise imposthumes. It relieveth against whatsoever may occasion any putrefaction in a man's body if the use of it be continued for some time.

THE PREPARATION OF THE TINCTURE OF CORALS

Seventy-Fourth Sheet

Take red Corals, break them to pieces and pour on them a common Spirit of Salt and the Corals will be dissolved. This being done, draw off by distillation the Spirit of Salt and edulcorate them well. Then take to one marck[416] of this power half an ounce of common Sulphur, pulverised, and having mingled it together, reverberate it very gently till all the Sulphur be burned away. Having done so, grind as much Camphor with the Corals and burn the Camphor likewise away. Then edulcorate well the Corals and pour upon them high rectified Spirit of Wine and digest them for eight days and the tincture of the Corals will elevate itself into the Spirit of Wine. Then pour off that which you have extracted and after that draw off the Spirit of Wine from it and there remaineth the tincture of Corals behind in the bottom like a red, fat oil of Olives.

THE USE OF THE MEDICINE

Six drops of this tincture given in a spoonful of Wine to those that are bereaved of their senses restoreth them again. This tincture comforteth likewise the brain and strengthens the memory, dispelleth sadness and melancholy, makes light-hearted, breedeth good blood and strengtheneth the heart. It is such a noble Medicine for which we are bound indeed to bless Almighty God.

OF THE TRUE SOLUTION OF PEARLS

Take very good Verdigris, grind it small and dissolve it in distilled Vinegar; pour off the clean and throw away the feces. Then distil off the Vinegar out of a glass body to a thickness and put it into a cold place and there will shoot from it a fair Vitriol. Put this Vitriol into another glass and pour on it a high rectified Spirit of Wine and dissolve therein the Vitriol very well. Separate the feces from it [and] afterwards distil off likewise the Spirit of Wine to a thickness and set it again in a cold place and the Vitriol shooteth again. Put then the Vitriol into a glass body and draw off by distillation the phlegm *in Balneo Mariae* till the matter becomes dry. Take it out, put it into a glass retort and distil once more with a stronger fire in sand and you will obtain a pleasant Vinegar. Dissolve in this Vinegar as many Pearls as it will dissolve, for this Vinegar worketh very well upon them, dissolveth the substance but not the shells. The Pearls being dissolved, draw off the Vinegar *in Balneo Mariae* till the Pearls be very dry, then take them out and edulcorate them with Rose-water. Put these Pearls thus prepared into a glass body and pour some Spirit of Wine upon them and digest them in [a] gentle heat four and twenty hours and there riseth a pleasant liquor from the Pearls which doth mount and swimmeth upon the Spirit of Wine like an *Aqua vitae* made of Cinnamon. Pour it off together with the Spirit of Wine and keep it.

THE USE OF THIS MEDICINE

Take of this Spirit of Wine half a spoonful so that four or five drops of the oil may go with it. It comforteth the heart, gives strength to the very marrow and bones [and] cureth swimming in the head and whatsoever may be hurtful to the eyes. [It] dispelleth rheums in the head and the noise in the ears, openeth the passage to hearing and is, moreover, a most precious treasure in many distempers.

A CERTAIN CURE OF THE STONE

Recipe. Of common Salt-peter, well purified, one pound and as much of common white Spirit of Vitriol. Pour the Spirit of Vitriol upon the Salt-peter and the Salt-peter will be dissolved altogether. This being done, distil from thence the Spirit of Vitriol in ashes to a thickness and set it in some cold place and the Salt-peter will shoot again from it. Take two ounces of this Salt-peter and the like quantity of the Salt of Wormwood; pour on them a little of the oil of Sulphur made *per campanam* so that the Salts may be like a poultice. Mix with it likewise one dram of Anniseed oil and as much of oil of white Amber, adding thereto a pound of Canary Sugar and mix all these ingredients very well together. Let him that is tormented with the stone take of this powder every day five or six time[s] as much as will lie upon a point of a knife, twice repeated, and this medicine will work upon the stone and break it and throw it out radically.

OF THE SOUL OR THE SULPHUR OF LUNE OR THE PHILOSOPHER'S SILVER

Take common Salt[-peter] and quick or unslaked Lime, reverberate them together in a wind furnace with the strongest fire, extract again the Salt-peter with warm rain water and coagulate it to dryness; mingle again with it new quick Lime, reverberate it and extract again; repeat this the third time. This being done take Calx of Silver, being after the dissolution in an *Aqua fort* prepared, and mix it with the prepared Salt[-peter]; put it into a glass viol, pour on it common *Aqua fort* such as the goldsmiths use, made of Salt-peter and Vitriol, and draw it off by distillation in hot sand. Pour on it some fresh *Aqua fort* and having distilled it likewise, repeat it the third time, giving at last [a] very strong fire, that the matter in the glass may flow very well. Let it cool of itself in the furnace and the Silver will become transparent blue in one piece. Extract this with Vinegar till you can extract no more. Edulcorate that which is extracted with water, that the Salt may be separated from it.

Cohobate Vinegar upon the dry Sulphur till it come over like a Saphire. Reduce the same Silver into small filings and add to it its weight of Sal-armoniack and sublime it in a glass body and the Sal-armoniack carrieth with it the Sulphur of Lune of a very pleasant sky-colour. Put this sublimate into a dish of glass, edulcorate it well with rain water, first distilled, and the Sal-armoniack will be separated. Then dry the Sulphur of Lune, put it into a little body and pour on it good rectified Spirit of Wine and set it twenty-four hours in heat and the Spirit of Wine doth imbibe the Sulphur of Lune, [a] fine transparent blue, like a Saphire or Ultramarine, and leaveth some few feces behind, which separate from it.

Seventy-Fifth Sheet

THE USE

Five or six drops of this tincture being taken in Wine doth dispel sad and melancholy thoughts. It preventeth unquiet sleep, cureth those as use to rise and wander up and down in the night and likewise that are lunatics and giveth rest to all such as are restless in the night.

THE SECRET OF THE QUICK OR UNSLAKED LIME

Take good, pure Chalk [and] burn it in a potter's furnace with a very strong fire to bring it to an exact maturity. Then grind it small upon a warm stone and pour on it, in a glass body, Spirit of Wine made with philosophical Tartar that the Chalk become like a thin poultice.

This being done, distil from thence the phlegm to the dryness of the Chalk, pour fresh Spirit of Wine on it and distil it off again. Repeat this six times, then grind the matter small and lay it on a stone in a cellar to dissolve and there will flow in a few days from it a liquor, which, when you have gathered, put it into a retort of glass and distil it in sand and the phlegm comes over first, which keep apart. After this there cometh a spiritual liquor which is likewise to be kept by itself.

Moreover take crystal stones, pulverise them and grind their weight of live or mineral Sulphur with them. Put then this matter upon a broad, earthen platter, stirring it continually, and burn away the Sulphur from it. Then reverberate it in an open, flaming fire for three hours. This being done, likewise put the matter into a glass and pour the liquor upon it. Take likewise crabs eyes,[417] put them into another glass and pour on them of the same liquor; let it stand pretty hot for fourteen days and nights and there will rise from both a moisture, which pour off together very clean into a little body of glass and rectify it *in Balneo Mariae* and the liquor remaineth behind. Three grains of which, being taken in wine, have wrought very great and admirable effects. This Medicine cureth likewise radically the stone of the bladder and kidneys, both in men and women.

Take this burned Chalk, pour upon it and then draw from it again several times an *Aqua fort* made of Vitriol and Salt-peter. Dissolve it afterwards in a cellar. Distil that which is dissolved into an oil with a strong fire. Digest with this oil a Calx of Lune, opened wth *Aqua fort*, for a month. Reduce this Calx by melting down with Salt-peter and Sal armoniack and refine it with Saturn; then separate it and you will have a white, fixed Lune, which lay for a day and a night in an *Aqua fort* and you have good Gold, which endureth all trials. *Laus Deo.*

THE PREPARATION
OF THE GREAT PHILOSOPHIC STONE

Our Stone is made out of its own proper Essence; for its transmuteth other metals into real and true Gold, which Gold must be prepared and become a better Stone. And though nothing of another nature must be used in the preparation of our Stone, which might obstruct its majestic excellency, yet the preparation of it in the beginning cannot be made without means. But observe that, as you will hear afterwards, all corrosives must be washed away from it and separated, so that our Stone may be severed from all poison and be prepared to be the greatest Medicine. Now I will show the work itself.

Take of the very best Gold you can have, one part; of good Hungarian Antimony, six parts; melt these[418] together upon a fire and pour it out into such a pot as the goldsmiths use; when you have poured it out it becometh a *Regulus*. This same *Regulus* must be melted again that the Antimony may be separated from it.

Seventy-Sixth Sheet

This being done, add to it Mercury and melt it again and cleanse it again. Repeat this the third time and the Gold is purged and purified enough for the beginning of the work. Then beat the Gold very thin as goldsmiths do when they gild and make an amalgam with common Quicksilver, which must be squeezed through a leather. Let the Quicksilver fume away little by little upon a gentle fire, that nothing of it may remain with the Gold and stir it about continually with a small Iron [rod] and the Gold is become subtile so that its water may the better work upon it and open it.

THE PREPARATION OF THE WATER

Take one part of Salt-peter, well purified, and grind with it the like quantity of Sal-armoniack and half as much of pebbles, very well cleansed and washed. Mingle all these ingredients together and put them into an earthen retort, that the Spirits may not come through and put the same into a distilling furnace. The retort must have a pipe behind and put as large a receiver as you can get to the retort. The receiver must lie in a vessel full of cold water and a wet linen cloth must be put round about it, which you must continually [change] with another wet cloth. Then again so much matter [must be put] into the retort [at intervals] till all is gone into it[419] and then your water is prepared.

Take then of the prepared Calx of Gold one part, put it into a glass body and pour three parts of the above made water upon it and place it in warm ashes and the Gold will dissolve in it; but if it should not altogether be dissolved, pour more fresh water upon it and it will dissolve it all. This being done, pour it out into another glass and let it stand till it become cold and it will let fall some feces, which separate by pouring the water from them to another glass. Set this glass *in Balneum Mariae* and put a head upon it. Let it stand in heat day and night and more feces will settle, which separate from it as before. Close up your glass very well after you have put on the head and lute another glass to the head and let it stand for fourteen days in a gentle heat that the body may be well opened. This being done, increase the fire and distil off the phlegm to a thickness that it remain in the bottom like an *Aqua vitae*. That which hath been distilled pour again into the body, having first made it warm, and lute again the head to it and let it stand to digest a day and night. Then draw off the water again by distillation and pour it again warm, upon it. Repeat this so long till the Gold is come over altogether into a low body with a flat bottom. Put this spiritualised solution of Gold again into a glass and pour on it a considerable quantity of rain water, putting thereto three parts of live Mercury to one of Gold but you must squeeze first the Mercury through a leather, and stir it very well together and you will see many wonderful colours. And if you do repeat this, stirring several times, there will fall an *Amalgama* to the bottom and the water will become clear.

This being done, decant the water and dry gently the *Amalgama*, which, having edulcorated it very well, put upon a broad, shallow, earthen platter under a cover. Stir it about continually with an Iron wire till all the Quicksilver be fumed away and there will remain upon the earthen [platter] a very fair powder of a purple colour.[420]

AFTERWARDS YOU MUST PREPARE YOUR SPIRIT OF WINE WITH THE PHILOSOPHICAL TARTAR IN THE MANNER FOLLOWING:

First you are to know that the Tartar of the philosophers, whereby the lock is unopened, is not like unto common Tartar as many do think; but it is another Salt and springeth from one root and is the only Key to open and to dissolve metals and is prepared as followeth. Take ashes of a vine which hath borne grapes that have yielded good wine; make of them with warm water as strong a lee[421] as possibly can be made. When you have a considerable quantity of this lee, boil it away and coagulate it to a dryness and there remaineth a reddish matter. Put this matter into a reverberating furnace and reverberate it for three days or thereabouts in an open fire, that the flame may play very well upon it and stir it continually till the matter is become white.

Afterwards dissolve this [re]verberated matter in fountain water and let it settle, pour off the clear [liquid] and filter it, that all the feces may be separated and coagulate it in a glass body and you will have a pure, white Salt of Tartar from which a true Spirit is drawn.[422]

Take now high rectified Spirit of Wine, fully freed from its phlegm,

[and] put the same into a glass phial with as long a neck as possibly you can get. But first of all put into it your Salt of Tartar and then the Spirit to the supereminency of three fingers. Lute a head to the phial and put thereto another glass, let it stand in a gentle heat, then distil gently off the phlegm and the Spirit of Tartar is opened by the Spirit of Wine and by reason of their reciprocal, wonderful love it comes over with the Spirit of Wine and is united with it. The remaining feces and some phlegm staying behind with them are to be put away.

Seventy-Seventh Sheet This is now the right Spirit of Wine, wherewith you may open that which the lover of Art desireth to know, for it is become penetrant by preparation.

Take now the powder of Gold of a purple colour and having put it into another phial, pour on it your Spirit of Wine. Put it, very close luted, in a gentle heat and it will extract the Sulphur of Gold within twenty-four hours of a high red colour like blood. Having done so [so often] that it doth not yield any tincture more, pour off the extraction very clear into a little glass body. The remainder is a white Calx. Pour upon this Calx the aforesaid Spirit of Wine and let it stand in putrefaction, having the glass well stopped, for fourteen days and nights and the Spirit of Wine will become of a white colour like milk, which pour off clear and pour upon it[423] fresh Spirit of Wine and let it stand a day and [a] night longer and it will be coloured again, but not much. Add this to the first and what remaineth do not dry, but leave it in the glass. Put the white extraction into a little body and distil the phlegm from it till it be reduced to a small quantity.

This being done, put the glass in a cellar and there will shoot from it fair and transparent crystals, which having taken out, put the remainder again in a cellar and you will have more crystals, which put together into a body of glass, for it is the Salt of the Philosophers, and pour half the extraction of the Sulphur of Gold upon them and they will dissolve immediately and melt like butter in hot water. And then distil it together out of a glass body in hot ashes and it will come over together in the form of a red oil, which falls to the bottom and the Spirit of Wine swimmeth upon the top, which separate from it.

This [oil] is the true Potable Gold, not reducible into a body, and my *Phalaia*, whereby I have cured many by the blessing of God, giving but three grains of it in Wine.

The other half of the extraction must be distilled gently *in Balneo Mariae* to a dryness [that] the Spirit of Wine may be separated. Pour on it this Oil of Gold or Potable Gold and it taketh the powder in a moment and becomes of a much higher colour than it was before; and this will dissolve in common Spirit of Wine and other Wine as red as a Ruby, which constantly and wonderfully cureth all such distempers of the body as have their origin from within.

Then take that other part of Mercury of Pure Gold which you have kept and pour all this, being its own oil, upon it and distil by an alembick, but not too strongly; and there comes over some phlegm and the oil doth precipitate its own Mercury and becomes white again, the greenness[424] being lost and gone.

This work being done likewise, get a philosophical egg, which the philosophers call their Heaven and you will find two parts of the oil in weight to one part of the precipitated Mercury. Put then the Mercury into a glass and add the oil of Gold to it, so that one part of the glass may be filled and three parts remain empty. Seal it well as Hermes teacheth and put it into the three-fold furnace so that it standeth not hotter than an egg which is under an hen to be hatched, and the matter will begin to putrefy within a month, and both become very black which, when it doth appear, it is then certain that the matter is open by putrefaction and you may be glad of the happy beginning. Increase now the fire to the second degree and the blackness will vanish away in time and change into many admirable colours. These colours being gone likewise, increase the fire to the third degree and your glass will look like Silver and the rays will become ponderous. Then, increasing the fire to the fourth degree, the fumes will cease by little and little and your glass will shine as [if] it were beset within with cloth of Gold. Continue this fire and the rays will disappear likewise and there will be no more rays be seen to rise, but you will see your matter lie beneath like a brown oil, which at length being become dry, doth appear like into a Granat,[425] which is both fixed and liquid like wax, penetrant like oil and mighty ponderous.

He that hath obtained this may render thanks to God his Creator, for poverty hath forsaken him, diseases will fly from him and wisdom hath taken possession of him.

Having thus prepared your Medicine, if you intend to multiply it proceed as follows. Take of the prepared powder of Gold of a purple colour, as you have done before, three parts. Add to it of the prepared tincture one part, in a new Heaven or philosophers' egg. Seal it again hermetically and set it again into the furnace as before and the matter will unite itself and dissolve and be brought to perfection within thirty-one days, which is a month, which otherwise will take up ten months. Thus you may multiply the Medicine *in infinitum* so that you may perform things which the world will account incredible.

Lastly you must know that this Medicine is a very spiritual and piercing one, which cureth any distempers of this world in all creatures

Seventy-Eighth Sheet

whatsoever. One only grain of it being taken, it penetrateth the whole body like a fume, cleareth out of the body all that is bad and bringeth that that is good in the room of it, reneweth the man and maketh of him, as it were, a new man, which it preserveth without any accidents to his age and the term prefixed by the Most High. *Contra mortem remedium non est.*

This Medicine, being first fermented with other pure Gold, doth likewise tinge many thousand parts of all other metals into very good Gold as I showed in a former process, whereby such Gold likewise becometh such a penetrant Medicine that one part doth tinge and transmute a thousand parts of other metals, and much more beyond belief, into perfect Gold. God be blessed and praised both now and for ever more. Amen.

ADDITIONAL PREPARATIONS FOR A FULLER DECLARATION OF THE SAME

SPIRIT OF MERCURY BY ITSELF OR MERCURIAL WATER

Put running Mercury into a retort and put to it a receiver, which must stand in a glass with water in it. Distil then, and the Spirit will precipitate itself and is resolved into a water. Pour out this water and put the Mercury which sticketh to the neck of the retort back again into the retort. Distil and rectify till you have brought and reduced it to a water. This spirit of Mercury cureth almost all distempers and doth extract the essence out of minerals and metals.

A TINCTURE BOTH UPON MEN AND METALS

Take the spiritual Gold of a purple colour, extract its Sulphur with distilled Vinegar and separate the Vinegar again from it that it become a powder. This powder being dissolved in Spirit of Red Mercury, that is Gold, put thereto Salt of Gold and fix it. This is an universal Medicine for sick and diseased bodies of men, likewise it is excellent to exalt metals to the highest degrees.

A TINCTURE UPON WHITE

Calcine Silver with Salt and Quicklime and extract its blue Sulphur, which elevate and rectify with Spirit of Wine that it remain a liquor.

Dissolve this in the white Spirit of Vitriol and in the Spirit of mineral Mercury.

I do not understand here the red Mercury, but the common, white, mineral Mercury, or rather that [which] is extracted out of Vitriol.

Fix it then, and you have an universal Medicine against all distempers and a tincture which doth tinge Lead, Pewter, Mercury and Copper into Silver.

TO MAKE AN OUNCE OF GOLD OUT OF HALF AN OUNCE

Take Spirit of Salt, rectify it with Spirit of Wine and it becometh sweetish. Pour this upon the Spiritual Gold of a purple colour and it will extract only the Soul or Sulphur of the Gold, but doth not touch the body of Gold. The Sulphur of Gold doth graduate Silver into Gold, yet no greater quantity of it than there hath been of Gold. The body of Gold must be as white as Silver. Reduce it upon a cupel with Saturn and a little Copper and the white body of Gold doth recover again its colour and property and becometh good Gold.

TO MAKE MERCURY OF GOLD OR THE PHILOSOPHICAL MERCURY

Take the Gold of a purple colour out of which the Sulphur is already extracted, digest it with the following water for a month, then revive it again by driving it through a retort in the neck whereof are to be laid Iron plates. Drive it into a receiver with some water in it and it runneth together and becometh a Quick Mercury of Gold.

THE WATER IS MADE AS FOLLOWETH

Take Salt of Urine of a young man that drinketh nothing but Wine and likewise Salt of Tartar and Sal-armoniack, *ana*.[426] Let all this dissolve into a liquor, which rectify with Spirit of Wine that it become very sweet. This is the Arcanum wherewith the body of Gold is reduced into a running Mercury.

TO MAKE THE SALT OF GOLD

Pour[427] Gold three times through Antimony, beat it into thin plates and dissolve them in *Aqua Regis*. Dissolve likewise Salt of Tartar in Spirit of Wine and draw off the phlegm that it remain like an oil. With this oil precipitate your Gold and separate again the Salt of Tartar from it by ablutions, then reverberate it fourteen days. Pour upon this Calx of Gold distilled Vinegar; let it boil gently a day and night and the Vinegar doth dissolve the Salt of the reverberated Gold. What remaineth in the bottom undissolved must be reverberated again eight days. Then boil it again in new Vinegar [and] put this afterwards to the first solution.

If anything remaineth behind it must be reverberated eight days more till the body is gone into the Vinegar. Then draw off the Vinegar *in Balneo Mariae* and you have the Salt of Gold in a yellowish powder which cureth all distempers.

SOLI DEO GLORIA

Seventy-Ninth Sheet

TO CONCLUDE THESE PREPARATIONS WITH A BRIEF DISCOVERY OF THE FIRST TINCTURE, ROOT AND SPIRIT OF METALS AND MINERALS, HOW THEY ARE CONCEIVED, RIPENED, BROUGHT FORTH, CHANGED AND AUGMENTED

OF THE FIRST TINCTURE, THE ROOT OF METAL[S]

Observe that the tincture which is the root of all metals is a supernatural, flying, fiery Spirit. It hath its sustenance and natural habitation in the earth and water, where it may rest and work. And this Spirit is found in all metals, and more abundant in other metals than Gold; for the Gold is very close, solid and compact by reason of its well digested, ripened and fixed body; therefore it can no more enter into the body than the body doth need. But other metals have not such a fixed body, but their pores are open and dispersed, therefore can the tingeing Spirit abundantly more penetrate and possess them. But because the bodies of other metals are unfixed, the tincture likewise cannot stay with these unfixed bodies, but must go out of them, and [it] being [the case that] the tincture of Gold doth in no other metal abound more than in Iron and Copper, as husband and wife, their bodies are destroyed and the tingeing Spirit from thence [is] expelled, which breedeth much blood in the opened, prepared Gold, and by its feeding doth make it volatile. Therefore when the volatile Gold is filled by its meat and drink, it taketh up its own blood, doth dry it up through its own internal fire with [the] help and addition of a moist fire and is again a conquest, which doth fix, nay produceth the highest fixedness, so that the Gold becometh a high fixed Medicine and cannot make a body again by reason of the superabundant blood, except there be added to it a superfluous body into which this [super] abundant fixed blood doth disperse itself, which joined metallic body is penetrated by the exceeding great heat of the fixed blood of the Lion, like fire, [is] cleansed from all impurity and immediately is ripened to a perfect maturity and fixedness.

I now pass to the birth and to the generation, how the *Archeus* doth show and pour forth its power and displayeth it, by which all metallic and mineral forms are exposed to the view and are made formal, palpable and corporeal through the mineral, incomprehensible, flying, fiery Spirits.

First you are to know that all the metals and minerals of the earth have one only matter and one only mother, by which they in general altogether have received their conception and perfect bodily birth. And this matter, which cometh from the centre, doth divide itself in the beginning into three parts to produce some corporeal thing and a certain form of every metal. These three parts are fed and nourished by the elements in the earth out of its body till they become perfect. But the matter, which hath its original from the centre, is framed by the Stars, wrought by the elements and formed by that which is terrestrial and is a known matter and the true mother of metals and minerals and is such a matter and mother out of which man himself hath been conceived, born, nourished and made corporeal, and may be altogether compared to the Middle World;[428] for whatsoever is in the Great World, that is known likewise in the Little and whatsoever is in the Little World, that is likewise in the Great. And thus what is in the Great and Little World together, that is found in the Middle World, which joineth the Great and Little Worlds and is a Soul, which doth unite and copulate the Spirit with the body. This Soul is compared to water and is indeed a right true water, yet doth it not wet like other water, but it is an heavenly water, found dry in a metallic, liquid substance, and a soul-like water, which loveth all Spirits and doth unite them with their bodies and bringeth them to a perfect life. Therefore it is certain that the water is a mother of all metals, which, being heated by a warm, aerial fire,[429] as is the Spirit of Sulphur, bringeth life into the terrestrial body through its ripening, wherein the Salt is apparently found, which doth preserve from putrefaction, that nothing may be consumed by corruption. In the beginning and in the birth is wrought first the Quicksilver, which yet lieth open with a subtile coagulation, because there is but little of the Salt communicated to it, whereby it showeth more a spiritual than a corporeal body. Other metals, which are all derived from its essence and have more Salt, which maketh them corporeal, do follow after this. I begin with the Spirit of Mercury.

OF THE SPIRIT OF MERCURY

All visible and palpable things are made out of the Spirit of Mercury, which is beyond all the terrestrial things of the whole world, and all things are made out of it and have their original from it. For herein is all to be found that can do all that the Artist doth desire to enquire into. It is the principle to work metals, being made a spiritual Essence, which is a mere Air, and flyeth to and fro without wings and is a moving wind, which, after its expulsion out of its habitation by Vulcan, is driven into its Chaos, into which it entereth again and doth resolve itself into the elements, where it is attracted by the Stars after a magnetical manner, out of love, from whence it went forth and was wrought out before, because it desireth to be united again with its like. But when this Spirit of Mercury can be taken and made corporeal, it doth then resolve itself into a body and becometh a clear, fair and transparent water, which is a true spiritual water and the first Mercurial Root of minerals and metals, spiritual, unperceivable, incombustible, without any commixtion of the terrestrial aquosity. It is that heavenly water of which much hath been written. For by the Spirit of Mercury all metals may be, if need requireth, dissolved, opened and without any corrosive reduced or resolved into their first matter. This Spirit reneweth both men and beast[s] like the Eagle,[430] consumeth whatsoever is bad and produceth a great age to a long life.

To declare further the Essence, matter and form of this Spirit of Mercury, I must tell you that its Essence is Soul-like, its matter spiritual and its form terrestrial, which yet must be understood by some incomprehensible thing.[431]

Touching the beginning of this Spirit of Mercury, this is needless to know because it is of no benefit, nor can it do you any good. But observe that its beginning is supernaturally from Heaven, the Stars and Elements, granted in the beginning of the first Creation to enter further into a terrestrial being. And because this is needless as I have told you, leave that which is heavenly to the Soul and apprehend it by faith. That which is of the Stars, leave likewise alone, because such impressions of the Stars are invisible and incomprehensible. The Elements have already brought forth this Spirit perfect into the World, through the nourishment of it, therefore do not meddle with them either, for no man can make any Element, but the Creator alone; and insist upon thy Spirit already produced, which is both formal and not formal, comprehensible and incomprehensible and yet doth appear visibly, and you have the first matter, out of which are grown all metals and minerals and is one only thing and such a matter which doth unite itself with the Sulphur of Venus or Copper and is coagulated with the Salt of Mars, so that it becometh one body and a perfect Medicine of all metals, not only to generate [them] in the beginning in the earth, as in the great world,[432] but also by [the] help of a moist fire to change and transmute [them], together with the augmentation, in the little world. Let this not seem strange to you, because the Most High hath thus permitted it and Nature hath wrought it.

But [as to] how the Archaeus worketh further by the Spirit of Mercury in the earth, you are to understand that after the spiritual seed is framed from above by the impression of the Stars and fed and nourished through the Elements, this seed is changed into and is become a mercurial water: as in the beginning the great world[433] likewise was made of nothing;[434] for the Spirit moved upon the water and thus was this cold, waterish and terrestrial creature revived to life by an heavenly warmth.[435] It[436] was in the great world the power and the operation of the Light of Heaven;[437] in the little world likewise, the power of God and the operation by His Divine and Holy Breath[438] to work in the earth. Furthermore the Almighty did grant and ordain means for the performing of the same that the creature might get power to work upon another creature[439] and one might help and promote the other for the forming and perfecting of all the works of the Lord. Thus was granted to the earth an influence to generate by the Luminaries of Heaven and likewise an internal heat to warm and to ripen that which was too cold for the earth by reason of its aquosity. And thus to every creature a peculiar Genius [is granted] according to its kind, that so there is raised a subtile, sulphureous steam by the starry heaven, not a common, but another, clarified, cleaned and pure steam, separated from others, which doth unite itself with the mercurial substance, by which warm property in a long time the humidity is dried up by little and little and then the Soul-like property,[440] being joined with it, which giveth the body and balsam of maintenance and worketh before too upon the earth by a spiritual and starry influence. Thus happeneth, then, a generation of metals according to the commixtion of the three principles and according as they take in more or less of these three, so the body is formed. If so be the Spirit of Mercury is directed and formed from above upon animals, then there is produced an animal being,[441] but if it seizeth upon vegetables, a vegetable work is brought forth. And if it falls upon minerals, by reason of its infused nature there will spring thence minerals and metals. Nevertheless everyone is differently wrought, the animals by another form by themselves, the vegetables after a manner proper to themselves and the minerals likewise on another fashion, every one after a singular way. Now I shall faithfully discover how this Spirit of Mercury may be had and obtained, the manner how to prepare it, that it may cure diseases and change and alter all metals of the ignoble kind, as they are generated in the little world by a transmutation and augmentation of their seed.

Eighty-First Sheet

Take, in the Name of the Lord, red mineral Quicksilver which looketh like Cinnabar and the best mineral Gold that can be gotten. Take an equal quantity of them both and grind them together before they have been in any fire; pour upon them an oil of Mercury made by itself out of the common, putrefied and sublimed Quicksilver; digest them for a month and you will have an extraction which is more heavenly then terrestrial. Distil gently this extraction *in Balneo Mariae* and the phlegm cometh over and the ponderous oil remaineth in the bottom, which taketh up into itself all metals in a moment. Add to this three times the quantity of Spirit of Wine, circulate it in a pelican till it becometh blood-red and hath recovered an incomparable sweetness. Pour off the Spirit of Wine and add to it fresh Spirit of Wine. Repeat this so long till the whole matter be dissolved into an exceeding sweet and ruby colour[ed], transparent liquor, which mingle afterwards together. Pour it upon white, calcined Tartar and distil it with a strong fire in ashes and the Spirit of Wine remaineth behind with the Tartar, but the Spirit of Mercury cometh over. This Spirit of Mercury being mixed with the Spirit of Sulphur Solis, together with its Salt, whosoever shall bring them over joined and united together, that they may not be separated *in infinitum*, he will have such a work (if so be it doth receive its Ferment in a due measure and prefixed term, with Gold, by a solution, and is brought in its proper maturity to a *plusquam* perfection) to which nothing may be compared for the preventing of diseases and poverty. This Spirit of Mercury cureth the dropsy, consumption, gout, stone, French pox and all other lasting sores. It is the only Key to make the corporeal Gold[442] potable.

OF THE SPIRIT OF COPPER

Venus is clothed with a heavenly Sulphur, which doth far exceed the Splendour of the Sun, because there is found much more Sulphur in her than in Gold. But learn what the matter is of the said Sulphur of Gold, which dwelleth and reigneth abundantly in Venus. [It] is a flying and very hot Spirit, which can search and penetrate all, as also digest, ripen and bring to maturity, namely [bring] the imperfect metals into [the] perfect. If you ask how the Spirit of Copper can ripen and bring to perfection other imperfect metals, it being itself, in its body, imperfect and not fixed, I answer that this Spirit cannot have or hold in Copper a fixed body for an habitation; therefore the habitation being burned by fire the guest goeth out of it likewise and must leave his habitation with impatience, for he dwelleth therein like an hireling. But in the fixed body of Gold he hath a protection that nothing can drive him out without the sentence of a peculiar Judge, because he hath taken possession like an heir and hath taken root in that fixed body [so] that [he] cannot be cast out so easily. The tincture which Venus hath obtained is likewise to be found in Mars, yea much more powerful, higher and more excellent[443] for Mars is the husband, Venus the wife. This tincture is likewise to be found in Verdigris and Vitriol as in a mineral, of which a volume might be writ; and in all things there is found a Sulphur which doth burn and yet another Sulphur which doth not burn, which is a wonderful work. The one is white, the other red in the operating birth, but the right and true Sulphur is incombustible, for it is a mere and true Spirit, out of which is prepared an incombustible oil and [it] is indeed the Sulphur out of which the Sulphur of Gold, out of one and the same root, is made and prepared.

This Sulphur may be very well called and christened the Sulphur of the Wise, because in it is found all wisdom, [444] if you except the Mercurial Spirit, which is to be preferred,[445] and with which it, together with the Salt[446] of Mars[447] must be united through a spiritual copulation[448] and [these] three may be brought to a correspondency and be exalted into one operation.[449]

This Spiritual Sulphur doth likewise and in the same manner derive its original from the Upper Region,[450] as the Spirit of Mercury doth, but with another form and fashion, whereby the Stars do show a separation in fixed and unfixed, in tinged and not tinged things. The tincture doth consist only in the Spirit of Copper and chiefly of its consort[451] and is a mere steam, stinking and of a very ill scent in the beginning. And this must be resolved in a liquid manner, that the stinking, incombustible oil may be prepared out of it. This oil is easily joined with the Spirit of Mercury and do[es] soon take up all metallic bodies, being first prepared according to the account I formerly declared. Venus hath much Sulphur; she hath been, together with Mars, digested and ripened sooner than any other metals, but because they have had but little help from the inconstant Mercury, being he had no room left him to work harder, by reason of superabundant Sulphur, they could not receive or obtain a melioration of their unfixed bodies. Now I will discover a mystery to you, that Gold, Venus and Mars have in them one and the same Sulphur, one tincture and the same matter of their tincture, which matter of the tincture is a Spirit, a Mist and a Fume, which hath penetrated and doth penetrate all bodies. If you can bring it into captivity and do accuate it with the Spirit which is found in the Salt of Mars and then do join with the same the Spirit of Mercury according to their weight and do separate them from all

Eighty-Second Sheet

impurity, that they become sweet and sweet-smelling, without any corrosive, you have then a Medicine to which nothing in the world may be compared. If you ferment this Medicine with the shining Sun you have made an ingress which is penetrant to work and to transmute all metals.

Lastly take notice that the root of the philosophical Sulphur, which is an heavenly Spirit, together with the root of the spiritual, supernatural Mercury and the principle of the supernatural Salt, is in one and is found in one matter, out of which the Stone, which hath been found before me, is made, and not in many things although the Mercury be drawn by itself by all the philosophers and the Sulphur by itself, besides the Salt apart,[452] that so [it may appear that] Mercury is found in one and the Sulphur in one and the Salt in one. Notwithstanding all this do I tell you that this is to be understood of their superfluity, which is found [al]most in every one — and particularly in many ways may be used profitably and prepared to a Medicine and [for the] transmutation of metals. But the universal, as the greatest treasure of terrestrial knowledge and wisdom and of all the three principles, is one only thing and is found in one only thing and is drawn out of it, which can reduce all metals into one only thing and is the true Spirit of Mercury and the Soul of Sulphur, joined together with the spiritual Salt, enclosed under one heaven and dwelling in one body; and [it] is the Dragon and the Eagle; it is the King and the Lion; it is the Spirit and the body, which must tinge the body of Gold to be a Medicine, whereby it getteth abundant power to tinge others its consorts.

Concerning the generation of Copper, observe that Copper is generated out of much Brimstone, but its Mercury and Salt are equal in the same, for there is neither more nor less in quantity of one and the other to be found. Now because the Brimstone doth exceed in quantity the Salt and Mercury, there ariseth from thence a great tingeing redness, which great redness hath so possessed the metal that the Mercury could not perfect its fixedness, that a more fixed body might have been produced out of it. You are further to know that the form of Venus' body is of the same condition that a tree is which hath and doth yield abundance of Gum, as is the pine and fir-tree, with other sorts of trees, which Gum is the Sulphur of the tree, which drives out sometimes this Gum at the sides of it by reason of its too great abundance and because it cannot harbour it all. Such a tree now, that is tinged with so much fatness by Nature and the ripening of the elements, burneth and taketh fire immediately; neither is it heavy and [it] is never so durable as oak and the like hard wood, which is solid and compact and hath not his pores so open[453] as that sort of light wood, that the

Brimstone might abundantly reign in it. But therefore hath the oak wood more Mercury and a better Salt than the pine or fir-tree. And such wood is never so much apt to swim upon the water as the fir-tree is, because it is [so] close, solid and compact that the air in it cannot bear it up. The same is to be understood of metals, but especially of Gold, which, by reason of its much fixed and well ripened Quicksilver, hath a most solid, compact, close, fixed and invincible body, to which neither fire nor water, neither air nor any putrefaction of the earth can do any hurt because its pores are closed up and the corrupting power of the elements cannot injure it. Which fixedness and solid and compact conjunction do demonstrate its natural ponderosity, which is not to be found or proved in other metals, which may be discerned not only by weighing it in a pair of scales, but you will find it likewise if you put but a scruple of pure Gold upon a hundred pound weight of Quicksilver, it will fall presently to the bottom, whereas all other ponderous metals laid upon Quicksilver swim upon it and do not sink to the bottom because their pores are more largely extended that the air or wind may pass through them to bear them up.

Concerning the Spirit of Venus or Copper in physick, you are, in fine, to observe that it is found very necessary and wholesome in its virtue and efficacy; not only that Spirit that lieth *in primo Ente*, but that Spirit likewise which is found in the last matter. Its virtue, power and operation is such that in the rising of the Mother it is to be preferred before any Medicine whatsoever; also against the falling sickness, the dropsy, the stone. If you have a special care of this Spirit of Copper it will work such wonders both inwardly and outwardly as will be accounted of all incredible and supernatural.

Eighty-Third Sheet

To conclude, the Spirit of copper is a hot Spirit, penetrant and searching, consuming all the bad humours and phlegm both in men and metals and may justly be accounted the Crown of physick. It is very fiery and piercing, incombustible yet spiritual and without form and, therefore, is capable, like a Spirit, to further in particular the ignition, digestion and ripening of things without a form.

OF THE GENERATION OF MARS, ITS SPIRIT AND TINCTURE

Mars and Venus have one and the same Spirit and tincture as the Gold and other metals have. Though this Spirit be found in every metal, in some [there is] a greater, in some a smaller quantity. It is undeniable and confessed of all that there are divers men and divers opinions, although men in the beginning are made out of one first matter and generated and born out of one seed, yet there is a manifold difference of their opinions because the operation of the Stars hath occasioned this and not without a cause. For the influence of the Great World worketh the other (namely the difference of opinions) after itself in the Little World, because all the opinions, nature and thoughts, together with the whole complexion of man, do derive their original from the influence of the Stars of Heaven and do show themselves according to the Planets and Stars, where nothing can withstand nor obstruct such an influence because the generation of their perfection is already performed and brought to a period or finished. For example, a man is naturally inclined to study, one hath a mind to Divinity, another for the study of the Law, the third for Physick, the fourth will be a Philosopher. Besides all this, there are many wits that have a natural inclination for mechanical arts, as one turneth a limner, another a goldsmith, this man a shoemaker, that man a tailor, another a carver and so forth. All this happeneth by the influence of the Stars, whereby the imagination is strengthened and founded supernaturally, wherein it resolveth to continue; as we do find if a man hath once taken up a resolution in his mind and laid a foundation upon it, that no man is able to bring or keep him from it, that he should not so obstinately stand upon it, death only excepted, which at last closeth up all. The same is undertood of chemists and Alchemists, who, having got once into the secrets of Nature, do not intend to give them over so easily except they have more exactly searched Nature and wholly absorbed[454] and finished the study thereof, which yet is no easy matter. Thus you are likewise to understand of metals that according as the infusion and imagination happeneth from above, so happeneth the form likewise; although metals are altogether called metals and are indeed metals, yet as you have understood by divers opinions of men, which are altogether men out of one matter, there may be manifold and divers metals, of which one hath got an hot and dry, another a cold and moist, another a mixed complexion and nature. Therefore because the metal of Mars hath before others been ordered by a gross Salt in the greatest quantity in its degree, its body is the hardest, most inflexible, strongest and coarsest which Nature hath thus appropriated to it. It containeth the least part of Mercury and little more it hath of Sulphur but the greatest part of Salt; and from this mixture is sprung its corporeal being and [it] is thus born into the world with the help of the elements. Its Spirit is in operation equal to other Spirits, but if the true and right Spirit of Iron can be discerned, I assure you one grain of its Spirit or quintessence, taken and administered in Spirit of Wine, comforteth and strengtheneth a man's heart, mind and courage not to fear his enemies. It stirreth up a lion-like heart within to fight Venus' battles. If the conjunction of Mars and Venus doth rightly happen in a certain constellation,[455] they have success, victory and conquest both in love and sorrow, in fight and peace and will continue of one mind though the whole world should bear a spleen and enmity against them. This spirit cureth wonderfully all martial distempers.

This Spirit of Iron, being rightly discerned, hath a secret affinity with the Spirit of Copper, that they may be so joined together that there riseth one only matter from them, of one and the same operation, form, substance and being, which will cure the same distempers and transmute the particulars of metals with profit and honour.

But Iron, together with its virtue, ought properly to be considered in the manner following, that it hath a terrestrial body only in its corporeal form, which body may be used to a great many things, to alter the blood, to outward wounds, to a graduation of Silver and inwardly to the constipation of the body, which yet is not always beneficial to use, neither in a man's body inwardly and outwardly, nor yet as concerning metals, because there is no great advantage to be made *per se* without the known right means, which do belong to Nature's secret knowledge. Observe one thing more, that the Loadstone and the true Iron are almost of one and the same use in bodily distempers and are almost of one and the same nature, even as it is according to a divine, spiritual and elemental sense betwixt the body, its Soul and the Chaos out of which the Soul and Spirit are gone; the body is framed last of all out of that composition.

Eighty-Fourth Sheet

OF THE SPIRIT OF GOLD

If you are desirous to get this golden Loadstone, your prayers must be rightly made to God in true knowledge, contrition, sorrow and true humility for to know and learn the three different worlds, which are subject to human reason;[456] as there is the super-celestial world,[457] wherein the immortal Soul[458] keepeth its seat and residence beside its first original[459] and is by God's creation the first moving sensibility, or the first moving sensible Soul[460] which of a supernatural being hath wrought a natural life. And this Soul and this Spirit is the root and the first fountain and the first creature existing in the life of anything[461] and the *primum mobile*,[462] which hath been so much controverted by learned men. Observe likewise the second celestial world[463] and take good notice of it for therein do reign the Planets and all the heavenly stars have their course, virtue and power in this heaven and do perform therein their service, for which God hath placed them there and do work in this their service by their Spirit [on] both minerals and metals.

Out of these two worlds ariseth yet another different world[464], wherein is found and comprehended what the other two worlds have wrought and produced. Out of the first Super-celestial World is derived the fountain of life and of the Soul; from the second Celestial World doth spring the Light of the Spirit[465] and from the third, the Elemental World, cometh the invincible, heavenly yet sensible fire, by which is digested and ripened that which is comprehensible. These three matters and substances do generate and bring forth the form of metals, among which Gold hath the pre-eminency because the sidereal and elemental operation hath mellowed and ripened the Mercury in this metal the more substantially to a sufficient and perfect maturity. And as the seed of a man doth fall into the womb and toucheth the *menstruum* which is its earth, [and as this][466] seed which goeth out of the man into the woman is wrought in both by the Stars and the elements that it may be quite united and nourished by the earth to a generation, so you are likewise to understand that the Soul of metals [is worked upon,] which is conceived by an unperceivable, invisible, incomprehensible, abstruse and supernatural, celestial composition, as out of water and air, which are formed out of the Chaos and then further digested and ripened by that heavenly, elemental light and fire of the Sun, whereby the Stars do move the powers, when its heat in the inward parts of the earth, as in the womb, is perceived. For by the warming property of the Stars above, the earth is unlocked and opened that the infused Spirit of the same may yield food and nourishment and be enabled to generate something as metals, herbs, trees and beasts, where every one particularly bringeth with it its seed for a further multiplication and augmentation. And as the conception of a man is spiritual and heavenly, whose Soul and Spirit, by nourishment of the earth in the mother's womb, are formally brought up to a perfection, so likewise it is to be observed and understood in every particular of metals and minerals. But this is the true secret of Gold, namely to instruct and teach you by an example and similitude, whereby the possibility of Nature and its mystery is to be found in the manner following. It is probably true that the heavenly light of the Sun is of a fiery property and of a fiery being, which the Most High God, as Creator of Heaven and Earth hath granted to it through an heavenly, constant and fixed Sulphureous Spirit for the preservation of its substance, form and body, which creature, through its swiftness is inflamed and set on fire by the air, which inflammation will never be extinguished as long as the motion doth last and the whole created, visible world doth continue and endure, not in the least diminisheth in its power, because there is no combustible matter extant which might be given to it, whose consumption might cause the decay of that great light of heaven. So is Gold by the superior [counterpart] of its essence⁴⁶⁷ thus digested and ripened and is become of such a fixed, invincible nature that nothing at all can hurt it, because the upper fixed Stars have penetrated the lower, that the lower fixed Stars, by reason of the infusion and grant of the upper, need not to give place to their equal because the lower hath received and obtained such a constant fixedness from the upper.⁴⁶⁸

Eighty-Fifth Sheet

I will add another similitude, according to the manner of philosophers, of the great light of heaven and of that small fire, which, being terrestrial, is here kindled every day and is made to burn before our eyes, because that great light hath a magnetical likeness and an attractive, loving power with that same small fire here upon earth, which is yet without form and impalpable and found only spiritual invincible, insensible and incomprehensible. It is remarkable, as it is proved and demonstrated by experience, that that great light of heaven hath a great love for and beareth an affection and inclination to the little fire, which is terrestrial, by reason of the Spirit whereby both are agitated and preserved from their utter ruin and destruction. For do but consider that as soon as the air, through [the] great moisture which it hath attracted, conceiveth any corruption, that so through mists and further coagulation and conjunction clouds are generated, the beams of the Sun are hindered and obstructed that the Sun cannot obtain its reflection nor have its due penetrating and searching power; so likewise this little terrestrial fire doth never burn so clear in dark and rainy weather, neither doth it show itself with that gladness in its operation as when the air is fair, pure and clear. The cause is this, for through the obstacle of the moist air the love is hindered that the attractive power, growing sad, cannot exercise its perfect love and operation as it ought to do, for the contrary element, the aquosity, causeth this obstruction. As now the Sun, that heavenly great light, hath a special communion and love with the small terrestrial fire to attract after a magnetic manner, so likewise hath the Sun and Gold a special correspondency and a peculiar attractive power and love together, because the Sun hath wrought the Gold through the three principles, which have their loadstone, and is nearest of all related to the Sun⁴⁶⁹ and hath attained to the highest degree, so that the three principles are found most mighty and powerful in the same. Next to it is Gold in its corporeal form, because it is framed out of the three principles, but hath its original and beginning from the heavenly and golden loadstone. This is now the greatest wisdom of this world. In this loadstone is and lieth buried the dissolution and opening of all the minerals and metals, their government as also their matter of the first generation and their power as touching health; moreover the coagulation and fixation of metals, together with the operation to cure all diseases. Take a special care of this Key, for it is heavenly, sidereal and elemental, out of which the terrestrial is generated. It is supernatural and natural together and is born out of the Spirit of Mercury, heavenly; out of the Spirit of Sulphur, spiritual; but out of the Spirit of Salt corporeal. Out of this spiritual essence and out of this spiritual matter out of which the Gold first of all is made corporeal into one body, the ancient[470] as well as modern Rosie Crucian philosophers do make potable Gold more substantial than out of Gold itself, which must be made spiritual before the potable Gold can be separated out of it. This Spirit cureth likewise the leprosy [and] the French pox, as being a super-fixed mercurial essence, dryeth up and consumeth the dropsy and all running, open sores, which have afflicted a long time; comforteth the heart and brain; strengtheneth the memory and breedeth good blood.

Thus can the Soul of Gold reduced into water, the Spiritual Essence of Pearls and the Sulphur of Corals, united in one, do such things which to Nature seem otherwise incredible; but because experience confirmeth this truth it is deservedly a cordial in this mortal life to be preferred justly before all other cordials by reason of its wonderful effects. The preparation thereof is this. Take Spirit of Salt and with it extract the Sulphur of Gold. Separate the Oil of Salt from it and rectify the Sulphur of Gold with Spirit of Wine that it may become pleasant without any corrosiveness. Then take the true Oil of Vitriol, made out of Vitriol of Verdigris, dissolve in it Iron; make again a Vitriol out of it and dissolve it again into an Oil or Spirit, which rectify likewise as before with Spirit of Wine. Put them together and draw off the Spirit of Wine from thence. Dissolve the matter which remaineth dry behind in Spirit of Mercury in a due proportion or weight. Circulate and coagulate it. When it becometh constant and fixed without rising any more, you have then, if you ferment it with prepared Gold, a Medicine to cure diseases and to tinge metals.

Eighty-Sixth Sheet

OF THE SPIRIT OF SILVER

The Tincture and Spirit of Silver is of a sky-colour, otherwise it is a[471] waterish Spirit, cold and moist and not so hot in its degree as the Spirit which is found in Gold, Iron or Copper; therefore is Silver more phlegmatic than fiery, although it hath been reduced by fire out of its waterish substance unto a coagulation. In the same manner have the stones likewise received their hardness, fixedness and tincture, as by one and the same influence. In a Diamond is found a fixed and coagulated Mercury, therefore this stone is harder and more fixed than other stones and is not to be broken as they are. In a Ruby is found the tincture of Iron or the Sulphur of Iron. In an Emerald, the tincture of Copper.[472] In a Granite,[473] the soul of Lead. In Pewter [is] the tincture which is found in the stone called *Topasius*. Crystal is attributed to common Mercury and in a Saphire is found the tincture and Sulphur of Silver,[474] yet everything in particular, according to its nature and kind, and in metals likewise according to their form and kind. And when the blue colour is separated and taken away from the Saphire, then is its garment gone and its body is white like a diamond. Thus when Gold hath lost its Soul, it yieldeth then a white body and a fixed white body of Gold, which is called *Luna fixa* by the searching students and novices in this Art.

What hath been said as concerning the stone called Saphire, for your instruction you may apply to the better knowledge of the nature of metals, for this blue Spirit is the Sulphur and Soul out of which Silver hath its life as well in the earth as above the earth by Art, and the white tincture of Silver upon white always, in a magnetical form of that one thing and creature, wherein the *primum ens auri* likewise is found. This Spirit of Silver alone containeth that which will perfectly cure and dispel the dropsy, even as the Spirit of Gold and of Mercury can radically cure the consumption so that even the centre itself of the said distemper may not be found.

But that Silver is not so provided in its degree with a hot substance and quality in the veins of the earth, but is subjected to a waterish kind, this fault is to be laid upon the Great Light of Heaven,[475] which by reason of its waterish influence hath planted this quality into the Second Creature[476] and into the second Planet of the earth[477] as into Silver. And though Silver doth carry with it a fixed Mercury or fixed Quicksilver, which is born in it, nevertheless it wanteth the hot fixed Sulphur, which might have exactly dried up and consumed the phlegm, which is the cause it hath not obtained a compact body,[478] except it be done afterwards by Art of the lesser World. And because the body is not solid and compact, by reason of its waterish substance, hence are its pores not well stopped up nor consolidated, that it might have a due ponderosity and endure a fight with its enemies. Which virtues ought altogether to be found in Gold, if so be it must conquer all its foes and endure all the trials without fault.

You are likewise to understand that the first matter of metals must be observed, studied and found out through the discovery of their last matter, which last matter, as there are the absolute and perfect metals, must be divided and separated that it may appear altogether naked to a man's eyes and then there may be learned and known by such a division what the first matter hath been in the beginning, out of which the last matter is made. Observe diligently this Arcanum.[479]

Take the sky-coloured Sulphur of Silver, which hath been extracted out of Silver and rectified by Spirit of Wine; dissolve it according to its weight in the white Spirit of Vitriol and in the sweet scented Spirit of Mercury and coagulate them together through a fixation of fire and you will get the possession of the White Tincture and its Medicine. But if you know the *Primum Mobile* it is then needless, because you may bring the thing to perfection out of one.

OF THE SOUL AND TINCTURE OF PEWTER

The benign Jupiter is almost of a middle nature amongst all the metals. He is neither too hot nor yet too cold, nor too warm nor too moist. He hath not too much of Mercury nor yet of Salt and of Sulphur there is least of all in him.[480] Pewter is found white in its colour, yet of these three principles one doth exceed the other[s] as it hath been clearly discovered in its division according to the true enquiry into Nature's secrets. Out of this composition and mixture of the three principles is generated and wrought and coagulated into a metal and brought to a maturity of perfection benevolent Jupiter. The Spirit of Jupiter doth protect and preserve from all distempers and diseases incident and hurtful to the liver. Its Spirit is naturally, as for its taste, like unto Honey. Its Mercury being made volatile doth get a venomous quality, for its purgeth vehemently and penetrates with violence. Therefore it is not always good that its unlocked Quicksilver should be thus simply used by itself; but if a correction goeth before, it may be very well used with exceeding great usefulness in those distempers and diseases which are immediately subject to his influence; that is to say, when you have taken away from Zadkiel[481] its venomous volatility and it is placed into a better and more fixed state, which doth resist poison. To conclude, if you do extract out of the benign Jupiter his Salt and Sulphur and make Saturn flow very well together with them, Saturn doth get a fixed body, is purified and becometh clear by them and is a total change and real transmutation of Lead into good Pewter, as you will find it upon a most accurate trial. And though this may seem to you not to be true, yet are you to understand that by reason that the Salt of Jupiter is made more Corporeal only by its Sulphur, it likewise hath received an efficacy and power to penetrate Saturn, as the vilest and most volatile metal, and to bring it to its own substance by making

Eighty-Seventh Sheet

it better and you will really find it to be so.

OF THE SPIRIT OF SATURN OR TINCTURE OF LEAD

Saturn, to generate his metal, which is Lead, is placed in the Upper Heaven, above all the Stars. But in the lower parts of the earth he doth keep the lowest degree.[482] As the uppermost light of Saturn is mounted to the highest altitude of all the lights of Heaven,[483] so likewise in imitation of the same hath Nature given leave and permitted that his children of the Lower Region have retired themselves by Vulcan to those of their quality according as Saturn hath been moved. For the Upper Light is the cause of it and hath generated an unfixed body of Lead through which go and are drawn open pores, that the Air can have its passage through this Saturnine body and bear itself up. But the fire easily worketh upon and consumeth it because the body is not solid and compact by reason of its unfixedness. This is well to be observed by a serious enquirer into all things because there is a vast difference betwixt fixed and unfixed bodies and then the causes of this fixedness and unfixedness. And though Saturn is of a singular ponderosity before other metals, yet will you observe that when they are poured out together after their conjunction in the melting of them, the other metals will always fall to the bottom, as, likewise, it happeneth with other metals by pouring them through Antimony. Whereby it doth appear that other metals have a more solid and compact body than Saturn can raise, because it must give place to other metals, make room for them and yield the victory; for it vanisheth away and is consumed together with those unconstant and unfixed metals. For there are the three grossest qualities of the three principles in Saturn and by reason that its Salt is altogether fluid in comparison to other metals and planets, therefore is likewise its body more fluid, inconstant, unfixed and more volatile than any metallic body.

[As for] how Saturn doth proceed towards his regeneration, you are to know that as common water, through natural cold, by the alteration of the Upper Heaven, is congealed so that it becometh a coagulated ice, so likewise it is demonstrated that Lead is coagulated and made corporeal reason of the great cold which is found in its Salt before any other Salt. The coagulated ice is resolved through warmth and so is the coagulated Lead made fluid by fire. It hath most Mercury in it, yet inconstant and volatile; but less of Sulphur and, therefore, according to the small quantity of the same, its cold body cannot be heated; and least of all of Salt, but fluid; otherwise the Iron would be more liquid and malleable than Saturn if the Salt alone could impart both the malleableness and fluidity, because Iron doth carry with it more Salt than any other metal. And being there is a difference to be found in these things, you must carefully observe how metals are to be distinguished.

All the philosophers, indeed, besides myself, have writ that the Salt causeth the coagulation and the body of every metal; and this is true; but I shall show by an example how this is to be understood. *Alumen plumosum* is reputed and probably accounted to be a mere Salt, and herein may be compared to Iron, which Salt of the aforesaid *Alumen plumosum* is nevertheless found to be as a matter and not liquid as Iron. On the contrary Vitriol doth show itself like Salt in a small quantity, yet liquid and open, and therefore its Salt cannot cause so hard a congelation in its appropriated metal as that other Salt doth. Although all Salts of metals are grown out of one root and one seed, yet there is a difference of their three principles to be observed. As one herb differs from the other, and likewise in men and beasts a difference is found as concerning the original of their qualities and their three principles, where one herb has something more of this, another herb more of that kind, which is likewise to be understood of men and beasts. The Soul of Lead is of a sweet quality, as also the Soul of Jupiter, and yet sweeter, so that as for sweetness there is hardly anything comparable to it, being first highly purified by separation, that the pure being very well severed from the impure there may follow a compleat perfection in the operation. Otherwise the Spirit of Lead is naturally cold and dry, therefore I do advise both men and women not to make too much use of it, for it over cooleth human nature, that their seed cannot perfect or perform its natural operation, nor is it good for the spleen and bladder. It doth attract the phlegmatic quality, which breedeth melancholy in men. For Saturn is a governor and such a melancholy one whereby a man is upheld and strengthened in his melancholy. Therefore if its Spirit be used, one melancholy Spirit doth attract the other, whereby a man's body is freed and released from its infused melancholy. Outwardly is the Soul of Saturn very wholesome in all sores and wounds, whether they be old or green, whether they happen by thrusting, cutting or naturally by means incident, so that hardly any other metal will do the like. It is a cooling thing in all hot and swelled members, but to eat away and to lay a foundation for healing in all corrupt and putrefied sores, which have their issuing forth from within, there the nobel Venus hath the pre-eminency because Copper is hot in its essence to exiccate and dry up, but Lead, on the contrary, is found to be cold in its essence.

Eighty-Eighth Sheet

That heavenly light of the Sun is much hotter than the light of the Moon, because the moon is much lesser than the Sun, which doth comprehend the eight[h] part of magnitude in the circle of measuring and dividing. And if the moon should exceed the Sun in this magnitude of the eight[h] part, as the Sun doth exceed the Moon, then all the fruit and whatsoever groweth upon the earth would be spoiled and there would be continual winter and no summer would be found. But the Eternal Creator hath herein wisely prescribed a certain order and law to His creatures, that the Sun should give light by day and the moon by night and thus be serviceable to all creatures.

Those children which are addicted to the influence of Saturn are melancholy, surly, always murmuring, like old, covetous misers, which do not good to their own bodies and are never satisfied. They use their bodies to hard labour, vex and fret themselves with troublesome thoughts and are very seldom so cheerful as to recreate themselves with other people, neither do they care much for natural love of women although handsome.

To sum up all, Saturn is generated out of little Sulphur, little Salt and much immature and gross Mercury, which Mercury is to be accounted like scum or froth which swimmeth upon the water in comparison to that Mercury which is found in Gold, being of a much hotter degree. Hence it is that the Mercury of Saturn hath not so fresh and so running a life as that which is made out of Gold, because more heat is found in this [latter], to which the running life oweth its original. Therefore it is likewise to be observed in the inferior world of the little Vulcan, in the augmentation and transmutation of metals, what description I have given you of these three principles of Saturn concerning their original quality and complexion.

And everyone is to know that no transmutation of any metal can arise from Saturn by reason of its great cold, except the coagulation of Mercury, [which can be achieved] because the cold Sulphur of Lead can quench and take away the hot, running Spirit of Quicksilver if the process be rightly performed; therefore it is rightly observable that the method be so kept that the theory may agree with the practice and concur in a certain measure and concord. Wherefore you must not altogether reject Saturn, nor vilify and disparage it, for its nature and virtues are but known to a few. For the Stone of the Philosophers hath the first beginning of its heavenly, resplendent tincture only from this metal and by the infusion of this Planet is the Key of Fixedness delivered to it through putrefaction, because that out of the yellow there cannot come any red thing except there be first made at the beginning of the black a white one.

To conclude these secrets I shall here insert Dr John Frederick Helvetius' letter to Dr John Dee,[484] how in less than a quarter of an hour, by the smallest proportion of the Philosopher's Stone, a great piece of common Lead was totally transmuted into the purest Gold by Elias Artista.

Dear Doctor,

Eighty-Ninth Sheet

The 27th day of December 1666, in the afternoon came a stranger to my house at the Hague, in a plebeian habit, honest gravity and serious authority; of a mean stature, a little, long face, with a few pock-holes, and most black hair, not at all curled, a beardless chin, about forty-four years of age (as I guessed) and born in north Holland. After salutation he beseeched me with great reverence to pardon his rude access, being a great lover of the pyrotecnian Art; adding [that] he formerly endeavoured to visit me with a friend of his and told me he had read some of my small treatises and particularly against the sympathetic powder of Sir Kenelm Digby[485] and observed my doubtfulness of the philosophical mystery, which caused him to take this opportunity and asked me if I could not believe such a Medicine was in Nature, which could cure all diseases unless the principal parts (as lungs, liver etc.) were perished or the predistinated time of death was come. To which I replied, I never met with an Adept, or saw such a Medicine, though I read much of it in your letter which you sent me[486] and have wished for it. Then I asked if he were a physician, but he, preventing my question said he was a founder of Brass, yet from his youth learned many rare things in chemistry of a friend, particularly the manner to extract out of metals many medicinal Arcana by force of fire, and was still a lover of it. After another large discourse of experiments in metals, this Elias asked me if I could know the Philosopher's Stone when I see it. I answered not at all, though I had read much of it in Paracelsus, Helmont, Ripley, Heydon etc., yet dare I not say I could know the philosophic matter. In the interim he took out of his pouch a neat, ivory box and out of it took three ponderous pieces, or small lumps of the Stone, each of them about the bigness of a small walnut, transparent, of a pale brimstone colour[487] whereunto did stick the internal scales of the crucible, wherein it appeared this most noble substance was melted. The value of them might be judged worth about twenty tons of Gold, which, when I had greedily seen and handled almost a quarter of an hour, and drawn from the owner many rare secrets of its admirable effects in human and metallic bodies and other magical properties, I returned him this Treasure of Treasures, truly with a most sorrowful mind, after the custom of those who conquer themselves, yet (as was but just) very thankfully and humbly. I further desired to know why the colour was yellow and not red ruby colour or purple as philosophers write; he answered that was nothing, for the matter was mature and ripe enough. Then I humbly requested him to bestow a little piece of the Medicine on me in perpetual memory of him, though but the quantity of a coriander or hemp seed. He presently answered: Oh no, no this is not lawful though thou wouldest give me as many ducats in Gold as would fill this room, not for the value of the matter, yet for some particular consequences. Nay, if it were possible, said he, that fire could be burnt of fire, I would rather cast all this substance into the fiercest of flames. But after, he demanding if I had another private chamber, whose prospect was from the public street, I presently conducted him into the best furnished room backwards, where he entered without wiping his shoes (full of snow and dirt) according to the custom of Holland, then not doubting but that he would bestow part thereof, or some great secret treasure, on me, but in vain; for he asked for a little piece of Gold and pulling of his cloak or pastoral habit, opened his doublet, under which he wore five pieces of Gold hanging in green silk ribbons, as large as the inward round of a small pewter trencher, and this Gold so far excelled mine that there was no comparison for flexibility and colour; and these figures[488] with the inscriptions engraven [upon them] were the resemblance of them, which he granted me to write out.

I being herewith affected with great admiration desired to know where and how he came by them, who answered; An outlandish friend, who dwelt some days at my house (giving out he was a lover of this Art and came to reveal this Art to me) taught me various Arts. First how out of ordinary stones and crystals to make Rubies, Chrysolites and Saphires etc., much fairer than the ordinary, and how in a quarter of an hour to make *Crocus Martis*, of which one dose would infallibly cure the pestilential dysentry (or bloody flux) and how to make a metallic liquor most certainly to cure all kind of dropsies in four days, as also a limpid, clear water, sweeter than honey, by which in two hours of itself in hot sand it would extract the tincture of garnets, corals, glasses and such like more, [all of] which I Helvetius did not observe, my mind being drawn beyond those bounds to understand how such a noble juice might be drawn out of the metals. Moreover he told me his said master caused him to bring a glass full of rain water and fetch some refined silver, laminated in thin plates, which therein was dissolved within a quarter of an hour, like ice when heated. And presently [continued this Elias] he drank to me the half and I pledged him the other half, which had not so much taste as sweet milk, whereby I became

Ninetieth Sheet

very light hearted. I thereupon asked him if this was a philosophic drink and wherefore we drank the potion. He replied I ought not to be so curious. And after he told me that by the said master's directions he took a piece of a leaden pipe, gutter or cistern and [this] being melted he put a little sulphureous[489] powder out of his pocket and once again[490] put a little more on the point of a knife, and after a great blast of the bellows in [a] short time poured it on the red stones of the kitchen chimney, which [poured out matter] proved most excellent pure Gold, which, he said, brought him into such a trembling amazement that he could hardly speak. But his master thereupon encouraged him saying, cut for thyself the sixteenth part of this for a memorial and the rest give away among the poor, which he did. And he distributed as great an alms, as he affirmed (if my memory fail not) to the church of Sparronda;[491] but whether he gave it several times or once, or in the golden mass or in Silver coin I did not ask. At last, said he, going on with the story of his master, he taught me thoroughly this almost Divine Art.

As soon as this his history was finished, I most humbly begged he would show me the effect of transmutation to confirm my faith therein, but he dismissed me for that time in such a discreet manner that I had a denial, but, withal, promising to come again at three weeks end and show me some curious Arts in the fire and the manner of projection provided it was lawful, without prohibition. And at the end of three weeks end he came and invited me abroad for an hour or two and in our walks had discourses of divers of Nature's secrets in the fire; but he was very sparing of the great Elixir, gravely asserting that was only to magnify the most sweet fame and name of the most glorious God and that few men endeavoured to sacrifice to Him in good works; and this he expressed as a pastor or minister of a church. But now and then I kept his ears open, interesting him to show me the metallic transmutation, desiring him also that he would think me so worthy [as] to eat and drink and lodge at my house, which I did so sagely that scarce any suitor could plead more to obtain his mistress from his corrival. But he was of so fixed and steadfast a spirit that all my endeavours were frustrate, yet I could not forbear to tell him further that I have a fit laboratory and things ready and fit for an experiment and that a promised favour was a kind of debt. Yea true, said he, but I promised to teach thee at my return with this proviso, if it were not forbidden.

When I perceived all this in vain, I earnestly craved but a most small crumb or parcel of his powder or Stone to transmute four grains of lead to Gold and at last out of his philosophical commiseration he gave me a crumb as big as a rape or turnip seed, saying, Receive this small parcel of the greatest treasure of the world, which truly few kings or princes have ever known or seen. But I said, this perhaps will not transmute four grains of lead, whereupon he bid me deliver it him back, which, in hope of a greater parcel, I did. But he, cutting half off with his nail, flung it into the fire and gave me the rest wrapped neatly up in blue paper, saying, it is yet sufficient for thee. I answered him (indeed with a most dejected countenance) Sir, what means this, the other being too little, you give me now less? He told me, if thou canst not manage this, yet for its great proportion for so small a quantity of Lead, then put into the crucible two drams or half an ounce or a little more of the Lead, for there ought to be no more of the Lead be put in the crucible than the Medicine can work upon and transmute. So I gave him great thanks for my diminished treasure, concentrated truly in the superlative degree and put the same charity up into my little box saying I meant to try in the next day, nor would I reveal it to any. Not so, [saith he] for we ought to divulge all things to the Children of Art which may tend to the singular honour of God, that so they may live in the Theosophical truth and not all die sophistically. After I made my thanks to him [I confessed] that while the mass of his Medicine was in my hands I endeavoured to scrape a little of it away with my nail and could not forbear, but scratched off nothing, or so very little that it was but an indivisible atom, which, being purged from my nail and wrapped in a paper, I projected upon Lead, but found no transmutation, but almost the whole mass of Lead flew away and the remainder turned to a mere glassy earth, at which unexpected passage he smilingly said, Thou art more dextrous to commit a theft than to apply thy Medicine; for if thou hadst only wrapped up thy stolen prey in yellow wax, to preserve it from rising fumes of Lead, it would have penetrated to the bottom of the Lead and transmuted it to Gold; but having cast it into the fumes, partly by [the] violence of the vaprous fumes and partly by sympathetic alliance, it carried thy Medicine quite away. For Gold, Silver, Quicksilver and the like metals are corrupted and turn brittle like glass by the vapour of Lead. Whereupon I brought him my crucible, wherein it was done, and instantly he perceived a most beautiful, saffron-like tincture stick[ing] on the sides and promised to come next morning by nine in the morning and then [he] would show me my error and that the said Medicine should transmute the Lead into Gold. Nevertheless I constantly prayed him in the interim to be pleased to declare only for my present instruction, if the philosophic work cost much or required long time. My friend, my friend (said he) thou art too curious to know all things in an instant, yet will I discover

Ninety-First Sheet

so much that neither the great charge nor length of time can discourage any, for as for the matter out of which our magistery is made, I would have thee know there are only two metals and minerals out of which it is prepared; but in regard the Sulphur of Philosophers, [it] is much more plentiful and abundant in the minerals, therefore it is made out of the minerals. Then I asked again, what was the *Menstruum* and whether the operation of working were done in glasses or crucibles. He answered [that] the *Menstruum* was a heavenly virtue, by whose benefit only the wise men dissolve the earthly metallic body[492] and [that] by such a solution is easily and instantly brought forth the most noble Elixir of philosophers. But in a crucible is all the operation done and performed from the beginning to the very end, in an open fire; and all the whole work is no longer from the very first to the very last than four days and the whole work is no more charge than three florins. And further neither the mineral out of which, nor the Salt by which it was performed was of any great price. And when I replied [that] the philosophers affirm in their writings that seven or nine months at the least are required for this work, he answered. Their writings are only to be understood by the true Adeptists, wherefore concerning time they would write nothing certain. Nay, without the communication of a true Adept Philosopher, not one student can find the way to prepare this great magistery, for which cause I warn and charge [you] as a friend not to fling away thy money and goods to hunt out this Art, for thou shalt never find it. To which I replied, Thy master (though unknown) showed it thee, so mayest thou perchance discover something to me, that, having overcome the rudiments, I may find the rest with little difficulty according to the old saying that it is easier to add to a foundation than begin anew. He answered, In this Art tis quite otherwise, for unless thou knowest the thing from the head to the heel, from the beginning to the end, thou knowest nothing; and though I have told thee enough, yet thou knowest not how the philosophers do make and break open the glassy Seal of Hermes, in which the Sun sends forth a great splendour with his marvellous coloured metallic rays, and in which looking glass the eyes of Narcissus beheld the transmutable metals;[493] for out of those rays the true Adept Philosophers gather their fire, by whose help the volatile metals may be fixed into the most permanent metals, either Gold or Silver. But enough at present, for I intend (God Willing) once more tomorrow at the ninth hour (as I said) to meet and discourse further on this philosophical subject, and shall show you the manner of projection. And having taken his leave he left me sorrowfully expecting him; but the next day he came not, nor even since, only he sent an excuse at half an hour past nine that morning, by reason of his great business, and promised to come at three in the afternoon, but never came, nor have I heard of him since, wherefor I began to doubt of the whole matter.

Nevertheless my wife (who was a most curious student and enquirer into the art whereof that worthy man had discoursed) came soliciting and vexing me to make an experiment of that little spark of his bounty in that Art, whereby to be the more assured of the Truth, saying to me, unless this be done I shall have no rest nor sleep all this night. But I wished her to have patience till next morning to expect this Elias, saying perhaps he will return again to show us the right manner. In the meantime (she being so earnest) I commanded a fire to be made, thinking (alas) now is the man (though so divine in discourse) found guilty of falsehood, and secondly attributing the error of my projecting the grand theft of his powder in the dirt of my nail to his charge, because it transmuted not the Lead that time, and lastly because he gave me too small a proportion of his said Medicine (as I thought) to work upon so great a quantity of Lead as he pretended and appointed for it, saying further to myself, I fear, I fear this man hath deluded me. Nevertheless my wife wrapped the said matter in wax and I cut half an ounce or six drams of old Lead and put [it] into a crucible in the fire, which being melted, my wife put in the same Medicine made up into a small pill or button, which presently made such a hissing and bubbling in its perfect operation that within a quarter of an hour all the mass of Lead was totally transmuted into the best and finest Gold, which made us all amazed as [if] planet-struck. An[d] indeed had I lived in Ovid's age there could not have been a rarer metamorphisis than this, by the Art of Alchemy. Yea, could I have enjoyed Argus' eyes, with a hundred more, I could not sufficiently gaze upon this so admirable and almost miraculous a work of Nature; for the melted Lead (after projection) showed us on the fire the rarest and most beautiful colours imaginable; yea and the greenest colour, which, as soon as I poured [it] forth into an ingot, it got the lively, fresh colour of blood, and, being cold, shined as the purest and most refined, transplendent Gold. Truly I and all standing about me were exceedingly startled and did run with this aurified Lead (being yet hot) unto the Goldsmith, who wondered at the fineness and, after a short trial of touch, he judged it the most excellent Gold in the whole world and offered to give willingly fifty florins for every ounce of it.

Ninety-Second Sheet

The next day a rumour went about the Hague and spread abroad, so that many illustrious persons and students gave me their friendly visits for its sake. Among the rest the General Say-master for examiner of the coins of the Province of Holland, Mr Porelius, who with others earnestly beseeched me to pass some part of it through all their customary trials, which I did, the rather to gratify my own curiosity. Thereupon we went to Mr Broctel, a silversmith, who first tried it *per quartum*, namely he mixed three of four parts of Silver with one part of the said Gold and laminated, filed or granulated it and put a sufficient quantity of *Aqua fort* thereto, which presently dissolved the Silver and suffered the said Gold to precipitate to the bottom, which, being decanted off and the Calx or powder of Gold dulcified with water and then reduced and melted, became excellent Gold. And whereas we feared loss, we found that each dram of the said first Gold [had] yet increased and had transmuted a scruple of the said Silver into Gold by reason of its great and excellent, abounding tincture.

But now doubting further whether the Silver was sufficiently separated from the said Gold, we instantly mingled it with seven parts of Antimony, which we melted and poured into a cone and blowed off the *Regulus* on a test, where we missed eight grains of our Gold. But after we blowed away the rest of the Antimony or superfluous *scoria*, we found nine grains of Gold more for our eight grains missing, yet this was somewhat pale and Silver-like, which easily recovered its full colour afterwards, so that in the best proof of fire, we lost nothing at all of this Gold, but gained as aforesaid. The which proof again I repeated thrice and found it still alike and the said remaining Silver out of the *Aqua fortis* was of the very best flexible Silver that could be, so that in the total the said Medicine (or Elixir) had transmuted six drams and two scruples of Lead and Silver into most pure Gold.

Dear Doctor.[494] I will for a conclusion give you a further testimony of divers illustrious authors of the Arcanum. First Paracelsus in *The Signatures of Natural Things*,[495] fol. 358. This is a true sign of the Tincture of the philosophers, that by its transmuting force all imperfect metals are changed, namely the white into Silver and the red into the best Gold, if the smallest part of it be cast into a crucible upon melted Lead.

Item.[496] For the invicible *Astrum* of metals conquereth all things and changeth them into a nature like to itself. And this Gold and Silver is nobler than that brought out of the metallic mines and out of it may be prepared better medicinal Arcana.

Item. Therefore every Alchemist who hath the *Astrum* of the Sun can transmute all red metals into Gold.

Item. Our Tincture of Gold hath Astral Stars within it. It is a most fixed substance and immutable in the multiplication. It is a powder having the reddest colour, yet the whole corporeal substance is liquid like Resin, transparent like crystal [and] frangible like glass; it is of a Ruby colour and of the greatest weight. Read More of this in Paracelsus' *Heaven of the Philosophers*.[497]

Item. Paracelsus in his *Seventh Book of [the] Transmutations of Natural Things*[498] saith: The Transmutation of metals is a great natural mystery, not against Nature's course nor against God's order, as many falsely judge. For the imperfect metals are [not] transmuted into Gold nor into Silver without the Philosophers' Stone.

Item. Paracelsus in his *Manual of the Medicinal Stone of the Philosophers*[499] saith: Our Stone is a heavenly Medicine and more than perfect, because it cleanseth all filth from the metals.

A second testimony I find in Henry Khunrath in his *Amphitheatre of the Eternal Wisdom*.[500]

I have travelled much and visited those esteemed to know somewhat by experience and not in vain etc. (Amongst whom I call God to witness) I got of one the Universal Green Lion and the Blood of the Lion, that is Gold, not vulgar, but of the philosophers. I have seen it, touched it, tasted it and smelt it. Oh! how wonderful is God in His works. I say they gave me the prepared Medicine, which I most fruitfully used towards my poor neighbour in most desperate cases, and they did sincerely reveal to me the true manner of preparing this Medicine.

Item. This is the wonderful method, which God only hath given me immediately and mediately, yet subordinately through Nature, Fire, Art and Masters' help (as well living as silent) corporeal and spiritual, watching and sleeping.[501]

Ninety-Third Sheet

Item. I write not fables; with thine own hand thou shalt handle and with thine own eyes see the Azoth, namely the universal Mercury of the Philosophers, which alone, with its internal and external fire, is sufficient for thee to get our Stone, nevertheless with a sympathetic harmony being Magic[o]-physically united with the Olympic fire by an inevitable necessity etc.

Item. Thou shalt see the Stone of the Philosophers (our King) go forth of the bed-chamber, of his Glassy Sepulchre, in his glorified body, like a Lord of Lords, from his Throne into the Theatre of the World. That is to say, regenerated and more than perfect, a shining Carbuncle, a most temperate splendour, whose most subtile and depurated parts are inseparably united into one, with a concordial mixture exceedingly equal; transparent like crystal, compact and most ponderous, easily fusible in fire, like resin or wax before the flight of Quicksilver, yet flowing without smoke; entering into solid bodies and penetrating them like oil through paper, dissoluble in every liquor and commiscible with it; friable like glass, in a powder like saffron, but in the whole mass shining red like a Ruby[502] (which redness is a sign of a perfect fixation and fixed perfection); permanently colouring or tingeing, fixed in all trials, yea in the examination of the burning Sulphur itself and the devouring waters and in the most vehement persecution of the fire, always incombustible and permanent as the Salamander.

Item. The Philosophers' Stone, being fermented in its parts in the great world transforms itself into whatsoever it will by the fire.[503] Hence a Son of Art may perceive why the philosophers have given their Azoth the name of Mercury, which adheres to bodies.[504] And further in the same place it is fermented with metals, namely the Stone being in its highest whiteness is fermented with pure Silver to the White, but the Sanguine Stone with pure Gold to the Red, and this is the work of three days.[505]

The Third testimony I take out of [Van] Helmont in the *Book of Eternal Life*.[506]

I have oft seen the Stone and handled it and have projected the fourth part of one grain wrapped in paper upon eight ounces of Quicksilver boiling in a crucible; and the Quicksilver, with a small noise, presently stood still from its flux and was congealed like to yellow wax; and after a flux by blast we found eight ounces wanting eleven grains of the purest Gold. Therefore one grain of this powder would transmute nineteen thousand one hundred and eighty-six parts of Quicksilver into the best Gold; so that this powder is found to be of similary parts among terrestrials and doth transmute infinite plenty of impure metal into the best Gold, uniting with it and so defends it from canker, rust, rottenness and death and make it in a manner immortal against all tortures of fire and art and transfers[507] it to a virginal of Gold, requiring only a fervent heat.

Item.[508] In his *Tree of Life*, fol. 630. I am constrained to believe there is a Gold and Silver-making Stone or powder, for that I have divers times made projection of one grain thereof upon some thousand grains of boiling Quicksilver to a tickling admiration of a great multitude. He who gave me that powder had so much at least as would transmute two hundred thousand pounds worth[509] of Gold.

Item. He gave me about half a grain and thence were transmuted nine ounces and three quarters of Quicksilver into Gold and he who gave it me was but of one evening's acquaintance.

The most noble, expert man in the Art of Fire, Doctor Theodor Retius[510] of Amsterdam, gave me, John Helvetius, a large Medal with this inscription: The Divine Metempsychosis etc. It was of Count Russe[511] his making, of Styria and Carynthia in Germany, of which one grain [of the powder used] transmuted three pound[s] of Quicksilver into pure Gold at all assays. Such a projection was made at Hannau in High Germany.

I cannot here pass by Dr Kuffler[512] in an extract of his Epistle.

First I found (in my laboratory) an *Aqua fortis* and another in the laboratory of Charles de Roy. I poured that *Aqua fortis* upon the Calx of Gold[513] prepared after the vulgar manner and after its third cohobation the tincture of that Gold did rise and sublimed into the neck of the retort, which I mixed with two ounces of Silver precipitated in a common way; and I found that [an] ounce in an ordinary flux transmuted an ounce and a half of the said Silver into the best Gold and the rest was the purest Silver fixed in all examinations of the fire; but after that time I could never find more of the *Aqua fortis*.

And I Helvetius saw this white Gold.

Another rare experiment done at the Hague.

There lived at the Hague [in] 1664 a silversmith named Grill, well exercised in Alchemy, but poor according to the custom of chemists. This Grill got some Spirit of Salt, not of a vulgar preparation, from one Kasper Knotner, to use, as he said, for metals. The which afterwards he poured upon one pound of common Lead in an open glass dish or platter; and after two weeks there appeared a most curious Star of Silver swimming upon it, as if it has been delineated with a pencil and a pair of compasses by some ingenious artist. Whereupon the said [Grill] told us with joy he had seen the Signet Star of the Philosophers, whereof by chance he had read in Basileus.[514] I with many others saw the same to our great admiration, the Lead in the interim remaining on the bottom of an ashy colour. After seven or nine days in July, the Spirit of Salt being exhaled by the heat of the air, the Star settled on the Lead or feces in the bottom and spread itself upon it, which many people saw. At last the said Grill took a part thereof and out of that pound of Lead he found by computation twelve ounces of cupelled Silver and out of that twelve ounces, two ounces of the best Gold. And I Helvetius can show some part that spongeous Lead with part of the Star upon it and also some of the said Silver and Gold. Now whilst this envious,

Ninety-Fourth Sheet

silly Grill, concealing the use, endeavoured to get more of that Spirit of Salt from Knotner, the said Knotner, having forgot what sort it was, or else not finding it, suddenly was shortly afterwards drowned and Grill with his family died of the plague, so that none could make further benefit or trial of the said process[515] afterwards. Indeed it would move admiration that the Lead's inward nature should appear in such a noble outward form by the simple maturation of the said Spirit of Salt; neither is it less wonderful that the Philosophers' Stone should suddenly transmute all metals to Gold and Silver, having its virtue potentially implanted within itself and raised to an active power, as is manifest in Iron touched with the Loadstone.

PART II

Clavis Chymicus

An Explanation of certain Chymical hard Words used in Dr Dee's works Alphabetically Digested.[516]

ALCAEST or ALTAEST. Prepared Mercury or Tartar.[518]   *First*
ALCALI. All manner of Salt extracted out of Ashes or Calx of any   *Sheet*
matter by boiling in lie.[517]
ALCHMYIA. A Separation of what's Impure from a Pure.[519]
ALCOL. A most subtle Powder of anything.[520]
ALEMBROTH. Salt of Mercury of Salt of Philosophers.[521]
ALEMBROT, purified, is Salt of Tartar and the Magistery of it.
ACETUM PHILOSOPHORUM, is a Mercurial Water or otherwise is called Virgin's Milk, wherein metals are dissolved.
ACETUM RADICALE, is Vinegar distilled out of its own root and Matrix and is called the Dissolving Water.
ADAMITA is a certain kind of Tartar.[522]
ALCOOL VINI is the Spirit of Wine rectified.[523]
ALCUBRITH or ALCUR or ALAZAR is the same that Sulphur is.[524]
ALCOFOL or ALCOSOL is Stibium or Antimony.
ALMIZADIR is Verdigris.
ALTEY PLUMBI is the sweet matter of Lead.[525]
AMALGAMA is the making of Gold, Silver or any other metal into a Past[e] with Quicksilver.[526]
ANIMA is our Mercury.
ANONTAGIUS is the Philosophers' Stone.
ANIMA SATURNI is the sweetness of Lead.[527]
ANOTASIER ⎫
ALIOCAB   ⎬ are Salt Armoniack.
ALEMZADAR[528] ⎭
ANTERIT is Mercury.[529]
ANTHONAR or ATHONAR is a furnace[530] or reverberatory.
AQUA CELESTINA is Mercurial Water.[531]
AQUA COELESTIS is rectified Wine, being in some sort made like to the Heaven for Subtilty and pureness.[532]
AQUA PERMANENS is that which is made of two most perfect

metalline bodies by a Philosophic Solution.[533]

AQUA SATURNIA is that which retains in itself the nature of the three Principles, as are bath waters which are naturally medicinable.[534]

AQUA SOLVENS is distilled Vinegar.

AQUILA PHILOSOPHORUM is the Mercury of metals, i.e., metals reduced into their first matter.[535]

ARCANUM in general, as it signifies anything hid, so among the Philosophers it signifies any secret, incorporeal virtue in natural things partaking of a perpetual, immortal life, derived upon it from heaven, which also may be multiplied by the Spagyrical Art above its former condition.

ARCHEIUS[536] is the highest exalted and invisible Spirit, which is separated from bodies, is exalted and ascends; the universal occult nature, operator and physician in all things. So *Archiatrus* is the Supreme Physician of Nature, which distributes to everything and every member this peculiar *Archeius* occultly by *Ares*.[537] Also *Archeius* is the first in Nature, the most secret virtue, producing all things out of *Iliastes*,[538] being supported by a Divine Power. *Ares* is the Dispenser of Nature hid in all the three principles, whence everything hath its being, and which disposeth to all things in a particular form, shape and substance, that it may put on its own proper, specifical nature and not another's. But you must note the difference betwixt these three in nature, to speak after the manner of the Schools. *Iliastes* is the substance of the highest *genus* or kind, consisting in the first universal matter of all things, which it doth first dispose into three kinds, namely into Sulphur, Mercury and Salt. The *Archeius* is the first dispenser of Nature and then it produceth all things into its next *genera* or kinds. Then comes *Ares*, another Dispenser of Nature, which produceth from kinds or *genera*, forms and species in individuals.

ASTRUM is in this place called the virtue and power got by the preparations of things, as the Star of Sulphur is its inflaming, which is turned into most excellent oil, which thereby receives more virtues than it had before. The Star of Mercury is its sublimation, by which it acquires a wonderful power and virtue, greater and more subtile than its natural.[539]

AURUM POTABILE is Liquor of Gold without any corrosive, which very few know.

AURUM VITAE is precipitated Gold and reverberated into its highest degree of redness, like ground Cinnabar. That is the best which is made and precipitated with its proper Mercury.

AVIS HERMETIS is the Mercury of Philosophers, which ascends and descends for nourishment.

AURUM VIVUM is sometimes taken for Quicksilver.

AUSTROMANTIA. The observation of the Winds, as when the Stars of the Winds break forth into great vehemency, contrary to their custom, shows a pressage of something good or ominous to come. *Second Sheet*

AZOTH is Quicksilver extracted out of any body and it is properly called the Mercury of the Body, but in Paracelsus and Arnoldus it is the Universal Medicine of things.[540]

BALNEUM MARIAE or MARIS[541] as many call it, is a furnace for distillation containing water, in which, being warm, chemical vessels are put for the putrefaction of the matter which they contain, as also for their separation and for the performing [of] the operations of that kind of moist Ascension.[542]

BALNEUM RORIS is a furnace in which the vessels of distillation are put over the vapour of the water only, that the water[543] do not touch the body. Also it is called a Vaprous Furnace.

BALSAMUM is a substance of bodies preserving things from putrefaction. It is internal and external. [The] internal in Man is a certain temperate substance, not bitter nor sweet nor sour nor mineral Salt, but the Salt of Liquor, which preserves the body strongly from putrefaction. [The] external is Turpentine, which hath never come to the fire, but is digested.

BALSAMUM DE MUMIIS is that which is extracted from flesh.

BALSAMUM ELEMENTORUM EXTERNUM is a Liquor of Eternal Mercury, i.e., the Mummie[544] of External Elements, one of the three principles, the firmamental[545] essence of things.

BERILLUS is a crystalline looking glass, magically consecrated by the Augurs.

BERILLISTICA is an art of observing visions in those kinds of glass.

BISMUTUM is the lightest, whitest and basest kind of Lead.

BUTYRUM SATURNI is that which [is] above called *Altey* and it is the sweetness of Lead.

CABELA or CABALIA[546] is a most secret science said to be delivered by divine inspiration together with the Law of Moses,[547] the Hebrew Rabbis asserting the same. The Persians were most diligent seekers of this Art, being also possessors of the same, as appears by their calling of their wise men.[548] They called their Priests wise men and most skilful of all secrets, such as were those three that came to Christ out of the East to worship Him and not Kings as the ignorant vulgar think them to be. It was not set down in writing, but delivered by word of mouth.

CALX MERCURII is precipitated Mercury.[549]
CALX VENERIS is Verdigris.
CALX SATURNI is Minium.[550]
CALX IOVIS is Spirit of Tin.
CALX MARTIS is Crocus of Steel or Iron.[551]
CALX SOLIS is calcined Gold.
CALX LUNAE is the Azure Flower of Silver.
CALX PERMANENS or FIXA is an incombustible matter.
CALX PERIGRINORUM is Tartar.
CALX LIGNORUM is the Ashes of wood.
CALCANTHUM is Vitriol.[552]
CALCINATUM MAGUS is called all that which is made sweet by the Spagyric Art, which, of its own nature, was not so, as the Sweetness of Mercury, of Lead, of Salt or the like, which also is called their Soul[553] and doth quickly consolidate any wound.
CALCINATUM MINUS is all that which is naturally sweet and is very healing, as Sugar, Manna, Honey of the Woods, Nostock etc.[554]
CHOAMANCY[555] is an Art of pressaging by the Air.
CHAOS, besides the confused and unshaped matter of all things, by some philosophy [it] is taken for the Air; it is also taken for *Iliaster*.[556]
CAPUT CORVI is Antimony.[557]
CAPUT MORTUUM is the feces remaining after distillation and sublimation.[558]
CARBONES COELI are the Stars.
CATHIMIA is the same as the Spume of Silver.[559]
CAUDA VULPIS RUBICUNDI[560] is Minium of Lead.
CINIFICATUM is the same as *Calcinatum*, i.e., burnt to Ashes.
CHEIRI, if it be put absolutely, without any adjection, and if it be spoken of minerals, it signifies Quicksilver; if of vegetables, flowers. But when it is found with an adjection after this manner *Flos Cheiri*[561] it signifies the White Elixir made of Silver, as *Flos Anthos* signifies the Red Elixir.

Third Sheet

CHERIO is the occult, accidental virtue of the external Elements and not the qualities of heat and cold and the like.
CHIFER MINERALE is of some interpreted Gold; by others the Sulphur of any metal.
CHRYSOCOLLA is a kind of green earth like Verdigris.
CHRYSOS is Gold.
CHYMUS is feces.
CINERITIUM is Ciment of Gold or Silver, which some call *Regale*.[562]

CITRINULUS is pale crystal.⁵⁶³
CITRINULUM is a transparent Salt made out of calcined Vitriol.
COAGULATIO is the making of a thing thick.⁵⁶⁴
COELUM PHILOSOPHORUM is any Quintessence or Universal Medicine, especially the Philosophers' Stone.⁵⁶⁵
COELUM SPAGYRICUM is the upper part of a philosophical vessel.
COELI PLANETARUM are the proper orbs and their Spheres.
CEMENTUM is a dry corrosion when any metalline body is calcined with Salts or such-like drying things.
COHOBATIO is the often drawing off [of] a liquor from its body, being oft put upon it.
COHOPH or COHOP is the same as Cohobation.
COLCOTHAR is calcined Vitriol or the *Caput Mortuum* of Oil of Vitriol.⁵⁶⁶
COLLIQUATION is melting as metals are melted.
COLERITIUM is a liquor compounded of the corrosive materials of metals.
COMPOSITUM, put absolutely, is a body not separated.
CONGLUTEN is that which by putrefaction is turned into a viscous matter.
CONSTELLATIO is the impression of Superior Stars or their virtues upon inferior bodies.
COR, among metals is called Gold.⁵⁶⁷
CORBATUM is Copper.
CORNU CERVI, amongst the chemists, is the nose of a still.
CORPORA COELESTIA SPAGYRORUM are Astral virtues in their matter.
CORPORA SUPERCOELESTIA are such bodies that are not known by sense but by reason.
CORPUS INVISIBILE is the Soul, which is corporeal in respect of its sustentation and invisible by reason of its spirituality.
CORTEX MARIS is the Vinegar of the philosophers.⁵⁶⁸
COTORONIUM is a Liquor.⁵⁶⁹
CRUOR SALIS is Salt separated from the first by fault of the second Digestion.
CUCURBITE is a vessel like a gourd.⁵⁷⁰
CYCIMA is Litharge.
CYDAR is Jupiter.⁵⁷¹

DESCENSORIUM is a chemical furnace in which the liquor falls downwards from the gross matter.
DERSES is an occult vapour of the earth by reason of which all kind

of wood grows and increaseth.

DELIQUIUM is a cold descension, when coagulated bodies are dissolved in liquor in any cold place.

DIAMETER SPAGYRICUS is a Temperament.[572]

DIATESSADELTON is precipitated Mercury.[573]

DIENEZ are Spirits that dwell among hard Stones.

DIGESTIO is a chemical operation alluding to the digestion of a man's stomach, in which and by which the matter is decocted into a separation of pure from impure.[574]

DISCUS SOLIS is Quicksilver made out of Gold.[575]

DIVERTALIUM or DIVERTELLUM a generation made by the Elements.

DUENECH is Antimony.[576]

DULCEDO SATURNI is *Altey* or Ceruse.[577]

DURDALES are corporeal Spirits inhabiting Trees.

DIOTA is a circulating vessel.

EDELPHUS is any one that prognosticates by the nature of the Elements.

EDIR is Steel or Iron.[578]

ELECTRUM is sometimes taken for Amber, but in Paracelsus it is a mixture of a compound metal made by melting all the planets into one body.

ELEMENTUM in Paracelsus is the corruptible and transient Essence of the World and of all things which are subject to change.

ELEPHAS is *Aqua fortis*.

ELIXIR is properly a ferment, the least part of which turns the whole mass of anything into its own kind; also it is the essence of anything.[579]

ELEVATION is making a thing subtile.

ENTALI is flaked Alum and sometimes it is made spagyrically of Salt Gemmae.

ENUR is an occult vapour of water by which stones are bred.

ERODINIUM is the sign of anything to come.

ESSATUM ESSENTIALE is the essential and power that is in vegetables and minerals.

ESSATUM VINUM is rectified Spirit of Wine.[580]

ESSENTIA QUINTA, according to Paracelsus, his definition, is a certain matter extracted from things purified from all manner of impurity and corruption, whereby it is made incorruptible.[581]

ESSODIUM is a certain pressage of things to come by their marks.

Fourth Sheet EVESTRUM is a prophetical Spirit which pressageth by signs, or something going before.

EXORCISTA is the Artist which calls up the Spirits.
EZEZICH is Salt.

FEL DRACONIS is Quicksilver out of Tin.
FEL VITRI is the Spume of Glass.
FERMENTUM is a fixed matter which reduceth a matter to its own nature and fixedness.[582]
FIDO is called Quicksilver and sometimes Gold.
FIDA is Silver and sometimes Gold.
FILIUS UNIUS DEI is the Philosophers' Stone.[583]
FILUM ARSENICALE is the Philosophers' Stone.[584]
FIMUS EQUINUS is a digestion made any way, either by horse-dung or warm ashes or water.
FILTRATIO is straining a thing through a woollen cloth or paper.
FLAGAE are Spirits which know the occult secrets of men.
FLOS CHEIRI is the essence of Gold.[585]
FIXATIO is making that which flies in the fire to endure the fire.
FOLIA DAURE are leaves of Gold.
FORMA RERUM are called the Influence of Celestial bodies, which inferior bodies receive from them or they are the virtues of anything.[586]
FONS PHILOSOPHORUM is *Balneum Maris*.
FULIGO METALLORUM is sometimes called Arsenick, and sometimes is taken for Mercury.
FULMEN is purified Silver.
FUMIGATIO is calcining anything with a sharp, corroding fume.[587]
FUSIO is melting or making anything flow in the fire.

GAMATHEI[588] are Stones in which Celestial virtues and supernatural constellations[589] are impressed, being marked with wonderful Characters and Images.
GAMAHEI are Images impressed by a supercelestial influence.
GAMONYNUM is that one only anatomy of all things.
GLACIES DUR is crystal.
GLADIALIS is an Art whereby according to the course of the firmament of the Stars, swords are forged that anvils cannot resist them, whence [they] are[590] otherwise called *Incusma*.[591]
GEOMANCY is the most known Art of the Earth, but in this place it is taken for the Stars of the Earth manifesting themselves to men so that thereby they may take sure ground for pressaging.
GEMMA TARTAREA is called the stone that is generated of diaphanous and perpiscuous Tartar.[592]

GIBAR is a metallic Medicine.

GNOMI are certain corporeal Spirits living under the earth, small, like pygmies.

GRAECA MAGIA is a curious Art invented by the Grecians by which they made things appear which really were not.

GRAVUS[593] is the stone *Porphyrites*, the use of which is as of a marble to dissolve things in the cold.

GUARINI are men living by the influence of the heaven.

GUMA is Quicksilver.[594]

HADID is Iron.

HAL is Salt.[595]

HENRICUS RUBEUS is the Colcothar of Vitriol calcined or the *Caput Mortuum*.

HELIOTROPIUM is Paracelsus his Balm.

HELIOMIDAN is Balsalmical Mummie.

HORION is the Mercury of Gold.

HUMOR VITAE is the radical moisture.

HYDROMANCY is an Art taken from the Stars of the water when they manifest themselves to men, as from unusual inundations and the like.

JESAHACH is supernatural.[596]

IGNIS LEONIS is the Element itself of Fire.[597]

IGNIS PRUINUS ADEPTUS is the Quintessence of Vitriol, rectified with Tartar.

ILECH PRIMUM is the first Principle.[598]

ILECH SUPERNATURALE is a conjunction of the supernatural and firmamental Stars with the inferior Stars of terrestrial things and with Wine.

ILECH MAGNUM is an Ascendant or a Star of a Medicine, which together is taken with it or in which also it is hid; and as the superior Stars are in the firmament, so also are the inferior in man.

ILECH CRUDUM is a composition of the First Matter of the three first Principles.

ILEIDUS is the Elementary Air, but in men it is the Spirit which passes through all his members.[599]

ILIASTER or ILIASTES or ILIADUM is the First Matter of all things, consisting of Sulphur, Mercury and Salt; and it is four-fold, according to the number of the Elements. The first is the Chaos of the Earth, the second is the Chaos of the Water, the third is the Chaos of the

Air, the fourth is the Chaos of the Fire. Also there are four *Iliastri* of men respecting long life.[600]

ILIASTER PRIMUS is the term of life or the life itself, or the balsam of life in man.

ILIASTER SECUNDUS is the term of the balsam and the life which we have by Elements and things elementated.

ILIASTER TERTIUS [is] the term of the balsam of life we have by the quintessence of things.

ILIASTER MAGNUS or QUARTUS is of the Mind or Soul, caught up into another World, as Enoch and Elias were.

Fifth Sheet

ILIASTER in general is called the occult virtue of Nature, by which all things are increased, nourished, multiplied, and flourish, of which you may read more at large in Paracelsus' *Book of the Generation of Meteors*.

IMAGINES are metallic figures or effigies in which the coelestial powers operate.

IMAGINATIO is a Star in man, a coelestial and supercelestial body.

INCUBUS is a nocturnal spirit, deceiving women in their sleep as if they coupled with them.[601]

INFLUENTIA is the acting of Superior bodies upon inferiors.

INNATURALIA are Supernatural Bodies.

JUPITER is Tin.[602]

JUMNIZUM is Leaven or Ferment.

KACHIMIA or KAHIMIA[603] is the unripe mine of any metal as it is in its first being.[604]

KALD is Vinegar.

KAMIR is Ferment.[605]

KAPRILI is Sulphur.

KIBRITH is Sulphur [Philosophical].[606]

KIMIT ELEVATUM is white Cinnabar sublimed.

KOBALT or KOBALTUM or COBLETUM is a metallic matter, blacker than Lead or Iron, without a metallic splendour, yet will be melted and malleated.

LABOR SOPHIAE is Paradise or another world.

LAC VIRGINIS is Mercurial Water.

LAPIS PHILOSOPHORUM is the highest virtue of all terrene things giving tincture.[607]

LATO is Copper tinged with *Lapis Calaminaris* into a golden colour.

LAUDANUM is a compound Medicine made of Gold, Coral, Pearl and Opium.

LEPHANTE or LEPHANTES is the first kind of Tartar or Bole, holding the middle betwixt stones and clay.

LEMURES are Spirits of the Element of Air, which some philosophers think to be the ghosts of men departed.

LETHARGYRUM is the Spume of Mercury or of Silver or of Lead, which is separated in their purifying and purging.

LIQUOR MERCUR is the Balsam of things in which the virtue of curing and healing consists.

LIQUOR MUMMIAE is the fat of a man.[608]

LIQUOR MUMMIAE DE GUMMIS is Oil of Gum.

LIQUOR SALIS is the Balsam of Nature, by which the body is preserved from putrefaction.[609]

LUNA COMPACTA is Quicksilver.

LUNA is Silver.[610]

LUSTRUM is the Cream of Milk.

LUNARIA is the Sulphur of Nature.[611]

MAGIA METAPHYSICA is an Art by which any occult secrets are discovered.

MAGIA in general is wisdom and it is natural when the grounds of all true physic and the occult wisdom of Nature is discovered. There is another sort of Magic Solomon used, whereby good Spirits are raised by invocation on some emergent occasion, though sometimes bad ones may intrude, but they are soon banished by the exorcist.

MAGISTERIUM is in Paracelsus any secret extracted out of natural things without any elementary separation, with which other things are wont to be prepared yet with the addition only of other things from which that which is extracted is separated.

MAGNALIA are peculiar works of God.

MAGNESIA is commonly taken for Marcasite, but that which is artificial is melted Tin, into which is put Quicksilver and both mixed into a brittle matter and white mass.[612]

MAGOREUM is a magic medicament or secret.[613]

MAJUS NOSTER is our dew and the philosophical Loadstone.[614]

MALEK is Salt.[615]

MARCASITA is an unripe matter of metals and is of as many kinds as there are metals.

MARTATH or MARTACH is Litharge.[616]

MATER MATALLORUM is Quicksilver.

MATRICES RERUM are Elements.

MELIBOEUM[617] is Copper.

MENSIS PHILOSOPHICUS is the full time of digestion, namely forty days.[618]

MERCURIUS A NATURA COAGULATUS is a solid metal.[619]
MERCURIUS CRYSTALLINUS is that which by often sublimations is brought into a clearness like Crystal.
MERCURIUS CORALLINUS is that which by yolk of eggs and other waters is brought into a redness like Coral.[620]
MERCURIUS CRUDUS is that which is not yet separated from its mine.[621]
MERCURIUS LAXUS is Turbith Mineral.[622]
MERCURIUS METALLORUM PRAECIPITATUS is Mercury extracted out of metals and precipitated.[623]
MERCURIUS MINERALIUM is an oiliness extracted out of the mines of Gold and Silver.
MERCURIUS REGENERATUS is the first being of Mercury.
MERCURIALIS SEVA is the Water of Allum.[624]
MENSTRUUM is a liquor wherein anything is dissolved or digested.
METALLUM CURRENS is Quicksilver.
MICROCOSMUS is a little world or Man.
MINIUM is the Mercury or rather the Crocus of lead precipitated.[625]
MISSADAM is Quicksilver.
MYSSADAR is Mercury.
MYSTERIUM MAGNUM is the First matter of all things.

Sixth Sheet

NECROMANCY is an Art, by some thought unlawful, used of old time to work with the Dead. He is a necromancer who can make the Dead appear and can draw words and answers from them, as when the Stars were manifested with the Dead.
NECROLICA.[626]
NIGROMANCY. When wicked Spirits suffer themselves to be commanded by men and obey them, though sometimes to their hurt.
NANUFARENI are Spirits dwelling in the Air.
NITRUM is Saltpeter.
NITRIALES are all burning things[627] which conduce to calcination.
NEBOCH is an instrument used in Necromancy.
NOSTOCH is called a falling Star.[628]
NYMPHAE or NYMPHIDICAE are spiritual men or women or corporeal spirits dwelling in waters. Such an one was Melusina.
NYMPHIDICA are Spirits of dissolving waters in the Spagyric Art.
NYSADIR is Salt Armoniack.[629]

OBRIGUM is pure Gold calcined by Art into a light red colour.[630]
OCOB is Salt Armoniack.[631]
OLEITAS RERUM is the Sulphur of all things.[632]

OLEUM ARDENS is the Oil of Tartar corrected to the highest degree.
OLEUM VITRIOLI AURIFICATUM is that[633] which is dulcified with Gold artificially.[634]
OLEUM COLCOTHARINUM is red Oil of Vitriol.
OLEUM SQUAMINUM is Oil of Tartar.
OLYMPICUS SPIRITUS is a Star in man that makes him to yield a shadow of himself.
OPERIMETHIOLIM is the Spirit of Minerals.[635]
ORIZON AETERNITATIS is the Supercelestial virtue of things.[636]
ORIZEUM is Gold.
ORIZEUM FOLIATUM is leaf of Gold.[637]
ORIZEUM PRAECIPITATUM is Gold brought into a Cross by the help of the Crocus of Mercury.[638]
OROBO is the glass of metals.
OVUM PHILOSOPHICUM is a glass of the form of an egg, which philosophers use in their operations.[639]
OZO is Arsenic.

PELICANUS is a circulatory or circulating vessel in Alchemy.
PENATES are Spirits of the Element of Fire, called Familiars.
PENTACULA are Sigils or delineaments painted on virgin[640] paper or parchment or on metals engraven with curious letters and images, which, being worn about one will preserve against evil Spirits or witchcraft.[641]
PHANTASMATA are Spirits of the woods or the desert, which live in any obscure place.
PHOENIX is the Quintessence of Fire, also the Philosophers' Stone.[642]
PHYSIOGNOMY is an Art whereby men's natures and conditions are perceived by their faces.
PLUMBUM PHILOSOPHORUM is that which is extracted.[643]
PRIMALES are called fallacious bodies, which are by the Stars put before our eyes.
PRUINUM is the first kind of Tartar.[644]
PYROMANCY is an Art [of] pressaging by Fire.

QUARTATIO or QUARTURA is the highest trial of Gold, and that this way, namely that nine parts of Silver be mixed with one part of Gold in a melting by the fire. Then let them both be dissolved with *Aqua fortis*. All the Silver is turned into water and the Gold settles to the bottom like a dark powder.
QUINTESSENTIA is called a certain spiritual matter, extracted corporeally out of herbs, plants and all things that have life, and

the exalting of it to the highest degree of purity by separating all impurities.[645]

QUINTUM ESSE CUJUSLIBET ELEMENTI PER SE SOLUM is an animal produced out of that alone.

REALGR is the fume of minerals, being properly taken, but being metaphorically [taken] it is any vicious matter in man's body of which grow apostemes,[646] ulcers and the like.[647]

REBUS is the last matter of things.[648]

REBONA is the same as Mummia.[649]

REDUC is powder whereby calcined metals and minerals are melted.[650]

REGALE is a cement whereby Gold is purged.

REGULUS is the purest metalline part of any metal, or the purest part of a mineral, the feces being separated.

RESINA AURI is a Crocus, extracted out of Gold.

RESINA TERRAE is Sulphur.

RESINA TERRAE POTABILIS is sublimed Sulphur brought into a liquor, balsam or oil.

REVERBERATORIUM is a furnace in which the matter is calcined by a flame.

RILLUS is an instrument alchemists use to pour their melted metals into long forms and it is called an Ingot.

RUBELLA is a spiritual essence extracting by its dissolving power the Tinctures out of bodies.[651]

SAGANI are Spirits of the Four Elements.

SALAMANDRI are Spirits dwelling in the fire or fiery men.[652]

SALADINI. The same as Salamandri.

SAL ANATHRON is Salt extracted out of stony moss.[653]

SAL CRYSTALLINUM is Salt made out of man's urine.

SAL COLCOTHARINUM is Salt which is made out of the Colcothar of Vitriol.

SAL CONGELATUM is Salt which grows in baths.

SAL ENIXUM is Salt dissolved.[654]

SAL MERCURII is the Spirit of the Wine which causeth drunkenness.

SAL PETRE is that which grows in cold places upon stones congealed by the cold air.[655]

SAL NITRUM is Salt which is boiled out of earth as in a stables or any place of excrements.[656]

SAL PRACTICUM is a mixture made of equal parts of Saltpeter and Sal Armoniack.

SAL SCISSUM and ALUM SCISSUM is all one Salt. *Selenipum* is brine.

SAL TUBERZET is whitest Tartar of all.[657]
SAL TABARI is *Sal Alembrot*.[658]
SALLENA is a kind of Saltpeter.
SAMECH is Tartar.[659]
SANDARACHA is *Auripigmentum*.[660]
SANGUIS CALCETUS is that which is of as quick a taste as Calx and as white.
SAPHIREA MATERIA is a liquor in which there is no impurity or corruption, the pure being separated from the impure.
SAPO SAPIENTIAE is common Salt prepared.[661]
SAXIFRAGA are all such things which break the stone or gravel.
SAXIFRAGUS is pale crystal.[662]
SCAIOLAE are the spiritual powers and faculties of the mind and are four according to the number of the Elements.[663]
SIBAR is Quicksilver.
SILO is earth.
SIMILITUDINES are called celestial appearances.
SOL IN HOMINE is the Invisible Fire flowing from the Celestial Sun, preserving and nourishing that natural fire in man.
SOLADINI are corporeal Spirits dwelling in the Invisible Fire.[664]
SORTILEGIUM, a pressage by Spirits.
SPAGYRUS or SPAGYRICUS, is he which knows to distinguish betwixt good and bad, to separate pure from impure, a chemist or alchemist.
SPAIRIA is commonly taken for Alchemy.
SPARA is the mineral virtue of the first being of metals.[665]
SPERMA AQUA FORTIS is its feculency.
STANNAR is called the mother of all metals; an occult fume out of which Elements are generated.[666]
STELLIO ADUSTUS is Cinnabar.
STIBIUM is Antimony.[667]
SUBLIMATIO is when any dry thing is forced upwards by the heat of [the] fire.[668]
SUCCUBUS is a noctural Spirit whereby men are deceived, thinking they are coupling with women.
SULPHUR VITRIOLATUM is Sulphur extracted out of Vitriol by common water swimming on the top.
SYLO is the whole world.[669]
SYLPHS are Pigmies.[670]
SYLVESTRES or SYLVANI are airy men or airy Spirits. Sometimes they are taken for wood-men, which are strong, gigantic men.
SYPHITA STRICTA is a fantastic Spirit of them that walk in their sleep.

TARTARUM. The Saltish dregs which stick to the sides of wine vessels.[671]
TERA AURI is Litharge of Gold.
TERRA ARGENTI is Litharge of Silver.
TERRA FIDELIS is Silver.[672]
TERRA HISPANICA is Vitriol.
TERRELATI are corporeal Spirits living in the earth.
THIRSMA are mineral veins.[673]
TINKAR is Borax.[674]
TRIFERTES are called Spirits dwelling in the fire.
TRIGONUM is a four-fold transmutation of the Spirits of the Stars according to the four Elements.
TURBA MAGNA. A great multitude of Stars and pressaging by them.
TURBITH MINERALE is Mercury precipitated into a sweetness without any corrosive.[675]

VILTRUM PHILOSOPHORUM is a strainer.[676]
VINUM CORRECTUM is the Alcohol of Wine.
VIRIDITAS SALIS is the Green Oil of Salt.[677]
VITRIOLATUM is Vitriol liquid and can never be coagulated.
VITRIOLUM NOVUM is white Vitriol.

WARNUS is Vinegar of the Philosophers.

XENINEPHIDEI are Spirits which delight to discover the secret or occult properties of Nature unto men, the power of which is granted to them.

YSOPUS is the Art of Alchemy, to separate pure from impure.

ZAIDAR is Mercury.[678]
ZAIDIR is Copper or Verdigris.
ZERUS is Gold.
ZELOTUM is stony Mercury.
ZORABA is Vitriol.
ZINCK is a volatile Marcasite and a certain natural mixture of four immature metals, whereof Copper is most apparent.[679]
ZINIAR is Verdigris.
ZUITTER or ZITTER is a Marcasite.
ZYMAR or ZYSAR is Verdigris.

FINIS

PART III

Of the Laws and Mysteries
of the Rosie Crucians[680]

Their Laws are six in number.[681] First that every of them who shall travel shall profess medicine and cure gratis.

First Sheet

The Brethren are solemnly sworn and strictly engaged to each other to keep and observe these conditions and articles. In all which we find nothing either prejudicial to themselves or hurtful and injurious to others, but that they have an excellent scope and intention, which is the Glory of God and the good of their neighbour.

The Author is nameless, but yet worthy of credit; unknown to the vulgar, but well known to his own Society. The reasons [for this secrecy] may be [that] we know that the ancient philosophers counted themselves happy in a private life, and why may not modern [philosophers] enjoy the same privilege since necessity may put these more upon it than them. The world is now more burdened with wickedness and impieties. Indeed the whole creation, as it flowed from God, was exceedingly good, but man's fall hath brought a curse upon the creatures.

Amongst the ancients men of learning, wisdom and authority set up laws in every city or nation; [as] Moses among the Hebrews. Amongst the heathen the first law-givers were called Zephyrians; after them Zaleurus, in imitation of the Spartans and Cretans (who were thought to have received ancient laws from Minos), wrote severe laws and found out suitable punishments. Afterwards the Athenians received laws from Draco and Solon, upon which they proceeded in all courts of judicature, from whom the Romans, who lived after the building of the city three hundred years, had their laws of the Twelve Tables published by the Decemviri, and these in process of time being enlarged by Roman magistrates and the Caesars, became our Civil Law, which at this time we use.

Other nations had their respective lawgivers, as Egypt had priests of[682] Isis, who were taught by Mercury[683] and Vulcan[684] (those were golden laws and such as owned their birth to the fire). Babylon had the Chaldeans; Persia had [the] Magians;[685] India had [the] Brachmans; Ethiopia had the Gymnosophists; amongst the Bactrians was Zamolsis; among the Corinthians was Fido; amongst the Nilesians was Hyppodamus; amongst the Carthaginians was Charonda; lastly amongst the Britons and French, the Druids.

The author was a private man and no magistrate, but in his particular relation he was invested with much authority, whereby he might oblige and bind others, be both Lord and Father of the Society and the first author and founder of this Golden Medicine and Philosophical Order.

SECTION THE FIRST

Of the First Law and the excellency of Medicine above all other Arts to which the Brethren are devoted. That whoever of them shall travel must profess Medicine and cure gratis without any reward.

Necessity hath forced men to invent Arts for their help; curiosity hath set others on to work to satisfy fancy; and luxury hath not been idle in seeking out means to please itself.

Now amongst these Arts and inventions some are more noble and excellent, both in respect of themselves and in the estimation of men.

Do not we count it a divine and majestical thing to govern? What more glorious than to wage war with success? There are merchants, handycraftsmen and husbandmen in a commonwealth and everyone acts in his proper sphere. In many profound points in divinity we consult the able clergy; in a doubtful and subtle case we go to an able and honest lawyer; in desperate sickness we seek an experienced and learned physician. But Medicine deservedly seems to have pre-eminence for a physician in sickness governs the Emperor, [of] prescribes rules and directions which the lawyer cannot do, for the law-giver being present the law has no force and may be changed and altered at his pleasure who first instituted them.

The physician likewise fights with the diseases of man's body and hath sharp battles with them; he overcomes to the preserving or restoring [of] health almost lost or decayed. Hence Aristotle places health amongst those things in which all men agree; for everyone knows that it is best and desires to be well and in the next place to be rich and wealthy.

Wherefore a physician's employment is so far from being contemptible that it is concerned in a man's chiefest outward good and happiness, in maintaining health and curing diseases. God at first created man. Nature, God's handmaid, conduceth to the generation of him from the seed of both sexes and it is the physician's office to recover man diseased and to restore him to his native health. So that this Art hath much in it of divinity, having the same subject with the creation and generation, viz., man, who being created after the image of God was His by creation, [and] being begotten was Nature's by generation; nay Christ himself, being incarnate, did not disdain to be as well as the physician of the Soul, so also the physician of the body. The prophets among the Israelites practised physick, [as did] the priests among the Egyptians, out of whose number the Kings were chosen. Lastly great princes have studied this Art, not covetously for the reward, but that they might help the sick. Wherefore since the profession of physick is so high, so noble and sacred, we need not admire that amongst other Arts and sciences in which they excel, these Brethren of the Honourable Society of the Rosie Cross should choose and prefer this above them all. I confidently believe that they, knowing the most intimate secrets of Nature, can naturally produce very strange effects, which as much amaze an ignorant spectator as the Gorgon's head, but Medicine was dearer to them, as being of most profit and greater value.

Second Sheet

But some, perhaps, may exclaim against the Brethren saying that they are not physicians but mere empirics, who intrude upon physick. Such, indeed, should first look at home and then abroad. These Brethren are great scholars, not fresh or raw in profound learning, but the greatest proficients. They compound their Medicine which they administer, it being, as it were, the marrow of the Great World.

To speak yet more plainly, their Medicine is Prometheus his fire, which, by the assistance of Minerva, he stole from the Sun and conveyed it unto man. Although diseases and maladies were afterwards by the Gods (as the poets feign) inflicted on men, yet the balsam of Nature was more powerful than the distempers. This fire was spread over all the world, conducing to the good both of body and mind, in freeing the one from infirmities, the other from grievous passions; for nothing doth more cheer and make glad the heart of man than this Universal Medicine. Precious stones wrought into subtile powder and leaf Gold are the ingredients of this powder, commonly called *Edel beriz pulver*. Aeschylus doth attribute the invention of pyromancy, the composition of Medicines, the first working upon Gold, Iron and other metals to Prometheus; hence the Athenians erected an altar common to him, Vulcan and Pallas, considering how much fire conduced to the finding out of the secrets of Nature. But we must know that a four-fold fire is required to bring this Medicine to perfection, and if one of them is wanting, the whole labour is lost.

SECTION THE SECOND

That the cure of diseases by specific remedies of occult quality, which the Fraternity useth, is most suitable to man's nature and prevalent against all distempers.

We must not suppose, by what hath been said, that the Brethren use Medicines which are not natural, for they have vegetables and minerals, but they, having a true knowledge of the secret and occult operation of things, know what will be most effectual for their purpose.

They have their *Panchresta*,[686] their *Polychresta*,[687] their Manus Christi,[688] their *Narcotica* and *Alexipharmaca*,[689] of which Galen and others do much boast, thinking them a present help at a dead lift[690] and, to colour their cheats, strictly command that none shall either prescribe or give them without a large fee, as if the price added virtue to them and the effect did much depend upon the cost.

The Brethren also have [a] variety of Medicines, some called Kings, some Princes, some nobles and others knights, each one being denominated according to its excellence and worth. But take notice that they prescribe not according to the purse but the infirmity of the patient; neither do they desire a reward beforehand; they likewise fit not a child's shoe to an old man, because a due proportion ought to be carefully observed; a dram is sufficient for the one and an ounce of the same Medicine for the other. Who would not think it absurd to apply the same plaster to the hardened and brawny hand of a ploughman and to the delicate and neat hand of a scholar or gentleman?

He that practiseth Physick aright doth consider the different temper of persons in the same disease, as a learned judge doth not always give the same judgement in the same cause, which circumstances may very much alter. The Brethren look chiefly to the constitution of the patient and do accordingly prescribe.

Third Sheet They have in all things experience to confirm their knowledge; they use very choice vegetables, which they gather when they are impregnated with heavenly influences, not deluded with common, idle Astrological notions, but certainly knowing at what time they have received a signature of effectual to such an end; and they apply these vegetables to such diseases for which they were intended.

It is a most rational thing when Nature hath afforded us simple Medicines, to correct and amend their deficiencies, that we should mix and compound with qualities hot, cold, moist and dry, so that one specific being, perhaps, secretly of a contrary operation to another ingredient, the proper virtues of both, if not lost, yet are much diminished.

The Galenists say that the first qualities do alter, that the second do either thicken or attenuate and so foolishly and ignorantly of the rest; whereas each vegetable hath in it virtue essentially to clear away that disease in which it may rightly be applied. It is here in Medicine as in an Army; if each soldier falls out with the other or they mutiny against their commander, the enemy gets strength and makes use of their weapons to slay them.

Some may ask what is here meant by Specific? I answer that I intend that which the illiterate Galenists call an occult quality, because it is neither hot, cold, moist or dry, because, indeed, true, profound knowledge was above their reach or understanding.

Valescus de Taranta, *lib.* 7, *cap.* 12, defines the Galenical occult quality. A question is started [as to] how a locust hanged about the neck doth cure a Quartane ague. To which they answer that if these empirical Medicines have any such virtue, they have it from their occult quality, which contains the specific form of the distemper conjoined with the influence of the Stars. But then we may ask what that total propriety is. Averrhoes calls it a complexion; others say that it is the substantial form of a compound body; some will have it to be the whole mixture, viz., the form, the matter and [the] complexion, which Avicenna names the whole substance when he said that a body hath neither operation from the matter, nor quality, but the whole substance or composition.

We hold that there is a natural virtue and certain predestination flowing from the influence of heavenly bodies, so particularly disposing the form to be introduced that it is (as it were) determined to its proper object, whereby, after due preparation of the matter and conjunction of the form, the whole substance or mixed body necessarily produces a proportionable effect. And Avicenna, perhaps, meant thus much; whence Arnoldus, in his book *De Causis Sterilitatis*, saith that the peculiar property of a thing is its nature, which proceeds from the right disposition of the parts to be mixed and this is called an Occult quality, to most men unknown because of its difficulty.

Hence it is that [that] nature is styled a complexion; not because it is so properly and found out by reason, its secrets being only discovered by experiment and practice; by this the understanding knows that experience is above reason, because there are so many experiments of which we can give no rational account, nor find out any method to satisfy ourselves concerning them.

By what hath been said it plainly appears that the whole propriety of anything is not the complexion; for if it were so, all things which have the same propriety would consequently have the same complexion, which is false, for Rhubarb and Tamarinds, from their whole propriety do attract and draw choler and yet are not of the same complexion. It is therefore evident that the true propriety of medicinal things is only known by experiment and not by the false Galenical rules of Art, which do not give us light into the nature of any simple. For instance, consider the Rose; it sends forth a most pleasant perfume and is of a ruddy, lovely colour, not in respect of the quality cold and dry, but of that proper virtue essentially in it; neither can there be any deduction from these qualities, being not subject to taste, to feeling [and] to hearing and consequently none at all, because specifics have another original.

How are the first qualities observed? Not from their essence and nature, but as sense discovers them, whence reason draws a conclusion. But we see not how reason can determine concerning the qualities of a rose, whether it is hot, cold, moist or[691] unless it hath been informed by the senses as by the colour, scent, taste or touch.

Fourth Sheet But the rules are altogether uncertain and fallacious, and there are more experiments to overthrow them than to confirm them; for who doth affirm that all cold things can have no scent; that all hot things have scent? That all scented things are hot; that all that have no scent are cold? Or that white things are cold or hot; that red things are hotter than white; or contrarily that bitter things are hot, narcotic cold etc.? For opium, the Spirit of Wine, the Rose and more things will confute such an opinion, so that the qualities do depend upon such uncertainties in respect of every simple, that it is far better to trust to experience, to search into the secrets of Nature, than vainly to trifle away time in gathering the second qualities from the first and the third from the second, or to gain reason by sense, a thing most ridiculous unless it be in the cure of diseases, where the qualities are in confusion.

When the Egyptians understood this they studied and most esteemed of that physick which was experimental and not rational, and therefore they used to place their sick persons in the streets, that if any one of the people that passed by had laboured under the same disease he might tell the specific remedy with which he was cured; whence it sometimes falls out that an old woman or an empiric in some certain diseases may effect more by one proper specific than many physicians by their methods and long courses.

I would not be misunderstood, as if there were no judgement to be used in the administration of physick, but that experience should be the only guide. Medicine, whether speculative or practical, must concur and meet in truth. I say we must not, as to the invention or prescription of physick, trust too much to reason informed falsely and concerning the nature of things, but when experience hath confirmed us in mysteries and secrets, because reason is too weak-sighted to teach them, we must not perversely slight them, disesteeming enviously what we cannot attain.

I do not account him a rational physician who hath only a large scroll or bill of simples in his memory and can tell you distinctly what are hot and dry in the first degree, what in the second, what in the third, and can run through the second qualities and third; and if at any time he is called to a patient, from this rabble, as from the belly of the Trojan horse, issue many receipts, many bands, when he is ignorant of the most inconsiderable simple and knows not how rightly to apply it. Shall not he who understands and is well acquainted with his Medicines be of more repute? A few select prescriptions that are infallible and effectual to the cure are of more worth than a rude multitude of Galenical receipts.

We have, indeed, now so great a variety of Medicines that it puzzles a physician more to choose what is best than to invent; for it is not the abundance of remedies that overcomes the disease, but the virtue, method, order and choice of time and place that give success.

We read in histories of the courage and skill of a Spartan King, who, with a band of four hundred stout Lacedemonians, possessed the straights by which Xerxes should pass with an army of one million, seven hundred thousand and made there a great slaughter of them. When the insulting Persian boasted that they would close the Sun with their arrows, the Spartan King answered that then we will fight in the shadow.

By these examples it appears that a select company of choice soldiers have great advantage against a confused multitude. And why are not a few choice remedies beyond a heap of vain receipts? Some have said that an army is complete that hath an hundred thousand, and if the number exceeds it will be tumultuous and in no order and discipline. We may assert the like of Medicine, if it increaseth to a great store or number it rather kills than cures; for every specific waging war or being opposite to another, must necessarily disturb Nature's peace and tranquillity.

SECTION THE THIRD
Although other Physicians may challenge, as indeed they deserve, a due reward, yet the Brethren do cure gratis, not valuing money.

We read in History that great persons, princes, Kings etc. have entertained famous and learned physicians, not only allowing them a considerable annual stipend, but have raised them to great preferment and honour. Eristratus found out the disease of Antiochus, viz. his

Fifth Sheet

love of his mother-in-law, of which he recovered him and received of his son Ptolemy one hundred talents. Democides restored the tyrant Polycrates for two talents of Gold. The same person, for curing Darius, had given to him a very rich chain of Gold and two golden cups. Jacobus Corterius, physician to Louis the second, King of France, had fifty thousand crowns yearly paid to him and Thaddeus the Florentine got fifty crowns daily for travelling up and down to cure the sick.

The rewards and gains physick bringeth in hath caused many students to employ all their time and labour therein, who for the most part look more to the[ir own] profit than [to the] health of their neighbour and [the] good of the commonwealth. Considering the infirmities we are subject to, we shall find physick to be as necessary as food and raiment, and thus able physicians are to be sought for, who may judiciously administer it; but no man will employ all his pains, cost and labour in that of which he shall reap no harvest. Who will be another's servant for no wages? Will a lawyer plead without his fee? Neither is there any injunction or law to command and oblige a Doctor to cure for nothing. Menecrates the Syracusan had nothing for his pains, but affected divinity; he would be thought and accounted Jupiter, which was worse than if he had required a reward suitable to his calling.

The Fraternity of the R.C. are so far from receiving a fee that they scorn it; so far from vain glory of their success that they will not have such a favour acknowledged! They have not one Medicine for a great man [and] another for the poor, but equally respect both [and are] frequent in visiting, comforters in affliction and relievers of the poor. Their labour is their reward — their pains to them [are] gain.

Coelius, *lib.* 16, *cap.* 10, tells us of Philo, a physician who found out certain Medicines which he called The Hands of the Gods;[692] but this great title was but as ivy hung out for a show to take the eyes of the spectators, to surprise the ears of the hearers, which promised more than they performed and rather deluded than helped any, having a glorious outside, but within [were] dregs and corrupt. But the Brethren, although they have the most efficacious Medicines in the world, yet they had rather conceal the virtues than boast of them. They possess the *Phalaia*[693] and the *Asa* of Basileus; the Nepenthes that drives away sorrow of Homer and Trismegistus; the ointment of Gold; the fountain of Jupiter Hammon, which at night is hot, at noon is cold [and is] lukewarm at sun rising and setting. For they condemn gains, they are not enticed with honour or preferment, they are not so overseen as one of whom Tully speaks, who wrote against others' affectation of esteem and placed his name in the frontispiece of his book that he might be the more known; they embrace security and are not busied, but live and are active in silence.

Is not this a rare society of men who are injurious to none but seek the good and happiness of all, giving to each person what appertains to him? These Brethren do not adore the rising Sun, mere parasites who conform themselves to the books of great men; their words and actions are [not] marked with cheats. It is reported that the statue of Diana by art was so framed that if a present was brought her by a pilgrim she would show a cheerful and pleasing countenance, but if anyone came empty she frowned, was angry and seemed to threaten. Even so is the whole world, wherein all things are subject to Gold. This dust of the earth is of no value with them, because these things are low in their eyes, which others most adore. They had rather find out a mystery in nature than a mine, and as Gold serves to help forward their studies, so they esteem of it. They wish and are ambitious of the age of Solomon, wherein there was so great plenty at Jerusalem as tiles on the houses, Silver as common as stones in the Street; so in the Golden Age its use was not known; men were contented with what Nature freely offered them, living friendly under the government of the father of the family without broils, luxury [or] pride, much less war.

SECTION THE FOURTH

Abuses in Medicine censured, as their long Bills for Ostentation, that the Physician may not seem an Empirick, and for the gain of the Apothecary, without respect to the benefit and purse of the Diseased, when a few choice simples might do the cure.[694]

We daily see how many weeds sprung from Gold have and still do overrun the whole world. It hath not only overthrown cities [and] destroyed commonwealths, but also hath corrupted the Arts and of liberal hath made them almost servile.

Cast your eyes upon Medicine, whose streams, the further they have run from the fountain, the more dirt and mire they have drunk up; and now at last they are full of stench and filthiness. We have said that Nature is contented with a little, which holds good as well in sickness as in health, for the more simple [a] diet is, the easier it is digested, because it is hard to turn many heterogeneous things into one substance. So likewise in diseases, the variety of ingredients distracts, if not totally hinders Nature in her operation in regard she struggles not only with the infirmity but the very remedy; and how can those things which are opposite and fight among themselves procure peace?

We confess that a judicious composition is necessary, because one simple specific cannot confer to the cure of complicated distempers,

Sixth Sheet

so that more simples united may effect that which one could not: neither would we be thought so absurd as to question so good and requisite a method.

That which we complain of is the great multitude of omnium gatherum put together of herbs, roots, seeds, flowers, fruits [and] barks, hot or cold in the first, second or third degree, so that you shall have thereby forty or more ingredients in one receipt, to show the memory and art of a dull and blockish physician and to help the knavish apothecary, who extols his gain for learning, the quick utterance of his drugs for experimental knowledge.

On the contrary, if anyone making conscience of what he undertakes shall prescribe a few rare and approved simples (as that famous Crato did, physician to three Caesars) he shall be thought an ignoramus, if not a mere empiric, although he excel those receipt-mongers by far in all parts of learning.

Take notice how the apothecaries slight a short, though effectual, bill, because it brings in little profit; but if they receive a bill of a cubit long, they bless themselves and thus the patient pays for his sickness, when, if he recovers, his purse will be sick.

Consider how injurious these are to each person and the commonwealth; by destroying the one they diminish the other; for if they remain, yet are they but poor members thereof. The disease is protracted by the contrariety of Medicines and Nature weakened. We account it absurd when a straight way leads to the wood, for haste to countermarch and make windings which may confound and not further. Multitude breeds in most things confusion, but especially in Medicine, when the essences of the simples are not known.

We may bring examples to confirm this from a Court, where if everyone at the same time may plead and declare his opinion, the case would be made more intricate, so far would they be from deciding the controversy. Wherefore a few wise counsellors on each side will clearly state the case and bring it to a sudden and safe determination. The same discord will appear in physick if each simple in the same disease should have its operation, when a few select ones may quickly do the business.

It is, therefore, an expedient course out of many things to choose a few and of those that are good to pick out the best, which may assist and strengthen Nature in her conflict. If these observations were taken notice of, a physician would not be reputed able for his large, rude bills, but for the quality of his ingredients; the apothecary would have more custom, because men would not be fright[en]ed with the charge and die to save expenses, but willingly submit to an easy and honest cure.

Everything is not to be esteemed according to its bulk; we see that brute beasts in body and quantity exceed man, but yet the less[er], being rational and wise, doth govern the other. A little Gold is worth more than a heap of stones, than a mine of base metals; so in Medicine a small quantity may have more virtue in it than a great measure of many simples.

It is sufficiently known to wise men that the same herbs do alter under several climates and [that] that which is innocent in one may be poison in another; wherefore it is not safe to compound India, Arabia, America, Germany and England together, for the Sun and planets have a different influx upon this or that country and accordingly alter the plants.[695] Nay we cannot be ignorant that the same field abounds as with wholesome, so with venomous herbs; we have example of this truth in minerals, for common Salt alone is harmless, as also our vulgar Mercury, but if these two be sublimed together, they become a venomous and rank poison. But perhaps some may think that this proceeds from Mercury, which indeed is false, for it may be brought by Art to run again, and then its innocency returns. So likewise the Spirit of Vitriol may be taken without danger, mixed with another liquor, and the water of Saltpeter may be received into the body, but if these two be distilled together, they make a water that will eat any metal except Gold and [is] certain death to anyone that shall take it. But if you add to the former Armoniack, its strength is increased and it will reduce Gold into a watery, fluid substance, yet its nature is pure and perfect.

It may be objected that Treacle,[696] Mithridate,[697] and confection of Hamech, with others, were compounded of many simples, which, being after long fermentation well digested, became most sovereign remedies and have been in use almost six hundred years and have helped many thousands of people.

We deny not but these compositions are excellent and have been in great esteem in foregoing and latter ages; we likewise approve perhaps of six hundred more, if they are grounded upon experience. For they who first invented these Medicines did not consider whether the qualities were hot or cold, but to their nature and essence as they either resisted poison or conduced to the evacuation of ill humors in the body, as in Treacle there is vipers flesh and many others of the same virtue. Our discourse is against the vain, extemporary ostentation in prescribing of Medicines compounded of plants hot, dry, cold and moist, either in this or that degree.

Seventh Sheet

We know a physician who was wont to boast that he knew not any one particular experiment, but all remedies were alike to him, respective the first, second and third qualities, and this surely proceeded from his ignorance of what was to be known; but a wise and prudent spirit searches more narrowly and descends to particulars. For indeed it is more easy by general rules to pass a judgement of simples than by experience to find out the proper virtue of specifics; and the reason is because each simple hath a peculiar property which distinguisheth it from another and sometimes contrary; nay the qualities do not only differ in respect of others, but the same simple may have effects differing in itself as it appears in Rhubarb, which in respect of its first qualities [as] hot and dry, it doth increase choler in man's body, but in respect of its essence and specific nature it purgeth it. To pass by Opium and Vinegar, with many others, we see how the same thing[s] in their first second and third qualities have many times contrary operations; so Rennet makes thin [the] thickened blood of the hare, but if it be very fluid it thickens it; so also Vitriol, according to its nature, doth penetrate and is astringent, yet it doth repel and disperse lead outwardly applied to it; though Quicksilver is most weighty, yet by the fire it is sublimed and ascends and though it is a thick, gross body, it may by Art be made to pierce any body and afterwards be reduced to its own native purity.

Many more proofs might be brought, for there is nothing in the world, how abject and low soever, but it hath a stamp upon it as a sure seal of its proper virtues, of which he that is ignorant hath hitherto attained but the husk and shell, the outside of knowledge.

That error in judgement may not corrupt practice and men's lives thereby should be in danger, I desire those who study Medicine to follow the Rosie Crucian method, who seek more after a few rare and certain specifics than to follow generals, which so commonly deceive.

Experience is the mother of Art and shall we now condemn her as having no need of her? As many experiments beget reason, so reason maintains and adorns experience.

SECTION THE FIFTH

That many Medicines, because of their high Titles, and the fond opinion of men who think that best which cost[s] most, are in great esteem, though others of less price, proper to the Country, are far above them in excellency and worth.

Besides the abuses before mentioned, another is crept in; the former were cheats in respect of quantity and quality; here by this the purse is emptied; for they fall in with men's humours, who think a thing good when they have well bought it.

Hence Galen concealed his Golden Emplaister for the Squinancy,[698] by which he got an hundred crowns, which indeed was in itself of little worth; for there are many things of excellent use, which, if they were divulged, would be foolishly despised because vulgar hands pollute whatever comes into them. Some reason may be why after[wards] they are not so successful, because the imagination and fancy works not so strongly and desponds as to the cure from such slight means and so hinders the operation; for although another man's imagination hath little force upon me, yet mine own much alters the body and either hinders or furthers a remedy in its working.

As this is clear in many diseases, so especially in hypocondriac melancholy, called the shame of physicians because rarely cured, wherein the non-effecting of the cure depends upon the prejudiced imagination of the patient, who despairs of help; for cares, grief and despair do alter and change the blood, corrode the heart, [and] overwhelm the spirits that they cannot perform their offices; if therefore these can first be removed, there is very great hope of recovery. Under this cloak many cover their knavery and covetousness, who seek nothing but gain by their practice; for they call their Medicines by great names that the imagination of the patient, closing with so rich and precious remedies, may promote the cure; and therefore they compound their Medicines of rare ingredients as Gold, Silver, Pearls, Bezoar,[699] Ambergris, Musk and many more, and then they christen them according to their birth. They call them the Balsam of Life, the Great Elixir, the Restorative of Life, Potable Gold, Butter and Oil of the Sun; and who indeed can reckon up their tricks by which they draw in and delude such multitudes of ignorant people? Yet their great names are not altogether insignificant; for by this Balsam of Life they mean that which maintains and keeps themselves alive.

But grant these costly Medicines to be good and useful, yet they must confess that others not so chargeable have greater virtues in them.

We may also question whether they deal honestly and do not sell a little Salt for Gold and rank poison for the Balsam of Life; we have known some at death's door by their Mercury. I speak this that others may be cautious. Think what would come of it when one mistaking administered Opium for Apium[700] or parsley. Thus they try experience upon men's bodies and kill one to save another.

Besides, though there may be very excellent cordials or antidotes, yet are they not appropriated to the disease, and so consequently little conducing to the grief. Consider, then, the abuse; the patient pays a great price for that which is of small advantage to him and scorns those means which are at an easy rate, wherein also there is no danger, as being by experience confirmed and by all hands received.

Eighth Sheet

It is not hard to prove that each country abounds with simples suitable to the diseases of that country and that we need not go to India or use exotic drugs.

This question has been handled by many learned men. We deny not the use of India[n] and Arabic spices in their food and physick, neither do we condemn other most excellent gifts of God; but here we find fault with the price. Let us, therefore, use them in their place and time.

Perhaps such precious things were intended for great persons, but yet great care must be used in the preparation that they be not sophisticated. I say rich men may afford to pay for these Medicines, who delight to eat and drink Gold and hope as by that they can purchase all earthly things, so they may buy health.

Neither would we be thought ignorant of the great virtues and efficacy of Gold, but we speak against the abuse of those imposters who instead [of making use] thereof do cheat and rob and we can assure all that there is no worth in the boiling and reboiling of Gold. They indeed give their menstruous stuffs for dissolved Gold, which, being reduced to a Spirit, may corrode (and let all men beware of it) imitating a careless cook, who, if he hath lost the broth in which the meat hath been boiled sets now upon the table [that] which hath no heart nor strength in it. So they, when they have consumed and lost their Gold with Salts and other ways, they sell that which remains. When the bird is gone they sell the nest, and this they call Potable Gold, spiritualised because invisible. It may be they put Gold into their furnace, but that they by those means can produce such Medicines we deny. There were many Alexanders, many called by the name of Julius, but yet but one Alexander the Great [and] one Julius Caesar; the others agree only in name.

Should anyone enquire into the excellency of our own country simples, he would have work enough upon his hands.

But besides the price may we not justly suspect the preparation; that they, instead of true, may well sell false compositions, failing in their art and profession? For the balance of human frailty being [weighted] at the one end by justice [and] at the other by profit, the last overweighs because honesty may be an hindrance to us, but profit brings pleasure and delight along with it. So now merchants count it part of their trade to learn and skill the adulterating of their commodities. The Thebans would admit no such persons to the magistracy unless they had left off their trade at least ten years before, by which time they might forget to cozen. But I will not here censure all of that calling. The same may be said of those who sell Medicines, whether physicians or apothecaries, if they abuse their profession.

It remains to show that specifics or vegetables and things of little worth are more powerful against any disease than those which are of so great price; neither is the reason fetched far; for they whose property absolutely resists the malady, they, I say, must needs be more effectual than those who accidentally suit the disease and by mere chance work a cure. In mechanic arts if a man excellent in one should boast of his skill in another which he never saw, you would find him a bungler in it, but employ the same in that trade wherein he hath been brought up and he will show himself to be a workman; so in diseases, when each specific doth its own office there is a happy issue, but applied to another [it] proves of no effect. Neither can it be expected from one man (though he had an hundred hands) to conquer an army, which yet choice bands of experienced soldiers may easily overcome.

SECTION THE SIXTH

That many are haters of Chemistry, others scorn the use of vegetables and Galenical Compositions, either of which may be useful in proper cases.

As the palates of men are not all taken with the same taste, but what is pleasing to one is loathsome to another, so men's judgements differ and what one approves the other assents not unto, both [of] which happen or are caused by sympathy or antipathy, drawing them on to embrace or provoking them to hate such a thing. So also by prejudice or reason corrupted, some dare not taste cheese all their life, some abstain from it for a few years, some drink only water, refusing wine or ale; and in these there is great variety. No less is the difference amongst minds, whence it is that two meeting, when neither hath seen or heard of the other, at the first sight shall desire and seek each other's friendship; and, on the contrary, whence is it that one hates another from whom he hath never received injury, as evidently appears by one coming where two are gaming, he shall presently find his affection to chose with the one and if his wish might succeed he should win, and he would gladly have the other lose, though he neither received courtesy from the one nor harm or ill word from the other.

Now as much as the understanding excels the taste and dull and sensual faculty, [by] so much a truly wise man surpasseth one that only outwardly seems judicious. One by reflection considers and weighs the matter, the other, not so acutely apprehending, is tempted to rashness. Thus many learned men, whose fancies have not been in due subjection to their understandings, have abused themselves and have heedlessly embraced this as good and cast off that as evil. It may

Ninth Sheet

seem as strange in Medicine that some Doctors should only prescribe vegetables and Galenical physick, perfectly hating chemistry, and that others, wholly inclined to novelty, should refuse all Medicines that are not chemically prepared.

Both parties (in mine opinion) are swayed more by fancy than by reason; for I suppose it absolutely necessary to study first your ancient, dogmatical Medicine, both as to the speculative and practical part and to correct the faults as we have already pointed [out] in the first, second and third qualities; and the same course is to be taken in chemistry, so that they be without suspicion and deceit; and first we will begin with the old and proceed to the new.

We have sufficiently proved that there are occult properties and specific virtues in simples, as no learned Galenist ever denied, who have also confessed that these did not work from their qualities or degrees, but their natures, to mitigate symptoms, take away the cause of the disease and to enthronize health in man's body.

If this be true, why are not physicians more careful in gathering and rightly understanding the nature of simples? Fernelius in his book *De abditis rerum caussi*, saith that this specific virtue, which he calls the form, lies hid in every part of a simple and is diffused throughout all the elements. Hence if by chemistry water is drawn off, oil is extracted and salt made out of the ashes, each of these, the water, oil and salt, hath the specifical virtues of the simples; but I suppose one not so much as another, yet all joined together are perfect and compleat.

These things being laid down and confirmed, we must confess that the outward, tangible body of any simple, that may be beaten, cut, sifted, boiled [or] mingled with any other, to be the bark, the carcass and habitation of the specific quality, which is the pith, the Soul, the householder. And now what shall we say of our common preparations in apothecaries' shops, which have good and bad, nay most corrupt, in them? Would not all laugh him to scorn who, being commanded to call a master out of his house, will needs have the house along too? That cannot use the birds unless the nest be an ingredient? That cannot[107] eat oysters unless he may also devour the shells? But the apothecaries think this lawful enough, because they can do no better. These Occult qualities, indeed, are so subtile that they make an easy escape unless they be narrowly watched and with a great skill housed or incorporated. Camphor loseth its strength unless it be cherished with flax seed. Rhubarb is preserved by wax and the Spirit of Wine. The Salt of goats' blood does evaporate if it be not close in stopped in glasses.

What shall we then say of these specifical qualities separated from their bodies? Will not they return to their first principles? For who can separate the quality of burning from the fire, the quality of moistening from the Water? But if this be impossible in simple bodies, how much more difficult in compound?

I could, therefore, wish that Medicines were used which were lawful, possible and reasonable, that laying aside ostentation and pride truth might flourish.

Perhaps we might allow of Syrups, Juleps [and] Conserves did not that great quantity of Sugar clog the natural operation of the Simple.

Perhaps we might approve of Electuaries, Opiates [and] Antidotes, unless the multitude of Simples confusedly put together did hinder, if not totally extinguish the true virtue.

Tenth Sheet

Perhaps Pills and all bitter, sour, sharp and stinking Medicines are good; but yet they destroy appetite [and] cause loathsomeness, [so] that a patient had better endure the disease than the remedy. If bitterness, sourness, sharpness and an ill savour are the specifical qualities, they should rather be checked than let loose, and indeed they are but handmaids to their Mistress, but subservient to the Specifical Quality and the true difference is discovered by Chemistry, for it separates the impure parts from the pure if rightly used. Yet mistake not. We say not that chemical preparations are altogether spiritual and without any body, but are more piercing and subtile, more defecated than gross bodies made heavy by a great quantity of Sugar so that they are not free and at liberty to act and play their parts.

Thus you may see the folly and madness of those who hate chemistry, which ought to be used, but with care and judgement; for it is not the part of a physician to burn, lance, cauterize and to take away the cause of the disease by weakening the patient and endangering of his life, but symptoms must be abated, [and] nature restored and comforted by safe cordials. One Archgatus was the first chirugeon that came to Rome and was honourably received; but coming to use lancing and burning he was thought rather an hangman and for the like cause at one time all physicians were banished from Rome. One Charmis, a physician, condemning the judgement of his predecessors, set up new inventions of his own and commanded his patients in frost and snow to bathe in cold water as Pliny reports; who saith also that he hath seen old men sit freezing by his direction. It is clear enough from what hath been said that Nature is best satisfied when profitable and wholesome Medicines are applied.

Asclepiades, an intimate friend of Cn Pompey, first showed the benefit of wine to sick persons, recovering a man carried to his grave. He taught to maintain health by a moderate use of meat and drink, an exact care in exercise and much rubbing; he invented delightful and pleasing potions; he commanded bathing and for ease to his patients invented hanging beds that sleep might surprise them in such a careless posture. Pliny saith that Democritus was a physician, who, in the cure of Considia, daughter to Consul Servilius, did forbear harsh means and by the long and continual use of goats milk recovered her.

Agron, as Coelius reports, *Lib.* 13, *cap.* 22, was a physician at Athens, who, in a great plague, when many were infected, did only cause to be made great fires nigh to the place; and thus did Hippocrates, for which he was much honoured.

Whence we may learn that mild and gentle usage in a disease is more efficacious to the taking away of the cause and to heal the symptoms, than harsh and rugged dealing. The mariner doth [not] pray for a full gale many times to force him into his desired harbour, neither doth the travailer go in a direct line, yet both in the end attain their hopes. We read that Fabius, by delay conquered his enemy, so that it is a masterpiece of prudence well and naturally to deliberate and then to execute; yet the method of curing remains and the anxious are firm, viz.: if the cause be taken away, the effect ceaseth; if the disease is cured the symptoms do vanish and wear away.

But chemistry stores and supplies us with Medicines which are safe, pleasant and soon perform that for which they were intended.

Let us take a view of these, who are mere chemists. These would be called young Theophrasts, asserting like their master a divine title, which he neither had by his father nor mother, but assumed it to himself as most magnificent and glorious. But without all doubt he was a man of eminent and admirable knowledge in the Art of Physick, yet surely it would be judged madness for his sake alone to forsake the Ancients and follow his new inventions.

It may seem an absurd thing for one to undertake to restore a very old man to his former strength, because Death is then approaching and every man at length must submit to his sceptre. Is not the world now ancient and full of days and is it not folly to think of recovering and calling back its youth? Surely their new Medicine cannot revive the dying world, it may [even] weaken it and hasten its end. Yet stay, I pray you, do not imagine that I do at present censure the excellent and plainly divine preparations of chemistry, but rather the persons who profess it, who make it their business to destroy but endeavour not to build, who trample on others to be raised and exalt themselves, as Thessalus of old did, and Van Helmont in our time, railing against all men who were not their followers. So Chrysippus, master to Eristratus, to gain pre-eminence, despised and changed Hippocrates.

These and such like men are wont to promise much but perform little; for we may certainly conclude that although such persons may affect greatness, yet they shall never attain it by such indirect means. I would many of the Paracelsians did not too much conform to their Master's vices. If many late writings were scanned and their abuses and bad language against others left out, I doubt [not] their volumes would very much shrink. It were much better that diseases, the common enemies, were more looked after than private grudges amongst physicians themselves revenged. Brute beasts do bark and show their teeth and spit venom; a man's weapon is Reason, by which he should foil his adversaries.

As touching chemistry, we highly commend and admire those things in it which are good, but yet so as not to despise Galenical physic, which in some cases is as effectual. My own opinion is that each ought to be used in its proper place. Men are not mere Spirits, but corporeal substances and therefore need not Medicines exalted to their highest degree of perfection, as least in every grief, applied to every person and to every part or member. There are some diseases, which, being hot and dry, are not to be cured by chemical prescriptions whose ingredients or preparations have the like qualities. In a commonwealth there is a merchant [and] there is a husbandman, but one ought not to supplant the other; so a prudent physician will make use of both as he sees occasion, the one for a countryman, the other for a delicate person; the one in a slight distemper, the other in dangerous cases; the one for pleasantness, the other for efficacy as necessity requires.

SECTION THE SEVENTH

Concerning the insufferable vices of many Physicians from which the Fraternity of R.C. is free.

We have not without sufficient cause said something of the abuses of Medicine, which the Brethren warily shunned by their first Law, which was that they should cure the sick gratis; for the greediness of physicians put them upon unjust and illegal actions.

Whence come those terrible, long bills, those short, dear bills, but from covetousness, every one more striving to enrich himself than to help the diseased; yet we deny to none their honest gains. Justice and truth should sway them in their practice; let them follow the method of Galen and Hippocrates, yet Nature is more to be looked after than either of them, as a sure guide into its own most intimate secrets. But from the faults of remedies we will come to the faults of physicians themselves, by which so many patients do and have miscarried.

They are commonly these: self-conceit, pride, malice, hatred, calumniation in word and writing, covetousness [and] ignorance, joined with a great stock of confidence, or, rather, impudence.

This self-conceit becomes no man. If a man is puffed up like a bladder, he may be sooner broken and his glory will vanish. His greatness increaseth his danger. Neither is pride to be allowed of; it spoils all parts and endowments and if the man escape the envy of others, yet death or a slight fever makes him fall and he who was even now lifted up through ambition is brought down to the earth. It is not true learning that causeth man to swell, but an emptiness; they suppose themselves to be knowing men, whereas indeed they understand not the depths of Nature. Socrates had learned a lesson of ignorance [when] after much study he found out his own unsufficiency. If these vapourers would turn over a new leaf, they would see their former presumption.

Mark how malice and hatred prospers; when two are set against each other, they endeavour, by making themselves a laughing stock, utterly to undo both and each at length is whipped with his own rod. There is this benefit in having an envious adversary, that he spends and wastes away; his malice feeds upon himself so that it is better for any man to deserve the envy of another rather than his pity, the one supposing him happy, the other miserable.

This vice, as the ivy by embracing trees doth spoil them; this vice, I say, clings to great persons and secretly corrodes their honour and fame. What noble exploits, what virtuous deeds have been performed, but yet they have been blown upon by some such pestilential breath? This was the cause of furious Cain's murdering his righteous brother Abel and that Jupiter struck Aesculapius with a thunderbolt. To avoid this many have forsaken their countries and lived among strangers, as did Iphicrates in Thracia, Timotheus in Lesbos, Chabrias in Egypt [and] Chares in Sigaeum, who were all Grecians. Amongst the Romans Pompey, after so many magnificent triumphs for his great and famous victories, withdrew into the country and came seldom in public that he might escape the envy and malice which he feared because of his innocency and greatness.

Twelfth Sheet What shall we think of that monster Aristotle, who (as it is reported) was so spiteful to his master Plato that he caused many of his works to be burned, that he might shine brighter. He was fearful his honour should be eclipsed by his master's greatness. Ajax hated Ulysses; Zoilus, Homer; and Didimus Alexandrinus was enemy to M. Tullius Cicero; Palamon, the grammarian to M. Vanno; Caesar to Cato; Adrianus to Trajan; M. Crassus to Pompey; Alexander to Achilles, at sight of his sepulchre; Julius Caesar to Alexander; and many others who were possessed all with this evil spirit; but in Medicine such practices are more dangerous because the body of man, being more worth than Arts or other trifles, is engaged as being the subject of Medicine.

This flame increaseth and most commonly breaketh out. Envy turns to calumniation.

Covetousness is another vice which hath infected many physicians, who make it their only study to heap up riches; and though their strength of body is decayed through age, yet with a most rigorous desire do they endeavour after money; nay, though they have one foot in the grave, they will have another in a bag to counterpoise them. Physicians indeed above others are tempted to this vice, for when they grow old they are most sought unto because of their experience and by this means they are encouraged to set Silver above justice and Gold above conscience. But if an apothecary be covetous and greedy, more mischiefs do ensue. All his compositions will be made up either of stale or false ingredients, so that the physician and patient are both cheated; the one is censured for ill success, the other is not only not cured, but may complain of the bad physic as of a new disease.

I shall speak nothing concerning the abilities and qualifications of a tried, examined and licensed physician, but of the unskilfulness of those who rashly undertake to practise when they want knowledge and learning to guide and direct them; they study impudence; and note that an illiterate, rude fellow in maintaining his opinion shall always appear most confident; their geese are swans, their absurd receipts are oracles and mysteries and they are enjoined to conceal what they know not. If anyone opposeth them, they either slander him or envy him perfectly.

These and the like vices have no place amongst our Fraternity. They are not emulous or arrogant; they are not spiteful and envious, but delight in instructing one another in mysteries; no brawling or disgraceful speeches are uttered amongst them, much less are they covetous.

SECTION THE EIGHTH

Whether one of the Fraternity being called to a patient is bound to appear? And whether they are able to cure all Diseases, as well those that are accounted incurable as those that are thought curable?

The actions of men as well as their persons are subject to many miscarriages; as the one may die, so the other may be forgotten; as the one may be infirm, so the other may be abused. Wherefore an Art was invented by which all worthy deeds might faithfully be kept and transmitted to posterity. Persons, indeed, whose offices are public, in performance of their duties in trust are necessarily bound, if occasion requires, to act publicly in their place; but if in the Little World any disorder happens, as a disease subverting health, the sick person immediately goes, not to a magistrate but [to] a physician; wherefore Medicine properly respects not the public but the private health of this or that patient; therefore it will follow that a physician, being not compelled by the law nor engaged by service, shall [not][702] be forced to visit any patient who sends for him; for a physician doth not prescribe to all, but to a particular sick man and is a servant to Nature but not to the diseased, whom he governs by his rules till he hath restored them to health.

We may enquire more strictly concerning these Brethren, whether, since they profess only Medicine as their first Law enjoins, if wrote unto or spoken to for the taking away of a difficult disease, whether in any particular place they must appear, being engaged thereto either by promise or charity?

We answer negatively; for if other physicians are not so straightened, much less are they who do their cures without price, who expect not a reward from men but from God, to Whom, as also to the lawful magistracy, they are obedient.

Furthermore, whether all diseases are cured by them, even those which others judge past help, as the leprosy, the dropsy, the pestilence, the cancer, the hectic,[703] the gout and many others? We answer that the Fraternity ingeniously confess in their writings that they know not the time of their own death and they acknowledge that all men must pay their debt to death, which cannot be hindered or prevented by any Medicine, if, according to predestination it seizes upon any man; and to endeavour against providence were impious and vain.

Thirteenth Sheet But there are three degrees considerable in the forementioned maladies, the beginning, the increase and the height.[704] At the first all or most of these diseases are curable; when they prevail somewhat over Nature, remedies may be had and doubtless the Brethren have Medicines which will effect the cure, God's providence assisting them in their lawful endeavours. Such diseases in their height which have a tendency to death are incurable. As for common sicknesses, we find that either Galenical or chemical preparations may remove them.

We will now declare the reasons why sometimes the most able physicians are foiled and disappointed. First we must know that diseases are the effects of sin and deserved punishment doth often times shut out favour, so that tedious sicknesses and death are means which God useth to check sinners or chastise his people; in vain, therefore, will man labour to frustrate the decree of the Almighty in His will and pleasure. The second reason may be drawn from the nature of diseases, which are either deadly in themselves or as they are consequences of others being produced by them. The plurisy or the inflamation of the pleura, although it is dangerous, yet if direct means be applied in time it is helped and cured. But if the matter inflaming is not evacuated by letting blood or by expectorations, there will follow a corrosion of the pleura and the corruption flows into the cavity of the breast and thus another disease is generated called empiema; and now if Nature stands not much the patient's friend and doth not carry this matter into the water courses, as often is seen, or also by art some muscles are opened and the corruption within forty days carried away, the lungs will be ulcerated and a consumption will ensue altogether incurable.

The question is whether curable diseases are by them helped? Such, indeed, would end without any application and Nature needs no assistance to such enemies, so that the Medicine were useless; for who will trouble himself to seek after means when his grief will shortly of itself cease and go away? Though here be many difficulties couched, yet we shall briefly state the case. Let those who [are] unsatisfied in large treatises show whether in the world it was always absolutely necessary that all things should be done which are done or whether they might have been otherwise disposed of. Cardanus and the Stoics do attribute all events to fatal necessity, to which they do subject God Himself as not being able to resist, so blasphemous are they.

We hold that god is a free Agent Omnipotent. He can do whatsoever He pleaseth; He hath made Nature His handmaid and she, having received a commission, doth accordingly act; she produceth all things either for the good and happiness of men or else to plague and punish them and of this rank are diseases, and death itself cometh from such prevalent diseases. But God alone disposeth of good and evil to everyone. He, indeed, generally lets Nature keep its course, but sometimes to show His freedom He interrupts that order and by a particular providence thwarts the intention of Nature, whether it tends to health or sickness. It is in His power to shorten a disease which to us may seem tedious; He can keep off death when we give over the use of means. Now if God foresees the evils which naturally hang over men and doth not prevent such evils but therewith will punish men, He is not the author of that evil foreseen and brought upon anyone by Nature, although sometimes He sends miraculous plagues upon His enemies. Hence is that saying: 'O Israel, thy destruction is from thyself, because thy wickedness hath drawn down judgement upon thy head.'[705] When some of the wise heathens had taken notice of this, they feigned pleasure and sorrow to be linked together, as if the excess thereof were to itself a sufficient punishment. They also said that a disease was brother to death; that by sweat virtue was attained; and to this purpose is that place in the Scripture: 'There is no evil in the City that is not from God,'[706] where is meant the evil of punishment, either brought upon any person miraculously and by the immediate hand of God or else miraculously falling upon him.

Hence we learn the birth and original of vice; it proceeds from the corrupted nature of fallen man; his will enjoys its liberty in respect of earthly things, but as to heavenly things it is not free. It is with a man as with a weak, inferior person, who cannot lift his hands to his head, but with ease he can let them hang downwards. So sinful man, naturally inclining to sinfulness, without any pains falls into wickedness; he needs no particular instinct from God; but the strength which must support his infirmities [and] exalt him to Heaven, so that he may obey God, is not from man himself, but from the free Grace and Mercy of his Heavenly Father, Who hath mercy on whom He will, but yet excludes none from His favour who, forsaking earthly things, do accept of the true means and receive the benefit thereof, who pray and endeavour to their utmost ability to be what they should be, committing themselves first and chiefly to God and then to Nature, who faithfully obeys Him in all things.

Fourteenth Sheet

SECTION THE NINTH

That the Brethren of the Fraternity do use only lawful and natural remedies.

The Holy Scripture makes mention of a King of Juda, who, being sick of the plague and [when] death seemed to approach, by divine providence was healed by having figs applied to the sore, and he lived many years after,[707] so that we see that God can miraculously direct to means which in themselves are natural, as indeed this was a very lawful remedy, and the reason is not unknown. So here we will examine whether the means which the Brethren use be of themselves lawful and warrantable.

A certain author, thinking to insinuate himself into the favour of the Brethren, speaks of rare blessings and exorcisms by which a man may promote the happiness of his patients and curse and endammage his adversaries. But who will esteem this lawful and good? Such things may catch some silly old women and by them be accounted secrets; they would be the greatest slander imaginable to the learned Fraternity, for the Brethren use natural means without any mixture of superstition, as we may see by the example of him at Wetzlar,[708] who with application of one simple took away the raging pain of an ulcerated cancer, whom Phanias applauds for his rare art, for by the same herb he also did the cure. The same Brother carried a bag of roots and herbs always about with him; he much commended the Briony root, but chose the bitter one; he taught also the occult virtue and proper use of many simples which are lost and forgotten.

We will not decide the controversy whether the simples ought to be gathered[709] according to particular constellations; many very learned men do favour this opinion, as first of all Barthol. Carictherus, who divided the most approved and effectual simples according to the four triplicities of the Signs of the Zodiac and in each of them made three degrees. I have known many who, addicting themselves to this study, have thereby been able to cure very dangerous sicknesses, especially old ulcers and outward griefs.

We will not decide the controversy whether the simples ought to be gathered[709] according to particular constellations; many very learned men do favour this opinion, as first of all Barthol. Carictherus, who divided the most approved and effectual simples according to the four triplicities of the Signs of the Zodiac and in each of them made three degrees. I have known many who, addicting themselves to this study, have thereby been able to cure very dangerous sicknesses, especially old ulcers and outward griefs.

That so many lights should be placed in the heavens to no end or purpose, it were profane to imagine, because God created all things to act according to their nature and surely the Stars were made to yield their influences; and there is not any doubt but that vegetables, minerals and animals do receive their occult qualities from them. He therefore is an happy man who can search out the effect by the cause and by the effect is able to judge of the cause.

Plants have relation as well to the heavens as to the earth, and he who knows this community is a great artist; but the Brethren employ all their time in these mysteries, as they confess as well in their *Fama* and *Confession* as in other writings.

We dare not affirm that this Astrology is the same with that which is vulgarly professed, or their Botany common; for theirs is founded upon certain and true axioms subject to no change, but always continuing the same worth and virtue.

Other axioms are so infirm that they oftentimes are proved false and admit of correction. It is an axiom that all wine is hot, which hitherto has been received as true; but if from some country be brought wine whose nature is cold, the falsity will appear. He who never saw a bat or doth not consider insects will immediately say that everything that flies hath feathers, when there are also flying fish, which make use of their fins, so that there are many exceptions [which] belong to the general rule. Who would not conclude this for a certain truth, that four-footed creatures cannot pass through the air as well as they pass on earth, but by flying? But experience confutes this, for the Indian cat, by spreading some membranes (not wings) from her hinder feet to her former [710] goes in the air whither she pleaseth. But the axioms laid down and followed by the Brethren are such which fail not; their principles always attain their end, so that there is nothing deficient in them which may exclude or diminish their perfection; wherefore cures wrought by properties truly brought down from the Stars and the Planets must necessarily be true and certain, for the effects do surely result from their causes, not anticipated or mistaken. He who promiseth with fire to heat, to dry, to burn, is not deceived, neither doth he deceive, because he hath that which can perform all these offices. So if they undertake a cure there is no doubt but that they can effect it because they know and can make use of the true and proper means, which mediums are purely natural, the hidden treasures of nature, the extraordinary gifts of God. They apply themselves only to the study of Natural Magic, which is a science containing the deep Mysteries of Nature. Neither is this divine knowledge given to any by God but to those who are religious, good and learned. Origen,[711] *tract, 5, super Matth.*, saith that the Magical Art doth not contain anything subsisting, but although it should, yet that must not be evil or subject to contempt and scorn. The same [author] *23 Hom. super Num.*, speaking of Natural Magic [712] doth distinguish it from the Diabolical. Many hold that Tyanaeus exercised the Natural Magic only,[713] and we do not deny it. Philo Hebreus, *Lib. de Legibus*,[714] speaks thus: 'That true Magic by which we come to the knowledge of the secrets of Nature is so far from being contemptible that the greatest Monarchs and Kings have studied it; nay among the Persians none might reign unless he were skilful in this great Art'.

Fifteenth Sheet

Magic (as some define it) is the highest, most absolute and divinest knowledge of Natural Philosophy, advanced in its wonderful works and operations by a right understanding of the inward and occult virtue of things, so that true agents being applied to proper patients, strange and admirable effects will thereby be produced. Whence magicians are profound and diligent searchers into Nature. They, because of their skill, know how to anticipate an effect which to the vulgar shall seem a miracle [715] as if anyone shall make roses bud in December, trees to flourish in January, shall cause a vintage in May, produce thunder and rain in the air as Joh. Baptista Porta teacheth, *lib. 2, De Magia Naturali*; also Roger Bacon did the same. Julius Camillus, a man to whom we may give credit, affirms that he saw a child formed by an alembic,[716] which lived some hours; a very strange thing if true. Coelius de Budda saith that he brought forth a Virgin out of his side, but we will not dispute the truth of these things, but leave them to the censure of the learned. We need not stand longer upon the praise of Magic, it being of itself so honourable, but yet[717] this noble science doth oftentimes degenerate and from Natural becometh Diabolical, from true philosophy turns to Necromancy, which is wholly to be charged upon its followers, who, abusing or not being capable of that high and Mystical knowledge, do immediately hearken to the temptation of Sathan and are misled by him into the study of the Black Art. Hence it is that Magic lies under disgrace and [that] they who seek after it are vulgarly esteemed sorcerers. Wherefore the Brethren[718] thought it not fit to style themselves Magicians but Philosophers. They are not ignorant empirics, but learned and experienced physicians, whose remedies are not only lawful but divine. And thus we have at large discoursed of their first Law.

SECTION THE TENTH

Of the Second Law of the Fraternity of the Rosie Cross, viz., That none of the Brethren shall be enjoined one Habit, but may suit themselves to the Custom and Mode of those Countries in which they are.

Many may think that I have been too prolix in expanding their Law, but weighty matters are not to be perfunctorily run over; transactions in the Little World may only deserve to be touched upon, but the affairs of the Great World ought to have an answerable consideration, for I could not wrap up the due commendations of such weighty subjects in so narrow a compass.

This second Law gives birth to the first; for without it the Brethren would have no opportunity of doing good, who by its benefit are secure and free and fear no danger. For as a bird, although it singeth not, is known by the colour of its feathers, so everyone accustoming himself to one habit is thereby distinguished. We find in history that many by their enemies have been discovered by their apparel and the disguise hath oftentimes procured liberty. Otho, being overcome and making his escape by sea, was taken by pirates who, not knowing him because he had changed his clothes, suffered him to ransom himself.

On the contrary King Richard, coming back from the Holy Land, affairs being there badly managed and to the displeasure of many, especially the Duke of Austria, [in] passing with his Navy by the Adriatic Sea, was described and became a prey to the said Duke, who was forced, to redeem himself, to pay a vast sum of money; and he was known and found out by his garments.

If danger attends Kings and great persons in such cases, much worse would be the condition of private men if they should have so sad a restraint upon them. Men in mean apparel do not fear the attempts of robbers, neither do they suspect a poisoned glass, whereas potentates are a prey to the one and very often are taken away by the other.

Besides, a poor habit is sufficient to cover learning and a cottage may become wisdom's habitation; nay men's parts and abilities are censured by their outside and that which is willingly concealed must not have a being; 'tis a courtier who must only be accounted a scholar But indeed the Soul is clothed with the body, which to add armament to it needs no help of tailors or painters; it is graved with true philosophy and secret arts are its glory.

Sixteenth Sheet Margareta, a Queen of France, is said to have kissed the beautiful Soul of Alanus, a philosopher, when he was asleep, through his body, the which action being much admired at, she answered that she thus perceived not the deformity of his body, being ravished with the amiableness of his Soul. Thus we see that a gallant Spirit may dwell in an unhandsome house and that a poor habit may be worn by the most excellent and profound philosopher.

There are yet many reasons which may persuade to a decent clothing, for by every vulgar eye the mind is judged by the garment; but very many instead of modest and comely apparel run into excess, as Poppea, wife to Nero, and Cleopatra, Queen of Egypt, to set forth their beauty. But this is not commendable, since Seneca's rule is to be observed, which requires a due moderation.

Our Brethren change their habit for a virtuous end, which, as it is not gaudy, so it is not contemptible; they are always civilly clad and not affectedly; they are especially careful of the inside, that their hearts are real and honest, neither would they impose on any by their actions.

There are many ways by which men may be deluded, as by a fallacy, equivocation or amphiboly,[719] but these do appertain to logic. The Brethren are vigilant as well in respect of disgrace as damage; it is a very difficult matter to cheat or deceive them.

Whereas others take the liberty to cozen a cozener and think it a piece of justice to repay in the same coin, the Brethren are not so revengeful; they count it a happiness to have an opportunity of expressing their patience; yet although they are as innocent as doves, they endeavour to be as wise as serpents, for there may be an harmless subtlety. We may judge easily that they affect not vanity by their often change of their apparel, because they would not be known but obscure their names and relation.

If the intentions are sincere, not thereby to wrong any but to do good, we may allow not only of a disguise in clothes but a change of names. The sign doth not alter the thing signified, neither doth an accident destroy the substance. Names are notes by which one man is known and distinguished from another; clothes are coverings; as the one hides our nakedness, so the other keeps from obscurity. The ancient philosophers and Egyptian priests did wear a linen, white robe, which distinguished them from others, as Pythagoras and his followers, to express both the cleanliness of body and unspotted innocency of Soul. Nature hath so befriended some birds that they change both voice and feathers in winter, and thereby being not known are safe from other ravenous birds. In some countries hares become white in winter, but in summer keep their wonted colours.

The Chamelion, by being like to everything she comes near, doth often escape. The ants and many insects have wings and can scarcely be known what they first were, so happy is that change which guides to safety.

Shall reason withstand the lawful dictates of Nature? Where necessity compels [and] custom forces, shall men run upon the one and to their damage slight the other? The Brethren, being in all points careful, will neither violate Nature's commands nor condemn civil rights; though they alter their apparel, their mind is unchangeable.

SECTION THE ELEVENTH

The Third Law enjoins each Brother to appear on a particular day[720] and at a certain place[721] every year, that they may meet all together and consult about their affairs.[722]

Every Society hath Laws and Rules binding them to some duties, so that the governor or chief, when he pleaseth and thinks it necessary, may summon all to one place to consider what is most fit and convenient to be done on some emergent occasions; for if a company be separated, their minds and counsels are disjoined, the one cannot be helpful to the other either in example or advice. Who knows not that most intimate familiarity and the nearest friendship is broken off by absence and want of visitation, so that they who were not long since highest in our thoughts are utterly forgotten; besides, wherein can a friend profit, who is distant from another; even brethren become as it were unnatural when thus separated. We confess that letters may supply this deficit, yet writing doth not so much delight and enliven as discourse. Papers are mute. If any doubt arise, they cannot frame a ready answer; but where a man appears he can resolve all questions, satisfy all scruples.

Seventeeth Sheet

Wherefore the Brethren of the R. C. thought it most expedient, if not altogether requisite, to meet at least once in the year in a certain prefixed place. This Law, as it is the third in order, so also in Dignity, by which the true Pythagorean assembly is obliged to appearance. Neither is their meeting vain and to gaze upon each other, for they do imitate the Rule of Pythagoras, who enjoined his scholars every day to examine themselves, where they had been and what good, memorable act they had performed. So the Brethren of the R. C., at their convention relate what rare cures they have done, what progress they have made in the Arts and Sciences and observe how their practice agrees with their principles; and if any new knowledge confirmed by often experience comes to them, they write it in books that it may safely come to the hands of their successors. Thus true and certain learning is increased till at length it shall attain perfection.

This School is not like to Aristotle, for there [there] were frequent, wrangling disputes, one opposing the other, and perhaps both [opposing] the truth; however they have no questions free from debate not contradicted by some of the same sect. For example: What is the Soul of Man, whether the First Act or something else, whether $ενδελεχ[ε]ια$[723] or $εντελεχ[ε]ια$,[724] whether born, generated or infused, given from heaven, and many other niceties, and at length they rest in opinion.

They have therefore framed a method to regulate disputes and supply terms, whereby they more darken knowledge and willingly shut their eyes. Let them discuss to weariness the nature and original of metals and whether there can be a transmutation and who will be better informed and satisfied? Thus idle disputation is a sport of wit and only a recreation of fancy; no solid and real truth is to be found out by it.

A certain philosopher, hearing some dispute what virtue is, made answer that as they could not come to an end of the question, so neither to the use thereof. If anyone professes himself to have a skill in physic, why then doth he not let the world see what he can do and, laying aside vain babblings, perfect the great work of natural tincture. But perchance he will utterly deny that there is any such thing to be found out and hereby gets a cloak for his ignorance, for he will censure all that he knows not.

But who will call him an horseman, who yet did never ride? Who will call him a smith who never wrought in that art? And why should we esteem him a philosopher who hath never experienced his philosophy, but hath only uttered some foolish and fantastical words?

But some may here object that one part of philosophy is contemplative, to which mathematics and metaphysics do relate, [while] the other consists in action, to which ethics and politics do guide. Plato was displeased that mathematics were brought [725] to sensible subjects as arithmetic to numbers, music to sounds [and] geometry to measures; but we must acknowledge that Plato in this was envious to mankind and [that] his passion prevailed over his reason. For what profiteth it any man by mere speculation to view the Mysteries of God and Nature? Is it a more commendable thing to think well than to be good? The same holds true in physics, for barely to contemplate of it is as unuseful as absurd and ridiculous. How can you call that a true cause of which you never saw an effect? There hath been some ancient philosophers who have searched after experimental knowledge and studied more Nature than Art, more the thing than the significance and name, as the Magicians among the Persians, the Brahmins among the Indians and the Priests in Egypt and now the Brethren of the Rosy Cross in Germany. Thus we see plainly they meet for a good end, for each court hath its appointed time in which justice may be duly executed and no wrongs further heightened. The Brethren assemble to vindicate abused Nature, to settle Truth in her power and chiefly that they may with one accord return thanks to God for revealing such Mysteries to them. If any man is prompted to a high office and neglects or contemns the Ceremonies and Circumstances of admission, the prince will immediately put him out as one slighting his favour and scorning of him. So since God hath been pleased to honour our Brethren with such rare endowments and they should not appear to show their gratitude, He might justly take from them His Talent and make them subjects of His wrath.

This Law hath a limitation; if they cannot appear they must either by others, their Brethren, or by a letter, tell the cause of their absence, for infirmity, sickness or any other extraordinary casualty may hinder the journey.

We cannot set down the places where they meet, neither the time.[726] I have sometimes observed Olympick houses not far from a river and a well-known city,[727] which we think is called S. *Spiritus*, I mean Helicon or Parnassus, in which Pegassus opened a spring of ever-flowing water, wherein Diana washed herself, to whom Venus was handmaid and Saturn gentleman usher. This will sufficiently instruct the learned, but more confound the ignorant.[728]

SECTION THE TWELFTH

Concerning the Fourth Law, that every Brother shall choose a fit person for his Successor after his decease, that the Fraternity may be continued.

Eighteenth Sheet

All things in the world have their vicissitudes and changes; what was today is not tomorrow; and this appears most of all in mankind, who are as sure once to die as they at present do live, wherefore God, out of His heavenly providence, granted generation and propagation, that though individuals do perish, yet the species may still be preserved.

And this is that innate principle which is the cause of multiplication, so that plants, animals, minerals and man, the noblest creature, shall to the end of the world be increased. Many philosophers have complained of the shortness of man's life, who, though he be more excellent than others, yet he lives not their ages. The Eagle, the Raven, the Lion and what not live longer than man, as though Nature was a step-mother to him and the others her true progeny.

Wherefore since that the Brethren being mortals must certainly once cease to be, and undergo the common lot of their nature, this wise Law-maker did not rashly make this Law, that each Brother should choose to himself a fit person to be his successor, in which choice they do not look to the obligations of friends, their natural relation[s], neither to sons or brethren, but purely to [such] qualifications [as] learning, secrecy, piety and other such-like endowments.

Amongst the Egyptians the sons did not only inherit their fathers' estate, but used the same trade and employment. The son of a potter was a potter, a smith's son was a smith. But the Kings were chosen out from amongst the priests and the priests from amidst the philosophers and the philosophers were always sons of philosophers, but many times there happened a great difference of parts between the Son and Father; outward goods may be conveyed to posterity and the son may be the father's heir, but the gifts of mind, especially such as this Fraternity hath, is rarely by generation communicated to the offspring. He that shall be enduced either by entreaty or hired with money to reveal aught to anyone but a truly virtuous man, doth injure the first giver of such a Talent[729] the Law-giver and the whole Fraternity, for perhaps enemies thereby would be able to further their designs, God would be dishonoured and virtue banished.

The philosophers would have mysteries revealed to none but those whom God Himself shall enlighten, that their understandings being refined they may apprehend the deepest sayings and profoundest secrets. Others say that we must not trust him with whom we have not eaten a bushel of Salt; that is him with whom we have not had much converse to the sure experience of his abilities and faith, for friendship is not to be compared to horses that bear price according as they are young, but to wine and Gold, which are bettered by age. So the Brethren entertain no man to be a Member of the Fraternity but men of approved parts and very virtuous.

There were certain Rites and Ceremonies done at Athens in the honour of Prometheus, Vulcan and Minerva after this manner: Many were appointed to run into the city with lighted torches and he whose light was out gave place to others, so that the victory was obtained by him who could come first at the goal with his flaming torch. The meaning was to express the propagation of secrets; for the putting out of the torch is the death of a predecessor, so that another living with his lighted torch succeeds him, by which means the rare mysteries of chemistry come safe to after generations.

Chemistry indeed is a science above all sciences, the Minerva that sprang from Jupiter's brain, an heavenly ray which doth display itself to the comforting of things below. This is the birth of the understanding, whose propagation is as necessary as that of the body. We may observe the antipathy of some bodies to others and we may see as great difference in minds. Men's dispositions are to be fully known lest a sword be put into a madman's hand; for a good thing may be evilly used, as wholesome wine put into a stinking cask doth change both colour and taste.

Archimedes boasted that if he could fix his foot in a sure place he could by his skill move the whole world, and what would not ill affected persons do if there were matters of such secrets known? Doubtless they would endeavour the accomplishment of all their wicked devices.

Some may ask why they have such an election and do not rather let their knowledge be buried with them (or if not so unworthy) why do they not print, that everyone may have, read and understand their Mysteries; or else why do they not choose more to augment the Fraternity? We shall answer to each of them to satisfy those who question.

First, why do they select a few persons and will not have their secrets perish? We answer there is good reason for both. Augustus Caesar would not suffer the Aeneids[730] of Virgil to be burned, although he had designed so by his will, lest Rome's glory should suffer thereby; and yet this Poet, as Homer amongst the Grecians, had instead of Truth produced fictions. And is there not a greater cause why [the] Brethren of the R.C. should endeavour the keeping in memory [of] such secrets? May this learning never be forgotten in which there are no fables but true and divine experiments.

Nineteenth Sheet

We may woefully lament the loss of secrets which, being writ, have unhappily been burnt, [and] not [being] writ have been forgotten; therefore, for the preservation of both it is convenient that they should be entrusted in a few hands and by those careful to be transmitted to others. Before the Flood the arts were engraven on two pillars, lest either fire or water should blot them out and afterward (as some write) the Cabalistical Art was found out and by word of mouth communicated, and the Rabbins have at this day rather a shadow than the substance of that Science.

The heathens had their colleges, in which were admitted none but such as were of unblameable conversation and of choice parts, so that everyone who was educated in a scholastic way was not thought a fit person to be of their Society, but they would choose of the most able, and they were few, the which rule is observed by the Fraternity of the R.C., who admitted few and those upon good desert.

In the next place we come to the reason why they do not print and make their knowledge public. There are many things in policy, more in divinity [and] not a few in Nature, which ought not to see the light, but are to be kept in private breasts lest thereby [they should be revealed, and though] some have written of the secrets of the Commonwealth, no one yet durst reveal the Mysteries of God.

Alexander the Great, being in Egypt, learned of Leon the priest that the Gods there and those which were everywhere else worshipped as Jupiter, Dionysius, Mars and others were no Gods, and he by letter informed his mother but commanded that the letter should forthwith be consecrated to Vulcan lest the multitude adoring those gods should run into confusion. So likewise in Nature, if their mysteries were known, what would become of order? But indeed how can that be called a secret which is revealed to many? Though many may be judged fit persons to receive the knowledge, yet few have such command over themselves as to keep them [secret]. Who will tie his tongue and deny himself the liberty he might otherwise enjoy? Very few will let their words by long abiding there corrupt in their mouths. An ancient philosopher, being accused of a stinking breath, said that it was caused by letting secrets putrefy in it.

Why all who are desirous of the Fraternity are not chosen is not their fault but the others' lottery. In courts they are somewhat promoted who are most pleasing to their princes and they who are known [are] preferred before the strangers, although their parts be better.

SECTION THE THIRTEENTH

The Fifth Law, that the Letters R.C. shall be their Seal, Character and Cognizance.

The Egyptians had two sorts of letters, the one holy, called hieroglyphics, only known to the priests, the other prophane, commonly known. The holy letters were the images of animals, vegetables or mathematical figures, engraven in marble, which yet are to be seen at Rome, being yet brought whole thither in Augustus his reign, for the impression being inward it will endure long. The prophane were made by lines as the Greek and Hebrew. The priests used both, the one to the Commonwealth, the other to the wise and learned.

Hieroglyphics were signs and characters of deep knowledge, which none might expound to others [except] under oath and pleasure of the Gods. Junior philosophers have employed all their pains and study to find out the meaning of these hieroglyphics. The Phoenix (properly belonging to chemistry) was accounted a creature dedicated to the Sun and this emblem agrees to all the holy marks; so likewise the R.C. have divers letters to discover their minds to their friends and to conceal it from others.

Their characters are R.C., which they use that they may not be without a name, and everyone according to his capacity may put an interpretation upon the letters as soon as their first writing come forth. Shortly after [this event] they were called Rosie Crucians, for R may stand for Roses and C for Cross, which appellation yet remains, although the Brethren have declared that thereby they symbolically mean the name of their first author.[731] If one man could pierce into another's breast and enjoy his thoughts, we should need neither words nor but this being denied us and only granted to Angels, we must speak and write each to other.

These letters do contain the whole Fraternity and so darkly that you cannot by their names know their families, by their families know their persons, by their persons know their secrets.

Twentieth Sheet

Each order hath its formalities and coat of arms or emblems. The Phodians have the double cross, they of Burgundy the golden fleece, others a garter in honour of a woman who left her garter in a dance. The Brethren have the letters R.C., and as some of the others are hieroglyphics and serve to cover Mysteries, so the Brethren have a particular intention in this. Is not this a Claw of the rosy Lion, a drop of Hippocrene?[732] And yet I have not been so unfaithful as to publish their Holy Mysteries, for no man can pick anything out of it unless he is very skilful both in words and things. Some out of proper names will make anagrams. See what is included in R.C., the Rosie Cross, γλυκιπικρον,[733] Ha, Ha, Eheu, in the same is contained laughter and a complaint, sweetness and bitterness, joy and sorrow; for to live amid Roses and under a Cross are two contrary things. Man being about to be born, partly by change of places, partly by the navel string cut, is said most commonly to shed tears and rarely to rejoice; so their whole life is but a continued sorrow and has more of the Cross than the Rose in it. But I rather take R for the substantial part, C for the adjective, which holds not good in that interpretation of the Rosy Cross.[734]

The Caesars of Germany, Charles the Great and his successors, were wont to use hand seals and to set them to their subscriptions. It was meet that the Brethren should not be deficient in this and therefore, ingenious persons, judge of this anagram:

For in this R.C. are acrosticks; diligence will find out the rest. I hope none will think virtue to lie hid in this Figure, we mean nothing less, but we have only given out our verdict and the others have freedom to have their opinions. But we mutter not words but look more after things, for things should be although they were unnamed, but words are, without things, vain and insignificant.

When a certain King threatened the Laconians for their long letter and desired a speedy answer, they sent back one, these letters, $o\nu$, by the one meaning that they would not, by the other that they valued not his threats one jot, so that [a] multitude of words are oftentimes to no purpose and a few, carrying weight in them, may be sufficient.

Hence the elements of the letters are not to be slighted. R., Rabies, madness and the Middle, L., Luna, the Moon do express, for if the Sun be between them they make an heart,[735] which is the first thing in man, and if it be sincere, it may be an acceptable sacrifice unto God.

SECTION THE FOURTEENTH

Concerning the sixth and last Law which is That the Fraternity of the R.C. shall be concealed an hundred years.

When the common people take notice of the secret managing of public affairs, they, because of their ignorance, suspect it to be a plot upon them and openly censure it as not fitting to see the Sun; for treacheries and wickedness desires the night and darkness to cover and conceal them and therefore actions are bad because they are private.

Besides the rude multitude, many graver heads have inconsiderately called apparent things good and the other nought, saying that if they be virtuous, why should they not be known, that they may be embraced by honest men? As if all lawful secrets, because of their lawfulness, were to be made public. Would it not savour of folly if a prince's treasure, because it [were] rightly gained, should therefore be exposed to all men? Surely such an opinion would only become a thief and a robber.

The Brethren are thought guilty of concealing themselves, for they might probably do more good if they were known because they should be sought after and have opportunities put in their hands, and why will they keep close both their persons and place? But let us consider that they travel and they, as all wise men else, acknowledge no particular country but the whole world to them is as their own native soil. Now in travel divers entertainments are to be found, much flattery, little sincerity, much falsehood and deceit, no truth nor honesty. He who is known by his family name or office may be taken notice of to his disadvantage. The Scripture calls men pilgrims, who have no true country and home but heaven, so that men are strangers and travellers in their own land, in their inheritance, and why then may they not scarcely be known to live when they shall not abide long? Their actions are such as becomes those who hope to appear and shine in heaven, though they are obscure below.

Twenty-First Sheet

How great is their madness who spend their times in drunkeness and gluttony, who are known by their vices, or imitate him who boasted that he never saw rising or setting sun and had no God but his belly. Whatever is rare and brought from a far country, that they desire to eat, as though the whole world in short time should be devoured by the filling of their guts more than their brains. Perhaps these may have rational Souls,[736] but so clogged that they cannot soar aloft who drink not, eat not that they may live, but live to eat and drink.

The Lacedemonians placed drunkards before a company of children that they, seeing the abominable naughtiness and deformity, might shun and hate that vice as Lycurgus commanded; but such beastly persons do very often draw in others who keep their company and the sight is too often dangerous and destructive; wherefore such vices should be covered as filthy that others may not be provoked and stirred up to the like enormities; nay, let such things not only be concealed but buried, and things more profitable be used in their room.

But if all good and honest secrets were brought to light, I dare say the Fraternity of the R.C. would be the last, as having no cause of fear upon them, but I doubt whether yet we shall see those happy days.

There are many things bad, which by custom have been in good esteem and the continuance of vice makes it be thought at length a virtue.

The Brethren would give no occasion for suspicion, for that which is not known cannot be practised; without practice [there is] no custom; without custom [there is] no such mistake, although they being altogether honest, need not to be censured or [any such fears] entertained.

Besides, perhaps the first author, by the Law that the Fraternity should be concealed an hundred years, would give the world time to lay aside their vanities, folly and madness and by that time be fitted to receive such knowledge.

And truly every man that hath eyes may see a great and happy change in the world, that many rare inventions are discovered, many abuses in the arts rectified and that they shall shine to perfection, and what, then, should hinder but that the name of the Fraternity should be published in their *Fame* and *Confession*?

Two hundred years are passed since the first Law was made, namely *ab anno Christi* 1413, *in anno Christi* 1613, about which time the *Fama* came forth. Although there is no clear manifestation of the discovery, yet it may sufficiently be gathered out of it, and afterward, the tomb of the first author being opened, which was *anno Christi* 1604, to which add the year of the prophecy, after one hundred and twenty years I will be known,[737] for one hundred and six *ab anno Christi* 1378 do make 1484, and afterwards one hundred and twenty do make 1604.[738] Some having this from their predecessors have certainly affirmed this truth.

SECTION THE FIFTEENTH

Concerning the advantage or disadvantage arising to Learning from the total concealment or discovery (as now is) of the Fraternity of the R.C.

I cannot imagine that any man can justly accuse me for my prolixity on the Laws of the R.C. Perhaps some may suck spider-like out of wholesome flowers destructive poison, and that which to others is pleasant and sweet, to them, [being] disaffected, may seem loathsome and ugly. They erring and being vain in themselves, scoff and laugh at our Fraternity [and] scorn their Laws. Say they, what benefit shall we receive from the discovery of them? Indeed we do hear that many under that title do abuse themselves and cheat others, for by such relations they vest their sophisticated drugs and confuse all method in Medicine.

We do not deny but that the best thing may be abused, but that is not to be charged upon the thing itself, but upon the person so employing it. So none can truly say that the Fraternity and Laws thereof are unlawful, whose institution and intention may be justified; but envious persons, who have devoted themselves to malice, may carp at them and endeavour the dissatisfaction of men's minds, wherefore I shall plainly demonstrate the profit and disprofit arising either from them detected or concealed.

There are four kinds of good; necessary, honest, pleasant and profitable. By each of them men may be drawn to the affectation or disrelish of any subject. The first two among them have the pre-eminency, the others are of less authority, but yet very often the latter prevail above the first and many had rather enjoy pleasure and profit suitable to their natures than the others, as being somewhat harsh, wherefore we will treat of them, but not as separated from necessary and honest good.

To what purpose should there be such a Society if the profit and benefit thereof should be wholly concealed? The Ethiopians and Indians, having never heard of their *Fama* and *Confession*, are not taken with their Fraternity, but if they should believe that there is such a select company of men, yet would they be heedless because they should receive no advantage by them. We care not for the richest mines if we cannot enjoy them and affairs translated at a great distance from us are nothing to us; we do not take notice how the Indians fight and they neglect our Arts.

Twenty-Second Sheet

If the Fraternity had not made known themselves there might seem to have no great damage thereby accrued to learning, since it is not more augmented; for heretofore [the] cure of diseases and [the] preservation of health were practised and professed; the sciences have been so reformed, especially the last hundred years, that they have attained their utmost perfection. On the contrary, if the Fraternity had been concealed, many might have great hopes and expectation of profit, for all kind of curiosity had been laid; men would not have vexed themselves with searching diligently after them, whom they should with the greatest difficulty hardly find; so many desires had not been unsatisfied, so many promises frustrated, so many sighs and tears vain; lastly no occasion of confusion [would have arisen]. But because all these things are so false and absurd, we shall not think them worthy of an answer; we shall therefore proceed to the profit of the Fraternity as it is detected and made known. There is in the world such an abundance of all things by the diversity of species and multitude of individuals, that it is almost impossible to discern either their increase or decay. Hence is it that persons of quality, being taken away by death, are not missed because others do succeed them and the rising Sun makes us take little notice of the set.

Had the Fraternity not been discovered, the world would have lacked nothing, for that which is unknown is not desired or sought after and the absence of it is no loss and we doubt not but that there are very many such things in Nature. Who ever dreamed of a new world now called America before it was found out; [and] who thought of the usefulness of writing and printing till they were invented? But now it is sufficiently well known what benefit the whole world received by them, although there seemed to be no want.

For as no line is so long, nor any body so big, to which something cannot be added, so the perfection of the world was not so absolute but that it was capable of addition.

Thus the detection of the Fraternity did increase the world's glory and we shall show after what manner, namely by revealing secrets and finding out others, much conducing to the profit of mankind.

The Poets report of Antaeus that he, fighting with Hercules, and by him beaten often to the ground, did as often recover himself by virtue received from the touch of the earth (for he was thought to be son of the earth), by which help he was always victorious till he strove with Hercules, who, finding out this mystery, caught him in his arms, and, holding him in the air, crushed him to death. By Hercules is understood a laborious and skilled philosopher, by Antaeus the subject to be wrought upon, in which are contrary qualifications. This matter is not easily known because it lies hid everywhere and at the same [time] lies open. Under the first in respect of men's intellect, the other in respect of sense,[739] and if it were known, yet the preparation is so difficult [that] little good can be expected. The philosophical earth is his parent, whose virtue is not easily attained. Hence it is that Antaeus is secretly strengthened from his mother and so all endeavour of killing him, Antaeus, is in vain and to no purpose.

Therefore Osiris, being about to travel into India, did not unadvisedly consult with Prometheus, join Mercury as a Governor and Hercules as President of the Provinces, by whose direction and his own industry he always accomplished his end. He used Vulcan's[740] shop, the golden house wherein Apis[741] is fed and nourished, for those three forementioned have their several offices in the philosophical Work. But some may say, what is this to the Fraternity of the R.C.? It properly appertains to them for they have overcome Antaeus, they have sufficiently declared their Herculean strength, the wit of Mercury and the providence of Prometheus. This, this is the knowledge in which the Fraternity is skilled, fetched from the innermost depths of Nature, which to neglect or to suffer to perish were folly and madness. There is no chemist who understands not what we mean.

They who take a voyage to the East Indies cannot be without sweet, fresh water, and if they find out a spring, they take a special notice of it [and] set it down in their writings that others travelling that way may enjoy the like benefit. Much greater reason is there in the philosophical voyage, having gotten a fountain sending forth pleasant streams, which can easily quench thirst and satisfy, how great reason is there that this should be highly esteemed and valued. I mean here the philosophers' living water, not any dead, which when once attained, the whole business will succeed; for the whole Work is perfected by one artifice, by one way, by one fire, which is natural (not neglecting the other three — unnatural, against Nature and occasional) in one vessel, at one time, with one labour, which must be cautiously understood.

Twenty-Third Sheet

2. The Book M, always in the hand and mind of the Fraternity and transmitted still to posterity, doth sufficiently lay open the knowledge of this Nature, in which Book is contained the perfection of all the Arts, beginning with the heavens and descending to lower sciences. For the mind of a wise man covets after the knowledge of all truths, to confute errors and to adorn itself with glory and excellency; but this is not obtained by idle, vain speculation, but by diligent practice, which is the only true wisdom.

3. Sufficient hath been said of their remedies for the cure of diseases which hath made them famous.

4. The Brethren have a secret of incredible virtue, by which they can give piety, justice and truth the upper hand in any person whom they affect, and suppress the opposite vices, but it is not my duty to expose what it is. I beseech the Great God Who governeth the whole world by His providence so to dispose of all things that such mysteries may never be lost, but that the whole world may receive benefit thereby and that hereafter men may not think it sufficient superficially to look into Nature, but deeply prying into it may have more knowledge of God the Centre and always praise Him for His goodness.

SECTION THE SIXTEENTH

That many Fables have passed under the name of the Fraternity, raised by the Multitude who always misjudge of that which they do not understand.

It cannot be otherwise, the Fraternity being in respect of itself well known, in respect of the persons thereof concealed, but that many strange, horrible and incredible falsities should be cast upon them. For if we hear, see or by any other sense have experienced anything, yet in discourse this will be altered, if not altogether changed, because he that relates will either add or diminish and the other, not apprehending it aright, or perhaps failing in memory or for affection favouring or envying the business, will unfaithfully report it. They who want these two faculties of Memory and Judgement are not competent judges in matters of so great concernment. What can a blind witness affirm he saw, one deaf that he heard or one not capable of understanding that he apprehended? For all these mistake one thing for another; they blame the subject and not themselves; they suppose all things as low as their parts and because they want abilities they acknowledge no deficiency. Whoever they are who ignorantly or maliciously do cast out any words aiming thereby to wrong the Fraternity, do only expose themselves; but let these geese, kept only to fill the belly, leave off to hiss at our Swans. The water of which we now speak is not that in which fishes do swim, neither is this a fit study for such dolts and blocks. Leave off to discover what you are by your idle words; learned and wise men are not censored by them and why should they receive evil for good? But some may ask what fables are thus vented against the Fraternity? We answer that many have detracted and traduced their innocent *Fama* and harmless *Confession*, that they have accounted them heretics, necromancers, deceivers, disturbers of the commonwealth. O harsh times, O evil manners! What is the world to come to when slanders shall pass for truths and they who devote themselves to God [and] holiness and make the Scripture their rule shall be called heretics; when they who study the depths of Nature shall be accounted conjurors; when they who make it their business to do good to others shall be esteemed cheaters; lastly when they who do to their utmost power advantage their country shall be held for the greatest enemies thereof?

    I can think these absurd railers to be none other than those who are employed in the distillation of simple waters for the apothecaries; they hate nothing more than learning and count themselves so much happier by how much more ignorant; but [742] some, (I confess) acting from a more noble and divine principle, have enlarged minds, willing and desirous to contain the Universe, who do not only employ their time in study and meditation, but experiment what they learn. A wise man endeavours after knowledge of all things as a Prince hath intelligence of all transactions and as by the one he is distinguished from a fool, so by the other from a peasant. But the Fraternity do imitate both, so that nothing is wanting to hinder their perfection.

As for that reproach they live under concerning their disturbing of the commonwealth, it is altogether false and by them coined; therefore let it return upon the first broachers of it, to whom it properly belongs as being their own. They might justly complain of such indignities offered to them, but they account it virtuous to suffer.

That there are so many heresies abroad in the world is not to be charged upon the Holy Scripture, but the obstinacy of man forcing the text to confirm their will is to be checked; so it is no fault of the Fraternity that they are abused, but theirs who are so wicked as to calumniate them; for if to accuse any man were sufficient to prove him guilty, justice and injustice, truth and falsehood, white and black, would not be distinguished, which is altogether unreasonable.

Twenty-Fourth Sheet

SECTION THE SEVENTEENTH

That the Brethren of the R.C. do neither dream of, hope for or engage in any Reformation in the world by Religion, the Conversion of the Jews or by the Policies of Enthusiasts, which seemingly would be established by Scripture, but that they both acknowledge and show themselves lovers of truth and Justice.

As that which in the Day-time most runs in men's thoughts doth in the night disturb and work upon their fancies, so every man is careful to let no opportunity slip of endeavouring to accomplish his intention. They who set their minds upon rules are very laborious and painful to advance their estates; they who bend their thoughts to change commonwealths, to alter religion, to innovate the arts, make use of very often most despicable instruments to do their business. From this spring head hath issued many murmuring streams. Such causes (I say) have produced many tumults and confusions in commonwealths, where men have been act[uat]ed by vain thoughts and foolish dreams, as it evidently appears in the Anabaptists and Enthusiasts. Are there not many, even in this our age, who, being ambitious to be ringleaders in new ways, instead of a Reformation have disturbed all Order and Law? They, forsooth, would have Religion and Learning suit with their fantastical opinions.

As soon as those had heard of this honourable Society, they assumed themselves that their desires would have an happy issue; for knowing that these Brethren were able in learning and riches, they doubted not but that they would employ both these talents to cause an Universal Reformation in the world. They therefore immediately promised themselves one Religion, Unity and Concord; but in all these things they were belied and abused, for they never did affect any such things, neither is there any ground of them out of their writings. Out of their Books something may be gathered concerning the Reformation of the Arts, which was endeavoured by the first Author about 217 years ago, about *Anno Christi* 1400, and at that time they had need of a Reformation, [as] witness the labour and study of eminent men, who have to good purpose spent their time to promote learning, as Rudolphus Agricola, Erasmus, Roterodamus, D. Lutherus, Philippus Melancthonus, Theoph. Paracelsus, Joan Regiomontanus [and] Copernicus, with many others. And there is no doubt but the Arts may be more increased, their lustre more polished [and] many more secrets discovered. But herein Religion is not concerned. Let Rome, therefore, that whore of Babylon, and her idolatrous affecting an Ecclesiastical tyranny, who with menaces makes not only inferiors but Kings their slaves and vassals, who belch out proud words against the true Church of God, without any attempt of the Fraternity, forsaking their toys and vanities, their blasphemy and profaneness, return into the right way, so may a reformation be produced and piety and religion shall flourish. I fear yet that these, as they who are rich and powerful, will not judge that true which may anyways prejudice them. They, I doubt, will not embrace naked Truth [and] honest simplicity. But such Reformations belong more to God than Man, who can turn the hearts of men at His pleasure, and so dispose all affairs that a severe check may be put to the growth of popery. However the Brethren (as all good men ought) count it their duty to pray for and expect such a reformation. The business lies more in the enlightening of the understanding than changing the will, which is God's own work, for He gives to do and will as He thinks fit. Who can (although he had the power of miracles) convert the obstinate Jews when the Scripture more confounds them and becomes a stumbling block? Observe how their own writings do disagree; how one thwarts another; and yet they consider not that wherein is concord. As for your Enthusiasts, their Revelations of which they so much boast of are sometimes to Sin, but that cannot be from God. Do they not dream interpretations on Scripture and when either the Devil doth delude them or they are distracted, they count their conditions happy. They acknowledge no superiority though commanded and allowed in the Scriptures. But our Brethren have always had one amongst them as Chief and Governor, to whom they are obedient. They pity such persons whom they find cheated and often possessed. Lastly as it is impossible to separate heat from fire, so it is as impossible to separate virtue from this Society. They bestow their time in duty to God, in diligent search of the Scripture, in charity, in healing gratis, in experimenting the secrets of Nature. They have the true Astronomy, the true Physics, Mathematics, Medicine and Chemistry, by which they are able to produce rare and wonderful effects; they are very laborious, frugal, temperate, secret [and] true. Lastly [they] make it their business to be profitable and beneficial to all men, of whom when we have spoken the highest commendations, we must confess an insufficiency to reach their work.[743]

REFERENCES

1. No table of contents appears in the MS.
2. See the Biographical Preface to *The Alchemical Writings of Edward Kelly*.
3. See Helvetius' *Golden Calf* in the *Hermetic Museum*.
4. Mr Waite might have added that it is almost a verbatim transcription of the English edition of the *Themis Aurea*, which appeared in 1656.
5. See Charlotte Fell Smith's *John Dee*, Appendix II, p. 320.
6. See p. 112 herein.
7. That is to say Part I only.
8. He alludes to the folio of the MS and not to the sheets of Dr Dee.
9. See *The Brotherhood of the Rosy Cross*, 1924, p. 400.
10. See note 4.
11. In this connection it might be mentioned that even so critical a scholar as Mr Waite seems to regard Michael Maier as a member of the Order, in which case it would seem not unreasonable to assume that he would have had some opportunity of verifying the statements made by the unknown authors of the *Fama* and *Confessio* and that the dates given by him for the birth and death of C∴R∴C∴ may well be accurate. See p. 256 herein.
12. I am fully aware that the *onus probandi* rests with those who would support such a tradition. I am not concerned at the moment to do so, but would point out that the responsibility rests equally with those who for any reason would wish to prove the tradition untrue.
13. See *The Brotherhood of the Rosy Cross*, pp. 397-401.
14. *Loc. cit.*
15. An example of his amazing impertinence in *Elharvareuna* will be mentioned later.
16. This must be obvious, seeing that it is difficult to find anything in Heydon that even appears to be original.

17. The source of much that appears in the Rudd MSS can be traced, but there remains a certain residuum still untraceable, and many of the very numerous illustrations I have been unable to find elsewhere.
18. The full title of this small work is *Euclide's Elements of Geometry, the first Six Books in a compendious form contrasted and demonstrated, whereunto is added the Mathematical Preface of Mr John Dee*. This Preface is No. 33 in the list of Dee's works in the *Athenae Cantabrigiensis*. It is described as *A fruitfull Praeface, specifying the chiefe Mathematical Sciences, what they are and whereunto commodious: where also are disclosed certain new Secrets Mathematicall and Mechanicall, until these our daies greatly missed*.
19. See p. 117 herein. It is to be observed that this marginal note comes later in the MS than the *Elharvareuna* section.
20. See p. 13, para. 3.
21. See *The Brotherhood of the Rosy Cross*, 1924, p. 401.
22. Mr Waite, *idem*, p. 186, note 2, points out that he formerly held this opinion and still realizes the difficulties of the belief. He prefers, however, 'the honour of a long departed theologian before the validity of a literary judgement.' This is refreshing, but we also find that he 'thinks the place of the Romance in Rosicrucian debate can be assigned more easily by accepting the author's statement.' Mr F.N. Pryce, in his Introduction to the facsimile edition of the *Fame and Confession* (1923), finds the same difficulty, but evades it by believing Andreae's statement that he wrote it and discrediting his statement as to when he did so, a liberty which appears somewhat unwarrantable. He further endeavours to substantiate a weak case by saying that *The Chemical Marriage* 'contains a passage describing the hero as decorating himself with four red roses and ribbons bound cross-wise in a manner obviously reminiscent of Andreae's family arms — a St Andrew's Cross with four roses.' 'This' he says 'confirms Andreae's authorship of this tract.' In point of fact the hero stuck the roses in his hat and wore 'a blood-red ribbon bound cross-ways over my shoulder', obviously meaning as one would wear a sash, and not at all implying a St Andrew's or any other cross.
23. Mr Waite published an only slightly condensed version of *The Chemical Marriage* in his *Real History of the Rosicrucians*, 1888.
24. Of the German editions; only a few being in German. Foxcroft has naturally followed this plan, leaving the Latin untranslated, while he has rendered the German notes into English.
25. The fact that it did deceive certain bibliographers nearly two

centuries later — if indeed a deception was practised on them — is no evidence that it could or would have deceived at the time.
26. Of all the alleged borrowed material, this letter is the only example of a considerable variation in sequence and phrasing. A comparison will show that there are many differences in both respects from the *Golden Calf*.
27. See the biographical preface to *The Alchemical Writings of Edward Kelly*.
28. See *Dictionary of National Biography*, Vol. xx., p. 345.
29. See, for example, *Theomagia, The Holy Guide, The Rosicrucian Infallible Axiomata*.
30. Unfortunately we have no knowledge as to the whereabouts of the original MS, which may be lost or destroyed. The absence of an original, however, is no proof that an alleged copy is in fact a forgery.
31. Certain passages are not to be found in *Elharvareuna*, and these I have indicated by footnotes. I have not been able to trace these passages elsewhere.
32. John Heydon.
33. Thomas Vaughan.
34. These passages are all indicated in footnotes to the text. Although I have described these passages as considerable, in relation to the bulk of the work they only represent a small proportion.
35. See his *Theomagia*.
36. Not including, of course, Helvetius' letter.
37. See pp. 63-64.
38. See note 11.
39. I say 'unexpected corroboration' advisedly, because Yarker, though likeable and sincere, is altogether uncritical and credulous, so that a large proportion of his statements are most unreliable.
40. On what exact grounds the journey is discredited other than that the name Damcar does not appear on the map I have not been able to ascertain even from a most painstaking reading of their books. They profess to find a few contradictions in the narrative, which exist largely in their imaginations, and Mr Waite hazards a query as to financial difficulties.
41. I am fully aware that the I.A.O. is to be found not only in R∴C∴ writings and Masonic studies, but also in use among the Gnostics, in whom some thinkers have seen a possible common ancestor for the other two traditions; but it seems to me that its origin is older than the Gnostics and is definitely traceable to Semitic sources. Apart from this I am prepared freely to admit that to

find I.A.O. in any writings *may* simply mean that the writer was acquainted with Gnostic ideas and that such mention can hardly be considered as evidence of either R∴C∴ or Masonic influence *unless there are other indications*. These, I think, are definitely to be found in Sebottendorf, to whom I must refer the reader.

42. See the biographical preface to *The Triumphal Chariot of Antimony*. Some authorities give his date of birth as early as 1413.
43. See Vaughan's *Coelum Terrae* in Waite's *Works of Thomas Vaughan*, p. 208. I am reluctant to make unnecessary assertions, but I feel convinced, after a careful and minute analysis of the passage quoted, that it bears the unmistakable stamp of Rosicrucian teaching. At least the Qabalistic element is unmistakable.
44. There is, for example, the statement made that in the Vault was discovered the *Vocabularium* of Paracelsus (a manifest impossibility if the Vault had been sealed since 1484). It is, of course, possible to put this interpretation on the words of the *Fama* (see Vaughan's edition, p. 23.), but it is equally easy to read the text as implying that the *Vocabularium* was a volume in the possession of the Brethren in addition to those discovered in the Vault.
45. See the Introduction to *The Fame and Confession of the Fraternity of R.C.*, 1923.
46. *Idem.* p. 11. Note 1.
47. *Idem.* p. 48.
48. *Idem.* p. 49. No reason is given for the implied qualification.
49. As regards what may be termed 'the earlier date hypothesis' F. de P. Castells points out in his *Our Ancient Brethren, the Originators of Freemasonry. An Introduction to the History of Rosicrucianism*, dealing with the period A.D. 1300 to 1600, that Inigo Jones designed costumes for a masque ball held at Whitehall on Jan 6th, 1604 and designated one as 'a Rosicros' (see pp. 90-92). See also *Ben Jonson's Works*, Vol. VII, cap. vii. This would seem to indicate that the Order was not unknown in England at that date.
50. Mr Waite, in *The Brotherhood of the Rosy Cross*, p. 36, note 3, says that 'among Ashmolean MSS at Oxford, the vellum flyleaves of No. 360 contain "Letters of Frater Johannes Gardiannus ... receiving Richard Ghonge (or Young) into a Fraternity. Dated in the Epiphany, 1450."'
51. Charlotte Fell Smith, *John Dee*, p. 217.
52. That Vaughan definitely belonged to some Society is borne out by his statement in the final paragraph of *Aula Lucis* that he wrote it by the 'command imposed by my superiors etc.'
53. I do not wish to take up unnecessary space by giving all the

evidence in any detail, but those who are interested may refer to Waite's *The Brotherhood of the Rosy Cross*, where most of it is discussed. No one can justly accuse Mr Waite of over-anxiety to establish a case for any individual as a member of the Fraternity.
54. *Idem*, p. 96.
55. *Die Praxis der Alten Türkischen Freimauerei*, p. 23. See also my previous allusion to this work on page 18.
56. I have said 'according to Sebottendorf' when writing this sentence, because, naturally enough, the signs are given cryptically. However it cannot be denied that if the three signs given by him are correct — and his practice affords an opportunity for experimental verification — they may very well be indicated in the manner suggested. In this case the versicle accompanying the figure becomes more interesting.
57. His list of some fifty private and imprinted works is admitted by him to be incomplete.
58. See, for example, his unacknowledged quotation from Maier's *Themis Aurea* in his preface to the *Fama* and the quotation from an unnamed source in his *Coelum Terrae* already mentioned on p. 18. Also see King's *The Gnostics*, 2nd edtn., p. 398, where the statement is made that a scarce tract entitled *An Essay on Spirit* (1647) contains a Rosicrucian Creed. King quotes three clauses, which are identical with the first three of Vaughan's *Magical Aphorisms*, printed at the end of *Lumen de Lumine* (1651). The probability is that Vaughan and the author of the essay borrowed from a common source. It should perhaps be mentioned that Castells attributes the tract to Eugenius Philalethes (pointing out that this was Vaughan's pseudonym) giving King's *Gnostics* as his authority. For this, however, he has no excuse, neither name being mentioned by King.
59. It may be suggested that in my use of the phrase 'by implication' I have definitely understated the case, and the following passages from Vaughan's Preface to his edition of the *Fama et Confessio* may be quoted against me, namely pp. 4a, verso, b3 and c3. While I freely admit the force of his denials in the first and last of these (that on p. b3 is not so definite) I feel that they are greatly diminished in value by his admission that (a4, verso) 'I know they are Masters of great Mysteries' and (c3) 'Their Doctrine I am not so much a stranger to.' Vaughan was a careful writer and would not have made these statements without strong grounds, but unless we admit a really close connection between him and the Order, it is difficult to explain how he could have obtained any

positive knowledge as to their doctrines or their right to be described as Masters of so great Mysteries.
60. The first paragraph of this Preface appears in the Epistle Dedicating to Prince Rupert in John Heydon's *Elharvareuna* (1665).
61. Compare *Aesch Mezareph* cap. 2, where it has been wrongly translated as yellow gold.
62. These two sentences appear almost exactly as they stand in Thomas Vaughan's *Aula Lucis* but no acknowledgement is made. The remainder of this paragraph, down to the words 'red gold' in its last line, is also used, almost verbatim, but about a page or two further on.
63. MS. has 'in'.
64. cf. *Tabula Smanagdina*.
65. A whorl or vortex.
66. Taken in conjunction with the 'emptiness' used a few lines previously the Telesma at this stage is obviously analogous to the 'formless' and void of *Genesis*, a parallel in frequent use among alchemical writers.
67. *Exod.* vii.i.
68. By this is obviously meant the Rational Mind or Ruach (Spirit) which must dominate and bring into complete harmony the Nephesch (Lower Soul, Animal Nature), alluded to later as 'the flesh'.
69. MS. has 'Could'.
70. *Col.* iii.3.
71. *II. Cor.* xii.2.
72. The whole of this paragraph is omitted in *Elharvareuna*.
73. From here to the point indicated on page 112 the text is substantially that of *Elharvareuna*, though the latter is written in the form of a dialogue.
74. These are the figures in Geomancy.
75. It might well be suggested that Luna and Chasmodas in Silver prepared would be efficacious. The employment of Jupiter is not advised on the same principle. In any event an alternative is suggested immediately afterwards in Sol and Gold (though Sorath is not named). But this would apply in any other case as *aurum potabile* is the Medicine of the Philosophers *par excellence*.
76. This phrase 'in his own nature' is most important as indicating the true and fundamental *locale* of the work.
77. Presumably this should read 'than'.
78. According to whether the Symbolical Regimen is that of the Planets, Sephiroth or Zodiac.

79. The first matter of Metals.
80. Philosophical.
81. But note the definition of this given in the Preface.
82. Thick Water or Permanent Water as it is often called.
83. MS has 'and'.
84. Root.
85. MS has 'moistness'.
86. Geber, *Lib. de Origine Metallorum.*
87. MS has 'tinctureth and coloureth'.
88. MS has 'no'.
89. Janus Lacinius Therapus in *The New Pearl of Great Price* by Peter Bonus of Ferrara, says of form that it is 'The intelligent outward influence (the Master)', which gives being to The Perfect Being or to The Formative Tincture. It goes forth from Chaos.
90. MS has 'proceding of'.
91. MS has 'is'.
92. MS has 'it is'.
93. MS has 'it entereth'.
94. This theory affords a clue to the correspondence between the metals and planets.
95. MS has 'their'.
96. Saturn, Jupiter and Luna are the White natures, while Venus, Mars and Sol are the Red natures and, alchemically speaking, the Red flows after the White.
97. C.f. The Tree of Life in the Qabalah.
98. The reason is to be sought in the planetary and zodiacal governance of the different countries, districts and cities.
99. It must be realized and remembered that the Mercury of the philosophers does not, in point of fact, exist apart from its own internal fire or Sulphur.
100. 'The Stone is One, the Medicine is One, to which we add nothing, nor take away anything, only in the preparation removing superfluities'. Aquinas. *Resar. Abbrev.* Tract. iii and v.
101. C.f. *Tabula Smaragdina.*
102. A common appellation for the Hermaphradite of the philosophers is their Brass. See note 307.
103. Who was, of course, created Male and Female according to *Genesis.*
104. i.e. as regards their functions. They are, however, often spoken of as male and female respectively or King and Queen.
105. Regarding the whole of this section, there is no real contradiction with what has gone before; for here Sol and Luna are regarded

purely functionally and, therefore, as Agents or Male; whereas symbolically Sol is male and Luna is female.

106. Note the emphasis laid on the feminine nature of the Spiritual, which is in Harmony with Qabalistic teaching.
107. There are two Mercuries recognized by the Alchemists, one of which is Masculine and one Feminine. Their union is the First Matter or Mercury of the Philosophers, namely a Mercury containing its own Internal Sulphur.
108. There are, of course, two masculine sperms or Sulphurs, namely the Red and the White, the one tingeing to Gold, the other to Silver.
109. Presumably this should read: 'that Silver is not the Luna'.
110. That is to say *Luna Philosophorum*.
111. The MS has 'unmixed' but this should presumably read 'unfixed'.
112. That is to say it is their Permanent Water.
113. Note this sentence, which affords an explanation of the term 'permanent water' so often employed.
114. C.f. *Elharvareuna* pp. 30/31. 'Out of which they did draw Gold out of the bottom of his body, and which they found quicksilver etc.'
115. *The Summary of Philosophy*.
116. This is the *Lunaria* of the philosophers, called by Geber and Eirenaeus Philalethes the Herb of Saturn. It is a term used by some for Mercury and also for the Sulphur of Nature. Compare *Maria Practica*: 'Take the white, clear and dignified herb that grows upon the little mountains ... for in it is the genuine body which evaporateth not, neither does it at all flee from the fire.' Geber says: 'There groweth a Saturnian Herb on the top of a hill or mountain, whose blood, if it be extracted, cureth all infirmities.' According to Thomas Vaughan (*Lumen de Lumine*) these mountains, commonly called the Mountains of India, are the same as his Mountains of the Moon, which were composed of the Philosophic Salt. Of this Khunrath speaks thus in his *Amphitheatrum Sapientiae Eternae*: 'Salt of Saturn, the Universal son in Nature ... reigns ... universally in all things ... self-existent in Nature. Hear and attend! SALT, that most ancient principle of the Stone, whose nucleus in the Decad guard in holy silence. Let him who hath understanding understand. Not without weighty cause has Salt been dignified with the name of Wisdom.' This is the 'The Stone in High Places' of Geber and should be compared with *Prov.* viii, 1-2, which is only intelligible in the light of knowledge of the Qabalistic Tree of Life. Compare

also with Lully's *Lunaria*, whose water shineth by night and by day has a glutinous, viscous faculty. Note also that Lully calls the Medicine Vegetable, Mineral and Animal. Vaughan also, in his *Anthroposophia Theomagica*, says it is a system, as it were, of all three. See also the passage referred to by note 121.
117. The Microcosm.
118. MS has 'casually'.
119. *Tractatus Aureus*, sect. 1.
120. Our author is rather diffuse in his explanation, but, alchemically speaking, it is quite clear seeing that the Mercury contains in itself a Sulphur that is essentially one with it. See note 307.
121. See note 116.
122. MS has 'condigested', to which form the word 'undigested' has been altered.
123. In other words the figure 3 is used to signify the First Matter or Mercury of the Philosophers because it is a third thing arising out of the combination of Sulphur and Mercury the Agent and Patient. It is thus able to be described as triune in nature or a trinity in unity.
124. That is to say it depends upon the radical positions in each case and upon what Paracelsus terms the internal planets.
125. The whole of this section down to the end of p. 62 is to be found in Vaughan's *Lumen de Lumine*, iii and iv. It also appears as a long speech of Eugenius Theodidactus (not Philalethes) in Heydon's *Elharvareuna* pp. 48-67.
126. Active darkness.
127. The visage of cold.
128. Divine darkness.
129. Ain אין .
130. In respect of us.
131. Unveiled Deity apart from all vesture.
132. A Tartaro ad primam ignem.
133. MS has 'Supernatural', but this seems an error. A Divine darkness has, indeed, just been mentioned but this hardly equates with Tartarus.
134. Let him receive it who can.
135. Dissolved and flowing water.
136. Something melted.
137. A solution of earth and a certain plasticity of earth.
138. Son of the Earth mixed with Water.
139. Mixed earth and marriage of earth.
140. Divine and living Silver, an union of spirit in matter.

141. Thomas Vaughan has 'Jews' instead of 'Rosie Crucians'.
142. This paragraph is a variation of the analogy of Dew, which is so popular among the alchemical writers.
143. Compare note 163.
144. The mother shall bring forth a budding flower, which she will nurture at her own milky breast and, being helped by the father, will turn herself into food for it utterly.
145. Afflontus or Assotes. c.f. the 36th Dictum of the *Turba*.
146. It hath the likeness of the Sun and Moon, and in such water it hath appeared to us, not in spring or rain water.
147. Compare the Green Stone mentioned in the 20th Dictum of the *Turba*, the Green Lion, so often encountered in alchemical works, and the Green Salt of Thomas Vaughan, described in *Lumen de Lumine*, x. Note also the Spermatick Green Gold mentioned in the preface to the present work.
148. *De Naturalibus Aquis*, Lib. iii.
149. Pure potency.
150. In the beginning God created heaven and earth.
151. In the Hebrew the words translated 'The heavens and the earth' are: את השמים ואת הארץ. The word את, according to the Qabalistic Rabbis, implies more than merely 'the' which is 'ה' and means 'essence' or 'substance of the'.
152. The *Zohar* definitely makes a distinction between the first and second earths.
153. This is hardly a fair statement, but the letter ש which is the difference between them is the symbol of Ruach Elohim, the Spirit of God, which moved upon the waters. It is also the Mother letter to which is attributed the Element of Fire, so that Hashamaim offers us an image of the Philosphers' Water containing its inward Fire or Sulphur.
154. Be-Chokmah.
155. Sometimes termed an Iron Key (as in *Aesch Mezareph*) because of the relationship between Iron, Mars, Geburah and Fire.
156. This sentence is not used in Vaughan.
157. Probably 'Dramaah'. See p. 62.
158. 'As it were inbreeding fire.'
159. Vaughan has 'magicians'.
160. Horse's belly.
161. Horse-dung.
162. Neither of the sea nor of dew.
163. Namely two living Mercuries. cf. ante p. 54. Compare with this Thomas Vaughan in his *Euphrates* where he says: 'Join this living

male to a living female, for in this lies all the mystery, namely in the union of a particular spirit to the universal, by which means nature is strangely exalted and multiplied.'
164. The name given to the first of the philosophic vessels, the second being called an Aludel.
165. cf. The blood of the Lion and the gluten of the Eagle.
166. Within the horizon of Eternity.
167. *Sepher Yetzirah*. Cap. I. § 7.
168. *Sepher Yetzirah*. Cap I. § 4.
169. The Secret of the Art, which is said by some the secret of rousing the Spheirema and the activating and equilibrating currents which precede it. This cannot be done without a previous dissolution, decension and coagulation, so that the prime secret is the dissolution, which is the Solution of the Sophic Salt.
170. He shall be worthy to take a seat at the table of the twelve peers.
171. The MS has 'eight' but this should presumably be 'eighth'. The inference is that this relates to the Qliphoth.
172. According to the *Zohar* the chaos, i.e. the formless and void 'earth' was composed of the fragments resulting from the fall of the 'Kings of Edorn' or the seven Lower Sephiroth in Atziluth, which fell first into Briah, the creative world of the Elohim.
173. Light was the separating principle.
174. Allusion is here made to the first division.
175. MS has 'this'.
176. MS has 'this'.
177. Note that here Fixation is omitted and that Multiplication in quantity and virtue are reversed in their order. The present arrangement would seem to be the best in this respect.
178. The 'and' would seem to be an error.
179. Presumably this should be 'reserve'.
180. Which is, presumably, elsewhere called the blood of the Lion.
181. See pp. 70, 99.
182. Just as in the theurgical practice there are two mystical marriages so-called, a point which is not as a rule made clear.
183. Strengthened.
184. MS has 'is'.
185. An unusual term. We would have expected 'number'. There is, however, such a close and accepted correspondence between sound, number, colour etc. that the point is one of curiosity rather than significance.
186. MS has 'Balneo'.
187. Burning.

188. Chaomodai.
189. This should probably read: 'Observe the Harmony of Geomancy in this Preparation.' See p. 73.
190. See pp. 66, 99.
191. MS has 'Sole', which would seem to be an error.
192. MS has 'ferment', but the verb and not the noun seems indicated.
193. See p. 67, para. 10.
194. Mercury.
195. Presumably this should read 'Inceration'.
196. MS has 'proof'.
197. MS has 'appeared' instead of 'appear red'.
198. See p. 66 and p. 70.
199. Cf. Raymund Lully. *Lib. Mercur.*, p. 103.
200. Presumably this should be 'shut'.
201. The sentence ends abruptly thus in the MS. There should be added something to the following effect: '. . . you shall see it at first black, then white and, at the last, red.'
202. Any matter from which a good tincture can be made.
203. Elsewhere called Augmentation or Multiplication. See p. 67, *et aliter*.
204. An unusual term, but see Thomas Vaughan in his introduction to the *Fama et Confessio Fraternitatis Rosicrucianis*. Paracelsus does not use the word Pantarva. See, however, *Aurora*, cap. xiii, where he speaks of the supercelestial Marriage of the Soul.
205. MS has 'prose'.
206. The place where Christian Rosenkreutz, according to the *Fama*, first came in touch with the mysterious Order, of which he afterwards founded the German branch, was Damcar in Arabia. The significance of this name is Blood of the Lamb. It is not a usual alchemical term.
207. This 'yet' seems superfluous and spoils the sentence.
208. See note 206.
209. The words 'and body' appear to be an error.
210. This last paragraph does not occur in Heydon.
211. This phrase is to be noted. Alchemical writers were not wont to be so open in their indications of when they were speaking symbolically and when literally.
212. The words 'of which Raymund saith' do not occur in Heydon.
213. Sublimation in virtue.
214. Rhasis.
215. Whether red or white. MS has 'poverty' instead of 'property'.
216. Note here and elsewhere the definite distinction made between

Mercury and Quicksilver. This particular example given would seem obviously only to have been inserted for the purpose of making this distinction unmistakably clear.
217. Note the gradation of relationships: Mercury, Quicksilver and Lead or Tin.
218. The whole of this section down to para. 2, p. 87, is to be found in Vaughan's *Lumen de Lumine*, ix. In *Elharvareuna* it is put into the mouth of Eugenius Theodidactus as usual.
219. Heb. i. 3.
220. Should be $\delta \upsilon \nu \alpha \mu o \pi \theta \iota o s \ \delta \upsilon \nu \alpha \mu \iota s$.
221. Compare Simon Magus *The Great Announcement*.
222. In *The Great Announcement* the symbol of the Boundless Power and Universal Root was fire. In the Qabalah also the symbol of Ruach Elohim was *shin*, the Mother letter to which was attributed the element of fire.
223. Vaughan adds 'or Prester'.
224. Qabalistically the world of Briah, the second of the four Worlds.
225. According to the *Zohar* the development of God from negative existence to positive manifestation was from Ain, the Negative, through Ain Soph the Limitless (cf. the Boundless of *The Great Announcement*) to Ain Soph Aur, the Limitless Light.
226. Vaughan has 'perpetual'.
227. Vaughan adds: 'As Campian was altered by the music of his mistress.
> When to her lute Corinna sings
> Her voice enlives the leaden strings;
> But when of sorrows she doth speak
> Even with sighs the strings do break;
> And as her lute doth live or die,
> Led by her passions, so do I.'
228. Our author is, of course, speaking symbolically.
229. Vaughan has 'Prester'.
230. Compare the Oracle: 'So, therefore, first the Priest who governeth the Works of Fire, must sprinkle with the Water of the Loud-resounding Sea. And when, after all the Phantoms, thou shalt see that Holy and Formless Fire; that Fire that darts and flashes through the Hidden Depths of the Universe, hear thou the Voice of Fire.'
231. *Matt.*, iv, 4.
232. *Acts*, xvii, 27.
233. *Ibid.*, xvii, 28.
234. Vaughan adds: 'A glorious, incomparable discourse; but you will shortly find it in English.

235. The reason being obviously that it is the Spirit. Vaughan has 'grows' instead of 'goes' which appears to be a mistake.
236. Remember how it has been constantly reiterated that in the process of Augmentation or Multiplication there is a projection. In the Multiplication of the fire or spirit there is also a projection.
237. This appears to equate with the 'Condensed' Aether a few lines lower.
238. Note the interchange of terms and compare note 222.
239. *Aurum fulminaus.* Fulminate of Gold. Compare the alchemical process of Solomon Trismosin.
240. The whole of this section down to the end of the paragraph is to be found in Vaughan's *Lumen de Lumine* xii.
241. Each thing whatsoever bears within it the seed of its own regeneration.
242. The Qabalistic name of Jesus according to the Christian mystics was יהשוה or the letter ש, the symbol of the spirit, inserted in the Tetragrammaton. Now the four letters of the latter were referred to the four elements. The Eternal Unity is, of course א while the *Ternarius*, on the plane of Spirit is ש . These two letters form the word אש meaning fire, to which element, as we have previously pointed out, the Mother letter *shin* (ש) is attributed, so that this single letter symbolizes 'the Eternal Unity and *Ternarius*' as our author expresses it. Furthermore Jesus is בן , Ben the Son, and the numerical value of this word is 52 or 5+2=7.
243. This is the main thesis of Theurgical theory.
244. I *Corinthians*, xv, 51-52.
245. Cf. Arnold in his *Rosary*. See p. 69 herein.
246. At this point Heydon (p. 127) inserts a short diatribe against Nicholas Culpeper, the herbalist.
247. The sense appears to be: 'This is only on account of . . .'
248. The perfect metals.
249. There is no paragraph marked 3 in the MS.
250. 'but to' would be better.
251. MS has 'Consurgeat'.
252. Abscesses.
253. Lupus
254. MS has 'seed', which is a manifest error.
255. The following paragraphs from here to the end of para. 3, p. 93 will be found in Vaughan's *Coelum Terrae*. Mixed with them therein, however, there is some other matter. Heydon begins a paragraph or two earlier in Vaughan with, 'And now give me leave to look about me . . .' and goes onto the end '. . . I seek not any man's applause . . .'

256. Celestial Slime.
257. MS has 'all' instead of 'powerful' or, perhaps the latter word was omitted accidentally.
258. Meaning, of course, the Creation.
259. MS has 'is in', an obvious error.
260. Cf. note 224.
261. From here to the end of the next paragraph is quoted by Vaughan in his *Coelum Terrae*.
262. Vaughan has 'Hejanthe' instead of *Beata Pulchra* and inserts several lines before coming to the next sentence.
263. Vaughan again inserts a few lines before coming to this sentence.
264. Heydon continues from Vaughan down to '. . . it is Truth if they can understand it.'
265. Mecuries. Compare Zaibar (used by Paracelsus for Argent vive). It is spelt in the MS as Zaibeth, Ziabeth and Zabieth. The word appears to be of Hebrew origin from a root meaning to flow. One of the two Zaibeth is called Kibrith (see *Maria Practica*). It is sometimes written Zabech.
266. See note 116.
267. MS has 'congealeth' corrected to 'congealed', but though this makes sense grammatically, it is a property of the odour of coagulated Mercury with which I am not familiar. See also section 12.
268. Khunrath in his *Amphitheatrum Sap. Isag.* says 'which in its proper tongue is called Saturn, i.e., the Lead of the Wise'.
269. Minium. Sometimes said to be the matter of the work at the red stage.
270. See note 307.
271. See pp. 66, 70.
272. Hermes (cf. p. 106).
273. MS has 'or'.
274. MS has 'is'.
275. MS has 'preparative'.
276. MS has 'taste'.
277. MS has 'to'.
278. Freed from acids, salts or impurities by washing.
279. These three paragraphs which yield this discovered unity of teaching among the philosophers are most important, as they reveal the whole process from the spiritual or Theurgical point of view, which is, of course, analogous or parallel with the physical or material in as much as the requisite formulae have one root. At the same time he is not quite straightforward, seeing that he

introduces a confusion between the body and the Lower Soul which is, in a sense, its basis. The apparently homogeneous, but imperfectly united and balanced, trinity of Body, Soul and Spirit. Gup, Nephesch and Ruach — must be dissolved, i.e., its bonds must be loosened so as to allow of a separation of its three elements. The Nephesch and Ruach, after due preparation and purification may then be brought into harmony and truly united, this being the first Mystical Marriage, namely that of the King and Queen or the Red and White natures. From this union is born the true microcosmical infant or son, made in the image of the Higher Soul or Self, the Neshamah. The second Mystical Marriage is that of the Regenerated Man and his Higher Self.

280. MS has 'to contrary'.
281. *Coelum Philosophorum.*
282. There is an illegible figure in the text. Paracelsus wrote *Archidoxorum Librix* and *Archidoxes Magicae* (seven books). Amber is alluded to in the seventh book of the former and the sixth of the latter. The illegible figure alluded to looks more like a six than a seven. See further note 295.
283. Compare the process given on page 161 under the heading 'Of the True Solution of Pearls'.
284. *Sol centralis.*
285. Presumably a glass-making furnace.
286. This should probably be 'or' and not 'of'. See note 290. The bell of Trithemius was made of Electrum, see Paracelsus, *De Compositione Metallorum*. At the same time Electrum and Amber are not usually interchangeable terms, but perhaps our author identifies them because of their colour.
287. MS has 'Amongst which this is to be found none'.
288. To be consistent he should say one third stone, one third mineral and one third metal, seeing that their natures are correlated with Salt, Mercury and Sulphur respectively.
289. See note 286 and note 290 below.
290. Is this to be taken literally, and should we therefore suppose that our author was familiar with the electrical phenomena associated with Amber? The derivation of Electrum is, of course, from the Greek *electron*, meaning Amber. It seems possible that the natural Electrum is Amber, but the artificial Electrum is certainly not synthetic Amber.
291. MS has 'of'.
292. Probably Lapidisic.
293. See note 288.

294. *Coelum Philosophorum.*
295. *Archidoxes Magicae.* See note 282.
296. Presumably one ounce may be allowed to do so, seeing that the total weight of Electrum produced at the end of the operation is seven ounces.
297. MS has 'pour it upon them.'
298. Presumably this should read 'Electrum.'
299. Paracelsus mentions the Magical Bell in his *De Compositione Metallorum* but he does not mention Trithemius or Virgil Hispanus. He speaks of a necromancer in Spain who had such a bell and suggests that the reader will 'have no difficulty in believing that Virgil's bell (Nola) was of such a kind as this.' There is no record, incidentally, that Trithemius ever visited Spain.
300. After this *Elharvareuna* breaks away from our MS for its remaining four pages.
301. Mercury.
302. Sulphur.
303. Sulphur.
304. Late Latin-Redness.
305. 'The' would seem more apt.
306. As it stands this sentence is meaningless. The intention would however appear to be that when the matter is subjected to a gentle heat the undigested Mercurial Spirit dissolves and then magnetically attracts the Sulphurous Soul, which, in turn, being dissolved, attracts the Salt.
307. The Mercury of the Wise, or the matter considered during the putrefaction, i.e., at the black stage, when it is the same as the Head of the Crow. The general meaning is that of the fixed nature dissolved with the volatile. The latter, which is the Mercurial part or Azoth, is that which whitens the Laton itself and when this whitening is achieved success is assured and we have the White Gold. When this is made red by the internal Sulphur or seed of Gold it becomes their Golden Sulphur or Salamander. Laton is also Copper or Brass. Both these may be regarded as Hermaphrodite by nature. With regard to Copper, compare the symbols of Venus and the Egyptian Ankh. Furthermore remember that although Copper, *per se*, is feminine, nevertheless in its close kinship with Sulphur it is masculine. As regards Brass, whose symbol shows its mercurial nature, see *Aesch Mezareph*, cap. v. It is a veil for that Mercury which contains in itself its own hidden, internal incombustible Sulphur. All this is in line with the notion of a double Mercury and the two Zaibeth.

308. MS has 'but'.
309. MS has 'are' instead of 'consists of'.
310. *Succus Lunaria*.
311. cf. Arnold de Villa Nova in his *Speculum*, also the *Turba*.
312. This process Dr Dee had from Dr R. set down in a letter October 19th 1605.
313. The unshot.
314. MS has 'this'.
315. MS has 'being'.
316. MS has 'Those I divided . . .'.
317. MS has 'peebles'.
318. MS has 'lost'.
319. The White Solar Body.
320. MS has 'and'.
321. MS has 'the other'.
322. MS has 'with'.
323. Equal parts.
324. MS has 'iterated a third time'.
325. Matter (?).
326. MS has 'transmitted'.
327. See page 121.
328. This should probably read 'Mercury'.
329. See note 462.
330. To make this sentence intelligible one must suppose that 'of' should read 'to' and that 'take' should read 'add'.
331. 'The Salt of Saturn, the Universal Son of Nature, has reigned, does reign and will reign naturally and universally in all things; always and everywhere universal through its own fusibility, self-existent in Nature.' Khunrath, *Amphitheatrum Sapientiae Eternae*.
332. MS has 'iterate it a third time'.
333. This should read: 'See that they do not . . .'.
334. Slag.
335. MS 'Lib. semis'.
336. Aqueous extract.
337. MS has 'it'.
338. MS has 'tissing'.
339. MS has 'flagrant'.
340. This would appear to be the sense of the sentence, but the MS actually has: 'Six times as much of Sol is precipitated than above the ponderosity the compound did weigh.'
341. See the end of the first paragraph of the previous section.
342. The numbers from 1 to 5 added yield 15 = יה, Jah. The letters

Yod and He are the symbols of Abba and Aima, who, conjoined are the Elohim of *Gen.* i. As applied to the creation 15=1+5=6 the number of the Son or Microcosm. As 'The Rescuer unto the Light' the Son is also 'The Stone that the builders rejected.' *Ps. cxviii,* 22, *Matt.,* xxi. 42, *Mark,* xii. 10, *Luke,* xx. 17, *Acts.* iv. II, I. *Peter,* ii. 7.

343. Energy manifesting as Light.
344. Separative Art.
345. i.e., a thick water, the aqueous form of the Internal Sulphur, Permanent Water, often called Igneous. Compare that thick water mentioned in II. *Maccabbees* i. 19-22, where the sacred fire, having been buried in a pit, is found to have become a thick water, from which fire is again extracted.
346. The Male or Sol or Sulphur.
347. The unripe mineral basis of all *menstrua*. From it are drawn two viscous Spirits. The first is white, opaque and like milk, whence it is called *Lac Virginis,* and sometimes Gluten of the Eagle. The second spirit is Red and is called Blood of the Green Lion. Compare the Siren of the Philosophers, the Goddess 'born of our deep Sea, who pours milk and blood from her breasts'. This is admirably illustrated in Basil Valentine's *The Azoth of the Philosophers.*
348. MS has 'it'.
349. Spirit of Mercury.
350. Gold's.
351. The Tincture.
352. White Gold.
353. The use of a comma after the word 'original' is particularly to be noted. The common original is the Sulphur.
354. Soul.
355. Body.
356. MS has 'in'.
357. That is to say coagulate it.
358. Our author, however, seems also to be deliberately misleading on this point. For while he is speaking the literal truth, he is liable to be misunderstood. 'Common' in this context, if he is to be understood aright, must be read in its sense of universal, that which is to be found everywhere. The same observations apply to the use of the word common in connection with the word matter in the next paragraph, for it is the *prima materia,* the origin of all things. That he is, indeed speaking in the sense indicated seems to be made apparent by the last sentence of the next

paragraph: 'So is our Glass likened to the Globe of the earth.' No one but a Rosicrucian would have expressed himself in this manner, and those who are in any way familiar with the tenets of the Fraternity will appreciate the allusion to their Magical and Spherical Mirror.

359. MS has 'being'.
360. MS has 'then'.
361. Four processes are indicated, namely solution, fixation, calcination and sublimation or volatilization.
362. In Arabic called Asimat, and in Hebrew Puk or Stibium.
363. MS has 'and'.
364. Instructions for the making of this Star are given by Basil Valentine in his *Triumphal Chariot of Antimony*.
365. Usually the Mercury of the Alchemists or their feminine sperm.
366. Lupus.
367. Cf. *The Triumphal Chariot of Antimony*. Kirchringius, the commentator, says: 'The Serpent is that which mingles with the King, and he (Basil) calls it a serpent of stone, because it is a Salt.'
368. Sal Armoniack?
369. Quality?
370. Presumably referring to the Salt.
371. MS has 'fixer'.
372. MS has 'of'.
373. Presumably this should read 'the red'.
374. Calcined Vitriol or the *Caput Mortuum* of oil of Vitriol.
375. MS has 'and'.
376. Kin(?).
377. By distillation.
378. Salad oil.
379. MS has 'it'.
380. Sulphur.
381. MS has 'cinober'.
382. Crabs' eyes, in *materia medica* are concretions formed in the stomachs of crayfish, formerly, when powdered, in much repute as antacids.
383. Compare what is said under the heading Tartar herein, that Salt is generated of a vegetable seed. See p. 145.
384. Meaning: 'That is to say with Tartar'.
385. An allusion to the internal Sulphur of the Philosophic Mercury.
386. Cf. note 383.
387. Vitrified?
388. It is their Mercurial Water, *Lac Virginis*, Pontic Water, Universal Solvent etc.

389. Burned or scorched.
390. MS has 'his'.
391. Burnt Wine.
392. The Paracelsian *Mumia* is here intended.
393. The Mineral Stone.
394. Which is hid in Wine as we saw at the beginning of the previous section.
395. See p. 119, *et seq.*
396. The allusion is to the process of recapitulation, indicating first the three principles of Sulphur, Salt and Mercury and then the seven metals distinguished by their planetary colours in the rainbow scale.
397. It seems clear that the meaning intended to be conveyed is that the second half *Aurum potabile*, though only able to be described as half, is infinitely preferable to that prepared by the first method. As a matter of fact it seems to be rather more than half.
398. See p. 124.
399. The Primary Radix.
400. A Sarment is the same as *Sarmentum*, a botanical term for a runner; a name given to a running stem giving off leaves or roots at intervals, as that of the strawberry; it is applied also to a turning stem which supports itself by means of others.
401. This, again, is no ordinary Vine but the matter whence is drawn the philosophic Mercury. It has but one root though many shoots.
402. Compare with the process given on p. 165.
403. MS has 'Take'.
404. See note 382.
405. Gouty.
406. Swollen.
407. What was called Unicorn's horn was formerly in repute in medicine. It was prepared from the horn or tooth of the Norwhal or Sea-unicorn.
408. Epilepsy.
409. Compare the Fire-Stone of Basil Valentine.
410. Quartation is a technical process in gold refining, described in some detail on p. 193.
411. MS has 'distilled'.
412. Sublimate?
413. MS has 'as'.
414. That is to say the aforementioned sublimate which had to be fixed with Saltpeter water.
415. Lupus: sometimes also known as *Noli me tangere*.

416. Marck or Mark, a weight still used in some parts of Europe for various commodities, especially Gold and Silver. Its weight varied, but was always something more than half a pound.
417. See note 382.
418. MS has 'this'.
419. The receiver.
420. Cf. The *Turba*, where frequent mention is made of Purple, and the Tyrian dye.
421. Solution.
422. Compare this process with that given on p. 151.
423. The remaining Calx.
424. Presumably this should be 'redness'.
425. Garnet.
426. A medical term implying equal quantities of each.
427. Presumably it should be 'pass' and not 'pour'.
428. The Formative World, Yetzirah, as the Greater is Briah and the Little is Assiah. Such is the normal meaning put on these terms, which in the make-up of Man correspond, as we have elsewhere said, to the Higher Soul (Neshamah), Spirit (Ruach) and Lower Soul (Nephesch). Yet in this context we are dealing with the Trinity of Body, Soul and Spirit, so that each world is, as it were, taken one step lower. Here, then, the Nephesch or Soul is the medium through which Spirit acts on Body. It is not unusual for the body to be called a water, although its more general description is an earth, for the philosophers agree in saying: 'Our earth is a water.' Compare with notes 431-437.
429. The symbol of Ruach is Skin, Fire, its meaning is Breath or Air. See note 435.
430. Cf. *Ps.* ciii. 5.
431. That is to say, a terrestrial form does not imply something simple and well-known, but is an allusion to that relationship which exists between that mysterious, spherical and magical mirror of the universe, of which mention has already been made and the Nephesch. Confirming this, the student is referred to the word אספירכא used for Mercury in Gemara Tract. Gittin, Cap. 7. fol. 69. This is ASPIRKA, Espherica, meaning Spherical Water. This word also occurs in *La Très Sainte Trinosophie* by the Comte de St-Germain, where it is the name of a bird. The 'spiritual matter' is connected with Ruach and the 'Soul-like Essence' with Neshamah.
432. At first sight the analogy between the earth and the great world may seem confusing, but the idea intended to be conveyed is

probably that of the earth in its aspect of Malkuth or Assiah, the material world, the lowest of the four great Qabalistic Worlds, while the little world, mentioned in the next sentence, is man, who, in his present stage, is the Microcosm of the Macrocosm of Assiah.

433. Qabalistically the distinction between the greater and the lesser worlds here would be apt as between Yetzirah and Assiah, and the *Zohar* distinguishes between the two earths in the story of creation. (For further details see my article *The Kings of Edom* in the *Occult Review*, Vol. LIII, No. 6.) This suggestion is further borne out by the use of the word revived towards the end of the sentence. The intention of the thought expressed seems clearly to imply an acquaintance with this somewhat recondite Qabalistic doctrine.

434. As far as the earth is concerned, in its aspect as the great world previously commented upon, the word 'nothing' can only be taken in the sense that in the beginning it was 'formless and void'. Only the great world of Atziluth can be said to be evolved *ex nihilo*, and then only because it is the first manifestation of, or rather from, the third great Veil of the Negative Existence which is called *Ain Soph Aur*, the Limitless (but uncreated) Light.

435. By gematria Ruach Elohim, RVCh ALHIM is 300, the number of the letter Shin, Sh, the Mother Letter referred to the element of fire.

436. The Warmth.

437. The Heaven World is Briah, the World of the Elohim, sometimes called the Fire-World or Light-World.

438. Breath, Pneuma, Spirit, Ruach. See note 435.

439. Here the idea indicated in note 433 is further developed and the inter-relationship of Yetzirah and Assiah is considered.

440. The Essence of the Spirit of Mercury.

441. It would hardly be possible to produce better evidence for the assertion that the Philosopher's Mercury is no common mercury than this sentence.

442. Note the distinction here made between the corporeal and spiritual Gold.

443. The close proximation of Mars to Gold is traceable through the Alchemical Tree of Life /cf. *Aesch Mezareph*) whereon Mars and Iron are referred to Tiphereth and Sol and Gold to Geburah, which attributions are normally reversed in the ordinary forms.

444. Sulphur is referred to the third Sephira, Binah, Understanding; the Salt of the Wise (or Sophic Salt) is attributed to Chokmah, Wisdom, the second Sephirah.

445. Mercury is referred in the same form of the alchemic Tree of Life to Kether, the Crown, the first Sephira.
446. See note 444.
447. This section deals with Mars, but the implications are the same, seeing that each Sephira has its ten Sephiroth, forming a complete Tree of Life.
448. Qabalistically it is, of course, Venus, Copper, the Spouse of Mars, that unites these three, but she does this in collaboration with the Airy and Mercurial natures.
449. The correspondency and one operation is, of course, the birth from the Divine Parents Chokmah and Binah, the Father and Mother of the Son, Tiphereth, Gold. If we are considering the Martian Tree, then, as the *Aesch Mezareph* says, when Gold is referred to Geburah, it signifies the Tiphereth of Geburah.
450. That is to say from the Supernals proper and not merely from those of a particular Metallic Tree.
451. Mars.
452. MS has 'a part'.
453. MS has 'often'.
454. MS has 'absolved'.
455. Probably in Pisces, the House of Jupiter, the Exaltation of Venus and one of the Signs of the Watery Triplicity ruled by Mars.
456. There are properly speaking only two worlds open to human Reason, Yetzirah and Assiah; Atziluth and Briah are intelligible rather than intellectual.
457. Briah.
458. Neshamah.
459. Yechidah.
460. It is of the World of the Elohim, and corresponds, thus, to the Ruach Elohim or Spirit of God, which moved upon the face of the waters in the beginning.
461. The Higher Soul, as summed up in Neshamah, is triune, being composed of Yechidah, Chiah and Neshamah, corresponding to Kether, Chokmah and Binah respectively. Both the first two imply Life, while Neshamah in its plural form Neshamoth, is used for breath (and thus Spirit) when it is said (*Gen*. ii. 7.) 'and breathed into his nostrils the breath of life'. Not till then did man become Nephesch Chiah, a living Soul.
462. The *primum mobile* is the Rashith ha Galgalim of the *Zohar*, the beginnings of whirling movements, and the first of the Heavens of Assiah, the Material World. Our author here indicates the sphere represented by the Kether of Assiah. The idea which it enshrines is, however, consonant with the World of Atziluth if

we regard this primordial motion in its most recondite sense, far removed from matter or even form.

463. Properly speaking we are now dealing with Yetzirah, which follows on the previous consideration of Briah. At the same time the sequence initiated by the introduction of the *primum mobile* is continued, and we are given the second Heaven of Assiah, Masloth, the Sphere of the Zodiac, which is then described. Observe that he calls it 'the second celestial world' however, following on the super-celestial. His purpose is to differentiate between the world of 'the stars in the sky' as Iamblichos would put it and the celestial world of the Angels, which is Yetzirah.

464. Assiah, the material or elemental world.

465. Yetzirah is the habitat of the Ruach or Spirit.

466. MS has 'but thee'.

467. The Sun.

468. This seems rather involved but the idea is probably that the lower or visible fixed Stars have been to such an extent impregnated by the upper and invisible fixed Stars of the World of Yetzirah that their energy is in no way diminished by their work on the metals.

469. The sense of this obscure phrase would seem to be '. . . which have as their loadstone the Spirit of Gold, which is nearest of all related to the Sun.'

470. It is of interest to observe that our author refers specifically to the ancient as well as to the modern Rosie Crucians. The date of the birth of C.R.C. is given as 1378 and he died about 1484, the discovery of his tomb being in 1604. It is not of importance to the present argument whether these dates are correct or fictitious; they were the accepted dates at the time the present work was written. The point is that the word 'ancient' is hardly justified by them, and substantiates the tradition that the Order of the Rose and Cross was older than the time of C.R.C. who thus may be regarded as the founder of the Fraternity in Germany only.

471. MS has 'of'.

472. The allusion is to the colours attributed to Mars and Venus. There is, of course, neither iron nor copper in either.

473. Garnet. This contains Iron and not Lead.

474. Another allusion to the colour of Luna. As a matter of fact the chemical compositions of Saphires and Rubies are the same, and the former can be turned into magnificent blood-red specimens of the latter. Compare the fact that the body of Gold from which

its Soul or Sulphur has been withdrawn, leaving it white, can again be brought to a perfect redness.
475. Here this signifies Supernal Luna (Briatic).
476. Medial Luna (Yetziratic).
477. The Moon of earth or Assiah.
478. In comparison with Gold.
479. Compare the theory of Thomas Vaughan who suggests that the original Seminal Viscosity, sperm or seed from which the earth was made disappeared in the Creation (for it was the Waters of Creation). The world, however, now yields us, he says, a secondary seed, which is the very same essence with the primitive, general one. This sperm is generated from the mixture and marriage of the inferior and superior natures in the vapours. See his *Euphrates*.
480. Tin, however, according to *Aesch Mezareph*, has an excess of Sulphur.
481. MS has 'Zedekiel'.
482. Saturn may be said to be placed in the Upper Heaven inasmuch as among the Sepiroth he is referred to Binah. At the same time he may be said to hold the lowest degree if he is considered in respect of his reference to the connecting Paths.
483. Planets.
484. The issues raised by this sentence are fully discussed in the preface. The letter forms Chapter III of Helvetius' *Golden Calf*.
485. Flor. 1603-1665. Digby was, *inter alia*, an Alchemist and as such was concerned also with medicine. He first described his weapon-salve or powder of sympathy in a discourse at Montpellier in 1658.
486. It is not known to whom Helvetius' letter was addressed, and we therefore do not know to what letter he here alludes.
487. Compare the description of the Stone given by Van Helmont, who says: 'I have divers times seen it and handled it with my hands: but it was of colour, such as is in Saffron in its Powder, yet weighty and shining like unto powdered Glass.' J.B. van Helmont: *Life Eternal* (see *Oriatrike*, translated by J.C. 1662 or *Van Helmont's Workes*, translated by J.C. 1664.) Compare also Paracelsus in *Signatura Rerum*: 'It is a powder having the reddest colour, almost like saffron, yet the whole corporeal substance is liquid like resin, transparent like crystal, frangible like glass.' See also the fourth quotation from Khunrath's *Amphitheatrum Sapientiae Eternae* given herein on p. 195.
488. They occur at fol. 376 in the MS.
489. MS has 'such sulphureous . . .' See note below. Should we understand that the first powder was sulphureous and not white?

490. The word 'again' occurring here confirms what one would have expected, namely that the Silver did not just melt in the rain water, but that something was added thereto. In the version of this letter contained in *The Hermetic Museum*, where it is included in Helvetius' *Golden Calf*, the phrase used is 'a glass full of warm water, to which he had added a little white powder.'
491. Sparenda or Sparrendam.
492. This statement is of the greatest importance, indicating as it does that the solution is produced by something other than a physical solvent.
493. This whole sentence would seem to be a direct and clear allusion to the Rosicrucian 'Magical Mirror of the Universe.'
494. From here to the end we have Chapter II of Helvetius' *Golden Calf.*
495. *Signatura Rerum*. This is Book the Ninth of *Concerning the Nature of Things*. The quotation (or rather paraphrase) is taken from sect. 4. 'Concerning Mineral Signs.'
496. We have italicized *Item* to show it is the Latin also or again. He might equally well have used *Idem* as the next three passages come from the same source and paragraph.
497. *Coelum Philosophorum.*
498. *Concerning the Nature of Things, Book VII, Concerning the Transmutation of Natural Objects.*
499. *Das Manuale de Lapide Philosophorum*, or *The Manual Concerning the Philosophers' Stone*. The paraphrase given as a quotation is taken from sect. 3, 'The Remainder of the Preparation.'
500. *Amphitheatrum Sapientiae Eternae.*
501. This quotation is one of singular importance.
502. Cf. note 487.
503. Note the words 'it' and 'itself'. These are very important to the whole theory of the relationship between the Stone and the Self.
504. He might well have said 'because' instead of 'which.'
505. From the careful instructions regarding the fermentation given by the Alchemists, we can see that this period of three days is to be taken symbolically.
506. See *Oriatrike*, translated by J.C. 1662 or *Van Helmont's Workes*, translated by J.C. 1664 pp. 751 *et seq.*
507. Presumably this should be 'transforms.'
508. *Van Helmont' Workes*, p. 807.
509. The word 'worth' is an interpolation.
510. Theodor Ketjes(?).
511. Rusz(?).
512. Dr Kiffler(?).

513. There is probably an error here and the sentence should run: 'First I found (in my own laboratory) an Aqua fortis and next in that of Charles le Roy I poured it upon the Calx of Gold etc.'
514. Compare what Basil Valentine says of the Signet Star of Antimony in his *Currus Triomphalis Antimonii*.
515. MS has 'progress'.
516. Few of these words actually occur in the writings of Dr Dee or the present MS, but this has been dealt with in the Preface.
517. Lye. Usually a solution of one of the fixed alkalis, potash or soda, in water.
518. A liquor which dissolves all visible bodies and disposes them to generate. Rullandus says it is not Tartar.
519. The Separative or Spagyric Art.
520. Otherwise the substance of a body free from all earthly matter. Sometimes it is Vinegar.
521. Sometimes Salt of Tartar.
522. White Tartar or foliated earth.
523. *Essatum Vinum*.
524. Sulphur vive or Ambrosial Sulphur, reddish, transparent, like fixed Orpiment. The philosophic matter at the Purple stage during the first preparation; their Gold, their *minera* of celestial fire, their Prometheus.
525. Extracted by Vinegar. Also Salt of Saturn. See *Butyrum Saturni* and *Anima Saturni*.
526. Or the union of Sulphur and Mercury.
527. See *Altey Plumbi, Calcinatum Magus*, and *Butyrum Saturni*.
528. Alinzadir.
529. Antarit, Antaris or Antaric.
530. Usually Athanor.
531. See *Acetum Philosophorum*.
532. Not ordinary Spirit of Wine but their Mercurial Quintessence.
533. Philosophic Mercury.
534. Or the water that filters through the pores of the earth, from which are made the precious stones.
535. Mercury after sublimation.
536. Usually Archaeus. The *Sol Centralis*. Also the Universal Agent of Spagyrists; the dividing, differentiating and individualizing power of the Supreme Cause.
537. The spiritual principle.
538. Usually written *Iliaster*. The first Chaos. The three principles united in the *minera* from which they are extracted, and also sometimes the matter in putrefaction because the three principles

then appear confused. See *Iliaster primus, secundus, tertius, magnus* or *quartus*.

539. The fixed and igneous substance, the principle of multiplication, extension and all generation.
540. Paracelsus and Arnold only use it in this way in the sense that the Mercury of the Philosophers is so used. 'In our work we need only fire and Azoth' says Basil Valentine. 'The fire and Azoth wash and clean the Laton or black earth and remove its obscurity.' *Clangor Buccinae*. 'The fire and the water, which is Azoth, wash the Laton and cleanse it from its blackness.' Arnold de Villa Nova. 'The coagulated earth must be divided into two parts, of which one will serve as Azoth for washing and mundifying the other, which is called Laton, which must be whitened.' Nicholas Flamel. When the Philosophers say that *ignis et Azoth tibi sufficunt*, they mean that the prepared and well purified philosophical Mercury will suffice the artist for the commencement and perfection of the whole work, but the Mercury must be drawn from its *minera* by a subtle artifice. Bernard Trevisan says that everyone sees this *minera* altered and changed into a white and dry matter, after the fashion of a stone, from which the philosophic Argent vive and Sulphur are extracted by a strong ignition. Many names have been given to this Azoth, such as Astral Quintessence, Flying Slave, Animated Spirit, Ethelia, etc. According to some Azoth is a means of union, of conservation and the Universal Medicine. Also it is the beginning and ending of all bodies, enclosing all Qabalistic properties even as it contains the first and last letters of the Hebrew, Greek and Latin languages.
541. Otherwise called *Fons Philosophorum*.
542. It is also the furnace of the Sages and the secret furnace. Sometimes the name is given to the Philosophic Mercury. The term Bath is also given to a matter reduced to the form of a liquor, as for example, when speaking of the projection they say it must be in the bath; that is the metal must be in a state of fusion.
543. MS has 'vapour'.
544. Mumia.
545. Heavenly?
546. Cabbala, Kabbalah or Qabalah, from the Hebrew root QBL, to receive. It was a part of the Oral Tradition, of which the Talmud was originally also a part.
547. *The Torah*.
548. The Magi.
549. Also known as *Diatessadelton*.

550. Cf. *Cauda Vulpis Rubicundi*, The Mercury or Crocus of Lead precipitated. It is Red Lead; but also Red Sulphur or *minera* of celestial fire.
551. Also called Colcothar.
552. Atrament, Flower of Copper, Water of Copper, Copperas, Chalcitis, etc.
553. As for example in *Anima Saturni*, q.v.
554. A kind of terrestrial sponge. It is called by some a falling Star.
555. Chaomancy.
556. See *Archeius*.
557. See herein under *Duenech*. The Head of the Crow is the Matter in putrefaction.
558. Also Ashes. In it is preserved the principle of body, and that one principle being saved the whole life is restored from it. Khunrath calls it 'Our Pigmy' and 'The Diadem of the Body'.
559. Probably the same as the Spume of the Moon of the *Turba*, also called therein the Green Stone and the Spirit of the most intense Brass.
560. See *Calx Saturni*.
561. Under the heading *Flos Cheiri* it is called the Essence of Gold. Both meanings seem to be used. Some authors use *Cheiri* or *Cheizi* for Antimony and others for Potable Gold.
562. *Regale* is a cement whereby Gold is purged. We can, therefore, conclude that Ciment is an error. See *Cementum*, which we see is a dry corrosion when any metalline body is calcined with Salts or such-like drying things.
563. See *Saxifragus*.
564. It is only the beginning of the fixation.
565. Or the Elixir perfected to the Red.
566. Also the brownish-red peroxide of Iron which remains after the distillation of the acid from Sulphate of Iron. Otherwise called *Crocus* or *Crocus Martis*. See also *Henricus Rubeus*.
567. Gold, Sol, Tiphereth, the Heart is the Qabalistic correspondence. Sometimes *Cor* signifies the fire.
568. Vinegar is said in the *Turba* to be the foundation of the Art, and is also called Clean Water, Water of Mundane Life, Divine Water, White Magnesia, Mercury, Sea Water, Virginal Milk, Pontick Water etc.
569. More usually written *Cotonorium*.
570. Sometimes also the secret furnace of the Philosophers.
571. Tin.
572. The equilibrium or temperament of the elements in the Stone.

573. *Calx Mercurii.*
574. The act of putting a liquid body with a fluid for the purpose of making a partial or total mixture, of extracting the tincture, of disposing them to dissolution or putrefaction, of causing them to circulate, thus fixing the volatile and volatilizing the fixed.
575. Or mixed with Gold.
576. Green Duenech is Antimony, otherwise Duenech is the matter at the black stage, when it is still called the Laton that has to be whitened.
577. Ceruse is white Lead.
578. Philosophical.
579. The Elixir, according to Trevisan, is extracted from the mercurial water into which the matter is reduced. It is an animated Spirit; it is Hermes' Ixir, which is a vivifying ferment. It is the second part of the Great Work as the *Rebis* is the first and the Tinctura the third. There are three Elixirs in the Magistery, of which the first was termed by the Ancients the Elixir of Bodies and was made by the first rotation proceeded with to the black stage. The second was made by seven imbibitions as far as the white and red. The third, called Elixir of Spirits, is made by fermentation. It is also called the Elixir of Fire.
580. *Alcool Vini. Vinum Correctum.*
581. It is also our Seed, Sperm or Ferment.
582. The Tincture, the true philosophical earth wherewith the water of Mercury is tinged. The Seed or Sperm. Is also called Theriac, Male, Shadow of Gold, Flower of Gold, Key of the Sages, Vinegar of the Sages, Acetum, Vitriolum, Golden Tree, Body and Quintessence.
583. This is an important definition in view of the Qabalistic interpretation of Alchemy and the relationship between the Son, Tiphereth, Gold, Sol, Ruach, the King etc.
584. Presumably an error. *Filum Arsenicale* is sublimed Arsenic.
585. See *Cheiri.*
586. See also note 89.
587. Rendering metals friable by exposing them to the vapour of melted Lead or Mercury.
588. *Gamalei* or *Gemetrei.*
589. See *Constellatio.*
590. MS has 'is'.
591. From *Incus*, an anvil.
592. Otherwise stones engendered in the human body.
593. *Granus.*

594. The Philosophers' Mercury or their Luna.
595. Otherwise called Malek.
596. Sometimes Jesichach.
597. The fire of the Sulphur of the Sages.
598. Chaos, Hyle.
599. Compare with Ruach and Pneuma.
600. See also *Archeius*.
601. Certain of the philosophers have given this name to their Luna, who is also called Wife of the Sun.
602. Sometimes, also, Pewter.
603. Or Kakimia.
604. A half-metal or metal in embryo.
605. Leaven or Yeast.
606. Sometimes written *Kibrich* or *Kibric*. See *Maria Practica*, where it says that we should take Lunaria and 'grind it fresh when it is its appointed hour, for in it is the genuine body which evaporates not neither does it at all flee from the fire. But after this it is necessary to rectify Kibrith and Zaibeth upon this body; i.e., the two fumes which comprise and embrace each other in the two Luminaries, and to put upon them which softens them, which is the accomplishment of the tinctures and Spirits and the true weights of the wise'. These two correspond to Soul and Spirit.
607. Also spoken of as the Powder of Projection.
608. This seems rather an insufficient definition. Mummia is the essence of life contained in some vehicle, as in parts of human, animal or vegetable bodies, separated from their oganism, which retain their vital power and their specific action for a time.
609. Spirit of Salt prepared philosophically.
610. Luna has, in point of fact, several significations; sometimes it signified Silver, sometimes Mercury, sometimes the Matter at the white stage. When they say that their Stone is made with the Sun and Moon, the latter signifies the volatile and the former the fixed. They also call Luna their White Sulphur or White Gold. The reign of Luna commences at that point in the operation when the matter, after the putrefaction, changes its colour from grey to white. When the Sages speak of their Luna in this state, they call her Diana and say that fortunate is he who has been able to see Diana naked, that is to say, the Matter in its White Perfection. He is so indeed, because the perfection of the Red Sulphur or Philosophic Gold is only a matter of continuing the fire.
611. It is the Saturnine Herb of Thomas Vaughan, Vegetable, Mineral

and *Animal, whose juice, *Succus Lunariae*, is the Philosophers' Mercury, also called *Sputum Lunae* etc.

612. Magnesia is the matter whence the philosophers extract their Mercury. Sometimes they use it as a name for their prepared Mercury or for their Lead or for the Matter at the black stage. Lully (*Theor.* cap. 30.) uses it for the foliated earth or the Matter arrived at the white stage. 'This earth' says he, 'is our Magnesia, in which the whole of our secret consists; and our final secret is the congelation of our Argent vive into our Magnesia by means of a certain Regimen. Planiscampi gives the name of Magnesia of the Philosophers to an amalgam of fluid Silver and Mercury.

613. Which acts without one being able to discover the physical cause.

614. Though here dismissed thus briefly yet in the analogy of Dew with the Philosophic Work we have the Key to the whole Art. The philosophers, in using this symbol, regard the air as a vast circulatory. In it is contained all the idea of the action of opposites upon one another, for the fire and water, i.e., heat and moisture, are always busy with one another and according to Anaxagoras in the *Turba*, 'The thickness or spermatic part of the fire falls into the air. The thickness or sperm of the air, and with it the thickness or sperm of the fire, falls into the water and all these fall upon the earth.' (This idea should be compared with body, soul and spirit, or the Qabalistic divisions of the soul.) Now the water is the middle nature between air and earth, while the air, on the other hand, is the middle nature between fire and water, hence in the reactions and interactions of these two the air is a vast circulatory where inferiors and superiors meet like agent and patient or where Sulphur and Mercury are mingled. Here things are resolved into their first principles by the action of wind, i.e., vibration and contrition, whereby they are resolved into moisture, which then descends as Dew, so that there is a perpetual rarefaction and condensation, or circular process going on, that which is generated in the air being taken up by the water, which acts as the body as it were. This is the fire involved in the air and taken up by the water, when it is called Starry Milk or Air of Luna, so that the water is like a flying bird (cf. Hermes) and the milky moisture which is found in her crystal breasts is called Milk of Birds, and thus some of the philosophers have said that 'Birds do bring their Stone unto them' while others have said the same thing of Fish. To explain the sublimation of the metalline essences with the water in the foregoing, Vaughan and others, such as Sendivogius, postulate an Archeus or Central Sun, 'For

where the rays of the one and the other meet', says the former authority, 'the central, breaking forth to meet the celestial, suffers a sort of ecstasy. So then, in Winter the face of the earth being sealed, Magnesia is generated, but in Spring and Summer the sperm ascends more freely.' Qabalistically the air, which involves in itself a fire, is the Spirit or Ruach (air or breath), whose symbol is fire. This fire, in the Soul is the Neshamah or Higher part, to which the alchemic Sulphur is referred. From the gross earth of the material self or Nephesch, therefore, the subtle or watery part, which shall dissolve the volatile or airy Ruach, must be distilled. This in turn being thus wedded to the water, dissolves the fire or Neshamah, and when these are returned to the earth as dew the purification takes place. Again, in the *Zohar* we learn (*Sepher Dzenioutha*, i. 10) that the Skull of Macroprosopus is filled with a crystalline Dew, which is Aur or Light. This is called the second conformation, the third being the Skin of Ether or Auira, which occultly signifies Light, Fire and Air. In Macroprosopus this Dew is White, but in Microprosopus, where it finds its counterpart, it is White and Red. (*Idra Rabba Qadisha*, sect. 548.) From this dew the dead are raised up and this is the Manna prepared for the just, and Manna, MNA is by metathesis AMN Amen, which bears out the saying (*idem*, sect 552) that all things are contained in that Dew, for the mystery of Amen embraces the whole of the Sephiroth. Again Auira is related to Irach, the Moon, which, like Dew, contains the idea of air and water, and by which name the Matter of the Work is called. And it is pointed out in *Aesch Mezareph*, cap. 8, that Irach is one with azia, Arcana and Rabui, a Multitude for, the this matter are found not only the secrets of multiplication, but a multitude of arcana.

615. Also called Hal. It is sometimes spelt Malech.
616. Also Marthat.
617. Or Melibocum.
618. Quite obviously a symbolical period. Note, however, the connection between digestion, liquor, water and the letter Mem, whose numerical value is forty.
619. Used of all solid metals.
620. Red precipitate of Mercury.
621. At other times it is the Solvent of the Sages.
622. Mercury precipitated into a sweetness without any corrosive.
623. *Mercurius Corporalis Metallorum*.
624. The Principle of Mercury (Planiscampi).
625. Red Sulphur or *minera* of the Celestial Fire.

626. This word appears at the turnover of this folio of the MS, suggesting that we should find it over-leaf. It seems, however, to have been omitted. It is the same as *Necrolium* or *Necrolia*, and is a sovereign remedy for the preservation of health.
627. Stones.
628. A kind of terrestrial sponge, naturally sweet and healing.
629. Also *Nysoe*.
630. Also *Obrizum*.
631. Also *Ocab*.
632. Sulphurs are Souls. The Oil is also sometimes the Secret Fire.
633. Oil of Vitriol.
634. Properly speaking it is the incombustible oil of the philosophers.
635. Which assists in the formation of metals and minerals. *Oprimethiolim*.
636. Cf. *Lumen de Lumine* sect. 4.
637. Or the philosophic Gold in dissolution.
638. In this definition, Cross is probably an error for Crocus. It is Gold like Saffron.
639. While this is certainly true chemically and exoterically, yet the inner signification intended to be conveyed by the Sages referred not to the container, but to the contents, for it is that which is contained which is the true Vase of the Nature, being the egg and not the shell containing the egg. It is the matter of the magistery, however, which contains the Mercury, Sulphur and Salt.
640. MS has 'virgins'.
641. The theory underlying pentacles and talismans goes somewhat deeper than this. They are, when properly constructed and consecrated, said to be *foci* for and conductors of certain arcane forces in the universe, and can thus be used to bring about a desired effect.
642. Also the Red Sulphur of the Philosophers. In any case note the equation of the Stone with the Quintessence of Fire, and compare with our various remarks on Qabalistic Alchemy.
643. This is rather vague, as various things are extracted. We have, however, seen elsewhere that according to Khunrath and others great emphasis is laid on the Salt of Saturn, which has to be extracted from it. Salt and Antimony, we have also seen to be closely linked, and the Lead of the Philosophers is said by Planiscampi to be Antimony. Artephius tells us that Antimony must be taken from Saturn.
644. Planiscampi calls it *Privinum*. Cf. *Ignis Pruinus Adeptus*.

645. Paracelsus, Vaughan and others have said that this term is a misnomer. The latter says that it is, however, no element but a certain miraculous hermaphrodite, the cement of two worlds and a medley of extremes. Elsewhere he says of this cement and balsam that it is the Spirit of the Living God. Others describe it as the specific magnetism, the bond and seed of the elements, one only thing, from one matter or subject, in which resides the form, a material essence in which the celestial Spirit is enclosed and in which it operates. Again it is described as the fifth principle of composites, comprising the finest portions of the four elements. It is also the Mercury of the Philosophers. Lully and Rupescissa have each written a treatise entitled *De Quinta Essentia*, in which they take advantage of the ignorant to suggest that the Hermetic Mercury is made with common Spirit of Wine instead of the Philosophic Wine. However Lully says that the Spirit of Wine is absolutely mineral and not vegetable, though sharpened and rendered more potent with vegetables according to the purpose to which it is to be put. See also *Essentia Quinta*.
646. Imposthumes or Abscesses.
647. The magistery at the red stage. Red sulphide of Arsenic (Arabic).
648. Usually *Rebis*. It has been described as the Matter of the Sages during the first operation of the work. Trevisan says it is the crude mineral spirit, which, like water mingles itself with its body in the first decoction and dissolves it. Hence it is called *Rebis*, because it is composed of two things, namely male and female, that is to say the solvent and the dissolved body, though fundamentally it is but one thing and one matter. The philosophers also used the term for the Matter at the white stage, because it is then a Mercury animated by its own Sulphur, and because these two, drawn from the same root, are but one homogeneous whole. See Elixir.
649. Sometimes it is dung calcined in the fire.
650. Planiscampi says it is a metallic powder made by calcination. It is reduced to a water and then used.
651. Such are the Spirit of Venus and the Alkahest of Paracelsus and Van Helmont.
652. Cf. *Penates*.
653. Red Salt of the Indies. Salt Nitre. Also called *Sal Andaron*.
654. Dissolved in oil.
655. The Saltpeter of the Sages is the philosophical Nitre.
656. Compare, however, the definition of *Nitrum*.
657. Also written Taberzet.

658. Purified Salt of Tartar or the magistery of it.
659. This name for Tartar is Qabalistic and indicates its place in the scheme. Compare the other name for Tartar, *Calx Peregrinorum*. Samech is also Salt of Tartar.
660. Auripigment reduced to powder. Sometimes burnt Arsenic.
661. Reduced to oil. Also used for *Azoth*, because it washes, cleanses and purifies the Laton, taking away the blackness.
662. Pale citrine. See *Citrinulus*.
663. Sometimes *Scariolae*.
664. Compare Saladini.
665. The Seed of metals.
666. Sometimes Starmar.
667. Its Chaldean name according to Basil Valentine and *Aesch Mezareph*. Also Puk.
668. This is the exoteric or ordinary chemical meaning of the term. In alchemy it signifies something more profound. It is the purification of the matter by means of dissolution and reducing it into its principles. It is the first preparation necessary either to turn the matter into Mercury or to form the Sulphur or the Stone. D'Espagnet says that it is the preparation of which the philosophers have not spoken, because it was a manual operation, able to be performed by anyone, even by the uninstructed. It is probably that preparation of the agents of which Flamel said that it was difficult above all other things in the world, but very easy to those who knew it. It is the second degree that has to be passed through to arrive at the transmutation of bodies. It is alluded to under the name of sublimation, but also it is called fixation, exaltation, elevation. It is even very near to distillation, for even as in this the water rises and separates itself from all phlegmatic and purely aqueous parts, and leaves the body in the bottom of the glass, even more in sublimation does the spiritual separate itself from the corporeal, the volatile from the fixed, in such dry bodies as are the minerals. Admirable things are extracted from minerals by sublimation. Many are fixed and rendered able to resist the most violent fire. To succeed fully the sublimate must be ground with the feces and the sublimation repeated, this process being reiterated until nothing more sublimes. When all is fixed, it is taken out of the glass and exposed to the air or put in a cellar to become an oil, which is then digested in a slow fire to reduce it to a stone.
669. Compare *Silo*.
670. Air Spirits.

671. Apparently, therefore, not to be confused with Alchemical Tartar.
672. In the sense of Luna of the Philosophers.
673. Sometimes *Thisma*.
674. Mercury of the Sages cooked and digested to the white. Also Verdigris. Sometimes written *Tincar*.
675. It is yellow. Also called *Mercurius Laxus*.
676. MS adds 'Or an Alembic'. Sometimes the Philosophers' Filter is used as a name for their Mercury.
677. The matter from which the philosophers extract their celestial water.
678. Zaibar.
679. This is according to Planiscampi. It is not the common or vulgar Zinc.
680. Apart from a number of minor variations this tractate is substantially the same as the English translation of Maier's *Themis Aurea*, published in 1656.
681. See the *Fama et Confessio*, Vaughan's English edition, pp. 14-15.
682. MS has 'and'.
683. Hermes or Thoth.
684. Ptah, by the Greeks called Hephaistos.
685. MS has 'Magicians'.
686. Panchrest or Panacea.
687. Polychrest, a medicine that serves for many uses or cures many diseases. Polychrest Salt in old chemistry was Potassic Sulphate, also Sodio-potassic Tartrate.
688. A kind of lozenge.
689. Alexipharmaca are just remedies. (Gr. *alexo*, to ward off, *pharmakon*, a drug or remedy.)
690. Extreme emergency.
691. MS has 'and'.
692. Cf. *Manus christi*. See note 688.
693. True potable gold.
694. In transcribing this heading, the copyist has been guilty of an unconscious sarcasm in writing 'Deceased' instead of 'Diseased'.
695. MS has 'planets'.
696. A medicinal compound of various ingredients formerly believed to be capable of curing or preventing the effects of poison, particularly the effect of the bite of a serpent.
697. An antidote against poison or a composition in the form of an electuary supposed to serve either as a remedy or preventative against poison.
698. Quinsey.

699. Bezoar is a word of Persian origin from *bâd*, wind, and *ʒahr*, poison, that which blows away or dispels poison. The Bezoar Stone is a name for certain calculi or concretions found in the stomach or intestines of some animals, especially ruminants, formerly supposed to be efficacious in preventing the fatal effects of poison. Many varieties have been mentioned, but the most value was put on Bezoar from the East Indies and from Peru. Bezoar mineral is an oxide of Antimony or antimonic acid, especially that produced from butter of Antimony by the action of nitric acid.
700. Celery.
701. Compare Nature's rebuke to Madathan, who thought to make the Stone without dissolution: 'Dost thou think to eat oysters or crabs shells and all? *Aureum Seculum Redivivum.*
702. The omission of this word seems tolerably obvious. In any event it is confirmed by the opening sentence of the next paragraph but one.
703. Hectic fever.
704. MS has 'state'.
705. I have been unable to trace this text.
706. Cf. *Amos*. iii, 6.
707. Hezekiah. See *II Kings*, xx, 7.
708. An account of this alleged Frater was published in 1616 by George Molther, Doctor of Medicine and Town Physician of Wetzlar in Hesse under the title: 'Complete History of an Unknown Man who travelled through the town of Wezlar in 1615 and not only professed himself a Brother of the Rosy Cross but by his manifold accomplishments and universal knowledge aroused general astonishment'.
709. The sense in which the word 'gathered' is here used would appear to be 'classified'. It has already been stated in Section 2, para. 4 that the Brethren gather their vegetables when they are impregnated with heavenly influences, knowing certainly at what time they have received a signature effectual to a desired end.
710. Cf. *Pteromys Sabinus* or *Pt. Alpinus*.
711. The remarks on Magic from here to the word 'divine' at the end of this whole section are also to be found with variations as to wording sequence and the quotation of sources in Rudd's *Liber Mallorum Spirituum*, folio 1. recto and verso. The reference to Origen is not in Rudd.
712. The words 'The same . . . Magic' are omitted in Rudd who merely substitutes 'and'.
713. Rudd has: 'Tyaneus only exercised the Natural Magic and adds:

'by which he performed wonderful things.'
714. The reference is omitted by Rudd.
715. This paragraph is to be found verbatim in Rudd, fol. 1. recto.
716. Cf. The various remarkable accounts of *Homunculi*.
717. The continuation of the sentence down to this point is in Rudd, fol. 1. verso.
718. Rudd substitutes: 'And the Fraternity of the Rosy Crucians . . .' I would recommend that the whole of this section on Magic be carefully compared with Ashmole's notes to Norton's *Ordinall of Alchimy*, pp. 113 to 117, but especially pp. 114 and 115. Such a comparison will emphasize the relationship I have suggested between Maier, Ashmole and Rudd.
719. Ambiguity.
720. According to the *Fama* they were to meet 'on the day C.'
721. 'At the House S. *Spiritus.*'
722. Anyone unable to be present had to 'write the cause of his absence.'
723. Continuance, constancy.
724. Absoluteness, actuality.
725. Reduced, applied.
726. See notes 720 and 721.
727. Compare The *Assertio* or *Confirmation of the Fraternity* R.C., by 'B.M.I., least of the Brethren of the R.C., while on his third journey at Hagenau . . . September 1614.' He says 'We dwell in a monastery which our Father called 'of the Holy Spirit.' A smooth but famous river runneth by; and not far away is a well-known town.'
728. Thomas Vaughan quotes this passage in his Preface to the *Fama*, but does not name the author.
729. i.e., God.
730. MS had 'Eneads.'
731. Cf. The *Assertio*, whose author says: 'Not rightly doth the common man style us "of the Rosy Cross," because we are named after the first Father of our body. How then was he named? That we shall steadfastly hold secret.'
732. The stream sacred to Apollo and the Muses, brought forth from double peaked Parnassus by a blow from the hoof of Pegassus. This is the fountain of Bernard Trevisan.
733. Bitter-sweet.
734. The only interpretation of the letters R.C. with which I am familiar in which the former is the substantive and the letter the adjective, is *Roris Cocti*, an allusion to the alchemical coction of Dew. The usual acceptation, however, is *Roseae Crucis* or *Rosatae Crucis*.
735. The L or Luna here mentioned is a glyph for the C of R.C. If

then the circle or O symbol for the Sun be inserted between C and R we have *Cor*, the heart.

736. Qabalistically this is the Ruach, the volatile part, the aerial nature uniting two worlds, that part by virtue of which alone the 'soaring aloft' can take place. According to the *Zohar* there are those who do not possess it.

737. The words '*Post centum viginti annos patebo*' are said to have been found written on the door of the Vault wherein was discovered the tomb of C.R.C.

738. These dates are to be found in the *Confessio*, where 1378 is given as the year of the birth of C.R.C., and one hundred and six years as the span of his life.

739. This is interesting as being a definite statement that the matter of the Work is sensually perceptible.

740. Ptah.

741. Apis was regarded as the renewed life of Ptah.

742. MS has 'and'.

743. The MS ends with the words: '*Finis Coronat Opus* — 1713'.